O9-AID-549

SAM AND CHUCK GIANCANA

DOUBLE CROSS

WARNER BOOKS

A Time Warner Company

WARNER BOOKS EDITION

Copyright © 1992 by Sam Giancana and Chuck Giancana
All rights reserved.

Cover design by Tony Greco
Cover photograph by Bettmann Archives

Warner Books, Inc.
1271 Avenue of the Americas
New York, NY 10020

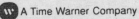 A Time Warner Company

Printed in the United States of America

Originally published in hardcover by Warner Books.
First Printed in Paperback: March, 1993

10 9 8 7 6 5 4 3

Until 1969, our family was held captive by the legacy of Chicago Mob boss Sam Giancana. At that time, we mistakenly thought that by changing our last name, we could escape the very real stigma attached to being related to a notorious "gangster." It was an act whose logic ultimately proved faulty, for it succeeded in stripping us of our rich Italian heritage, to say nothing of our friends and family. Hiding behind a mask, we denied our very existence, creating merely the illusion of normalcy. It was an illusion only we could dispel. This book is dedicated to the person who showed us that only by removing the mask can we ever truly hope to see ourselves.

The saga of Sam Giancana, its social and historical significance aside, would never have reached a single reader without the sincere enthusiasm of our literary agent, Frank Weimann; for his tireless efforts and friendship, we are indebted. Nor could this story have come to life with such grace and power without the expert guidance of our editor, Rick Horgan; for his tremendous vision and encouragement, we are deeply grateful.

AUTHORS' NOTE

In writing *Double Cross*, we've attempted to impart the essence of an enigmatic man as well as to portray, as accurately as possible, his involvement in national and global affairs as he himself related it. However, what follows is not an investigative treatise on the life and times of Sam Giancana—nor, do we believe, should it be. Too many important political revelations have gone unnoticed by the U.S. reader due to tedious journalistic research, which results, unfortunately, in tedious reading.

Instead, the subject of Sam Giancana's life has been approached with every attempt to engage the reader—to tell a good story—while maintaining historical accuracy. Most of the information contained in these pages is the result of conversations, held over five decades, between Sam Giancana and his brother. The balance is the natural by-product of being on the inside of Chicago's Outfit: information gleaned from personal experience (as younger brother to Chicago's most powerful Mob leader) and contemporaneous conversations with various Outfit members. We've made every attempt to relate these conversations and events as unerringly as recollection will allow over the span of more than five decades.

What has emerged from this endeavor is something that is far greater than the sum of its parts. *Double Cross* is, in the end, more than a biography of a mobster, more than an exposé of organized crime, more than a steamy report featuring all the right players, more than a true crime narrative, and certainly more than a gripping political drama filled with Presidents, spies, and secret agents.

But despite these acknowledged assets, *Double Cross* may still be criticized for its lively approach. Bringing Sam Giancana and his times to life in a fashion more common to the novel than the exposé, all the while presenting the Mob leader's own point of view, has made *Double Cross* a disturbingly entertaining story. And a subject such as this should not, by most accounts, be entertaining. Because of this approach, however, far more people can be expected to read *Double Cross*, and the historical purist will be forced to concede that no amount of journalistic research could ever replace the personal perspective offered by Sam Giancana himself.

Although most Americans have known little up until now about Sam Giancana's impact on the nation, it's precisely this lack of knowledge that has made writing *Double Cross* so necessary. Tired of the blatant misinformation and inaccuracies that have continued to be reported on topics ranging from the St. Valentine's Day Massacre to the death of Marilyn Monroe to the assassination of John F. Kennedy, we decided it was time, once and for all, to tell the story of these events as Sam Giancana related it. The resulting revelations contained in *Double Cross*, although shocking, speak for themselves.

Thus, we now present what was confided to Chuck Giancana by his brother Sam Giancana as the truth of the times. It should be added that we do so with much sadness and no small measure of fear. This is a sordid and difficult legacy—and one we did not choose. It's therefore our desire that, after completing the book, the reader will not find those bearing the Giancana name guilty, by association, with a man who so destructively changed the course of history.

We do believe there may yet be a positive outcome to the saga told here. Once armed with a truer account of our nation's past, the reader—no longer enslaved by an apathy borne of falsehood—may possess a renewed ability to affect America's future. And, in the final analysis, that may be what *Double Cross* is all about. Perhaps the reader, like these authors, will conclude that the ultimate double cross was not perpetrated against one individual but was, more significantly, committed against the people of this nation and the citizens of the world.

SAMUEL M. GIANCANA
CHUCK GIANCANA
August 1991

CHAPTER 1

Everything was right; it was a beautiful night for a murder. Above the rustling treetops lining the quiet Oak Park, Chicago, suburb, occasional streaks of heat lightning flashed in the night sky. Although it was after ten o'clock, the sweltering humidity hadn't lifted; the air was thick and hot and still. A dog barked in the distance. The sounds of crickets and humming air conditioners muffled the killer's heavy, measured footfalls as he stealthily made his way along one side of the modest bungalow and down the concrete stairs to the basement below. He felt the .22 target pistol against his waist, hidden beneath his belt, reminding him of the task at hand.

He had nothing to fear—nothing to hide; he and his intended victim were friends. When he reached the bottom of the stairs, the heavy steel door swung open as it had a thousand times before and the familiar smell of cigar smoke, mingled with sausage and garlic, slapped him with countless memories spanning a lifetime of trust and loyalty. He looked Mooney Giancana squarely in the eye, and smiled.

If he knew what was coming, Mooney showed no fear, not the slightest inkling. Instead, he turned his back to continue nursing the fat sausages that sizzled in the pan. Hunched over the stove, he looked old from the back, like a graying hound past his prime.

The metal of the gun had grown warmer against the killer's spine. The six-inch tube placed over the barrel's nose pressed insistently. Mooney had always told him timing was everything—and the killer knew it was time now. He stepped up behind his friend and in one swift motion pulled the gun from its hiding place. Pressing it against the base of Mooney's skull, he pulled the trigger. A sharp crack rang out and his victim lurched forward and then back again, falling faceup on the floor.

The killer stood over Mooney, a man he'd known for thirty years, and watched as he fought for air, gurgling in his own blood. And then he placed the gun into the gaping blue-lipped mouth and fired again. The bloody face shuddered; its vacant eyes fluttered and rolled. He shoved the gun under Mooney's chin and lodged five more bullets in what was left of a brain.

His job accomplished, the killer calmly glanced from his watch to the sausages browning nicely on the stove. Then he walked back out the door into the summer night air. And vanished.

"Mooney's dead."

The words echoed through the night, shaking Chuck Giancana into consciousness. He felt the phone go cold in his hand. He wanted to ask how and why and a million other questions, but the voice on the line continued: "It sounds like a hit . . . he was shot in the head."

There was no emotion in the telling, just a strange formality. True to form, even his brother's death was a sort of business, to be reported from a safe distance, like everything else connected to the Outfit.

For a while, Chuck just sat on the side of the bed, listening to the dial tone. He wanted it to sink in, to really feel it. It was June 19, 1975, and his brother, his childhood hero—Chicago's great and powerful underworld boss, Sam "Mooney" Giancana—was dead. It was finally over. Once and for all.

Two days later, Chuck attended his brother's wake. Hundreds of reporters, curious onlookers, FBI agents, and police officers crowded the chapel parking lot, lending a carnival-like atmosphere to an otherwise somber affair. "Where's their respect?" Chuck mumbled angrily to his wife as they rushed past the photographers and through the heavy double doors.

Inside, two bullnecked Outfit guys were posted at the doorway. Guarding this entry was an honor, and one they weren't taking lightly; Chuck watched as the men skillfully assessed him from a distance and then, recognition in their eyes, nodded in deference and stepped aside.

Chuck Giancana had been to Chicago's Montclair Chapel countless times over the years; it was popular with the Italians. Plenty of unlucky Outfit soldiers had been laid out within the grim silence of its elegantly decorated walls, but nothing prepared him for the magnitude of Mooney's wake.

He suddenly felt awkward, out of place—"like a whore in church," he'd later recall—as he moved past the men and through the arched door into the chapel. A hush enveloped the red-carpeted room and the heavy scent of flowers took his breath away; he'd never seen so many at Montclair before. But this wasn't just any Outfit wake, he reminded himself; this was Sam Giancana's.

Lining the chapel walls were wreaths piled on wreaths, and buried beneath them was his brother's bronze casket; it was the most beautiful Chuck had ever seen. Torch lamps guarded each end and cast a golden glow across red roses cascading from two stately brass urns.

Confronted with such opulence, Chuck thought a person could almost forget Mooney had been murdered. No one, it seemed, wanted to dwell on the truth—the cruelty, the brutality of his brother's life. Or the double-dealing that had ended it.

There were a lot of things about his brother's life and death that bothered Chuck. But the questions that burned within him most were who and why?

Chuck knew it had to be somebody Mooney trusted; although in the Outfit, who pulled the trigger and who ordered the hit were two very different things. The press said it was just another gangland slaying aimed at silencing a fellow mobster. But that didn't make sense; Mooney might have been scheduled to go up before the Senate Select Committee on Intelligence, but he never would have talked.

Nor had Mooney been moving in on anybody's territory; Mooney's territory was the world. The very idea his brother had overstepped his bounds in Chicago was the craziest thing Chuck had ever heard.

It wasn't that Mooney wouldn't share the spoils of his international victories, either, as some people speculated.

Mooney always took care of the guys in the Outfit. He wasn't greedy. And he sure as hell wasn't stupid.

No, none of those explanations made sense to Chuck. So he guessed it had to be another angle, one he and everybody else just hadn't thought of yet. True, it looked like a mob hit. And true, it had to have been carried out by a trusted lieutenant—which meant only a handful of Outfit guys. But something was wrong with the story. And that something was lack of a motive; the Outfit just didn't have one.

Shit, things sure can change.

He'd loved Mooney more than he'd ever loved anybody in the world. And he'd hated him, too. But in spite of that, he'd always thought he was untouchable, never thought Mooney would be double-crossed like this. But who? And why? That was all he wanted to know.

He also wished he knew what it was about the past that made it seem so goddamned good. How could anybody in their right mind call those days the good ones? It sounded crazy. But crazy or not, here he was a half century later, in 1975, wishing he could have them back. Wishing he could see his big brother walk through the door of their crumbling little flat, cussing and raising hell as he stepped over sheets of newspaper carefully placed by their sisters on the freshly scrubbed floor.

That was before Mooney really hit it. It had all seemed like a game to Chuck back then; all he'd really known was that his brother was important, a "big guy" in something people called the Syndicate.

Chuck laughed bitterly to himself. Had he known as a punk kid what he knew now, he would have run so far, so fast, he never would have stopped. But hell, as a kid you think you're immortal. There aren't any stakes too high, because nobody ever calls their marker. And there aren't any consequences too great, because you're too smart or too tough or too good to get caught. That's the irony of living, he guessed. You never realize the truth until it's too late. And a lot of good the truth does when you're an old man and the game is over.

For some reason, the New Year's party Mooney threw back in 1955 came to him now—it seemed like years ago. Mooney was riding high that night and everybody who was anybody in the Outfit was there; it was a big formal blowout.

Chuck grinned to himself. Damn, Mooney was an elegant bastard and he'd gotten pretty high that night, all right. Chuck could still see him with that can of shaving cream. What the hell had possessed Mooney to start a shaving-cream fight? The feds would never believe a story like that: Mooney Giancana, all-round fun guy. It was more like a fraternity party than a Mob celebration; before it was over, Mooney had shaving cream all over his face and tux. Then the other men had found more. Pretty soon, everybody was throwing champagne. It was wild, really wild. And it was probably the first time he'd seen Mooney laugh since his brother's wife, Ange, had died; he'd laughed until Chuck thought he'd die laughing, right there in front of God and everybody. Well, Mooney hadn't died laughing, goddamn it. No, some fucking bastard had gone and killed him, instead.

Chuck took a deep breath, stepped up to the casket, and looked down at the waxen face. He suddenly realized he'd never seen his brother sleeping—at least not in a long, long time. Mooney. His childhood hero.

He couldn't help staring at Mooney's body. What had been a tall, robust man now seemed shrunken and gnarled—reminding Chuck of the old tree he'd cut down in his backyard almost a decade before. That was the very day he'd decided to change his name. And he'd never spoken to Mooney again. Never seen him again. Not until now.

Chuck stood before the casket, looking down at his brother, thinking about that old tree. Had the tree felt something, had it understood—in some strange way—that its days were numbered? It was a silly idea, of course.

He'd stood by that day as the landscaper's ax tore through the rotted bark. Once down, the old tree lost its former majesty; it looked like any other broken pile of sticks. He never would have imagined it had been so big and strong and proud. It was the same with Mooney, lying in front of him now.

A flash of metal caught his eye. It was the silver cross of a rosary placed across Mooney's hands. Chuck looked up from the casket.

And suddenly, he knew.

It wasn't the Outfit that had wanted Mooney dead. But he knew who had. He might not be able to prove it; that didn't even matter. All that really mattered was that he *knew*.

The sound of the tree as it fell to the ground—the terrible cracking noise of bone when a bullet finds its mark—filled Chuck now with a pulsing fear. He felt his heart leap in his chest, could hear it pounding in his ears. It hadn't been the Outfit that wanted his brother dead. Mooney had another, far more powerful ally that *would* have feared his testimony before the Senate committee. Over the years, its commitment to secrecy had hung over Mooney's head like the sword of Damocles, waiting, just like the woodsman's ax for the tree. Waiting, until it dealt its fatal blow.

Chuck turned from the casket. He had his answer.

CHAPTER 2

For most children, a tree stands as a sentinel, a rite of passage. A gauge by which to judge time and the changing seasons; one's height in relation to its knotted trunk; one's strength and agility in climbing its perilous branches. Over time, it becomes a haven for games of hide-and-seek, a permanent carving board displaying life's accomplishments and passions. But for six-year-old Mo Giancana, the big oak tree behind the family's two-story flat on West Van Buren stood as a different symbol. . . .

Antonio Giancana's dark eyes focused glaringly on the small child cowering in front of him. The boy plainly required more discipline; the beatings Antonio had meted out daily had had no effect on him. He was more rebellious than ever.

Like the old mare that dumbly pulled Antonio's cart loaded down with fruits and vegetables along the streets of Chicago's Little Italy, little Mo could also be broken, beaten into passive submission. A man's will was stronger than a mere child's, Antonio had declared to his wife, and he was determined to teach his son this fundamental truth.

Without another word, he gathered up the struggling boy, carried him into the twilight, and chained him to the towering oak that stood behind their sagging tenement. There he proceeded to beat his tethered prisoner with a razor strap until Mo turned bloody and knelt on the ground, begging him to stop. Then Antonio went inside to his dinner of pasta and vegetables, leaving the whimpering child to face his pain and the encroaching nightfall alone.

The moon was up and full in the sky before Antonio unchained Mo and dragged him inside. From that night forward, the skinny little six-year-old slept on the floor in the corner of the kitchen and would come to know the oak tree well.

Faced with such brutality, there are some children whose character will slip into oblivion, to be lost forever. But others reach inside themselves and find an anger so deep, a rage so violent and strong, that it never subsides. And instead, with each fresh inequity, a sense of self is fanned that can't be extinguished. That fire blazed within Mo Giancana.

Although he celebrated his birthday on June 15, records show he was born on May 24, 1908, to Antonio and Antonia Giancana, in Chicago's Little Italy, a neighborhood known as the Patch, and christened Momo "Jimmy" Salvatore Giancana. Antonio called the little boy Mo, and, if nothing else, was proud to have a son.

The Giancana family was little different from the other Italian families who squeezed between Taylor and Mather streets. It was a neighborhood—once the sole domain of the immigrant Chinese—that bordered row after row of thriving, glittering brothels lining the riverfront district known as the Levee. Those who settled there were largely from the southern provinces of Italy or the island of Sicily; Antonio and his wife were natives of the Sicilian village of Castelvetrano.

Between 1890 and 1910, the Italian population in Chicago swelled to more than forty thousand, and their numbers continued to grow until the olive-skinned strangers spilled over into streets and ghettos once occupied mostly by Irish and Jews. Resentment and prejudice soon followed. For an Italian—a dago, a *greaseball*, as the Irish called these Sicilians—to cross over the imaginary line that separated the Patch from the Irish neighborhood on Halsted Street meant certain retribution from the burly, ruddy-faced mick immigrants settled there. Consequently, sidewalk brawls and bloody battles broke out in the streets bordering the Patch almost daily.

It was an easy transition for these frightened immigrants to view the Irish coppers—who did nothing to intervene in the ethnically inspired skirmishes and showed little if any sympathy for a battered dago—as the enemy. They'd brought little else with them from the Old Country save their culture—a peculiar assortment of odd customs and habits—which had at its heart an enduring mistrust and fear of those in power and the laws they made. In Sicily, their ancestors had borne the hardships imposed by a system of government that hailed back to the days of feudalism—one in which roaming bands of armed men both protected and punished at will. To Italian immigrants, Chicago police harkened back to those times, serving only to punish. And without the authorities for protection, the Italians turned to each other for support and safety in the New World, clinging to their heritage with all the tenacity of a drowning man to his ship.

The hills and valleys of Sicily may have held little more than rocky, barren soil—hardly an opportunity for future agrarian wealth—but the factories of the Industrial Revolution that regurgitated soot and fumes over the Patch presented even less attraction for Antonio and his friends and neighbors. Had the fat-cat Anglo industrialists welcomed the cheap labor the Italians represented, which most did not, it was still unlikely that men like Antonio Giancana would have been drawn to heavy industry's dark and stinking confines.

A people accustomed to making their living under the sun and at the mercy of the elements, they were slow to abandon their culture; many had been peddlers in the Old Country, and, once in the Patch, they quickly purchased carts and set off into the squalid streets to hawk a variety of Old Country favorites: popcorn, fruits and vegetables, lemon ice, and corn on the cob.

For pleasure, Antonio Giancana and his neighbors gathered in the evenings with their wives and children to play bocci and laugh and tell jokes and sip homemade wine— as their ancestors had done for centuries in some distant yet still-beloved village.

As more immigrants came, the Patch became a riot of smells and sounds and colors: a place where garbage, vegetables, and spoiled meats rotted beneath teeming flies on the wooden sidewalks, and packs of stray yellow dogs fought for a taste of the bloated horses and manure that steamed and stank for days in the mud-filled streets. Disease was quick to spread. Few children lived and fewer thrived.

The two Giancana children somehow managed to survive in the neighborhood's harsh environment, but Antonio considered his son—unlike frail, unassuming Lena, Mo's older sister, whom Antonio adored—a curious and troublesome child. Mo's stubborn independence and inquisitive nature were viewed by his father not as redeeming qualities but, rather, as confirmation that Mo was rebellious and meddlesome.

When Mo's mother, Antonia, died—as had so many other women in the Patch—from a miscarriage on March 14, 1910, the boy was not yet two. Precocious, he seemed to understand that he'd lost his only human ally, and any childhood spark he possessed was quickly buried with her; little Mo became sullen and quiet.

Antonio, a traditional Italian male, didn't waste any time seeking out another wife, one who could bear more children and care for the two he already had. He expected no more or less than any other man in the Patch: a clean house, proper meals on the table, and a child every two years. And with those expectations, he married Mary Leonardi.

After Mary joined the Giancana household, Mo fell asleep to the nightly sounds of Antonio's violent outbursts and the piteous cries of his battered stepmother. What the woman did to incur his father's wrath, he never really knew.

She wasn't a beauty, but rather a solemn-faced woman resigned to her lot in life. Mary became a stoic and dutiful wife, giving birth to her first child, Antoinette, in 1912; then to another, Mary, in 1914, when six-year-old Mo was just entering first grade at Reese Elementary.

Antonio turned to the oak tree with regularity over the next four years, believing in his ignorance that the chain and beatings he delivered would eventually tame his unruly son. He also looked to the stern disciplinarians at Reese Elementary for added support, making sure new teachers were fully aware that Mo was a troublemaker and sadly in need of reform.

The legacy his father bestowed on him became a self-fulfilling prophecy. By the time he was ten years old, and in fifth grade in 1918, Mo's teachers pronounced him a hopeless delinquent. He was sent to St. Charles Reformatory for six months, where, Antonio believed, the boy would learn his lesson. If not, he warned him, he'd take care of him when he returned.

In the late spring of 1918, Mo did come back—but not to his father's household, now laboring under the strain brought on by the births of two more children, Josephine and Vicki, nor to the grim walls of Reese Elementary.

Instead, Mo slept mostly in abandoned cars or beneath back porches. He wandered the streets and stole food from vendors. Thus, it was inevitable, as he skulked up and down the streets of Chicago throughout 1919 and 1920, that little Mo Giancana would finally find a home within a gang.

They were a band of crazy dago punks from the Patch, a gang called the 42s. They'd started out with Joey Colaro—a smooth-talking tough guy they nicknamed "Babe Ruth"—as their leader. At first, Colaro, along with Vito Pelleteiri, Mibs Gillichio, Pete Nicastro, and Louis Pargoni, stole clothes from lines around the Patch and made money selling them on street corners. When petty crime lost its luster, the boys turned to stealing "shorts"—cars left unattended, which they could either strip for parts or sell outright. But they soon graduated from stolen goods to bombings and murder, developing a reputation as the meanest, most vicious dagos anywhere around.

Historians would later suggest that the gang came to the name 42 one day when one of the more literate of their group recounted the story of Ali Baba and the forty thieves. And although there probably were never more than twenty members of the gang at any given time—someone was always getting killed or being sent to the reformatory in St. Charles—the name 42 stuck.

The people of the Patch called gang members "smart-heads" and spoke of them in a manner that conveyed a strange mixture of awe, respect, and fear. They frankly admired the gang for its ability to outwit the mick coppers, who they believed interfered in the affairs of Italians. Like the 42s, the immigrants neither trusted nor revered outside authorities, but felt mostly resentment and contempt for their presence in the Patch. The young gang members might break the American laws, might even settle disputes with murder and violence, but to the people in their neighborhood, they were a welcome reminder of the type of law and order they were accustomed to in the Old Country. Hence, the 42 gang was more often extolled by Italians than railed against.

Much to their glee, the 42s were also notorious outside the neighborhood, making newspaper headlines by terrorizing the streets in souped-up cars. They became well known for their ability to "whip" corners—a getaway method in which a driver took a corner as fast as possible on two wheels.

Mo, a homeless and starving boy with little else to occupy his time, joined up with this unsavory cast of characters. He quickly decided to win a place of leadership and respect among his fellow gang members and practiced his skill at whipping corners at every opportunity, using barrels set up in alleys as a makeshift obstacle course. It wasn't long before skinny little Mo had earned a well-deserved reputation as the 42s' best wheelman.

Skill like Mo's often came in handy. There could be no doubt that a hair-raising getaway was preferable to being "pinched." If that happened, they had to come up with enough money to pay off, or "fix," the coppers. Gang leader Joey Colaro was considered king of the fixers and took monthly collections of ten dollars from each gang member to cover such inevitabilities.

It didn't take Mo long to realize that the coppers represented not the fair hand of justice but, rather, a hand outstretched, looking for a payoff. If there was a copper or judge who couldn't be bought, for the right amount of money, he and his friends hadn't found one.

The going rate to have charges dropped by a judge or police captain was five hundred dollars—more than most of them could muster. This forced the boys to turn to their parents, who barely had enough money to survive as it was. But no decent Italian family could completely turn its back on a son in trouble, no matter how heinous the crime, and consequently, if they were arrested, most 42s found themselves out on the streets again in no time at all, thanks to a payoff made by their debt-ridden parents.

Common people might believe the police were on the side of good and right, but not Mo and his friends in the 42; they knew better. All that separated cops from robbers were a few dollar bills; it was that simple. There was no honor, no virtue; those ideals were the stuff of fairy tales. Reality in the Patch dictated a different code of survival, and Mo, already calloused by life at the tender age of twelve, embraced that code as his own.

His friends were a Mad Hatter's assortment of screwed-up kids and sociopaths whose limited choice of role models consisted of either hardened criminals, celibate priests, or poverty-stricken parents who couldn't speak English and knew little if anything of the new American laws and mores.

It wasn't a hard choice for members of the 42, for as Mo Giancana said, "We're not a bunch of fuckin' rum-dums." They fashioned themselves after the more visible gangsters, such as whoremaster Big Jim Colosimo or his nephew, Johnny Torrio; the young Al Capone and his cronies; or the Black Hand sugar baron, Diamond Joe Esposito. These were men who had money and power and women—men to whom even their uneducated parents bowed with respect.

With that in mind, 42 gang members became gross cari-catures of their heroes, and did their best to go them one better, dreaming up outrageous schemes for burglaries, sexual assaults, and, should they deem it appropriate, mur-der. If parents were aware of their sons' bizarre activities, they gave no indication, but went stoically about the busi-ness of survival.

When bored, Mo and the rest of the gang hung out at Goldstein's Delicatessen, Mary's Restaurant, or Bonfig-lio's Pool Hall. For fun, they turned to the sport and refinement of exquisite torture—Mo was particularly good at entertaining fellow members with new methods of blud-geoning the numerous cats that slinked along the neighbor-hood's alleys.

For sexual release, gang members excelled in gang shags—gang rapes—or engaged in elaborate public "pull-ing" contests, masturbatory challenges to determine who could ejaculate first or the farthest.

By the time he was thirteen, in 1921, Mo had become known as the craziest, the "mooniest" of them all, earning him the nickname "Mooney." They said the hollow-eyed boy would do anything on a dare, anything for two bits, a beer, or a cigarette. Nothing mattered, nothing except this newfound family and winning its esteem.

Street gangs had been a fact of life in the United States long before the turn of the century. Ethnic lines were typically drawn between neighborhoods, and in response, gangs of brawling young men formed for protection.

The oldest gangs in Chicago, the Black Hand, dated back to 1890, when the Italians were congregated between Oak and Taylor streets and Grand and Wentworth avenues. They had mystically inspired names such as the Camorra, the Mysterious Hand, and the Secret Hand, but unquestionably the most ferocious were the Sicilian Black Hands.

They were not a secret society or sect whose rites were closely guarded by the Italian people, but, instead, a loosely organized means of inciting terror for profit. The Black Hand traditions were brought over from the feudalistic Old Country, and featured as core elements kidnapping and extortion. The Black Hand protected its loyalists and severely punished its rebellious detractors.

Innocent fellow immigrants became its chief prey and provided the fodder necessary for expansion. Local police authorities—paid off by wealthy Black Hand dons—turned a deaf ear to any cries for justice from the Italian citizenry.

By 1900 in Chicago, several other gangs of differing ethnic persuasions emerged. The Irish Market Street gang had become a strong force by 1902 and even had a juvenile division—the Little Hellions, with an up-and-coming young choirboy named Charles Dion O'Banion as its leader. Another Irish band of toughs, the Valley gang, controlled the bloody Maxwell Street section and concentrated on burglaries, pickpocketing, and, eventually, contract murder.

But the most formidable Chicago Black Hand gangs centered around two Italians: Diamond Joe Esposito and Big Jim Colosimo. Diamond Joe had established himself as padrone, or boss, as early as 1905 by utilizing the familiar Old Country tactics of extortion and payoffs to gain political and union ties. Big Jim Colosimo took a different and—wisely—noncompetitive road to fortune through high-class prostitution, establishing a widespread enterprise of gilded, red-velvet brothels that generated millions of dollars and considerable influence.

Both Italians operated cafés; Colosimo's became a hangout for fast-living celebrity idols of the day such as Enrico Caruso, George M. Cohan, Al Jolson, and Sophie Tucker. Esposito's Bella Napoli was a meeting place for up-and-coming gang leaders.

Gang expansion also occurred in New York during the early 1900s. And as in Chicago, the most important of the gangs, the Morello gang, had as its heritage the Black Hand. Other New York gangs formed rapidly; among them the James Street gang and Five Points gang—the latter led by Chicago's Big Jim Colosimo's nephew, Johnny Torrio.

In 1909, Big Jim found himself in need of additional services. Continued extortion by opposing gangs—rivals of Diamond Joe Esposito's, as well—had begun to nibble at his profits. Colosimo appealed to Diamond Joe to intervene on his behalf. It was a request that required additional organizational muscle and inspired Diamond Joe to bring in Colosimo's nephew from New York.

Johnny Torrio was a hardworking hustler who'd already proven with the New York Five Points gang that he possessed the tough leadership necessary. Once settled in Chicago, he soon had his uncle's brothels running more profitably than ever before.

To further control his own burgeoning territories, Diamond Joe Esposito sponsored the six Genna brothers from Sicily in 1910. With assistance from Esposito's right-hand man, Joe Fusco, the enterprising and ruthless Gennas launched their criminal careers as Black Hand enforcers, extortionists, and brothel operators.

Smaller, loosely organized neighborhood gangs like the 42 provided the fresh recruits sorely needed by gang leaders such as Esposito. Profiteering businessmen of the time also took note of street-gang tactics, viewing them as a resourceful means to further their own legitimate enterprises. Thus, it wasn't uncommon for young gang members to be employed to protect a legitimate company's interests or influence potential consumers.

In 1919, Johnny Torrio, who was looking for additional muscle, brought in Five Points gang member Al Capone from New York to help run the Colosimo empire. Capone had witnessed the bootlegging successes of fellow Five Points gang members Lucky Luciano, Meyer Lansky, and Bugsy Siegel, and Torrio hoped that, together, he and Capone could convince Big Jim to shift his operations from prostitution to a more lucrative liquor enterprise.

Their pleas fell on deaf ears; Big Jim wasn't interested in amassing greater fortune, and neither man could convince him to move into bootlegging. Frustrated, Torrio ordered his uncle's execution, and Colosimo was gunned down in May of 1920.

During the following years, Chicago's gangs made feeble, halfhearted attempts to work together, but—with so much money to be made—greed, double-dealing, and strong ethnic hatred ultimately won out. An all-out fight for territory ensued.

Amazingly, during this turbulent period, Diamond Joe

Esposito went unchallenged and managed to retain ultimate gangland power. Because he controlled the sugar distribution from Cuba, a license he claimed was granted as a personal favor by President Calvin Coolidge in 1923, Esposito remained in a somewhat neutral position. Since sugar was an ingredient critical to the distillation of alcohol, and Cuba was the major supplier to the United States, Esposito could rise above the day-to-day gangland battles. Not only was he secure in controlling a commodity everyone needed but he was also able to influence gang operations and "legitimate" politics throughout the country.

By the time fifteen-year-old Mooney started working for Diamond Joe running sugar and alky in 1923, many Black Hand leaders across the country had disappeared, victims of prison or rival-gang slaying. Those like Esposito were a new breed, using bombs called "pineapples" as their chief terrorist tactic.

Esposito utilized the muscle of the West Side Genna brothers to patrol his illicit moonshining activities in the Patch. The immigrants called them the "Terrible Gennas," and under the padrone's direction, they ran alky from the hundreds of stills that bubbled and cooked in as many Italian households. Both murderous and devoutly religious, the Gennas strutted menacingly from flat to flat, carrying a crucifix in one pocket and a gun in the other. There were few coppers patrolling Maxwell Street who were not on their payroll. On the day payoffs were made, over four hundred officers came and went from the Gennas' Taylor Street alky plant. Should the Gennas discover a still not controlled by them in the Patch, they'd send the coppers over to smash it up and make headlines in the process.

Business boomed for the Gennas. Each week on Taylor Street, bands of young Sicilian muscle—Mooney now among them—collected over three hundred gallons of the prized liquid from each of the homes. From the Gennas' operation alone, Esposito collected over a million dollars a year. In exchange for their trouble, the Italians in the Patch were paid handsomely—a half-dollar for each gallon of alky, an average of $150 per still. It was more than they could make in six months of honest menial labor and most were grateful; those who weren't kept quiet.

There wasn't an Italian in Chicago who wouldn't bow to Esposito; if he required it, he even had their women. Particularly fond of young brides, Esposito was apprised of all upcoming Italian nuptials, demanding to bed the more desirable women on their wedding night, before they were soiled by their husbands. Although many men longed to kill him, Esposito's lascivious humiliations were never denied during his twenty-year reign.

By the close of 1924, Diamond Joe Esposito was undeniably the most powerful man in Chicago, perhaps in North America. All of the day's hoodlums, in one way or another, were in his debt. Men such as Al Capone, Johnny Torrio, Jake Guzik, Paul Ricca, Murray Humphreys, Frank Nitti, Jack McGurn, and Tony Accardo had all either been sponsored from New York through Esposito's political connections or handpicked for their guts and daring off the streets of Chicago.

Esposito's Black Hand touched enterprises far beyond the confines of Chicago's Patch. The padrone routinely boasted of meeting with Calvin Coolidge and dispensing votes and favors at the President's request.

According to Esposito, in the early fall of 1924, when asked once again by Coolidge how he could be repaid for his recent political assistance, he requested a promise that the President not interfere with a Chicago takeover of all union operations—coast to coast. Under the guise of generosity, he also asked that the men he supplied with sugar—Joe Kennedy in Boston, Sam and Harry Bronfman of Canada, Lewis Rosenstiel of Cincinnati, and Joe Reinfeld of New Jersey—receive special protection and all rights to bootlegging.

Esposito insisted he got exactly what he wanted from Coolidge, and, given the national power he wielded, there wasn't a soldier in Chicago who doubted him. Just as Esposito had promised, Capone and his boys went after unions totally unimpeded by law enforcement, while Esposito's sugar customers remained protected. It was a smart move and it made Esposito filthy rich.

Although Diamond Joe Esposito preferred neutrality, this traditional Italian, ethnic heritage was a tie that couldn't be broken. He was unswerving in his support of Torrio and Capone, forming an alliance that would prove formidable to the north side O'Banion gang. Together, the Italians had at their disposal an enormous thousand-man multiethnic force that was well structured and organized for any effort.

The Torrio-Capone gang had a Jew, Jake "Greasy Thumb" Guzik, as its financial whiz, while Italian Paul Ricca and Welshman Murray Humphreys served as lieutenants. Frank Nitti, William "Klondike" O'Donnell, William "Three-Fingered Jack" White, "Machine Gun" Jack McGurn, and Charles Fischetti were the gang's chief enforcers.

Chicago gangs often formed loose alliances to gain dominance and strength over their adversaries. Torrio and Capone could rely on the unswerving support of several.

Although always double-dealing, the Genna brothers were at their fellow Italians' disposal when it came to a dispute with north siders. They had carved out an alky empire in the west and south sides of the city under the sponsorship of Diamond Joe Esposito.

Ironically, cooperation with the Italian gang leaders was based more on geography than ethnic heritage. The Irish Valley gang, led by Frankie Lake and Terry Druggan, was a solid supporter in the battle against north side domination—as were the Sheldon gang, the Saltis gang, and John "Dingbat" O'Berta's gang.

They referred to their principal opponents as "those Irish bastards" under the leadership of Dion O'Banion. O'Banion held complete control of the north side and used his right-hand man and enforcer, Hymie Weiss, along with George "Bugs" Moran and Vincent "the Schemer" Drucci as his primary weapons. For added strength against Capone and the Italian gangs, O'Banion brought in the south side and West Side O'Donnells.

It was O'Banion's superior bootlegging product and his fanatical Catholic aversion to allowing prostitution on the north side that had led to a confrontation with Torrio and Capone. The war that followed resulted in more than a thousand gangland slayings and, in November of 1924, O'Banion's murder, as well.

But despite fierce fighting, the gangs, and many of those who worked with them, managed to amass considerable fortunes by the mid-twenties. Smaller operators such as the Genna brothers were netting over $100,000 a month, while men at the top such as Al Capone brought in $5 million a year.

Such a large sum was evidently not enough for Capone, who Mooney would later say tired of Johnny Torrio's unwillingness to share the wealth. In any case, with the encouragement of Paul Ricca and Murray Humphreys, Al decided his partner should step aside; with that in mind, he enlisted two of Esposito's young toughs for the job—rather than the gang's own enforcers, who might be unduly loyal to Torrio. One was Mooney, now a coldhearted seventeen-year-old who was becoming well known in the Patch for his abilities both behind the wheel and the barrel of a gun.

Mooney took his sidekick and friend Leonard "Needles" Gianola along—just as he'd done countless times before—to give Torrio the signal to retire in January of 1925. Although the press conveniently gave credit for the ambush to the north side O'Banion gang, Torrio knew better. He knew who fired the shotgun blasts that nearly gutted him on the spot—and for whom his attackers worked. After a touch-and-go recovery, Torrio took the $40 million he'd accumulated during his brief but profitable reign and got out of town.

Mooney's work evidently pleased the Capone forces, because just five months later, in May of 1925, they enlisted his skills again, as part of a gang that would remove another obstacle to Big Al's power. This time, they were six men Mooney knew well: the Genna brothers.

The first to go was Angelo Genna. Helplessly pinned behind the wheel of his car after a cat-and-mouse chase through Chicago streets, he could do nothing to save himself when his attackers pulled alongside and shotgunned him to death.

Believing wrongly, as did the police, that Angelo's death was the work of the north side gang, Mike Genna immediately set out for revenge with two enforcers at his side: Alberto Anselmi and John Scalise. Unknown to Genna, the two had switched their allegiance to Capone. Before Scalise and Anselmi could carry out Capone's orders to murder Genna, the three were engaged in a gun battle with police and a critically wounded Mike Genna was captured. Anselmi and Scalise fled. Genna was hospitalized and died just hours later. That left "Tony the Gentleman" Genna as Capone's last real stumbling block. Fearful for his life, Tony Genna made plans to go into hiding and set a meeting with one of the few men he thought he could trust, Giuseppe Nerone. When Genna and Nerone met later in an alley, Mooney and Needles stepped out of the shadows and cut Genna down in a blaze of gunfire.

Not long after Tony's death, the three remaining Genna brothers escaped the city with their lives and little else. Years later, after promising they'd stay clear of Syndicate activities, the Gennas would return to Chicago to run a legitimate cheese and olive oil business.

With Torrio and the Gennas out of the way, Capone filled his time by systematically eliminating any remaining rivals for his empire and by gradually consolidating smaller gangs under his rule.

Contact with the big gang leaders elevated Mooney's stature among other 42s to near idolatry. He reveled in it, swaggering down Taylor or Maxwell Street in classy suits, with a revolver in his pocket and a loose girl on his arm. Unfortunately, neither his gangland connections nor his 42 cronies could get him out of a jam with the coppers that September of 1925. At seventeen, he received his first arrest and conviction—for auto theft—and was sentenced to thirty days in the Joliet state pen.

It was a turning point for Mooney. Sitting in the cell in Joliet gave him time to consider just how far he'd come since those days as a child when he'd been chained and beaten beneath the tree on West Van Buren.

He'd learned to rely on his own wits and cunning to get by in the world—and up until now they'd served him well. He knew the power of the bullet and the baseball bat. And he knew he was different—different from the other greaseball smartheads, different from men like his ignorant father, different from the other convicts who lined the cell block in Joliet. Those men were hindered by their own stupidity and victimized by emotions such as love and suffering; he'd left those fetters behind long ago. The realization that he could kill, do whatever was necessary to reach his ends without the ponderous moral questions that might plague others, opened his eyes. He counted the days until his release from prison. He would return to Taylor Street and face the only man who'd ever humbled him: his father.

Antonio had seen Mooney from time to time, had caught him when he was younger sneaking into the house late at night to steal a loaf of bread or, if it was cold outside, looking for a place to sleep—and he'd always beaten him and kicked him out the door. In later years, he'd tried to erase Mo from his mind altogether; he knew what his son had done on the streets of the Patch with hoodlums like the Gennas, Esposito, and Capone—and he wanted no part of it. His business was beginning to prosper; he had a partner and a small store where they sold lemon ice along with the obligatory fruits and vegetables. His wife, Mary, had served him well and he had a new brood of children now. Two boys, Joseph ("Pepe") and Charles ("Chuck"), had been added to his family, bringing their number to seven—four girls and two boys, plus Lena. The dreams he'd had before coming to the New World were beginning to come to fruition. Then his son walked back into his life.

It surprised and angered Antonio to see Mooney walk right into the flat so boldly one night. The family was asleep and he'd been sitting at the table nursing a glass of wine when the door opened.

"You should know better than to come around here," he yelled in Italian at the thin, sunken-eyed seventeen-year-old who stood staring at him from within the shadows of the doorway.

Mooney said nothing, but stepped out into the lamplight.

"What the hell do you want?" Antonio asked. "Come one more step and I'll beat the hell out of you," he threatened, shaking his fist. There was something about the way the boy just stared at him that was unnerving, as if he was looking right through him. "Get out," he yelled again.

Mooney smiled a distant smile and wordlessly edged closer.

"Well, what do you want, then? What? Tell me now and then just get out."

Mooney took another step and, without raising his voice, said evenly, "What I want is what you took away."

A look of puzzlement crossed Antonio's face and then was quickly replaced with red-faced rage. He got up from his chair and stood to face the boy, now taller than he, before replying. "And what is that? I have nothing of yours. . . . You don't belong here."

Mooney came right up to his father's face and looked him in the eye. Finally, the boy began to laugh, an odd high-pitched cackle. "It's over, old man," he said softly, and turned his back to walk across the room. Nonchalantly, as if he'd lived there all his life, he leaned against the sink and began to light a cigarette. Through the glare of the orange-sulfured flame, he glanced up and said, "You can't push me around anymore, old man. And you can't hurt me. . . . It's over." He blew out the match.

The words left Antonio momentarily speechless. "Why . . . you . . . you little bastard," he cried at last. "You lousy little son of a bitch . . . you might scare old women . . . but it won't work here. Not with me. . . . Now get the hell out of my house before I kick your ass out."

Mooney took a long, deep drag and exhaled before he uttered a barely audible reply. "No," he said, and dropped the cigarette in the sink. It hissed in the momentary silence.

"Why, I'll kill you," Antonio screamed, and he lunged across the room.

He was no match for his son; with one quick gesture, Mooney rammed Antonio against the wall and reached into the sink, his hand emerging with a large butcher knife.

Placing its cold steel edge against Antonio's throat, he whispered, "Listen and listen good. Don't ever touch me again or I'll cut you open like a slaughterhouse pig. You hear me, old man? I'll kill you. From now on, you'll do as I say, *capisce*? I'll come here when I want and I'll go when I want. From now on, things will be different. . . . You'll do what *I* say. And never forget that I let you live tonight. I could've slit your throat . . . but I didn't. Remember that. Because if you ever forget it . . . I promise I'll kill you." He loosened his grip.

"You'd kill your own father?"

Mooney laughed as he dropped the knife into the sink with a clatter. "Don't try me," he said over his shoulder as he swaggered out the door.

No one in the family knew what had come over Antonio, but when Mooney came to the Giancana household on

Sunday, it was with a new air of authority; Antonio seemed to welcome him with open arms. Nor did he speak up when Mooney defiantly took his father's own place at the head of the table. It looked as if Mooney was home for good.

From then on, if he felt like it, he stopped by his father's house for a nap or a good meal or simply to keep the kids in line; he quickly usurped Antonio's role as father and household disciplinarian. But largely, his days and nights were filled with crazy 42 stunts and robberies; his brief stay in Joliet had done little to dampen his enthusiasm for the outrageous.

Unlike the older Capone men whom Mooney needed to impress, the 42 smartheads were his friends and he could let his hair down with them. When he wasn't on a job for Esposito running sugar shipments and alky or breaking a few union or political legs for Capone under Murray Humphreys's direction, he was hanging out at Bonfiglio's Pool Hall with other 42s. His expertise at wheeling had also begun to pay off; he now frequently chauffeured Machine Gun Jack McGurn, the flashy Capone enforcer.

Though 1925 had been, in many respects, a good year for Mooney, it turned out to be a very bad year for his fellow gang members. Newspapers began a feverish attempt to paint the 42s as a blight upon the land and sprang on the smallest incident for their headlines. Even nonmembers received publicity if they were young, Italian, and lived in the Patch. Carl Torsiello's brawl with a neighborhood bully and one-night stay in jail became a ''42 gang war with felony conviction'' when the press made its splashy reports.

In reaction to public outcry, the coppers turned up the heat. First, there were the raids on 42 warehouses filled to overflowing with stolen goods; next, a two-mile car chase in March, led by Pete Nicastro and another 42, with the police cars screaming in hot pursuit, their bullets flying. Then two days after curbing Nicastro and throwing him in jail, seventeen other gang members were arrested for attempted robbery.

Throughout it all, Mooney remained unscathed, although the detectives hauled him in for questioning almost daily. The Giancana family's lives changed dramatically in response to Mooney's presence; 42 smartheads such as "Tumpa" Russo and "Fat Leonard" Caifano started to come around to visit over a plate of pasta. Most of the time, the children lived on a tightrope, captive to Mooney's new role as head of the household, his radical mood swings, and seesaw outbursts. And, whenever there was a robbery or shootout in the news, they came to anticipate the inevitable knock at their door.

Their father maintained a low profile; when Mooney set up a still in the basement of their home, Antonio, without the merest hint of agitation, ran it. There was little the older man could do. Like the other immigrants dominated by gangland rule, he resigned himself to the steamy odor of sour mash that hung throughout their flat and gladly took the few dollars Mooney threw his way as token payment. In some strange way, he even began to admire Mooney. His neighbors praised his son for his guts and street smarts, his catlike way of always landing on his feet, and Antonio found himself feeling a surge of pride at the mention of Mooney's name.

Things were going along smoothly from Mooney's point of view until July, when he and two other 42s, Joey Sypher and Dominic Caruso, came up with the idea of burglarizing an expensive north side dress shop. In the dead of night, they broke in and got away with over fifty dresses. Pulling out into the street, they were spotted by coppers patrolling the area.

The chase was what Mooney lived for, what he loved more than anything he could think of. More than banging mick girls in the backseat of a car or whores up on Michigan, he loved the opportunity it provided to prove his prowess as a wheelman. With Mooney at the wheel, the trio sped off, with the police car in hot pursuit. He finally lost control of the car. "The only time in my life," he would tell friends. Mooney managed to get away on foot. Caruso and Sypher, however, were nabbed and, under questioning, broke down.

The next morning, while the eight Giancana children were gathered for breakfast, hungrily eating their bread and coffee, the knock on the door came. Mooney was sitting, bleary-eyed, at the head of the table, holding the smallest child—three-year-old Chuck—in his lap while drinking a cup of coffee. At the sight of the officers, he stood up, handed the little boy to his stepmother, and gave Antonio a hard look. Without saying a word, he let the detectives make their arrest and lead him off to jail.

Down at the station house, he was charged with burglary; bond was set at five hundred dollars. Antonio had understood what Mooney's look meant; he was to get the money from Diamond Joe Esposito to post bond and pay off the coppers. He did exactly that and soon his son was back home and ready to hit the streets again.

As repayment to Esposito, Mooney gratefully drove a sugar shipment to Louisville. Once there, he cooled his heels in seedy bars and on the riverboat city's sidewalks while waiting for a return shipment of Kentucky bourbon whiskey.

Kentucky coppers, like those in Chicago, were always on the lookout for suspicious types, and Mooney Giancana, a fast-talking Italian, stuck out in their slow-moving town like a horse with knickers. Mooney was picked up as a vagrant and later released. A few days later, he got his carload of booze and hightailed it out of town. The experience left a bad taste in his mouth; he always hated Kentucky after that, saying it was full of dull-witted degenerates, lazy shines, and coppers who could be bought too cheap.

Back in Chicago, the air took on a crispness indicative of the coming fall. Antonio no longer peddled his lemon ice, mammoth watermelons, and ripe tomatoes, but squashes and dried fruits instead. Wagons laden with coal creaked up and down the streets of the Patch and residents chattered like squirrels as they scampered to and fro, gathering the necessities required for survival during the harsh Chicago winters.

For Mooney, it was business as usual. There were the runs for Esposito, the calls to drive McGurn, the nightclubs where he wore expensive suits and flashed wads of cash while giving fast girls with blond bobs long looks. And naturally, there were the 42 heists.

Late one night in mid-September of 1926, he and two other 42s, Diego Ricco and Joe Pape, were sitting in a club, bemoaning their boredom, when they suddenly got the idea to hit a store in the brothel district of the infamous Levee. To Mooney, such jobs were as much for the thrill as for the cash they brought. He drove and served as lookout on most heists and jumped at the chance that night to demonstrate his getaway skills, whipping corners and laying rubber.

The robbery backfired miserably. Everything was going

fine, Mooney would later recall, until the crazy shopkeeper, a man named Girard, decided to be a hero and went for a gun. With that, all hell broke loose and gunfire was exchanged, bringing scores of people running toward the shop and wounding both Pape and Girard. The trio managed to make their getaway, but the next morning the detectives were knocking at the Giancana door, arrest warrants in hand, thanks to a witness, Alex Burba. Girard, the foolhardy shopkeeper, had died and Mooney, Pape, and Ricco were jailed. Bond was set at $25,000 on charges of robbery and murder.

Antonio received an envelope stuffed with cash from Diamond Joe Esposito and once again, money in hand, trudged down to the station house to win Mooney's release. The trial was scheduled for April of the following year.

Out on bail and at home, the strain began to show. Mooney became more aggressive with the children, as well as with Antonio. He largely ignored Mary, his stepmother, although he seemed to brighten at four-year-old Chuck's antics and didn't try to hide that the small rough-and-tumble boy was his favorite.

Like the rest of the neighborhood, Mooney was both impressed and amused by the little guy's sassiness and daring, his fearless acrobatics on the curbs and street corners. Not a day passed that Chuck could not be found swinging precariously from electrical wires, jumping from stoops and second-story rooftops, or dashing into the street to make a game of dodging the constant stream of carts and cars—behavior that drove Chuck's mother to near distraction as she anxiously watched for speeding cars and gangland whippers.

In October, Chuck's daring would lead to tragedy. The

four-year-old was playing in the street when a car barreled down on him. Ever alert, Mary ran from the stoop to save her child. Most certainly, he would have been killed if it hadn't been for what she did next. In one of those rare moments—when what a person is truly made of crystallizes—Mary Leonardi Giancana ran directly into the path of the car and threw her son, with every bit of strength she had, across the street. Within seconds, she was dead, dragged over a block by the speeding car. Three days later, she was buried. And Chuck was left with guilt instead of a mother.

Mary's funeral flooded Mooney with memories he'd never realized still slept within him: his own mother's eyes, her soft, comforting voice, the emptiness he'd felt so long ago. The feelings aroused in him an emotion long dead, one unfamiliar to him during his years as a 42. An affection stirred, stronger than ever, for four-year-old Chuck, who was standing by his side. Mooney tightened his grip on the little boy's hand. They had a kinship; they shared this loss. What had followed in his own life after his mother's death, all the brutality and pain, Mooney would never allow to touch this little boy. There had been no one to protect Mooney when his mother died. But he could change that for this child. He would protect him from all the madness, push him in a different direction from the one he'd chosen. Chuck wouldn't grow up to be a common greaseball, not now, not with him at his side.

Mooney stayed close to home over the next months. He quietly and solemnly watched Chuck as he reflected on his own mother—her face now no more than a vague memory.

In December, the dress shop burglary trial came up and Mooney and Caruso were acquitted for lack of evidence, but Sypher got one to ten years. A darkness still enveloped Mooney's days; he had the trial for murder to contend with in April. The possibility of prison and the electric chair haunted him at night when he fell asleep on the sofa and greeted him with the sunrise. There was no way he would allow either to occur; and therefore, he came up with a plan to make sure of it.

As the 1927 winter turned to spring, and the murder trial date drew near, Mooney launched an intimidation campaign against the only witness who could testify against them, Alex Burba. First, he and Ricco tried husky-voiced phone calls and whispered sinister threats—all with no effect. When this failed, they redoubled their efforts, the three driving over together to pay Burba "a little visit" at his soda shop. But the man remained steadfast. The trial date was only days away when Mooney decided to resort to bribery—offering Burba two thousand dollars in cash to keep his mouth shut. Still, he wouldn't back down. As Mooney saw it, they had no other choice at that point but to "kill the stupid bastard." And on the evening of April 20, at Mooney's bidding, Diego Ricco went back to Burba's shop alone and plugged him twice—once in the shoulder and once, a fatal wound, in the back of the head. No one came forward to finger them in Burba's death, and ten days later the Girard case was dropped for lack of evidence. Mooney's spirits lifted.

Things went back to normal and he started driving fast and hanging out with the guys at Bonfiglio's again. In the smoky pool hall, while his fellow 42 members grumbled about Joey Colaro's leadership, his rules against girls and guns, his heavy-handed domination, Mooney had his own ideas. Abiding by the rules set by Colaro no longer concerned him; there were other, more important men to reach and he thought he was almost there. Driving for McGurn had put him among the Capone gang and impressing them was all that mattered now. Once he made it with those guys, he'd bring his own band with him: Fat Leonard Caifano; Needles Gianola; Fiore "Fifi" Buccieri; "Willie Potatoes" Daddano; Sam "Mad Dog" DeStefano; "Milwaukee Phil" Alderisio; Chuckie Nicoletti, and the English brothers, Chuck and Butch.

Scanning the room, Mooney saw what would become the underworld's future, its "Youngbloods." The other thing he saw was an empire.

While other people were still heralding the May transatlantic flight of Lindbergh, Mooney's attention was fixed on other concerns, specifically, removing any obstacles in his path to leadership. And as fate—assisted by an anonymous phone call made by Mooney to the police— would have it, Mooney's one stumbling block to control of his fellow 42s—Joey Colaro—was gunned down in November. The press described the event as the "end of the 42s." Mooney described it as his "lucky break."

His next big break came when he got a call from the Capone gang in March of 1928. Most men might have shunned the request, might have wanted no part in the betrayal. But Mooney readily, eagerly complied.

He stood in the telephone booth, collar turned up on his topcoat, and stared vacantly out the dirty plate-glass window at the people milling around the aisles of Chesrow's Drugstore. Then he turned his back and dialed, glancing over his shoulder one last time before covering the mouthpiece with a crisp white handkerchief. His muffled voice echoed against the booth's wood-paneled walls when he spoke, his words pouring out in a low snarl. "Get outta town or get killed," he said to the man on the line, the man who had saved him from petty gangs and petty crime and starvation on the streets. Then he smiled a cruel smile and hung up the phone.

CHAPTER 3

Among the branches of the budding hedges, a lone mockingbird chirped the final notes of its evening song. Nearby, a sleek black roadster lingered along the curb, camouflaged by the nightfall. Stealthily, almost imperceptibly, it had been edging forward. At the wheel, a young man, oily black hair slicked back and a cigarette drooping from his lips, smiled as his passengers nodded at their approaching victim.

Unaware, Diamond Joe Esposito walked to his death with arrogance, swaggering confidently down the sidewalk toward his assassins—his jowls jiggling up and down as he chewed on a smoldering fat cigar. His bodyguards, the Varchetti brothers, seemed nervous, glancing from side to side.

The car fairly twitched in anticipation, its engine racing ever so slightly. The exhilaration of the coming kill quickened the driver's pulse; he longed to spring forward, but waited for his moment. When it came, he shifted the car into gear and lunged with a guttural roar toward the man.

Diamond Joe cried, "Oh my God!" at the sight of the oncoming gunmen and, instead of shielding their charge, the Varchettis fell to the ground.

Riveting machine-gun fire caught the padrone first in the chest, and his eyes registered fear as he stared knowingly into the driver's face for one brief second before falling forward, succumbing to the gnawing bullets that tore at his flesh. The hot lead ate through him, chewing the layers of clothing and fat—ripping them into open, flapping pieces of skin. Another round pitted and splattered what remained. Convulsing in a foam of blood, his arms and legs jerked spastically.

The driver paused long enough to watch Esposito's wife, Carmello, rush from her home. "Oh my God, is it you, Giuseppe? I'll kill them for this, I'll kill them!" she screamed, and threw herself on her husband's mutilated corpse.

The car sped off, swerving in the distance and—with brakes shrieking victoriously—rounded a corner, disappearing from sight.

Before he was gunned down in March of 1928, fifty-six-year-old Esposito had been a mentor to Mooney and hundreds of other boys languishing on street corners—as well as a benefactor to a great many struggling Italian families. He'd passed out 2,500 turkeys each year at Thanksgiving, played Santa Claus to the children of the Patch, and supported the local Italian charities.

Despite these philanthropic endeavors, Antonio Giancana, like many of his fellow immigrants, believed it was "a service his enemies have done this neighborhood . . . a service to rid us of such bloody tyrants as Diamond Joe."

But in the Patch, there were always new tyrants to replace the old, new rules to follow and lessons to learn. Carving out a life in the sprawling Italian section was difficult at best. The only apparent route to a better future, the only hope to escape the poverty, was a life of crime—and even then, the more ambitious, like Mooney, recognized power was not handed down; it was taken.

With Esposito out of the way, Capone eyed illicit operations throughout the entire Midwest; he began consolidating the ragtag assortment of south side gangs and made plans to eliminate his north side competitors. He and Paul Ricca continued Esposito's political friendships, hoping to extend the gang's influence still further.

Viewed more as a public servant than a criminal, Capone gave the people of Chicago what they wanted—booze, sex, and gambling—and his popularity in the city soared.

Capone's consolidation of power meant more power for his loyal followers. And Mooney was fast to take advantage of his own dominance in the Patch. In April 1927, he got another chance to prove his worth to Capone during the Republican party primary.

Incumbent Mayor Thompson was being challenged by what the Capone forces derided as a "do-gooder," Senator Charles Deneen. It was critical to the gang's operations that Thompson remain in power, and they made every effort to see to it that the appropriate number of vote floaters—people who went from precinct to precinct voting again and again—were out on the streets on the day of the primary.

But the Twentieth Ward had the gang worried; Thompson's political crony Morris Eller was being challenged by Octavius Granady, and rumor had it that the black attorney might actually win.

Mooney got the word to get rid of Granady—"the up-start, moolie, shine troublemaker"—on the morning of the election. Later that day, as the polls were closing, Granady was shot to death by four men in a sedan.

Morris Eller remained in power and Mooney was taken in for questioning but released—"Of course," he would later say.

Three months later, in June of 1928, Mooney Giancana was twenty years old, and every man, woman, and child in the neighborhood not only feared him but revered him, as well. His recent scrapes with the law, the murders he was known to have committed, his brutal intimidation tactics—all became legendary. Rather than diminish his stature, the stories the immigrants whispered among themselves only served to make the swaggering Mooney a larger-than-life figure. To the Italians, hoods like Mooney who'd roamed the streets as youths and now were pulling themselves up by the bootstraps to achieve financial success were simply symbols of a dream come true.

And you had to have a dream to get by in the Patch.

Mooney's little brother, five-year-old Chuck, didn't think any of the thousands of poor, uneducated immigrants who littered their neighborhood had a dream—at least not one like his.

He liked to pretend he was someone else—and ever since Mooney and Fat Leonard had taken him to see his first cowboy picture, he'd thought Tom Mix would be a good choice as a hero. But the best hero of all was Mooney. To Chuck, Mooney, at twenty, was a bona fide adult. Mooney came and went as he pleased. He had money and respect; he could even smart-mouth their peddler father and get away with it.

As long as Chuck could remember, the bigger boys had

spoken with unabashed reverence of Mooney and the 42 gang. Sometimes Chuck and the other kids would congregate on the stoop to watch the neighborhood men, fueled by homemade wine, play craps under the streetlight. One of the men served as a lookout for the Irish coppers who roamed the streets, ever ready to grease the patrolmen's palms if necessary, while the others rolled the dice, laughing and swearing in turn. Even *they* discussed his brother Mooney, and though Chuck couldn't always make out the exact words, their tone conveyed respect.

Chuck pretended not to pay attention to the bigger boys' whisperings as he checked his shoes for scuff marks, methodically rubbing each one off with the plaid patch on his sleeve. But in truth, he listened, enraptured, to their narration of his brother's escapades. They said the newspapers called Mooney the generalissimo of the 42, that he'd killed at least fifty men for Diamond Joe and Capone without blinking an eye—and they played games trying to name them all: "There's the one guy on the train tracks; there's the politician, Granady; there's . . ." And they reenacted heists and shootouts, describing in vivid detail the accompanying car chases.

Hearing tales about Al Capone's men and Mooney's 42 gang was better—even when Chuck had the nickel for admission in the pocket of his worn knickers—than going to any picture show at the Broadway over on Roosevelt Road, even one starring Tom Mix.

Esposito's death and Mooney's handling of the Granady murder catapulted Mooney to new acceptance by the Capone gang. He swiftly found a place among the older gangsters, supplementing his job driving for McGurn with that of executioner. It was easy money—and he was good at it. The rise in status brought him the adulation he'd craved so desperately from his old 42 cronies. Guys like Willie Potatoes, Fifi Buccieri, Mad Dog, "Teets" Battaglia, Milwaukee Phil, and Fat Leonard followed him around like lapdogs.

But with his prominence also came jealousy and rivalry; other gangs resented Mooney's ties to the big-name gangsters and looked for any means possible to knock him from his throne as reigning smarthead. His was a precarious crown and only through cunning was he able to survive their continual attempts to topple his authority. One such attempt changed everything for the Giancana family.

It had been late, probably well past midnight, one chilly September night in 1928, and Chuck had waited until he knew everyone else was asleep before propping himself up on the coarse flour sacks his sisters painstakingly stitched into pillowcases. He folded his thin olive arms behind his head and gazed past the cracked window. He never could tell whether there was a moon in the sky—or stars, for that matter—but boys didn't dwell on such things, anyhow. Chuck thought that was for sissies and queers.

He preferred to drift into his own secret world and cherished these moments in bed at night, though they weren't exactly ones of solitude. He was never really alone, since his brother Pepe and three cousins shared the bed. Since his father had married his widowed sister-in-law, Catherine, earlier that year, things in the small Giancana flat had become cramped and overcrowded. His stern-faced stepmother had seven children of her own, three boys—Vito, Chuckie, and Joey—and four girls—Pearl, Victoria, Rose, and Gracie.

It was hard to fall asleep with the sharp wire bedsprings squealing as they poked through the thin mattress. Or with

Cousin Vito's knobby toes wriggling in his face and Joey's knees nuzzling at his groin. To avoid such unwelcome intimacy, Chuck scooted up on his pillow and curled into an upright fetal position, pulling the covers tightly under his chin. A slumbering tug-of-war ensued as his brother and cousins wrestled drowsily to maintain their rightful portion of the blanket.

He amused himself by listening to the usual late-night cacophony of police sirens, screeching brakes, and the occasional staccato of gunfire echoing up and down the alleyways. Mentally rehashing the stories about Mooney he'd overheard earlier made him smile in the darkness; there was nothing he would rather be—in the whole wide world—than head of a gang like Mooney's 42. And he was determined that someday he would.

Suddenly, a thunderous blast ripped through the Patch. The little panes of glass in the window rattled like aggies in a tin can. He sat bolt upright, rubbing his eyes as much in amazement as to awaken fully. All the while, the brick walls of the flat shuddered and waffled in response to the explosion. He thought the entire room might come down around him and, terrified, he leapt from the bed, feeling the cold wood floor quake beneath his bare feet.

The shaking stopped and someone screamed in the street below. Grabbing his pants, he rushed over to the window and opened it, leaning out as far as his small frame would allow, stretching into the cool night air. The acrid scent of smoke filled his nostrils. He could just make out a red glow; it tinted the skyline and lit the shadowy figures of people running in its direction. Hundreds of lights shot on from as many households.

This wasn't your routine pineapple bombing, no sirree, he thought excitedly as he scampered through the window and onto the rickety wooden porch. It groaned beneath his weight and a few of the more rotted timbers sank spongily with each hesitant step. His heart fluttered when he looked down two stories to the rubble illuminated below. Had it been daylight and had he had an audience, he would have been fearless; he was always jumping from stoops and rooftops and he was proud of the reputation he'd earned as the neighborhood's foremost daredevil. But tonight, the darkness made him uneasy. He forgot any thoughts of such antics and, using one hand to steady himself, slipped on his pants. He could hardly wait to find out who had thrown such an incredible bomb, and called in to his brother and cousins; they sat frozen in the bed. "Sissies," he mumbled to himself.

Those who lived in the Patch had long gotten used to the nightly bombings, shootings, and fires—but in Chuck's short life, there had been nothing to equal the magnitude of this bombing. He heard a furious pounding at their front door, then heard it slam. Moments later, he caught sight of his father, still dressed in his nightclothes, running toward the blaze with his vegetable and lemon ice store partner, Gremilda.

Before Chuck could steal down the porch to follow, his sister Antoinette burst into the room. She stood in the doorway, dark eyes searching for him, tapping her foot angrily on the floor. Of his four sisters, Antoinette had the highest spirit and strongest constitution. After their mother had died, she'd taken on the task of mothering herself, caring for her five younger brothers and sisters with a courage and conviction uncommon for a girl of sixteen, but expected by Italians from the Old Country and certainly by Mooney and her father. Old habits died hard, and although the children now had a new mother, Antoinette still clung to her role of protectress.

Chuck's brother and cousins laughed as he sullenly trudged back to bed. Not until he'd pulled the rough sheets around his shoulders and fallen asleep did Antoinette close the door.

The incident would make Chuck understand, as best any child could, what the violence of the Patch meant to its victims: Thanks to the bombing of his father's lemon ice store, the entire Giancana family fortune, paltry as it was, was lost.

Less than two weeks later, on September 17, Antonio and Gremilda were shot and brutally beaten by young thugs from a rival gang of the 42, and, with the assistance of one more bomb, what little was left of the lemon ice store was demolished. The two men felt lucky to escape with their lives.

The boys on the street told Chuck that everybody thought his father and partner had been muscled by some guys Mooney had crossed. And that the same hoods had murdered one of Mooney's friends, a smarthead everybody called "Dibbits," after Mooney shotgunned one of their gang. Nobody expected the police to do anything about this latest wave of violence; they were too busy roughing up the remaining 42s or shaking them down to care about real trouble.

After the bombing, the mood in the Patch became strangely tense. Old women carrying baskets stacked high with loaves of bread, salami, and provolone lowered their heads and scuttled hurriedly to the other side of the street when punks under Mooney's spell—the Battaglia brothers, the DeStefanos, and crazy Patsy Tardi—strolled brazenly among the fruit and vegetable stands spreading the word: Mooney Giancana was declaring war.

There was no doubt Mooney, once he'd pinpointed the perpetrators of this latest offense, would take care of things his own way in the Patch. "Mooney'll give the guy who bombed his father's store a good taste of his own medicine," Chuck heard one boy say. And it was true. Even a child like Chuck knew Mooney would mete out his own brand of justice, that it was just a matter of time.

Unknown to Chuck, people of the Patch did have dreams of their own. But like him, they kept them to themselves, not daring to voice them for fear they would somehow hope too much—and fail. His father's dream had been to prosper in his lemon ice business. Antonio Giancana had lain awake at night, planning and worrying. It was a special pleasure to wonder where he'd get enough lemon or whether he'd have enough shaved ice to serve his growing enterprise. Now that dream had been blown to smithereens—lost in a rubbish heap with all the rest. And Antonio lay awake wondering where he'd get enough food to feed his children.

No one in the family could recall Antonio speaking up to Mooney; but now he didn't hide the fact that he blamed his son for their misfortune. They bickered and argued, screaming obscenities back and forth like two Sicilian fishwives. When Mooney was in the house, which had suddenly become rare, he sulked and stormed through the flat, smashing dishes against the walls and, more than once, his fist.

It wasn't so unusual for Mooney to be ill-tempered—unyielding in his control, he was always throwing his weight around in the Giancana household. But it was unlike Antonio to be so vocal. At twenty, Mooney had already murdered more men than Antonio cared to imagine, and he was now more afraid of his son's violent unpredictability than ever.

In the midst of this family infighting and economic collapse, Chuck and two of his friends stole a bag of money containing thirty-five dollars from the old pieman's car parked along Taylor Street as it made its deliveries of fresh fruit and cream pies.

"This is how the Forty-two got its start," they crowed among themselves and, victorious, the boys paraded through the Patch to spend their fortune on Maxwell Street—where a few nickels could buy food and clothing and a million other things about which most children in the Patch could only dream.

No one seemed to wonder why three ragamuffins had so much money; people in the Patch learned not to ask too many questions. The Italian vendors accepted with an open hand whatever came their way—whether stolen goods or cash. So for three dollars, a hunchbacked old man gladly sold them a red bicycle. And a pretty girl, who made Chuck blush when she smiled at him, took a crisp one-dollar bill for a pair of roller skates.

By five o'clock that evening, the bicycle lay in a twisted heap of spokes and rubber—a victim of the boys' overzealous acts of daring. Undaunted, Chuck next entertained himself by devising acrobatic feats on the skates. As the sun slowly disappeared behind the redbrick tenements, his friends departed for home and dinner. Chuck was left alone, shivering in the damp air. He sat down on the stoop to unstrap the skates and was so entranced by them that he jumped when Mooney's voice intruded on his daydreams.

"Where did you get those?" Mooney asked nonchalantly.

"From a friend," Chuck answered, barely looking up.

"A friend?"

"Uh-huh." Chuck's hands began to shake, which made the wheels of the roller skates twirl ever so slightly. But he was sure Mooney saw them—sure Mooney knew he was lying. He pushed a matted forelock of black hair from his eyes and looked up. Gone were the casual posture and friendly smile. In their place was the coldness he'd seen so many times.

In one swift gesture, Mooney leapt from the stair and lifted Chuck by his collar. He held him, squirming, and slapped him hard across the mouth as he whispered between clenched teeth, "Don't ever lie to me. Understand?"

Chuck nodded. Tears dribbled in milky streaks down his face.

"Okay. We'll try again. Where did you get the skates?"

It was hard to talk but he managed to choke out a reply: "I found them."

Mooney raised one hand ominously and, with the other, grabbed Chuck by his ear, jerking his face right up to his own. His breath was hot and smelled like cheap wine and stale cigarettes. "What? I don't believe it for a minute. Did you steal them?"

"No, honest I didn't . . . honest."

Mooney slapped him hard again. "Tell me the truth. Now!"

Chuck began to sob. "Okay, okay. Don't hit me no more. Please," he begged. "I'll tell you. I promise. Please."

"I'm waiting."

"Nickie and Tony . . . they stole . . . money . . . from the pieman."

"Were you with them?"

"Uh, well . . . yeah. But . . ."

"Did you help take the money?"

"Hm, uh sort of . . . maybe . . . sort of."

Mooney's pointed-toe shoe came out of nowhere to kick Chuck in the side with a sickening thud and he screamed, "Sort of? Did you or didn't you? Tell the goddamned truth or I'm gonna beat the living hell outta you."

Doubled over in pain, Chuck decided to tell it all. He'd spill his guts and Mooney would see that they were just like the 42. Just as smart and tough. "All right, I will. I will. I promise," he said.

Oddly calm, Mooney sat down next to him and listened to every word. When at last he finished, Chuck hesitantly looked into his eyes, hoping he'd gained approval—or at least a lighter sentence.

Mooney leaned over, still poised to strike, and hissed through his teeth, "Never, ever, be a stool pigeon, Chuck. That'll get you killed." He stood up and glowered. "You heard of *omertà*?" He screamed. "You keep your eyes and ears open . . . and your fuckin' mouth *shut*." The blur of Mooney's body rushed down upon him. Again the pointed toe of the leather shoe kicked him.

"*Omertà*," Mooney shouted. "Never forget that word. Never beef on anybody. You got that? Never."

Mooney picked up the roller skates, then stormed down the sidewalk until reaching a garbage can. Taking off the lid, he turned to Chuck, still cowering on the stairs. Mooney smiled and, with dramatic pomp, held the shiny skates above the gaping can. Dropping them, he slammed the lid down. The sound of metal against metal still clattered when he put his hands in his pockets and sauntered away.

Chuck stared blankly at the can. His beautiful skates

were gone just as quickly as he'd gotten them. He stayed on the steps for a while and cried. When he finally decided to stop, he sat whimpering and nursing his wounds and hating his brother. He'd remember what Mooney said, all right. He'd never beef on anybody again if it killed him. And besides, maybe it was time he'd learned his lesson: The consequences of telling the truth were just too great. He repeated the word *omertà* as he limped up the stairs.

In the following days, the first autumn frost blanketed the neighborhood, bringing with it new wares for the peddlers to display. Acorn squash and zucchini and pumpkins gleamed like brightly colored fallen leaves from the backs of wagons drawn by tired swaybacked horses. Emptied of their summer fare, each wobbly wooden crate and stand was now filled with the season's harvest, serving as a reminder of the approaching winter and the crisis it would bring; unlike in the Old Country, winter here sent bitter cold into the drafty, squalid flats and, with it, killers like tuberculosis and pneumonia.

This time of year, when Antonio could find him, Chuck carted the heaps of coal his father sold. It was a job he hated—which explained why he took his time getting home from school one crisp fall day just a little more than a month after the bombing of the lemon ice store.

Sitting on his favorite curb, Chuck threw the little stones he'd gathered on his wanderings, then picked them up and threw them again. He pretended they were dice. He could play like this for hours on end, which was exactly what he'd been doing when a man walked up beside him. Chuck paid no attention to the stranger standing there, leaning against the lamppost.

The man started to whistle. Finally, he stopped, bending

down to smile as he waved one hand toward the little stones and said, "Hey, kid. Can anybody play?"

Chuck looked up. The man was tall, an Italian. He hadn't seen him around before, which was odd. But he smiled back anyway. To people in the Patch, anyone who wasn't a mick, Polack, or a shine—in short, anyone Italian—was *paisan*.

"Uh-uh," Chuck said, shaking his head. "This is a one-man game . . . but . . . you can watch if you want."

"That's fair," the man replied, and continued whistling.

Chuck had just gotten up to retrieve his stones, rubbing his dusty hands on his ragged knickers, when out of the corner of his eye he spotted his brother. He was walking quickly toward them, and before Chuck could call out a "hello," Mooney stepped up to the stranger.

There was a loud *pop* and the man fell to the ground; blood gushed from his head like water from an open fire hydrant. It pulsed rhythmically—Chuck thought he could hear a slight *whoosh, whoosh, whoosh* as it spurted through a mangled hole of oozing brains and bone, bursting in torrents onto the pavement. And then, as quickly as he'd appeared, Mooney was gone.

Transfixed, Chuck stared down at the dead man; he couldn't make out a face.

Barbershop customers, lathered with heaps of shaving cream, ran out across the street and women tending children in buggies began yelling back and forth between second-story windows and stoops. Vendors threw down their wares, leaving vegetables to tumble down the sidewalk as they rushed to see what the commotion was about. The inevitable sirens of police cars rang in the distance as they made their way through the Patch.

Still Chuck stood there, mesmerized by the blood from the whistling man. It steamed in the cool autumn air. He didn't know there was so much blood in a person. It smelled like the warm iron in a blacksmith's shop and ran in sticky puddles around his feet.

Dozens of people milled around the body, pushing and shoving. Shaking their heads in disgust, the men shielded their women's eyes.

When the police arrived, one began questioning those standing closest to the dead man. He was a red-faced Irish copper with a notepad in one hand and a pencil behind his ear. Puffing out his barrel chest, he strutted over and squatted down to meet Chuck face-to-face.

"Let's make some room here," another officer shouted, forcing the crowd back with his nightstick.

"So what did you see, son? Did you see the person who did this terrible thing? Did you?" He grasped Chuck by his shoulders. His eyes were bullet blue and they made Chuck want to turn away, afraid they might puncture any words he might offer. In the crowd beyond, he caught sight of Mooney, standing as though invisible, enveloped within the onlookers. Mooney lifted one eyebrow and stared vacantly into his eyes.

Chuck looked back at the officer. "No, sir," his small voice trembled in reply.

"Well . . ." The copper scowled. "What were you doing, then, if you didn't see anything? You were right here?"

"Playing."

"Playing? Playing what?" He put one hand on the base of his nightstick with threatening authority.

"With these." Chuck opened his hand to display his treasured stones.

"With some rocks?" the officer exclaimed, standing up. "And you didn't see a thing? Not a thing? Well, then, go home to your mama . . . you, you little greaseball." Angrily, he slapped Chuck's open hand and the stones flew out, scattering in all directions. Chuck turned and ran.

That night, sitting on the stoop after a meager bowl of ceci beans, he listened intently while the older boys discussed the day's murder. Everyone figured Mooney and his friends had been behind it all; the man who'd been killed was a member of the same gang believed responsible for the bombing of Antonio's lemon ice store. All agreed things would be back to normal in the Patch—now that justice had been dispensed.

If only they knew, really knew that it was Mooney, Chuck thought to himself. He wished he could tell them, could share his deadly secret. As much as he wanted to tell his gruesome story, to see their faces blanch with the truth and his own stature rise in the telling, he said nothing. He chose to sit in silence, recalling Mooney in the crowd, the vivid image of his brother's victim lying in a pool of blood.

Certainly, losing his stones was a small price to pay. And lying to a mick copper to save his brother— why, he felt sure his own father would have done the same. Tomorrow, he'd hunt in the vacant lots for more stones.

"*Omertà*," he whispered softly to himself. Yes, he was sure he'd done the right thing. He'd learned the lesson well; the roller skates had taught him that. "Never beef on anybody," Mooney had said. "*Omertà*." Chuck said the word over and over again. He was proud to have done the right thing. The only thing. And he would do anything to make his brother proud. He'd earn Mooney's confidence and respect if it took him the rest of his life.

Mooney never mentioned the incident—nor did Chuck. Chuck referred to that afternoon in 1928 as "the day I lost my stones." Only years later would he use the word *innocence*.

CHAPTER 4

If Chuck had indeed gained Mooney's respect by keep-ing quiet about the whistling man, there was no sign of it. He even wondered whether the beatings had intensified. For days after one of Mooney's unwarranted tirades, his small back and legs sported reminders of his older brother's authority: the tender pink stripes left by a razor-sharp leather belt, the blue-black bruises that mottled his arms.

Strangely, whenever he investigated a mark left by one of Mooney's more recent admonitions, Chuck felt guilty—for letting his big brother down. And thankful—because Mooney cared.

Mooney said he wanted Pepe and Chuck to grow up right, "to show respect." That he didn't want them to turn out to be just common dago greaseballs. His sisters, he believed, required even more supervision; they would never grow up to be cheap painted tramps under his close scrutiny, and he forbade them to associate with what he called "whores and trollops wearin' flea-bitten furs with ugly animal heads danglin' around their necks."

He made it clear the children needed the strictest discipline. And if Mooney was inclined to provide it, no one in the family—including Antonio—was inclined to interfere. Indeed, following the recent slaying, attributed by most as retribution for the bombing of his lemon ice store, Antonio seemed to have settled back into meek submission in Mooney's presence.

Mooney ignored his stepmother's children for the most part. He felt no allegiance, no concern for their welfare. The three boys—Vito, Chuckie, and Joey—could have been invisible for all they mattered to Mooney. He barely looked at them or spoke to them; they didn't exist unless they got in his way. Of Catherine's four girls, only Gracie remained in the house; the other three had married.

Mooney's tactics were effective; the children avoided making waves. They tiptoed through the house. "Where's Mooney?" they'd whisper, and look over their shoulders when engaged in any activity, no matter how insignificant.

But what made it most difficult for Chuck, who wrestled continually with conflicting feelings of anger and love, guilt and resentment—and anyone else who dealt with the strong-willed Mooney—was that just as quickly as his hand could be raised in anger, it could also hold a gift or some small treasure. And both always came as a surprise, without provocation, depending on his mood at the time.

Everyone had long since given up trying to predict young Mooney Giancana's irrational state of mind—which was where they knew his nickname had come from in the first place. They just anticipated the worst and said a few Hail Marys.

Mooney walked through the door of the two-story flat

one winter evening after Christmas in 1928 with a box under one arm and a big smile on his face. Members of the Giancana family had to assume he was happy. And when he was, they were.

Grinning with uncharacteristic excitement, he handed his camel hair topcoat and fedora to his youngest sister, Vicki, and immediately motioned for Chuck to sit by him on the sofa. He placed the box between them.

"Well, open it up, Chuck. It's for you."

"Me? Really, Mooney?"

"Yeah, really. Come on . . . open it."

Chuck picked up the box. It was heavy. He held his breath; he hoped it was the chemistry set he'd seen in the window of the department store.

"Come on, I don't have all night. Your sisters are setting the table . . . and I'm hungry." Mooney laughed and took a wrinkled Camel from the pack in his shirt and lighted it.

Chuck lifted the lid. At first, he wasn't sure what the long black thing with little silver buttons could possibly be, but before he could examine it, Mooney grabbed it up and lifted one end to his lips.

"It's a clarinet, Chuck," he explained. "And you're going to learn to play it, real nice. Hey, everybody, Chuck is going to take music lessons . . . be a musician. Maybe play in a big band someday just like Benny Goodman."

The entire family gathered around the sofa, the girls oohing and aahing at the clarinet while the boys tried to conceal snickers of delight at Chuck's misery.

Chuck could hardly hide his disappointment and it made him wish for the chemistry set even more. Play an instrument? Take music lessons? He wanted to grow up to be a member of Mooney's gang—not a musician. He didn't think a member of the 42 would ever in a million years play a stupid clarinet; that was for girls and sissy entertainers. No, he wanted to have a 70 Chrysler and learn to drive it like Mooney did when he wheeled for Jack McGurn. He managed a halfhearted smile. "It's real nice, Mooney. Thanks."

"Is that all you're gonna say? Huh? After your big brother robs the bank to buy you a clarinet so you can have a trade . . . so you can grow up and be somebody?" He stood up and put his hands on his narrow hips, waiting for an answer. "Well . . . ?"

For a moment, Chuck wondered whether Mooney really had robbed a bank; after all, the money for the clarinet had to have come from somewhere. He thought of his sister Antoinette, who had been suffering with a toothache all week. Tearfully, she'd begged for money to see a dentist; Antonio had refused. He glanced up at Antoinette, her jaw still swollen, and wondered just how much the clarinet had cost and where the money had come from. But he couldn't disappoint Mooney.

"It's real nice. I like it . . . a lot. Really, I do," he said, trying to sound convincing. But his voice sounded pleading, like it did when Mooney started to use the strap and he begged him to stop. Chuck was no different from the people of the neighborhood or the rest of his family; he'd learned to say or do anything to appease Mooney, to avoid his brother's wrath at any cost. He put on his most convincing smile.

It must have worked because, after scrutinizing Chuck's face with the same thoroughness he might give the blueprint of a bank, Mooney seemed satisfied. "Good," he said. "It's settled. You start your lessons tomorrow after school, over at Mr. Cuchardi's."

"Okay, Mooney." Chuck glanced down at the hated instrument and then added, "Thanks."

Josie called to tell them dinner was ready; but she didn't have to: The heavy scent of garlic and oregano mingled with freshly baked bread made Chuck's mouth water.

There were no Roman Catholic words of grace spoken over meals at the Giancana household. No tablecloth or napkins, and few utensils. What dishes they had were a mismatched display of multicolored broken crockery. The table was filled with platters of pasta, barely enough to feed thirteen people. A melee of twisted hands and arms reached in all directions, grabbing for every morsel of food.

Between the forkfuls of pasta Chuck feverishly crammed in his mouth, he asked above the clamor, "Hey, Mooney . . . can me and Pepe go with you in your car tonight?"

Josie reached over to wipe his chin with the edge of her apron. "Leave Mooney alone, Chuck," she said. "Let him eat in peace."

His sisters glared at him now, disapproval shining in their eyes like coals in the wood stove. Chuck cast a sidelong glance at his stepmother; her reaction didn't matter, anyway. She wasn't their mother—and never would be, as far as he was concerned. After Chuck's mother had been killed, Antonio had paid Catherine a visit; soon after, they had married. Chuck knew it was a marriage of convenience, no more no less. And what had been a difficult, scrape-by existence to begin with got tougher. Catherine made a point of letting everyone know how little she cared for the Giancana brood.

Lifting his glass, Antonio shook his head at Chuck and mumbled his displeasure in Italian. He gulped at the wine and then set it down, wiping the red liquid from his mouth with the back of his hand. From under a canopy of bushy salt and pepper eyebrows, he shot a hard look at Mooney; he didn't want his other boys out on the streets.

Nor did Mooney. He often viewed them as his own children, his sole responsibility. Antonio, the naïve immigrant, had not the slightest idea what could happen to the boys out there on the streets.

But Mooney did. He'd seen punk kids as young as Chuck working for the gangs; they ended up dead by the time they were sixteen. That would never happen as long as he was around—he'd promised himself that when Chuck's mother died. No, he'd told Chuck over and over that he had other, more noble aspirations for him; he would have a trade and leave the poverty of the Patch behind forever. No matter that the example he set was one much different, if not in utter conflict.

"Don't you have something else to do? I think we'll have to go out another time," Mooney said, tearing a piece of hard-crusted bread from the loaf on the table. He scraped it back and forth, sopping up the red gravy until the cracked china shone. "Dinner's real good, Josie," he complimented. Then, twinkle in his eye, he added quietly, "But I can make better."

"Oh you can, can you?" Josie laughed, making the spindly-legged chair creak and sway beneath her. She was an excellent cook and had every reason to doubt his abilities. She looked at her other sisters and said, "Well, sometime you'll just have to show us."

"I will," he said, putting his fork and spoon down. "In fact, I'll make dinner for all of you next week . . . on Thursday."

The girls stared in disbelief. But Mooney was a man of

his word and if he said he'd cook them a dinner, he would. They'd enjoyed his meat-filled red gravies on special occasions over the years, but he'd never prepared a full dinner.

Mooney the cook. It seemed a contradiction, but he was full of those. He was a macho, swaggering smarthead who worked over a stove as readily as any woman. He was a man who, since he was just a boy, had learned to kill at another's bidding. And although one didn't talk of such things, it was common knowledge among girls of the Patch that Mooney was a man who—since he could first get it up—got it off banging fast mick and Polack girls in the backseat of a car. The same man who swore he would only marry an Italian virgin.

He leaned back in his chair and lit a cigarette. Dragging deeply, he smiled, making his thin lips curl around it in a crooked, half-cocked grin. He unbuttoned his shirt collar and loosened his wide silk tie and said in his most flattering tone, "Josie, you're the best ironer in the neighborhood." He fingered the heavily starched collar and added, "Matter of fact, I brought some shirts over for you to iron." He waved to a pile of laundry containing several dozen shirts.

He was feeling the warmth of the wine and seemed approachable, more talkative than usual, almost friendly. "I'll need them tomorrow," he said as an afterthought, and, fishing into his trouser pocket, brought out a wad of bills.

"See, Pa? Your son is doin' pretty well for himself. Don't you think?" He fanned hundred-dollar bills like a hand of cards.

His four sisters nudged each other under the table. They hadn't seen so much money in one place. Chuck saw Antoinette put her hand to her swollen jaw; he wondered whether Mooney knew about her toothache.

Antonio grunted and said in Italian, "Well, if I ever open my store again and my ice sells well, your father will have more money than that someday."

Chuck rolled his eyes at his brother Pepe. Their father always had a scheme. And it never worked out. Although he had to admit this time it might; the whole neighborhood seemed to mourn the demise of his father's lemon ice store. Maybe, he thought—maybe this time Pa is right and we will be rich.

Mooney flipped through the bills with his thumb and then, easing them back into his pants pocket, stood up. With a glass of wine in one hand, he walked across the room. The twenty-year-old had a way of commanding attention; there was a self-assurance in his stride that surpassed his years—and it let you know he was a man to be reckoned with. Around the Patch, people said that Diamond Joe himself had once remarked admiringly to Capone, "Mooney has the biggest *coglioni* [balls] I've ever goddamned seen. . . . He'd kill his own fuckin' father if he got in his way." Ironic, given Esposito's demise.

Even here at home, as he sunk down into the comfort of Antonio's velvet easy chair, he never let up; he was in total and absolute control.

He fondled the chair's fabric as if it were a woman's breast, admiring its sensuous luster. He appreciated the finer things and, thanks to his extraordinary skill as a burglar, the Giancana household was graced with exquisite Venetian tapestries on the walls, marble-topped mahogany tables, and the neighborhood's first refrigerator—trappings of wealth that, in spite of his efforts, did little to hide their poverty. And nothing to alleviate it.

"Pa, come here," he commanded. "I need to speak to you . . . in private."

Chuck was envious of the way Mooney managed their father. In spite of everything—the calls from the police station, the bail money that kept them poor, the fear and intimidation—it looked to all the world as if the old man clearly worshiped his eldest son.

But for Antonio, it was just a matter of acknowledging the obvious. Though Mooney might be on the wrong side of the law, no one could deny he was doing well for himself. And that made him feel a certain pride. In a time when everyone else groveled for nickels, his son drove a fast car, swaggered around in well-tailored, expensive suits, and carried bankrolls that might contain as much as five hundred dollars—no matter he never shared the wealth with him. After all, he was just a small-time vendor who wore clothes decorated with a quiltwork of neatly executed patches. Antonio's entire life savings was less than one hundred dollars. What little luxury he had, he was convinced he had because of Mooney.

Not yet finished eating his pasta, Antonio sighed wistfully and pushed his plate away to rise from the table. If Momo wanted his undivided attention, the pasta would have to wait.

Hours later and sound asleep, Chuck, Pepe, and their cousins were awakened by Mooney, standing in the middle of the room. His glazed eyes darted wildly back and forth.

"Get up, you thieving little bastards," he shrieked, ripping the covers off the bed.

"What's the matter, Mooney? What is it? We didn't do nothing. Honest," Chuck begged. He was afraid of him when he was like this; there was no telling what he might do to them. The boys all began to wail.

"All right, you goddamned ungrateful little punks, who did it? Who took my fuckin' money?" Mooney swung at

Chuck, who was nearest, knocking him from the bed with his fist.

"I'll teach you a thing or two about stealin'. . . . All of you get out of bed . . . now," he said, yanking Chuck up by the hair with a force that lifted him off the floor. He slapped Chuck square across the face before he could raise his hands to shield himself. Chuck let out a long, shrill cry.

Mooney turned on Pepe next, releasing his grip on Chuck's black curls, which twisted like knotted yarn around his fingers. The small boy crashed to the floor.

"So . . . who did it?" Mooney bellowed. "You?" he screamed at Pepe. "You? You?" He spun around, accusing each boy in turn. The room grew eerily still. Chuckie, Vito, and Joey stood along the wall, shaking their heads fearfully, not taking their eyes off Chuck as he writhed on the floor.

"Fine. None of you have the balls to admit it," he sneered, and took off his belt. "I'll give you one last chance." He waved the belt like a whip above his head. Still on the floor, Chuck began to cry again more loudly. Mooney reeled on his heels, towering above him.

"No, Mooney, no," Chuck pleaded. "I wouldn't take your money. I wouldn't ever do that. I promise. Honest, I do. Please don't, Mooney. Please . . . ."

The belt sliced through the air with a cutting hiss. It came down again and again. Chuck's body began to shudder involuntarily. The air seemed thick and full of blood. He could taste it when the belt sliced through his lip. His rib cage heaved and he thought he might vomit; the salt of the blood and bile in his mouth made him gag.

Like a machine, Mooney moved around the room, dispensing his punishment methodically and with precision, until each boy felt the full force of his rage and understood the terror it could bring.

Breathing heavily, he let the belt drop to the floor and said, "So no one's talkin'. Fine, then take off your clothes . . . all of you."

The boys stood immobilized.

"Now. I said . . . now." He repeated the command, smiling cruelly.

Chuck's hands shook so hard, he could barely pull his nightshirt over his head. He couldn't imagine what Mooney was planning to do to them and he wished, desperately, that whoever took the money would come forward. The unfairness of it all stung worse than any slashing belt or strap. He hated Mooney. Hated him more than he'd ever hated anyone or anything.

Mooney leaned against the wall and lit a cigarette. "Now we're gonna play a little game. I'm gonna take each one of you . . . one by one . . . into the bathroom. Then we'll see if you decide to tell the truth."

As promised, each boy was dragged—alone—into the bathroom. There, Mooney threw his young victim in the tub and, wielding a broken broom handle, pummeled him under a torrent of icy water. "Never fuckin' steal from me," he screamed with each blow. Again and again, the wooden club came down, until the water ran red and screams could be heard up and down the darkened hallway. Antonio and the other family members heard them but did nothing, staying in bed, as much out of fear as resignation.

Not one of the boys admitted to stealing his money. And when Mooney grew too tired to beat them anymore, he kicked them—shivering and crying and dripping wet with water and blood—with his stylishly sharp pointed-toe shoes all the way back into bed.

No one ever came forward to confess the theft, but Chuck overheard Antoinette tell their father that Cousin Vito had taken the money and given it to Catherine. Whether the story was true or not, Chuck never knew, but he did notice when his stepmother slipped on a new coat and hat. His father said nothing—to his wife or to his eldest son.

The following week, as the family sat around the table toasting Mooney's culinary talents, it was as if the incident had never occurred. His brother must have forgotten, Chuck thought to himself, gingerly stroking the bruises hidden beneath his shirt. But how could he forget something like that? Something so horrible? It didn't make much sense. But then, a lot of things Mooney did didn't make sense. Like the times he'd spot Chuck walking home from the YMCA over on Monroe and Ashland. He'd pull up in his car, Fat Leonard Caifano at his side, and open the door. "Come on," he'd say with a smile. "Get in."

They'd spin off down the street toward Hymie's Men's Store and Chuck would be trotted in for a new suit of clothes. Mooney would examine him with pride, spinning him around in front of the gilded full-length mirror. "Looks pretty sharp, don't you think?" he'd ask Fat Leonard. Each time, Fat Leonard would agree and they'd shuffle him back into the car for a trip to a soda shop.

The next day, Chuck would strut off to school, flaunting his new shirt and pants or sweater. And the other boys would admire them with unconcealed envy. "Wish I had a brother like yours," they'd say longingly as they tugged at pants too short and gazed down at shoes too tight.

So how could he not love Mooney? Chuck thought, looking across the table at his big brother carving the roast like some ritzy chef. It was the first meat they'd had in weeks. Mooney loved him and his brothers and sisters and showed it. So what if sometimes things got out of hand?

Chuck reprimanded himself for being so mad at his brother. He'd try harder to be good; that's what was wrong: He'd brought his brother's anger on himself. He'd tow the line and make him proud from now on.

As 1928 came to a close, Mooney's adventures—many unaffiliated with Capone's gang—grew bolder and more numerous. He was in and out of jail more times than his father could count, charged with everything from gang rape and burglary to suspicion of murder.

As in the Girard case, witnesses against Mooney always developed "amnesia" and disappeared, to be found later, living in another state—or dead. When the charges were more trivial in nature, such as theft or petty extortion, the arresting officer and station captain simply received a monetary gift in exchange for letting him off the hook.

Without Esposito's financial backing, the task of coming up with money for bonds and bribes fell to Antonio. His son might be affiliated with Capone, but so were many other punks from the Patch—that status didn't entitle hot-headed soldiers like Mooney to gain financial assistance every time they had a personal scrape with the law.

The cost of keeping his son out of jail continued to escalate; what little money Antonio's fruit and vegetable business earned was quickly spent down at the station house, stretching the old peddler to the breaking point. If need be, he would borrow the money, forcing the entire family to go without meat or bread or some other necessity of life for weeks on end. Yet, despite this hardship, Antonio never asked Mooney for a dime.

Stolen goods—ranging from plump turkeys at Christmas to the latest women's fashions—continued to be carted into the Giancana household in January of 1929. Mooney used them to control his father and the children, providing their survival, making them dependent on his crimes for signs of affection—and fearful of the consequences of his rejection. Deep down, they'd all come to believe that without him, they'd be lost. Antonio's righteous indignation from the previous year's lemon ice store bombing dwindled to nothing but a memory.

Mooney's nightly car chases, gunfights, and robberies—as wheelman for Capone's Jack McGurn—made good telling among the boys who hung out on Taylor Street on cold winter afternoons. It was no surprise to them that, when the murders of February 14, 1929, made headlines, Mooney and his friend Needles were picked up by the coppers for questioning. As a known driver for the Capone gang and one closely tied to McGurn—the suspected mastermind of the murders—Mooney was one of the first taken down to the station house. But he wasn't there long.

Back home and none the worse for his interrogation, Mooney lounged victoriously in the comfort of the velvet easy chair, perusing the paper with obvious pleasure. The gruesome photos of what Chicago was calling the worst gangland slaying in history—the St. Valentine's Day Massacre—were splashed across the front page.

He looked up and winked devilishly at Chuck, still seated at the dinner table with the rest of the family. Grinning, he tapped the paper with the back of his hand and called over, "Hey, Pa, Capone and McGurn must have had one hell of a gang to pull this off." Antonio didn't reply but simply shook his head and poured another glass of wine.

Mooney's behavior would have been inappropriate for a more mature gangster, but there was a novelty to what he was doing that hadn't yet worn off. And besides, he had good reason to gloat. It had been a job well done and one that would earn the respect of those men he needed to reach if he was ever to rise in power. Like McGurn said, "A good wheelman is hard to find, but a good wheelman with the smarts and guts to kill without question is a gold mine."

The St. Valentine's Day Massacre put everything neatly in place for Capone and fixed his position as undisputed boss of Chicago. Under McGurn's direction, Mooney and Needles had donned officers' uniforms and joined Fred Burke, who acted as wheelman, along with the duo of Alberto Anselmi and John Scalise.

But, as high as he'd been in February, by the time March rolled around, Mooney was facing another rap. This time, it quickly became apparent the neighborhood would be losing its most feared protector and that, likewise, the Capone gang would be losing what people said was the best wheelman—and hit man—they'd ever had.

The fact was, Mooney had run into the law once too often and this was one case, given its publicity, he couldn't fix. For a rather inglorious burglary, Sam "Mooney" Giancana was sentenced to three to five years at the Joliet state pen.

The Giancana family wouldn't have to put up with the oldest son's snarling domination, seesaw emotions, and frequent scrapes with the law much longer. Nor would they be receiving the counterbalancing perks.

Just days before Mooney was to surrender to the authorities for his stay in Joliet, Chuck tiptoed to Antonio's bedroom and cautiously peeked in. Mooney was alone and had his back turned to the door; he was looking out the window. The first streetlight flickered in the encroaching nightfall—its light reflected on the room's flaking plaster walls, dappling the cracks and fissures in a finger paint of shadows.

Sighing, Mooney pulled a pack of Camels from his shirt pocket and drew one cigarette out, tapping it on the window casing. He fumbled in his pocket for a match and struck it on the peeling sill. It flamed in the darkness. Catching sight of Chuck's silhouette in the doorway, he blew out the match.

"What do you want?" he asked in a tone that sounded more tired than gruff.

Chuck shrugged his shoulders and stuck his hands deep into his pockets. Looking down at the floor, he replied, "Nothin' . . . I dunno."

"Nothin'? Sounds pretty damned strange to me." Chuck saw a slight smile play across Mooney's face as he continued. "So what do you want?" He took another drag off his cigarette and leaned against the wall, waiting for a response.

Chuck came closer, hoping to assess Mooney's demeanor. In the darkness, he could make out the chiseled profile: the large nose shadowing thin lips. He searched for signs of annoyance, but his brother's features seemed unusually softened and he felt it safe to continue. "Mooney, what are we gonna do without you? Do you have to go? Do ya?"

As Chuck spoke, Mooney stared at the floor. After a few moments, he looked up, though his head didn't move. His dark eyes solemnly examined him. Chuck felt his chin tremble.

"Hey, there's nothing to cry about . . . it'll all be fine. I'll be back before you know it."

"When?"

"Well . . . soon. Real soon. I don't plan on stayin' away any fuckin' longer than I have to. Believe me, Joliet's no Garden of Eden." He turned to face the window once more.

"But Mooney . . ."

"Yeah," he said over his shoulder.

"Mooney, how's the neighborhood gonna be with you gone?"

"Shit, Chuck. Everything's gonna be fine." He sat down on the side of the bed. "Come here. And listen to me."

Chuck sat down next to him.

"Okay. Just remember somethin' about your big brother. . . . I can take care of anything that gets in the way. Anything that gets in your way . . . or Pa's way. Anything. You understand?"

"Uh-huh."

"You know why that is, Chuck? Do you?"

Chuck shook his head.

"It's real simple. People listen to you when you're a man to respect . . . a man of honor. Anybody that crosses Mooney Giancana is gonna fuckin' pay . . . and pay good. The people around here know that. They know my reputation. Don't ever forget that I'm the 'justice of the peace.' That means I know how to make things go smooth, real nice and peaceful, like they should. I know how to keep the peace, Chuck. You understand? And I know what to do when somebody steps outta line . . . and I don't mess around. . . . I do it. It's called justice, Chuck. And it takes guts. You gotta know how to handle people to get along in this world."

He cupped Chuck's face in one hand and lifted his chin, pulling him close, lowering his voice as if he knew some momentous secret that he was about to share. "Listen. Listen real good. If people do what I want, we'll take care of them. If they don't, well, we'll take care of that, too. You don't ever have to worry about that. It doesn't matter if I'm in jail or not. . . . I'll know what's goin' on . . . here at home and in the neighborhood. It doesn't matter where I am. I can make things happen. People respect that, Chuck. And they'll do whatever it takes to make you happy when they respect you. They know, without any question, they know beyond a shadow of a doubt . . . that I mean business."

His hand fell from Chuck's face and he began tearing at the pack of Camels to retrieve a lone cigarette. When he lighted it, the light made his face look sad. He turned away and said huskily, "Now go on and get the hell outta here."

CHAPTER 5

Winter in Chicago was always bitter cold. Maybe it was the wind, or maybe back then—during the Depression—things just seemed colder. In any case, for the Giancana family, the winter of 1932 was no exception. A metal gray sky pressed down on the Patch that year like a foundry worker's hand, holding the smog and fumes that regurgitated from the smelters and Model A's down on the redbrick tenements. The barnyard scents of fresh hay and horse manure, steaming in the icy ruts along Taylor Street, combined with freshly roasted chestnuts to create an earthy, sweet aroma.

In spite of their increasingly desperate poverty, people of the neighborhood maintained their joviality; perhaps the Neapolitans better than the Sicilians, but both understood hardship and both recognized the effectiveness of simply enduring.

They were a social people who could scarcely stand to be isolated inside during the winter months, so they gathered on the street corners and stoops—rebelling against the cold by bundling themselves and their children in a rainbow of ragtag coats and capes. Occasionally, a good joke led to a round of laughter that pierced the street's harangue of honking horns, trolley cars, and yelling vendors like a welcome footstep on dry, crunchy snow.

But it was bleak without end. The only relief from the oppressive skies came when it rained freezing-cold drops as big as Christmas pears. They formed great puddles and then froze, evoking cautious, icy perils for the older folk who crept along the sidewalks balancing sausages and cheese. Chuck and the other children, however, loved the slippery stuff, merrily pushing and pulling one another in orange crates across its glassy veneer.

Indoors, the men drank a bit more wine than usual and the women spent more time darning old socks and mending tattered clothes. Some fell in love.

Angeline DeTolve had fallen in love herself. A sturdy, broad-shouldered girl from a family better-off than most, she had a ready smile, classical profile, and wide-set eyes and hips. Considered both pretty and well-bred, she fit precisely Mooney Giancana's idea of the kind of woman a man should marry. Although she'd been somewhat attracted to Mooney before he was sent off to Joliet, much to her father's relief and satisfaction she hadn't fallen in love with him.

"You see," Francescantonio DeTolve had declared, "I told you Mooney Giancana's nothing but a lowdown, no-good bum. No convict will ever have my daughter's hand. . . . I'd sooner die. *Mama mia*, the disgrace such a thing would bring!"

Happily for her father, Angeline had instead fallen for a guy named Salvatore, "Solly." Nobody knew too much about him—except Mooney and those engaged in activities of Chicago's underworld. He knew all about the punk: Solly was a truck driver by day and jewel thief by night. He fenced his wares through some of the Syndicate's soldiers over on the north side. From his prison cell, Mooney kept abreast of Solly's comings and goings as well as the blossoming love affair.

Before Mooney was released on Christmas Eve of 1932, news of Angeline's engagement reached him and his heart went as cold as the bars outside his window. He recalled how Diamond Joe had managed to get his bride; Esposito simply had a couple of guys knock off her fiancé so the old padrone could have her for himself. And sure enough, not long after Diamond Joe's men took the guy for a ride out to the railroad tracks, Esposito married the fifteen-year-old girl.

Mooney made up his mind that the lovers would never be joined. No matter what the cost, no matter that he had another girl waiting for him back in the Patch—Angeline DeTolve would be his.

On New Year's Eve, only those brave enough to drive inched nervously down Chicago's roadways. Blasts of wind whistled around the corners, freezing the tattered shop awnings along Maxwell Street into stiffened submission. Cars creaked slowly through the streets like old arthritic men—their fenders prematurely grayed by soot and salt and cinders. Earlier, the roads had been wet and mushy, but now they were frozen into nasty chuckholes of ice and were glazed and treacherous. Occasionally, one of the more fainthearted hit his brakes, sending the car reeling against the embankments like a punch-drunk fighter.

In the twilight, a solitary black Ford came up on Solly's rear. It honked aggressively and, startled, Solly jumped.

"Stupido!" he yelled out the window, shaking his fist in the air.

The headlights behind him flashed off and on. In response, he swerved to the right and his car went slightly out of control, fishtailing to the left and right and back again. Like a shadow, the other vehicle mimicked his motions with amazing control and then moved up, pulling alongside.

Solly strained to see the other driver, but suddenly realizing the road took a curve, he slammed on the brakes. His car began a frenzied skate across the icy pavement and in seconds it was over. The Ford slowed to confirm he was dying within the wreckage and then quietly evaporated into the night.

Mooney waited until March of 1933, which he considered a reasonable period of time, before going by the DeTolves' to pay his respects. There, he found a woman grieving for herself as much as for her dead lover, a woman mourning the loss of her future and her dreams. Clearly, she was devastated.

Chuck's sisters, like other girls in the Patch, heard the local wags talk of how poor Angeline DeTolve sat alone for hours in her room, staring at Solly's picture. She refused to see anyone and cried until her parents didn't think there could be any tears left. But then, at the mention or thought of some forgotten memory, she would find still more pain buried in yet another hidden reservoir. Her grief didn't abandon her; when Mooney visited that spring, the emptiness was as fresh as the winter's recent graves.

At twenty-three and unmarried in 1933, a woman was considered on her way to spinsterhood. For Angeline, there seemed little hope for happiness; her life had been shattered by what everyone, including the police, called a "senseless accident.'' There was nothing left. This, Mooney set out to change. She was desperate. And he used that desperation to his advantage.

He had a gift when it came to reading other people, becoming increasingly astute as he matured. He accurately evaluated Angeline's vulnerability and was cognizant of how she brightened at even the tiniest compliment. His attentions were nourishment to the emotionally starved woman, and realizing this, he increased his efforts to make her feel pretty—and desirable—again.

By early summer, Angeline sat in front of her mirror, adjusting a ribbon in her hair, looking forward to a visit from Mooney. She began to see that he might provide a way out, an alternative to the cloistered life of spinsterhood she imagined loomed in her future. He gave her more than presents; he gave her a new beginning. And he made her smile. To her friends, Angeline said she'd fallen in love. To his, Mooney smugly said she had fallen.

In spite of the fact that their daughter's sorrow lifted in Giancana's presence, the DeTolves found acceptance of the hoodlum—now an ex-con—more difficult than ever. For Mooney, it was a challenge he relished, going so far as to command his father to visit the DeTolves in late July. Antonio took Lena as another representative of the Giancana brood. It was Mooney's idea to let Mr. DeTolve see that Angeline would be marrying into a hardworking, humble family—''Whose only crime,'' as Antonio put it, ''is that our eldest boy has made good.''

The DeTolves admitted that Mooney Giancana was the first person to come along since Solly who seemed to make Angeline happy. He brought her flowers and pretty little trinkets almost daily. And the young man did have an uncanny knack for laying his hands on money. A businessman himself, Francescantonio DeTolve told Antonio he liked that about Mooney, "no matter where it came from." He halfheartedly agreed to give his daughter's hand in marriage.

As doting as Mooney was during his courtship, and continued to be throughout the remainder of that summer after their engagement, it didn't escape Angeline that he was rumored to be seeing someone else—the same fast girl who'd waited for him to get out of prison: Marie Fanelli. Angeline told her friends it was all an ugly rumor; the idea of a betrayal so early in their relationship was probably more than she could bear to consider.

Mooney was skilled at portraying whatever emotion suited his purpose and was so sincere in his affections that it would have been hard for any woman, let alone one like Angeline who was on the rebound, to believe he wasn't the man he presented in the polite confines of her father's parlor. She defended him to her friends. Perhaps in the past he'd sought out the companionship of loose girls; that was normal; all young men did. But seeing someone else? Now, at this time in his life? She refused to discuss it.

Angeline had been correct in her assessment of Mooney's relationship with Marie: He didn't love her nor would he have ever wanted to marry her. Marie didn't fit his idea of the marrying type. All he wanted from her was physical release. And when Marie wasn't available for a little action, he stopped by Michigan and Twenty-second, as he told Chuck, to have one of the good-looking whores "cock his joint."

Mooney had a peculiar way of compartmentalizing his life, explaining to Chuck on a muggy summer afternoon in August why he was marrying Angeline. "A man's gotta marry a virgin, not a slut. You don't care how good a wife is in bed . . . you can fuckin' buy that. You want a woman who's well bred for your wife . . . remember, she's gonna be the mother to your children . . . so you want a woman who knows how to behave, one who looks halfway decent and won't embarrass you in front of the guys or out on the town in some swank joint. And if she doesn't look so good, well, you can dress her up real nice in a mink and some pearls and diamonds to give her style. . . . Money can give any woman class.'' He nodded knowingly. ''Now, remember what I'm tellin' you. Bangin' is different, Chuck. A woman who loves to bang . . . well, that kind of woman is trouble when it comes to being a wife. Anyhow, nobody said a man can't fuck more than one woman. *Capisce*?''

Carnal pleasure—the kind Mooney reveled in—and the word *wife* just weren't appropriate together; they were never used in the same sentence, and rarely found in the same bed.

As Chuck saw it, Angeline DeTolve would definitely make a good wife, but Marie, from what Mooney said, was good for banging—even if she did have a mouth like a dockworker. People said she was beautiful; but everybody called her a tramp.

Riding in the backseat of Mooney's car, less than a month before his brother's wedding date in September, Chuck listened to Mooney describe Marie to Fat Leonard as ''the best fuck this side of the Mississippi.''

Mooney laughed his gleeful laugh—the one he used when he beat somebody at poker—and went on to tell them how, after respectfully leaving barely the whisper of a kiss on the pristine cheek of his wife-to-be, he'd rush back to spend the rest of the night steaming up the backseat of a car with Marie.

Over the next weeks, before going by the DeTolves to see Angeline, Mooney continued to take Marie to the family's flat for an afternoon in Antonio's bed. One visit in particular stuck in Chuck's mind, probably because it was so close to the wedding and Chuck had wondered then whether Mooney really loved Angeline—at least with the same passion Chuck saw in the movies.

He watched the door to his father's bedroom close and heard the two laugh, locking it behind them. His sisters simply shook their heads, going about their daily cleaning, and prepared to change the sheets on their father's bed before he returned home for the evening.

Chuck could hear the iron bed heave and creak with the weight of their bodies as they fought to breathe, gasping and clawing. A distinct squeaking came from the bedroom and his sisters paused in their relentless scrubbing. Chuck sat down at the table, pretending to read a tattered newspaper he'd scrounged from the alley's garbage. When the obscene sounds began, he glanced up. His sisters were on their hands and knees, poised to obliterate some imaginary stain. Now distracted, they let their scrub brushes drip soapy water into iridescent bubbles on the floor as they listened intently to the slow, purposeful *squeak, squeak, squeak*, signifying each deep thrust of the two lovers. Antoinette caught her breath and put her brush to the floor, kneading it back and forth in unconscious rhythm. The other girls followed her example.

The squeaking sounds came closer together. *Squeak, squeak, squeak. Squeak, squeak—squeak, squeak— squeak, squeak*. Their brushes moved faster up and down each plank and methodically the tempo of their scrubbing increased in harmony with the lovers.

Chuck heard Mooney groan and Marie cry out in ecstasy, "Yes, yes, please, Mooney, please." Chuck felt his face turn hot.

The flat became still and Chuck's heart was pounding; he could hear his sisters' labored breathing. They sat trembling with their brushes, faces flushed and perspiration gleaming down their necks. "All done," announced Antoinette. And they rose from the floor, carrying the clanking buckets and brushes to the kitchen.

Certainly, a woman of Angeline's impeccable reputation would not have stooped to please Mooney the way Marie did—so shamelessly, so readily. That's what Chuck's sisters said, anyway. But after Angeline and Mooney were married in a small ceremony in her family's home on September 23, 1933, it became clear to Chuck that Mooney had a definite vision of what marriage would entail, and fidelity wasn't on the list.

His brother didn't stop seeing Marie; he just seemed to think that his adulteries should be discreet—that a good husband would avoid humiliating his wife at all costs. And should he be caught in an indiscretion, he made sure that Angeline would think long and hard before leaving him. Such a feat, he bragged to Chuck, was accomplished by providing one's wife with every possible material convenience and comfort. It didn't hurt that Angeline was a devout Catholic. And that his cronies knew better, under the threat of death, than to breathe a word about his philandering habits. Nor did he underestimate the effect pride and a woman's friends could have, and he used them to his advantage, setting out to make Angeline the envy of all.

From the beginning, Angeline—Ange as Mooney called her—had a maid. He moved her to a pleasant, spacious apartment over on the West Side and told her to furnish it as she pleased, with all the finer luxuries. To friends and family members, their standard of living was enviable, impressive, if in truth somewhat modest at first. But they had money in their pockets, beautiful, expensive clothes, jewelry to wear, and tasteful decor. Mooney brought home fine paintings and Oriental rugs. Ange began collecting such unheard-of amenities as porcelain, crystal, and sterling silver, which she proudly displayed while entertaining friends. It worked nicely; the men went outside to sip their scotch and talk Syndicate business while the women held lengthy discussions about children and the latest fashions over a game of gin rummy.

But whatever three-dimensional quality there was to the young couple's lives was an illusion. Angeline knew her husband continued to see Marie as well as pay for pleasure at the local brothel, and Chuck's sisters said the infidelity deeply wounded her.

As soon as he was married, Mooney started bringing Chuck over to spend the night, explaining to Ange that he was getting older—Chuck was eleven now—and needed a man around who wasn't afraid to use the strap. Chuck believed Mooney was genuinely worried that he might get in trouble and that he somehow planned to prevent that by keeping him busy and off the streets.

Mooney wasn't concerned, however, about the moral fiber of the rest of his family. Pepe, he said, was a "good kid" and would never get in trouble. As for his sisters—who were fast becoming spinsters—he forbade them to leave their flat except in pursuit of such acceptable womanly duties as selecting cleaning powders at the market. "You know better than to let me catch you going out with some two-bit hustlers. . . . I'd kill them . . . and I'd better never see you dolled up in lipstick and brassieres like a fuckin' slut," he threatened. He didn't expect any problems from them.

But Chuck's upbringing, as he explained to Ange, was another story: "I need to watch him like a hawk, and besides, he can help around the house and keep you company when I'm gone on business."

Mooney charged Angeline with the task of instructing the boy in the finer points of well-bred behavior. Here was an opportunity for his little brother to gain some class, to learn which fork to use at the table.

In spite of Mooney's thinly veiled intentions, Chuck loved his visits to his brother and Ange's home that fall in 1933; there was always more food than he could eat at one sitting and he could sleep alone, without the prodding knees and elbows. At Mooney's house, it was as if he'd died and gone to heaven. And he didn't mind helping his brother's wife; he truly liked Ange. She was pretty and, he thought, nice, even if she didn't understand men. But most of all, he treasured the time he had with Mooney.

Ange and Mooney were like a king and queen to people in the neighborhood. In December, with just a few days until Christmas, some of the little kids in the Patch caught sight of Mooney and Ange bringing Chuck home in their sleek new car. They rushed at them like beggars. "Can we help you, Mrs. Mooney?" one asked. "Do you need somethin', Mr. Mooney?" said another.

Mooney reached into the pocket of his double-breasted coat to retrieve a tightly wrapped wad of cash and handed them dollar bills as he shook his head. "No," he said as he climbed behind the wheel of his shiny roadster. "Just give it to your mama for some Christmas turkey."

With that, Mooney and Angeline spun off down Taylor Street, leaving Chuck standing once again in the old, familiar world of poverty and hunger. He hated coming back to the neighborhood, but seeing the way other people—both children and adults—fawned over Mooney made him proud.

By New Year's, things had gotten so bad at Antonio's home that many times they'd each just have a potato and a handful of beans for dinner. The comparisons seemed to make Chuck's life in the Patch even more intolerable. And he couldn't understand why his father didn't do something about it—he couldn't help but compare him to Mooney. In Chuck's eyes, Antonio would never measure up.

Despite the unspoken conflict early in their marriage, Ange and Mooney were popularly perceived as the picture-perfect postcard of a stand-up guy and doll. By mid-1934, the only thing that appeared missing was children. And Mooney didn't intend to be childless; there was a man's virility to confirm. Because of a heart condition caused by rheumatic fever as a child, doctors warned Angeline that pregnancy could be difficult, if not dangerous, both for herself and a baby. But her traditional views on childbearing and the insistent amorous encouragement from Mooney won out; she became pregnant before Christmas of 1934 and in June of 1935 gave birth prematurely to a three-pound baby girl. They named the frail infant Annette.

After Ange and the baby came home, Mooney brought Chuck over to see little Annette. Looking at the tiny face nestled in Ange's arms, Chuck felt old for the first time. He would be thirteen soon, not a man by any means—though he desperately wanted to be. But seeing the sleeping baby made him realize he wasn't a little kid anymore, either. The days of rubber-band guns, orange-crate wagons, and tin cans on his heels had ceased to amuse him.

Ange and Mooney celebrated their second anniversary

by going out on the town in September of 1935. Had there been a contest among Italians, the Giancanas would have been voted "most beautiful couple." Wherever they went, they made quite a splash. Considered the perfect pair, Ange and Mooney were stylish and fun. But little by little, in the harsh daylight of ordinary life, Chuck began to notice that they weren't like other couples he knew. They laughed, but it was strained sometimes, hollow in a way.

If her husband made it, she would spend it, he overheard Ange say angrily on the phone one day: "I'll spend so much, there won't be a dime left for him to spend on that tramp." He was sure she meant Marie.

For a while, Chuck thought about what Ange had said and it bothered him. Mooney had said that was the way men were supposed to be. He'd said it was different for them than for women. Sure, Ange had been sheltered by her parents, but his sister-in-law would have to come to grips with the real world if she was going to survive being married to someone as important as Mooney. Driving him home one night and mad as hell over something Ange had said, Mooney put it best, Chuck thought: "Ange needs to learn what her place is . . . and fuckin' stay there."

When Christmas came in 1935, even the beautiful tree standing in the corner of Mooney's living room, twinkling and sparkling, didn't seem to have the same magic it once would have had. The only thing Chuck looked forward to was the holiday food: "Enough ravioli to feed an army," they'd say at home in the neighborhood. He couldn't understand why Mooney and Ange didn't invite them over for Christmas; it was so much nicer at their house. And secretly, he hoped they would surprise them all with an invitation. But the holiday came and went without one, and he spent it sulking in the Patch.

He really didn't know how it came up, but all of a sudden one cold winter afternoon in January of 1936, Mooney began discussing politics. Everybody thought FDR was the finest man ever elected to the presidency, and, although just a boy, Chuck was no exception.

"Yeah, he's the perfect President all right. He's on our side." Mooney smiled knowingly.

"On our side?"

"The gang's, Chuck . . . the gang's."

"Oh," he replied, still not understanding the full implications of Mooney's comment.

"If he wasn't, he'd be dead . . . like Cermak. Like Huey Long. Plain and simple, we'd take him out."

Chuck was incredulous and yet pleased to be included in such an adult conversation. He wanted to act as if he'd been around, and he thought Mooney was pulling his leg. "No . . . come on, Mooney, you're kiddin' me, aren't you?"

"No, I'm not kiddin' . . . Jesus," Mooney snapped impatiently. "Read a little. Long . . . he was the senator from down south in Louisiana. The guy was on the take for years. Some of our friends in New York had him hit . . . worked it out with a New Orleans boss. They figured it out so it would look like a loony did it. All the papers picked it up." He laughed and then, a moment later, turned serious. "You know, Chuck, you'd think people would catch on." He shook his head in amazement.

Picking a nutcase—who was also a sharpshooter and in debt up to his eyeballs—to take the fall for a political assassination was "as old as the Sicilian hills" according to Mooney, who used the examples of Huey Long and Anton Cermak to prove his point.

Anton Cermak had been mayor of Chicago and a Capone

rival. "A real double-crosser," Mooney said. For years, he'd waged war against Capone on behalf of another mobster, a rival named Teddy Newberry.

After an unsuccessful attempt on the life of Capone enforcer Frank Nitti by Cermak henchmen in 1932, Paul Ricca, Capone's successor, turned the tables, killing Newberry. Rightfully fearing for his life, Cermak fled to Florida in December of 1932. In further retaliation, Ricca enlisted what Mooney called "a real patsy," a guy named Joe Zangara, to eliminate Cermak.

Thirty-three-year-old Zangara had been sponsored by Diamond Joe Esposito from Sicily just five years before and was placed in Florida to work the sugar runs from Cuba. A sharpshooter in the Italian army and a heavy gambler, Zangara was deeply in debt and in real trouble with his Chicago bosses. He was given a choice: Hit Cermak or die.

On February 15, 1933, while riding in an open car with President-elect Roosevelt in Miami, Cermak was shot and Zangara was quickly apprehended by the authorities. He immediately began spouting anticapitalist political pabulum, claiming he had missed his real target, FDR. But in fact, Mooney said his political rantings were a carefully devised smoke screen; Zangara had no connection to communism or fascism but was actually "a goddamned registered Republican."

Zangara's connections were to the Chicago Syndicate, something that escaped the attention of the press and was covered up by the paid-off coppers and investigators. Three weeks later, Cermak died. And as had been planned all along, Zangara was convicted of murder and sent to the electric chair. "Nice and neat," Mooney grinned. "Nice and neat."

Quizzed about Huey Long, Mooney told Chuck that for years the senator had worked closely with the Syndicate on everything from slot machines to casinos, becoming partners with Carlos Marcello in New Orleans; Frank Costello, Lucky Luciano, and Meyer Lansky in New York; Santo Trafficante in Florida; and Paul Ricca in Chicago. But by 1935, Long had "gotten out of hand" and another loony assassin was located. Unlike Cermak, Long was no turncoat traitor; he simply became too greedy, demanding over $3 million a year in payoffs from his "friends."

"He was cutting into profits . . . greed killed Huey Long," Mooney insisted. "It'll get you every time. Always remember, any profit is a good profit and always leave somethin' for the other guy. That's what Long forgot."

Chuck would remember that afternoon for the rest of his life. It marked the beginning of a new relationship with his brother; he was no longer a child in Mooney's eyes.

Over the past years, New York had had its own share of double crosses. Mooney said half the guys there were crazy. "It's not at all like Chicago," he explained with no small amount of pride in his voice. "Here, we got control, under one boss. We're organized. In New York, they've been backstabbin' and killin' each other for years."

Indeed, the gang wars had raged on in New York until Lucky Luciano seized power in 1931. But even Luciano's reign was cut short when, just five years later, he was arrested on charges of compulsory prostitution. In a case spearheaded by vengeful Special Prosecutor Thomas Dewey, Luciano was found guilty on ninety counts of direction of harlotry and extortion. With Luciano's sentence of thirty to fifty years in Clinton State Penitentiary,

Frank Costello—a man with whom Mooney would someday collaborate—took control.

By spring's first thaw in 1936, while other boys his age
were still in knickers and playing jerk-off games, Chuck
decided to leave such childish trappings and behavior behind forever. When he wasn't at Mooney's or on the corner
selling the season's first tomatoes for his father, he looked
at girls. On Saturdays, he hopped the bumper of some
"rich sap's car" and went up on California and Roosevelt,
to Douglas Park. There, he'd sit in the shade of the massive
oaks all afternoon, catching the scent of fresh pine.

The air smelled different in the park's wooded lawns,
clean and clear. And the sounds weren't those of boister-
ous, argumentative vendors or swearing, dissatisfied customers but of squeaky little sparrows and fat, chattering
squirrels. He liked to watch the young men in their starched
white shirts, hair neatly pomaded beneath straw hats, as
they paddled across the lake in canoes carrying pretty girls
with Carole Lombard bobs.

Much to his friends' dismay, Chuck even stopped entertaining the neighborhood with his crazy acrobatics—
swinging from electrical wires, jumping from stoops and
second-story rooftops. "Don't you know shit like that's
for kids?" he exclaimed in exasperation to his puzzled
friends.

It wasn't that he'd suddenly lost his guts; in fact, he'd
become more daring. But the childhood thrills were gone.
The only people that still put the scare in Chuck were his
brother Mooney—and the big Irish coppers. Both were as
constant as ever; the beatings from his brother hadn't ended
and the police hadn't gotten any smaller as he'd grown
larger.

It baffled him that one of the worst coppers around wasn't even a mick. His name was Frank Pape—no relation to Mooney's cohort Joe Pape. An Italian from the neighborhood, Frank Pape had joined the force in 1933 and over the previous three years had managed to make quite a name for himself. He didn't screw with Mooney, though, and on one of his increasingly frequent rides with his brother that spring, Chuck had an opportunity to see Mooney in action.

It was almost dinnertime and they were driving down Ashland in a Ford souped up for getaways when Mooney spotted Pape rounding a corner.

"Let's have some fun," he said to Chuck and Fat Leonard as he whipped the corner in pursuit.

"Cut in front of him," Leonard said, laughing. "Dare him, Mooney, just dare that son of a bitch to try to outrun us. . . . In this car the poor bastard don't stand a chance. . . . That'll get under his fuckin' skin real good." He looked back at Chuck. "Havin' fun?"

Chuck nodded and said nothing as his brother pulled up behind the police car, honking and yelling out his window.

"Hey, Pape . . . hey, you goddamned traitor greaseball . . . hey, asshole. . . ." They came alongside the copper. "Fuck you, Pape." With those words, Mooney cut right in front of the cop and hit his brakes. He and Fat Leonard were in stitches.

"Pape don't know whether to shit or go blind, Mooney," said Leonard, looking over his shoulder at the car behind them. "He's going fuckin' crazy."

Mooney looked back and gestured out the window. "*Va fa in culo*"—"Fuck you"—he yelled, and, with tires squealing, whipped the corner.

"Man oh man, that copper's gonna be mad tonight,"

Leonard said, hurriedly loosening his wide, striped tie and rolling up his sleeves.

"This is great," Chuck exclaimed. "Give it to 'em, Mooney." They were going fast and it was exhilarating. At last, he'd found a thrill to surpass the ones he'd left behind as childish.

"Someday, I'll give that motherfuckin' Pape more than this . . . right, Leonard?"

"Right."

Mooney slammed the car into second gear and left the mighty Frank Pape in a cloud of burning rubber. They laughed and laughed at the sight of the mad little wop swearing and shaking his fist behind them.

"That was nothin'," Fat Leonard remarked a few minutes later. "You should see when your brother catches one of 'em in a fuckin' alley. We give 'em a taste of what they do to our people in the neighborhood. Jesus, Mooney knows how to make 'em cry for their mamas."

"Shut up, Leonard," Mooney interrupted, giving him a stern look. "You're going home for dinner now, Chuck."

Pape was one of the few cops Mooney left pretty much alone, but when he wasn't on a real job for the Syndicate, he loved to corner the other mick officers in some clammy, dark alley within the safety of the neighborhood and beat the living hell out of them. Taking revenge on the coppers for all the abuse "his people"—as he called them—had taken for years made Mooney Giancana a hero to the Italians of the Patch.

Soon to be fourteen, Chuck had begun to think of himself as street-smart, someone who knew his way around, and that summer he spent time swaggering up and down the alleys shooting the breeze with smartheads. But whatever carousing he did, he did during the day. He might be a sharpshooter—a tough guy—but he still avoided the coppers, especially on Friday or Saturday nights, in spite of what the neighborhood men said about Mooney having them under control; cops were crawling all over, looking for trouble, and, as Mooney had warned him, "They'll pick you up for no goddamned reason and take you down to the station house, put your ass in a fuckin' lineup, and shake you down . . . or worse, set you up for some crime you didn't commit."

Sitting out on the stoop in front of the flat like he'd done most every hot summer night for as long as he could remember, Chuck got more insight into why people in the Patch had come to idolize Mooney.

A group of neighborhood men were playing bocci beneath the streetlight and started to talk about his brother among themselves.

"Until Mooney came along, you couldn't stand on this corner here and play craps or ball or anything," one paunchy Sicilian with slick-backed hair said to the rest of the group. "You know I'm right. The mick coppers . . . why, they used to just walk right up . . . and wop you real good with their nightsticks and yell, 'Break it up here, you dirty dago greaseballs.' "

They all nodded in agreement. "That Mooney's made a difference, he sure has."

They believed there was security in the neighborhood thanks to Mooney, and that the coppers knew better than to incur Mooney's wrath. "The police give Mooney plenty of room . . . and his family and friends, too," Chuck heard one say. "The most the coppers will dare these days is a shakedown," said another.

The men said the coppers had seen what lengths Mooney would go to in order to make an enemy pay, having found what was left of more than a few men Mooney's entourage had worked over. They said that had made all the difference in how they were treated in the Patch.

It was no secret that Mooney would get hold of some unlucky bastard and while two or three crazies from the old 42 gang held the guy down, Mad Dog DeStefano would shove a poker right up his ass. " 'Clear to China,' that's what the coroner says," commented one of the bocci players. "Yeah, all the way up the poor son of a bitch's innards 'til his eyes bug out."

If the guy was a stoolie who had talked too much or to the wrong people, and Mooney and his friends wanted to have a little more fun, the men said the hoodlums cut off his penis and crammed it right down his throat.

"*Mama mi*, that would hurt," the paunchy Sicilian cried, and they all grabbed their testicles in mock pain and laughed. He described how there would be blood everywhere and, at the sight, most rookies vomited all over the place. "The examiner always tells the new ones the same thing . . . that you can't cut off a man's dick without him bleedin' like a stuck pig, so they'd better get used to it." They laughed again. "That Mooney's put the fear of Jesus into them coppers and it's a good thing, too."

It was clear to Chuck, listening to the men rave about Mooney, that there were just some rules in the Patch you didn't break—even if you were a cop. Staying out of his brother's way was one.

" 'Better to take a bribe than a poker up the ass,' that's what the precinct captain tells his men," the Sicilian said, concluding their discussion. Chuck had to believe that the coppers followed that advice.

CHAPTER 6

Throughout the remainder of 1936, Mooney continued to harvest the rewards of dozens of lucrative illegal enterprises. When he'd married Ange three years before, he'd taken a "job"—which paid a measly forty dollars a week—at her brother Michael's factory, Central Envelope. He used this employment to satisfy the nosy, by-the-book probation officers concerned with his rehabilitation.

In actuality, Mooney frequently assisted the gang's clever Welshman, Murray Humphreys, on labor fixes that needed a "convincer." In 1934 and 1935, he'd still driven occasionally for Jack McGurn—enjoying the steady supply of blond show girls Jack brought his way. But by 1936, McGurn had fallen from grace and Mooney carefully avoided supporting him when seated at a table with one of the gang's bosses, Paul Ricca. The Syndicate's attitude toward McGurn had changed drastically since their St. Valentine's Day job; when McGurn himself was gunned down on February 13, 1936, nobody shed any tears.

"The guy didn't have a pot to piss in. High and dry, that's the way we left him . . . sellin' junk to the moolies. Somebody did us all a favor makin' Jack McGurn go away," Ricca commented at the news of his fellow gangster's demise, while daintily sipping an espresso.

Over the years, Mooney had developed a keen admiration for forty-five-year-old Paul Ricca. Paul could almost always be found at the Napoli, the haunt once owned by Diamond Joe Esposito and now controlled by his successors.

Mooney described Ricca, an enigma to most of those around him, as a cruel, heartless bastard who could laugh while cutting out a guy's liver with an ice pick—or cry with sincere sentiment at the birth of some soft-brained soldier's kid.

Ricca was a somewhat handsome man with strong Italian features and a firm square jaw that he clenched when angered. To those outside the underworld, he reflected the mannerisms of a wealthy country gentleman, slipping into upper-crust society and wealthy political circles with ease. He used this talent to cloak a violent criminal past, like cashmere around a leper. Mooney told Chuck that the ladies and crooked politicians loved him.

Ricca reached the shores of North American opportunity before his twenty-first birthday. In Italy, where he was known as Paul DeLucia, he'd served time for a murder he had committed at seventeen—and was personally responsible for at least two dozen more. After release in 1920 from his dank and stinking gray-walled Italian cell, he immediately killed the man who'd testified against him and fled the country.

Once in New York, he was passed on to Diamond Joe Esposito in Chicago, which was where Mooney had first met him. Under Esposito, Paul joined a stable of eager young immigrants with criminal backgrounds, working with the foul-tempered Gennas, running moonshine, and as a waiter in Esposito's Bella Napoli. There he earned the nickname Paul "the Waiter."

Ricca climbed up the ladder to win Esposito's favor, becoming closely aligned with Capone. Although Esposito's death didn't sadden Ricca at the time, when the Roaring Twenties became the Depressed Thirties, memories of the old regime started to give him twinges of nostalgia; Diamond Joe knew how to keep a low profile. Capone, on the other hand, had become an obstacle to "free enterprise," a larger-than-life figure on whom G-men, like Eliot Ness, and Treasury Agent Frank Wilson could build their careers.

After the public outrage accompanying the St. Valentine's Day Massacre, the Treasury Department, with Ricca's blessing, turned up the heat on Capone. Ricca hadn't been disheartened by Capone's prison sentence; as Mooney explained to Chuck, Scarface may have been Ricca's friend, but this was business—they had an operation to run and with Capone out of the way, there'd be no stopping Ricca.

The media might proclaim Frank Nitti Chicago's boss, but Mooney insisted it was a convenient ruse—intended to keep the likes of Eliot Ness confused as to the actual power structure in Chicago. Those on the inside knew better: Paul Ricca ran the show. For proof, one had only to look at obvious examples of Ricca's power; when major business deals were made with other bosses from other cities, Nitti was nowhere to be found. Nor would men like Jake Guzik and Murray Humphreys consult or take orders from a man of Frank Nitti's ilk—a barber turned enforcer, a man they believed possessed half their intellect.

While Frank Nitti served as front man, attracting the scrutiny of the press, Ricca was free to work the back rooms with Murray Humphreys, virtually unnoticed. Together, the two gangsters slapped more backs and lined more pinstriped pockets than a country politician, letting their old crony Greasy Thumb Jake Guzik take care of the money. If polite conversation didn't work, then, like Esposito and Capone before him, Ricca sent Mooney Giancana, ever the trusted executioner, to give the uncooperative a taste of hot lead.

Mooney told Chuck there was a "finesse" to crime the way Paul played it, and because of that, Ricca had won not only his respect but that of the President of the United States, politicians looking for votes, and police captains more interested in taking bribes than fighting crime.

A few years earlier Ricca had used the threatened loss of income resulting from Prohibition's end to formalize his national role. In Chicago's Bismark Hotel, he'd hosted a private meeting of the nation's crime leaders to discuss the Syndicate's future. Gangsters such as Lucky Luciano, Rocco Fischetti, Harry Ducket, and Sylvester Agoglia all attended, but Meyer Lansky, who'd come to town with his friend and colleague Luciano, wasn't invited to participate. Instead, Lansky was told to wait in the Bismark's lobby while Ricca made his pitch upstairs for a Syndicate takeover of unions, coast to coast.

Among Ricca's men, Welshman Murray "the Camel" Humphreys—"Curly," to his friends—was the most knowledgeable about union activity and the most visionary regarding its possibilities. Humphreys saw a time when the gang would completely control the unions. Entire industries could then be manipulated any way the Syndicate desired. Unlike Capone, who, according to Mooney, had more guts than guile, Humphreys had the brains to make it happen, and in the early twenties, he'd launched an attack on Chicago's south side dry cleaners union, plucking the gang's first real cherry.

Controlling this union brought home to Humphreys an important truth: Control a work force and you control the livelihoods of countless families sustained by those jobs. By threatening union members with loss of work, the gangsters could marshal the efforts of husbands, wives, sons, and daughters in support of virtually any scam the gang could dream up, including swinging an election.

But aside from valuable political clout, Humphreys also found union coffers, brimming over with a ready source of capital, highly attractive; thus, his representatives wasted no time raiding the funds of unions they took over.

With Ricca's organizational ability, Humphreys's foresight, and Greasy Thumb Jake Guzik's financial acumen, what had started out as merely another form of extortion—squeezing money out of rich businessmen in exchange for smooth labor relations—soon became an endless source of revenue. Unions were targeted for takeover and the word went out to the younger thugs such as Mooney Giancana, Willie Bioff, and Johnny Roselli to muster together bands of psychopathic hoodlums for shakedowns.

It was Mooney's chance to showcase his ruthlessness and guts, but also—more important—his ability to lead, and he grabbed the opportunity. For his muscle, he called on old 42s like Fifi Buccieri, Mad Dog DeStefano, Needles Gianola, Chuckie Nicoletti, and Teets Battaglia. He took pride in the fact that, after a few weeks or days of steady pressure from his terroristic hoods, union officials were more than willing to comply with whatever he had in mind. And with each success, Mooney's stock rose.

Following the conquest of the dry cleaners union, the building trades, barber's union, and motion picture operator's union rapidly fell. If there wasn't a union, Humphreys made one up. People suddenly became members of unions they'd never heard of and their employers began paying dues and fees to Syndicate front men in exchange for protection from violence.

In 1934, the Chicago gang became more daring and ambitious in its tactics and Ricca, Nitti, and Humphreys, who claimed to have gotten a foothold in Hollywood by financially backing fellow bootlegger Joe Kennedy's successful entry into the motion picture industry, decided to take their union rackets national by placing a local man, George Browne, along with Willie Bioff, in power as president of the International Alliance of Theatrical Stage Employees and Motion Picture Operators. The move gave Chicago absolute supremacy over Hollywood's film industry and the theaters in which films were shown.

To oversee California, Ricca sent one of Mooney's friends, the handsome, smooth-talking Johnny Roselli. Suave young Roselli took to Hollywood like a rising star, negotiating—"quicker than you could hum a few bars of 'Anything Goes,' " as Mooney would later recall—millions in extortion dollars from the major studios. In no time at all, stars whom Mooney described to Chuck as "gang-sponsored"—among them the Marx Brothers, George Raft, Jimmy Durante, Marie McDonald, Clark Gable, Gary Cooper, Jean Harlow, Cary Grant, and Wendy Barrie—were awarded extravagant contracts, as well.

With no federal, state, or local laws regulating union funds and their activities, Chicago had found the key to Fort Knox. By 1936, all major unions in the city had fallen under the Syndicate's domination and those that were occasionally rebellious soon got back in line.

A net had been cast upon the waters of gangland discord, creating an interwoven web of men who recognized that unity brought huge financial advantage. "With unions we caught the big fish," Humphreys would reminisce years later with Mooney, "all we had to do was reel it in."

To oversee the Syndicate's burgeoning enterprises, trusted "lieutenants" such as Louis Campagna, Tony Accardo, Charlie "Cherry Nose" Gioe, the Fischetti and Fusco brothers, Johnny Roselli, Frank Nitti, and Sam Hunt were given specific, agreed-upon territories. From within these protected areas, the lieutenants reigned over dozens of workers or "soldiers"—guys with more guts than brains—who handled the day-to-day hustling on the streets.

"Enforcers" like Mooney Giancana often acted as drivers and bodyguards for a "general" and his advisers or a high-ranking lieutenant. As hired killers, enforcers were considered a special breed; they had no territory and could be called on by any member of the hierarchy, with permission of the general, to ply their trade.

Roles were fluid and ever-changing; a man could rise among the ranks of the Syndicate through the death of a superior or by distinguishing himself as smarter, tougher, and more ruthless than his counterparts.

Monies from the unions, as well as from all other illicit activities, were pooled and distributed—the general receiving the largest cut.

Having made a successful push for power in 1937, it

was no secret in Chicago's underworld that Paul Ricca had nearly every local, county, and state politician eating out of his hand. His loyal followers, Mooney among them, maintained that he was also a welcome guest at the White House, granting and requesting favors with equal aplomb on the national level. In the space of two decades, Chicago's Syndicate, a dragon with many heads, had reached maturity.

Mooney made it known he liked the way Ricca and Humphreys took care of the unions; he'd liked Humphreys since the first time he'd pulled a job for him. He told Chuck he could tell back then that Humphreys was smarter than the rest of the morons who sneaked up and down the alleys, smarter than Nitti or Capone, for that matter. Humphreys had graduated from high school, whereas most of them had barely scraped through sixth grade. And, although Mooney hadn't done any better, he firmly believed they had this intelligence in common.

Mooney was well known for his uncanny knack at calculating and memorizing numbers. In his twenties, having a way with figures hadn't scored many points; all that counted then was his skill as an executioner and wheelman. But since he'd gotten out of Joliet, his mathematical ability had come in handy and was beginning to set him apart from the other hoodlums.

He'd even developed a habit of showing off his gift for numbers after a few drinks, telling Chuck it "puts other guys in their fuckin' place. Nobody'll ever short me and live to tell about it."

The threat wasn't lost on the thickheaded men he'd organized under his rule. Mooney had over fifty flunkies marching routinely back and forth between the shop owners in the Patch by 1937, picking up protection money. He said if he didn't keep a tight rein on them, they might give more than a passing thought to skimming a little extra off the take for themselves. Mooney's men weren't stupid and they took him at his word—making sure their payoffs to him were always to the penny.

Mooney created his own small empire in the Patch, one built on car thefts, burglary rings, moonshining, jewelry heists, extortion, and loan-sharking, as well as penny-ante gambling. And as his domination grew, he was able to dispense jobs like candy to the starving immigrants—or take them away. He reveled in the power his association with the Syndicate afforded; and the more he had, the more he craved. By 1937, union rackets were increasingly falling under his supervision and he was regularly called on by Ricca and Humphreys to supply the soldiers required for their control.

Ricca and Humphreys were impressed with Mooney Giancana, finding the twenty-nine-year-old astute and calculating. And Mooney, likewise, was impressed with them.

Since the days of Esposito, he'd been captivated by their style, listening intently, albeit most often from the sidelines, as they planned everything from political fixes and murder to getting fellow bootlegger Joe Kennedy out of a nearly fatal scrape with Detroit's Jewish Mafia, the Purple gang.

The Purple gang had put a contract on the mick's life for bringing bootlegged rum through their territory without permission, and Kennedy, fearful for his life, had gone to Chicago to beg Esposito to intervene on his behalf. Mooney had watched Esposito, Ricca, and Humphreys toy capriciously with the man's fate. Esposito had finally put in the requested phone call, and ever after, Kennedy was in Chicago's debt.

Whether required to knock off a friend or save the skin of an enemy, Mooney said he'd learned by watching two of the best—Ricca and Humphreys.

Mooney clearly admired Paul Ricca, but he reserved some of his highest praise for Humphreys, raving on and on to Chuck about the way Humphreys could analyze a situation and figure out a strategy, taking on whatever challenge the gang had and then, like some fedora-hatted Houdini, snatching a plan right out of thin air. But in the final analysis, Chuck knew his brother's appreciation of the Camel was far more simple and straightforward: "Humphreys gets the job done, and he gets it done smart."

At first, it had surprised Chuck to see his brother pull up a chair at the Bella Napoli, eager as a first grader, whenever Murray had something to say. But he soon realized that by watching Humphreys operate, Mooney learned tricks foreign to the muscle-bound world of the Patch. For Humphreys, violence was not always the best, or only, solution. "A live sucker is more valuable than a dead one" was one of his many pearls of wisdom. When Mooney heard that one, he'd laughed in agreement. He thought that was one of the sharpest things Murray ever said and went so far as to repeat it to Chuck one Saturday night after dinner. "Murray Humphreys is one of the smartest guys you'll ever fuckin' meet," he said as way of ending their conversation. "The guy's sly as a goddamned fox."

It wasn't that Humphreys abhorred violence, Mooney told him—he'd personally taken out his share of guys— but it was just that the Camel favored peaceful alternatives. And those alternatives invariably made the Syndicate money. "There's no denyin' it, Chuck, brains like Murray's can make the fuckin' difference between winnin' and losin' . . . put a big bullet in your gun. Take a guy with my muscle and put it with Humphreys's smarts and who knows? A man could be boss one day." He'd smiled when he said that, and Chuck couldn't help wondering whether that was exactly what Mooney had in mind. If so, he knew his brother could make it happen; there hadn't been anything yet he'd set his sights on that he hadn't gotten.

Mooney also liked Humphreys's style. And Murray had plenty of that. Early in his career, Humphreys had taken to wearing expensive suits and camel hair coats. The coats had become his trademark, hence his nickname the Camel. Mooney noticed how Ricca and Nitti appreciated Humphreys's elegant qualities, his ability to hobnob with the politicians and businessmen. Murray Humphreys—floppy ears and beady eyes aside—was, as Mooney put it, "high-tone . . . a class act. How a guy looks can open the door to the King of fuckin' England, Chuck. It gets Murray anywhere he wants to go, and where Murray goes, the Syndicate goes."

In deference to that fact, Mooney began to make an even greater effort to dress well, visiting Rothchild's each week and coming back with armloads of elegant gray flannel suits, double-breasted pinstripes, and foulard silk ties. He began wearing supple calfskin shoes and two-toned black and white oxfords. Soft felt fedoras to match each ensemble lined his closet shelves. And he didn't neglect Ange, making sure she dressed in the latest fashions; lounging pajamas, pearls, and a mink coat were among her ever-growing wardrobe.

It was late March of 1937 and Angeline had thrown another one of her jealous hysterics; they were becoming more frequent—and more irritating to Mooney. Before he stormed out the door, he sarcastically remarked to Ange that a few well-placed backhands might put her in her place; maybe that was what she needed.

It was impossible to explain anything to a woman, he complained to Chuck in the car later that night on his way to meet with Ricca and Humphreys. "Ange should have learned by now not to ask questions, that what men do isn't any of her business." He told Chuck she was getting pretty jealous, practically hysterical, accusing him of seeing other women just about every time he left the house.

Christ, Chuck thought to himself. Leaving home at night hardly ever had anything to do with sex. This was business. And the feeling you could get around the guys—well, Mooney was right, it was too goddamned good to pass up for a fuckin' whining woman. Not for a whore and especially not for a wife. At home, a man could play the husband role, and, Chuck thought, Mooney did a damn good job of it, too. But at the Napoli, you were a man.

As soon as they opened the door to the café, Chuck could feel it. It was electric.

"Paul and Curly wanna see you," a swarthy-skinned busboy whispered in broken Italian. "They're in back." He motioned with one hand toward two men seated at a table. Mooney, lapels turned up on his coat and the brim of a tan fedora pulled down rakishly to one side, strolled through the bistro tables. Chuck followed at a respectful distance and stood against the back wall.

His brother left his coat on, but out of respect took off his hat, placing it on his lap. He pulled the chair forward to face Ricca; Chuck thought the deep-set eyes across the table from his brother went right through him. Mooney had said Paul was like a wild dog—he didn't react well to jumpy, shifty guys—and Mooney knew better than to let him ever see any sign of real emotion. So he didn't flinch for an instant, but sat there for several moments waiting for Paul to say what was on his mind.

"Mooney, we got a little problem. . . . Curly and I know you can handle it." Ricca leaned back in his chair and unbuttoned the vest of his elegant sharkskin suit. He lit a long cigar before continuing, "It's like this . . . we gotta get the barber's union back in line. A couple of the old guys are squawkin' again. We're gonna have to persuade them to come along. They've got a barbershop over on Loomis and Taylor."

Mooney looked first at Ricca and then at Humphreys. Without another word, he put his hat on and stood up to leave. "Consider it done, Paul," he said, and signaled to Chuck to follow.

Driving always made Mooney's mind work better, and he took his time getting them home, whipping a few corners on the rain-swept streets. It was just like the good old days.

"Convincing the barbers that working with us is the next best thing to life insurance is gonna take some extra muscle," Mooney said suddenly. His wheels were obviously turning.

"I'll send a couple of the regular boys and . . . Carl Torsiello. Carl needs the money real bad, I know, because his sister-in-law told Ange they're havin' a hard time."

Mooney told Chuck that Carl had even stopped him one day to see whether he could get some work. "Anything, Mooney," the handsome Italian had said. "Anything . . . I got a wife and a beautiful little girl, Anne Marie. She's just five years older than your daughter, Mooney. I gotta feed and clothe her and our new baby. So I'd be real appreciative if you hear of anything.''

"If Carl plays it right, this could be the start of a whole new life for him and his family," Mooney added, and then smiled. "It'll sure make Ange and her girlfriends happy, too; I'll be a prince for helping them out." He paused for a moment and puffed thoughtfully on his cigar. "Besides," he continued, "I like Carl Torsiello. . . . We'll give him a chance and we'll see what happens."

At home, Mooney went right in and called Fat Leonard. He sent him to Torsiello with instructions for the job. Twenty years later, Carl Torsiello would tell Chuck about his chance to make it big with Mooney and how excited he and his wife, Tillie, had been at the time. "It was like manna from heaven," Carl said, shaking his head. "We needed money so bad back then, Chuck. Shit, it was smack in the middle of the Depression. You were lucky to have food on the table. Men would have killed for a chance to work anywhere . . . let alone for your brother Mooney. It was an honor."

Carl had realized right away that this was his big chance, maybe his only chance, to get in with Mooney and his fast-growing group of high rollers. When he came home from work that Thursday afternoon and looked around his tiny flat, he'd imagined how wonderful it would be to always have meat on the table and money in his pocket. He was tired of breaking his back eighteen hours a day out on the railroad tracks. And tired of being paid peanuts—fifteen dollars a week—to unload the endless crates of oranges and pears coming in from California.

"You're worn out, Carl," his wife had said. "All that will change now because tonight is a new beginning.

Things will be different from now on. You know what I mean? This is for Mooney, right?" She'd lowered her voice when she said *Mooney*—everybody did; it was a sign of respect, even if he wasn't around. "Think what a change this will make. You could quit your job and start making real money. We might even get a new table," she added, running her hand over the buckling veneer. "Or new clothes for the children."

He'd thought Tillie was right about it being a new beginning; he'd hardly been able to control his excitement, couldn't think of anything else all day. All he'd known for certain was that Mooney was going to pay him more money than he could make in six months of working at the rail station and that Fat Leonard had said they needed someone tough and strong for the job.

"Well, you fit the bill," Tillie had replied, laughing, when he told her what Leonard had said. "You're made to order if strong's what Mooney's looking for."

During dinner, he'd talked on and on about how this would be the lucky break they needed, but Tillie was a devout Catholic and wasn't about to give credit to Lady Luck. In all their married lives, she'd never thought luck had much to do with anything.

"No, it's not just luck; it's more than that," she corrected him. "This is sent from heaven, Carl. We should thank God."

He could tell Tillie had been proud of him. He'd felt so good about that. With him working for Mooney, the Torsiello family would finally be off and running. At least that's what Carl had thought.

The guys arrived at seven o'clock sharp that night to pick him up, but before Carl walked out the door, he planted a kiss on Tillie's cheek. "Whatever it is I'm to do, Til, you know I'll do my best for my family," he'd said.

He had to remind himself of that after they got to the barbershop. The dim light gave the room a certain eeriness. The mirrors lining the walls reflected each tool of the barber's trade in weird distortion. Razors, neatly lined along the counters, glinted like knives prepared for battle. He hadn't liked the look of things almost from the start.

He glanced over at the other guys and wondered what was next. There were three of them standing there together in the dark: James "Turk" Torcllo, Mad Dog DeStefano, and Fat Leonard. He knew their reputations; they were some of the meanest men in the neighborhood. He hadn't minded when they'd jimmied the lock and broken in; he'd known whatever Mooney had in mind couldn't be legal; he wasn't naïve. But the baseball bats, brass knuckles, and pistols the guys carried made him nervous. He thought of Tillie and the children and recalled her words. "From heaven," she'd said. He told himself he wouldn't let her down, that he'd act like a man.

Leonard smiled and pointed to a light coming from beneath the door of the back room and whispered, "In there."

It was the signal Mad Dog and Turk must have been waiting for, because they lifted their bats and stormed the door. When it fell with a crack of splinters and brass hinges onto the tile floor, Carl saw two old men. One was balding and had a dapper little mustache; the other was clean-shaven, with hair as white as Tillie's Sunday apron, Carl thought. He was short and round and probably pushing seventy. Their eyes met.

"*Mama mia*, what do you want?" the one with the

mustache cried. "You want money? Here's money. . . ." He waved at the desk between them and the steel cash box piled high with the day's receipts.

"They don't want money, Sal," the white-haired man said. "No, they're here about the union." He stood up and faced the four intruders. "That's right, isn't it?"

He was a brave old man, even if he was bluffing, and Carl suddenly wished he was somewhere else—anyplace besides standing in the barbershop, confronting an old man who couldn't hurt a fly.

Turk lifted his bat and slammed it on the desk, making the barbers jump half out of their skins, and swept a jumble of dollar bills and receipts onto the floor. The cash box fell with a clatter and coins rolled in all directions.

"That's right, old man," said Leonard. "We're here to talk about unions. We heard you have a few beefs. Maybe you wanna tell us what they are."

The barbers looked at one another. Carl could tell they were scared to death.

"Well? Cat got your tongue? What's it gonna be, assholes? You gonna make waves or vote for the union? . . . Either way, you're gonna keep your fuckin' mouths shut and mind your own goddamned business. Or else . . . you won't be cutting hair anymore. Got that? *Capisce?*"

"Come on, Leonard, can't you see the bastards are nothin' but trouble. They need a lesson in manners . . . gettin' cocky in their old age. Maybe they should retire," sneered Mad Dog.

"Shut up," Leonard hissed.

Carl glanced over at Turk and Mad Dog. As they fingered their bats, he thought that everything he'd heard about them was true; they were excited at the idea of letting the old men have it. Turk put one hand in the pocket of his jacket; there was a gun there and he looked as if he was itching to use it, but Leonard drew his first.

"Okay, old men, what's it gonna be?" Leonard said, waving the revolver. "You want us to leave you dead . . . or alive? I'm waitin', but I'm not gonna wait long."

Before they could say a word, Mad Dog sent his bat crashing onto the head of the white-haired man, and he crumpled to the floor like an old newspaper. Blood stained his snowy crown and poured down his face, clouding his frightened eyes. He looked up for mercy, but the bat came down again. This time, it hit his leg with a sickening crunching sound and he grabbed it, shrieking in pain. His eyes fluttered and he slumped, unconscious, on the blood-smeared tile.

"Nice piece of work, Mad Dog . . . you showed him pretty good," exclaimed Turk. "Give him another one."

They laughed and didn't seem to notice that Carl wasn't joining in their amusement. His first instinct had been to comfort the poor man. The blood made him sick. He'd been a goddamned fool to think he could ever be a part of Mooney's gang.

"You're killing him," the other barber screamed, and he began blubbering in broken English. "My friend of fifty years . . . you're killing him." He rushed for Mad Dog's throat but didn't reach him, catching Turk's pistol across his temple. He staggered against the desk.

"Hey, guys, what're you waitin' for? Teach the cocksucker a lesson he won't forget. Kick his ass . . . he'll remember who to vote for," Leonard ordered, and stepped back to light a cigar.

Brandishing brass knuckles, the two jumped on the man. When they broke his fingers—one by one—they cracked and snapped like kernels of corn popping at a fair. He screamed for a while and struggled against the blows that followed, but their youth was too much for him and he fell into a stupor on the floor.

"Is he dead?" Turk asked, chuckling as he lit a cigarette.

"No and he's not gonna be, either," Leonard said. "We didn't come here to kill 'em . . . we came here to teach the sons of bitches a fuckin' lesson. We want 'em to vote, you know, and dead men don't vote."

"Sometimes they do," said Turk, catching his breath as he smirked at his cohorts. They all laughed until they couldn't laugh anymore.

In the midst of the beating, Carl slipped to the front of the barbershop. He decided he'd tell Fat Leonard he thought he heard someone coming. But the truth was he couldn't stand it anymore; he'd walked straight out the front door of the shop to the curb. After he got a grip on himself, he stood beneath the red and white barber pole, thinking about Tillie and how he'd let her down. He'd lost his chance.

"So be it," he said out loud, alone in the shadow of the streetlight. He clenched his fist and wanted to cry at the unfairness of it all. He couldn't do it, no matter how much money it meant. And he decided then and there that somehow they'd make it—he and Tillie and the children—without Mooney and the Syndicate.

CHAPTER 7

Mooney hadn't said much besides "Later" when Fat Leonard started to tell him about Carl Torsiello and the night before as they pulled up to Louie's gas station on California and Lexington. Chuck was excited to be included on Mooney's rounds through his territory that spring; and as usual he stayed out of his brother's way that day, standing outside the open garage door in the bright sunshine, drinking a cold bottle of Coca-Cola from the cooler.

Each morning, when Mooney came to the gas station to conduct business, the owner and his wife thanked him profusely. "It's an honor, Mooney; just make yourself at home. The place is all yours . . . for as long as you like," they'd say, and then skedaddle, hastily leaving a customer's car waiting on the grease racks. Once the duo left, Mooney lit a cigar—he didn't smoke cigarettes much anymore—and got down to business.

It was easy to tell when the word had gotten out that

Mooney was at Louie's—because, one by one, neighborhood men from all walks of life, from low-life greaseballs to bankers and coppers, started to show up, waiting for a word with him. And it could go on like that until noon. Then, they'd sit around awhile before heading for Claudio's Bakery and Mooney's afternoon appointments.

Chuck sat down against the wall of the building and watched admiringly as his brother worked his magic. There was a big heavyset man in a suit, who looked like a businessman, asking for Mooney's backing to open up a bar. A disheveled guy in old dungarees waited on the sidelines, pacing back and forth smoking one Lucky Strike after the other; rumor had it he owed the Syndicate money and couldn't pay. Across the garage, two old fellows with shiny bald heads huddled in the corner. Chuck had seen them there before; they ran card games and book joints.

There were the usual down-and-outers, too, looking for a job at one union or another; three of them stood outside near the door, talking about how many mouths they had to feed. "And another baby on the way," one lamented.

A few new pock-faced recruits, whom Fifi had swept off the streets, were lined up against the wall behind the grease racks, tough-guy sneers permanently frozen on their faces as they waited to flex their muscle and prove their worth.

It always fascinated Chuck how people groveled and pawed their way in to talk with Mooney. They shuffled like shines on a plantation, eyes to the floor. His brother could've been the Pope the way they fawned and whined. To hear grown men ask permission to buy a house or a car amazed him. They begged and poured out their life histories when they needed a job. Cajoled and smiled and said, "Yes, sir, yes, sir," when they wanted to open a business—legitimate or otherwise. More often than not, they didn't come to ask for money; they came for his permission or advice. Or they brought him money in neat long envelopes and left without saying a word.

Something about the way Mooney made the entire Giancana family—including Antonio—come around with their tongues hanging out, whether they needed money or, in his sisters' case, Mooney's approval to go somewhere, rubbed Chuck the wrong way. Mooney treated them just like all the other common dagos who came off the street; and Chuck resented that. Until he'd started coming along with Mooney to Louie's and Claudio's Bakery and actually witnessed what went on, he wouldn't have believed it: Other people got the same treatment the Giancana family had gotten all their lives. His only consolation was that many got worse; at least Mooney hadn't killed any of his family.

More than once, Chuck had seen Mooney give one of his lieutenants a certain look after a guy had shown up with some sob story about not being able to pay a debt. And he started to put two and two together when shortly thereafter the newspapers would report that a man's body, twisted up like a busted tire, had turned up in a ditch. It didn't surprise him. Nothing Mooney did surprised him anymore.

Maybe it was Joliet; Mooney had become more reserved, quiet, since he'd come back. Before he'd left, not much moved his brother that Chuck could recall, but now nothing touched him; he was unreachable. Maybe he'd worn a mask so long that he'd become the mask. It was as if there wasn't a real person named Mooney sitting in Louie's gas station. Mooney had flesh and blood like everybody else, but he was a counterfeit person somehow. People who knew him—even Ange—didn't recognize that. Maybe they just couldn't believe it—or didn't want to.

Now, when he saw Mooney give one of his men that look, Chuck knew what it meant and he also knew it didn't mean a thing to Mooney one way or the other. Other people thought he had feelings like they did. That was their weakness. And Mooney's greatest strength.

The businessman got up and left, scurrying down the sidewalk. And the nervous guy sat down.

"I don't have it yet, Mooney; I will though. My pa, he's gonna help me come up with the money. I gotta stay away from joints with card games. I promise I'll have it next week."

"You've said that before, Rico. . . . We want it today. Not tomorrow. Not next week. Today. *Capisce*?"

The man started to cry, sobbing and sniffling and puffing on his cigarette. He was shaking like a leaf. "I don't know where I can get it, Mooney. There isn't anyplace. Please give me another week. I'll have it then. I will, just like I said."

"Get a grip on yourself, man. Pull yourself together. It's all right." There was a cool evenness to his tone. "Go home now; we'll talk again soon . . . when you're in better shape." Mooney turned to Needles. Chuck expected his brother to give Needles his special look, the one that said the guy would be lucky to make it until sundown. But he didn't. He smiled instead, a peculiar sympathy in his eyes, and said, "Take him home, Needles."

The man stood up and dried his eyes. "Thank you, Mr. Mooney," he cried out, joy in his voice.

Chuck watched, mystified, as Needles put his arm around the guy and led him to the car. No one, not even Mooney's closest associates, could predict his brother's reactions. But undeniably, just as easily as Mooney could order a man's death, he could also grant him life. He was that powerful.

Later that day, after the continuous stream of visitors had diminished to a trickle, Chuck joined his brother, Needles, Fifi, and Fat Leonard for a cigarette and a luke-warm cup of oily black coffee. He felt privileged that they let him sit there while discussing the morning's efforts.

"Now, tell me about Torsiello," Mooney demanded.

Leonard explained that the problems with the barber's union were taken care of, but added that Carl had gotten cold feet.

When Fat Leonard finished, Mooney displayed an un-characteristic sympathy, "Too bad, Carl's a tough son of a bitch . . . he would've made a goddamned good soldier . . . maybe even a lieutenant someday."

His reaction surprised Chuck, because such behavior was typically branded as "cowardly" by his brother and, from what he'd seen over the past months, swiftly pun-ished. But here was Mooney letting it go like it was noth-ing.

As if reading Chuck's mind, Mooney continued: "You guys got along fine without him . . . right? And he stayed outta your way. So, just forget about it," Mooney said, leaning back and putting his feet up on the table. "Some guys just don't have what it takes to go up the ladder. Carl's no chump, he just doesn't have the stomach for that line of work. He's not a bad guy. We'll leave him alone . . . help him and his wife, Tillie, if we can. And if a different kind of opportunity comes along, maybe I'll give him another try. But he won't get another chance like this one."

Chuck knew exactly what his brother meant by that and

it was the one thing that worried him about his own future. Not many guys made it to the top in the Syndicate without earning it, without breaking a few legs and killing their way up; he couldn't think of one. That's how Mooney got where he was. There didn't seem much getting around that. And Chuck didn't know what he would do if Mooney ever sent him along with one of his executioners to put a guy away.

Years before, Chuck had romanticized it all—as if it were something out of a movie—but little by little he'd realized this was for keeps and deep down he'd started wondering whether he could do it. Maybe he was more like Carl; maybe he didn't have the guts for it. He hoped Mooney wouldn't demand that kind of proof of loyalty from him, his own brother. Only time would tell. But he was getting older—he was fifteen—and Mooney had already built a well-deserved reputation in the Patch by the time he was twelve. Chuck didn't see how he could ever match that—not if he had to murder his way there.

Paul Ricca didn't have to brief Mooney on the Syndicate's answer to the end of Prohibition. He was well aware that they'd found more than one lucrative angle, and he was becoming increasingly involved in the workings of each.

Aside from the growing union rackets, the Syndicate still cooked the alky—only now they sold it to licensed distributors. Distributors, typically well-known bootleggers turned legitimate entrepreneurs, were always hungry for a better profit. Rebottled and passed off as a quality brand or import, booze costing five dollars a barrel to distill in a backwoods barn could bring the Syndicate—and a corrupt distributor—thousands in profit. Much of Joe Kennedy's so-called fancy scotch was, in fact, not so fancy after all, but rebottled still alcohol. "One hand washes the other," Paul Ricca told Mooney. "And right now, one of those hands is empty. . . . All the distributors want cheap booze . . . and to give it to 'em, we need more stills and more alky."

In response, early in the summer of 1937, Mooney sent a soldier, Guido Gentile, to find some property out in the country. "Way, way out, Guido," Mooney had told his scout. "This is gonna be a big operation and we don't want any fuckin' agents nosin' around our business, screwin' things up."

Gentile set out to find a barn and cooperative farmer in an appropriately godforsaken place. He did—in Garden Prairie, Illinois.

Gentile had a long wish list—a steady supply of grain and cookers as well as vehicles for transfer of the moonshine. Once Gentile got the operation in place, Mooney sent nine soldiers from the Patch to feed the stills. By January of 1938, they were producing enough alky to supply connections along the East Coast to Boston, north to Milwaukee and Detroit, and across to Cleveland. After giving Ricca and the guys their cut, the operation supplied Mooney with more money than he'd had in his entire life.

Throughout the summer, Chuck spent more and more time at Mooney's side or at his house, soaking up whatever he could of his brother's business savvy. After Ange had given birth in April to a surprisingly healthy baby girl named Bonnie, Mooney had become more willing than ever to take Chuck along. Whether or not there was a connection, Chuck didn't know, but for his part, he thoroughly enjoyed watching his brother in action.

It seemed Mooney conducted business everywhere he

went. It wasn't always formal as it was at the garage or bakery. Most times, it wasn't formal at all. Chuck would be sitting at Mooney's house, eating dinner with his brother, Ange, and his two nieces, and the phone would ring. Ange usually answered; Mooney had her screen his calls, and if it was somebody he wanted to talk to, he'd take the call in the other room. He'd set a time and place to meet later, usually that night. It might be on a street corner, in a parking lot, or just in the front seat of the car. A real office was something nobody longed for. The Syndicate guys reveled in the secrecy, liked slipping around corners and whispering orders, planning their next move.

It made Ange more comfortable when Mooney took Chuck with him; her jealous outbursts became less frequent. Chuck decided that she believed her husband would never have a romantic encounter when his younger brother was standing by—which couldn't have been further from the truth. After a few hours of meetings, Mooney liked to stop by one of the high-class whorehouses to unwind, suggesting to Chuck that he take advantage of the opportunity. "It's free," he'd say as they parked the car. "Other assholes gotta pay up to a hundred dollars to screw these girls . . . but not a Giancana. Anything you want, Chuck . . . you hear what I'm sayin'? Anything. It's yours, Chuck . . . anything you want and all you want. Free and clear."

The Italians they saw on Mooney's rounds were men Chuck came to know well. At the Bella Napoli, Paul Ricca let him stay at the table with Louis Campagna, Johnny Roselli, Tony Accardo, and Murray Humphreys, and Chuck felt honored to be included—even if all they talked about was how tasty the cannolis were. Chuck couldn't tell whether Mooney was grooming him for the day he'd join the Syndicate—he was afraid to ask—or if, by always taking him along, he was simply placating Ange.

Through Mooney, Chuck also met men from outside the neighborhood—guys like Jake Guzik, whom Mooney worked for. Guzik was a Jew who'd earned the nickname Greasy Thumb because of his knack at thumbing through stacks of bills. Mooney told Chuck that it was Guzik, along with Ricca, Sam "Golfbag" Hunt, Murray Humphreys, and Nitti, who held the Syndicate together after Capone had gotten pinched by the IRS.

But what really impressed Chuck about the man wasn't his business acumen, but his friendly manner and generosity; every time they went to Guzik's hangout—St. Huberts Old English Grill and Chop House—they'd leave with three or four old suits to take home to Antonio. Thanks to Guzik, their father had started looking like a regular Romeo.

Chuck enjoyed sitting at the table with Guzik, too. He was warm and talkative and, Chuck thought, different from the other men around Mooney. Jake Guzik just didn't have the eyes of a killer. Sitting at his table was like being at a happy-go-lucky payoff window; everybody from police captains and politicians to judges came and went all night. Between his wine and lamb chops, Guzik managed to make them all leave smiling, envelopes stuffed with cash in hand.

By August of 1938, Chuck was finding it old hat for men like Murray Humphreys to climb into the front seat next to his brother for a little talk while he sat quietly in the back. The men discussed things such as payoffs and labor disputes for what seemed like hours. After a few months, he saw a pattern to the visits; Mooney made his rounds at night just as he did during the day. But usually the night's events were far more interesting.

Mooney would never have taken him along, Chuck was certain, if he'd known what was going to happen one night in late October. It was strange, really, how Chuck had managed over the past months to block out his concerns about being able to cut it in the Syndicate.

Meeting Jake Guzik had gone a long way toward making him feel more comfortable; his fear of someday actually having to hit a guy in order to make it had all but subsided. Mooney said that Guzik didn't have the stomach for killing—and Chuck wondered aloud how Guzik could have gotten so far with Capone and the guys.

In reply, Mooney tapped his temple with his index finger and said, "Brains, Chuck. Brains. Guzik doesn't have to kill to prove he's valuable. He's a Jew, he's good with money, and he's as fuckin' smart as they come." Hearing that relieved Chuck; he figured that he'd just have to prove he was clever enough, that he had the brains, to be valuable.

He stopped worrying about having to hit a guy or being a part of a hit. The only time he'd seen a guy drop was as a little kid in the neighborhood and that seemed like a long, long time ago, but if he closed his eyes and thought about it, he could still see the pool of steaming blood and smell it in his nostrils, could still hear the tune the guy had whistled that day—sometimes he'd even wake up with it playing in his head, over and over. But that night in October, when he and Mooney climbed into the car, murder was the furthest thing from Chuck's mind.

It had started out just like any other night; Chuck was hoping to see a little action, maybe stop by the whorehouse or the Napoli.

But when Mooney pulled over to the curb and Needles got in, Chuck's delusions about it being just another night disappeared. Needles was all business. "We gotta do something about the son of a bitch," he said.

"Yeah, I know," Mooney answered. "So what do ya wanna do?" It was interesting to Chuck how Mooney always asked that question when a guy came to him with a problem. It certainly wasn't that the guy's opinion mattered; in essence, the guy was asking permission. But allowing him to speak gave Mooney "insight"—that's what Mooney called it—into how his mind worked, what he was thinking.

"Take the motherfucker out, that's what. I've fuckin' had it with his slimy double-dealin'. He's shortin' us . . . you know it and I know it. I say we fuckin' push him."

Mooney looked back in the rearview mirror at Chuck. "Well, let's just go pick up Fat Leonard then and pay the cocksucker a visit." He turned the corner and the tires squealed.

After finding Leonard, they ended up at a pool hall.

"Needles, go bring the fucker out," Mooney ordered, and looked back at Chuck. "You get up front with me."

Needles got out of the car and went inside. A few punks were milling around in front, playing tough, and Fat Leonard got out and yelled at them. "Hey, what you fuckin' lookin' at? Get lost . . . scram."

They took off down the sidewalk.

"Boy, Fat Leonard really got rid of them fast," Chuck said.

Mooney didn't reply but sat in silence, smoking his cigar. Something about the way Mooney had turned real cold all of a sudden made Chuck uneasy and he decided to light a cigarette. When he did, Fat Leonard leaned in the door and shook his head, saying, "Chuck, aren't you too young for those things?"

"I'm old enough," Chuck retorted, dragging deeply.

"Hey, Mooney, the kid thinks he's old enough. Gettin' pretty touchy in his old age, too," Leonard said, laughing.

Mooney sat at the wheel, not saying a word.

Pretty soon, Needles came out with a plump little Italian dressed in a blue pinstriped suit.

"Hey, goddamn it," the man said as he got near the car, shaking Needles off his suit coat. "You guys made me leave a nice fuckin' woman in there. Now, let's get this over with so I can get back to her."

"You ain't goin' nowhere, Mike. You're goin' with us," Needles said, and shoved him in the backseat next to Leonard. Needles got in beside him. Chuck looked back at Leonard. He smiled at Chuck and winked; it made him queasy when Leonard smiled like that.

They drove up and down the city streets until well after midnight. Back and forth, in no direction whatsoever. No one said a word. When they passed a streetlight, Chuck could see sweat trickling down Mike's forehead.

"So what's goin' on, Mike? How's business?" Mooney finally asked.

"Fine, Mooney . . . real good," Mike said hurriedly and then added, "So what's the problem? How come your guys wanna muscle me? I ain't done nothin'. I pay you on time and sometimes even a little extra. So what's the problem?" He looked at Leonard and Needles.

"Nothin', Mike. We just thought it was time for a little

talk," Mooney replied, his voice still even, his eyes never leaving the street ahead.

"Yeah, about what? Like I said, I ain't done nothin' to piss you guys off. Honest, Mooney." He was beginning to act real skittish, looking wild-eyed around the car.

"There's no reason to whine. I didn't say I was mad at you, did I? What would I be pissed off about? You say you're clean, that you been good to us, well, why shouldn't I believe you?" Mooney maintained his concentrated driving.

"I don't know why . . . but I don't think you believe me . . . no, I don't," Mike retorted, and went to take off his suit coat; Needles gave him a hand.

Looking back, Chuck noticed Mike's shirt had big wet spots where he'd been sweating.

"There's no reason you guys shouldn't believe me. Like I said. None," Mike whined.

"None?" Needles snorted. "Are you sure, Mike? Sure we can trust you?"

"Why yeah, sure . . . you can trust me. Hey, listen. Why the hell don't we go over to the Napoli for a drink or somethin'. It'll be on me . . . what do ya say? Huh?"

"Don't change the subject, Mike. We were talkin' about trust . . . you know, trust between *paisan*," Mooney said softly.

"Hey, you guys come on out and tell me what your fuckin' problem is. . . . I need to get home," Mike exclaimed, indignation brimming in his voice.

"Yeah, to your wife and kids," Leonard said, laughing.

"Mike, tell me . . . how much money you been makin'? Is it enough?" Mooney asked.

"You know what I make. Sure. Sure it is. I ain't got no beefs. You guys let me make a good livin'."

"Well, on the street they're sayin you're makin' a whole hell of a lot more . . . more than you're tellin' us about. Is that right?"

"Hell no . . . why, you guys know everything. You know about every goddamned nickle I make. I pay you your share, don't I? That should tell you, shouldn't it?"

"Yeah, but we're wonderin' if you're payin us *all* of our share, Mike. Now come on, it's no big deal. . . . Sometimes a man needs a little extra, so he just skims it off the top, real nice. He thinks nobody'll ever know. A lotta guys do it. But you gotta be straight with us. Have you been holdin' out a little on the side? Like a few dollars to take care of that whore you keep up in your apartment on Roosevelt?"

"No. I ain't never shorted you . . . never. As God is my witness, Mooney, never."

"Mike, Jesus Christ, do you think I'm fuckin' stupid? Don't you think I see your clothes, your nice new car? Don't you think I heard about the fur coat you gave to your whore?" Mooney remained collected, in total control, and didn't raise his voice, although there was a threatening hint of anger in his words.

"Well . . . I . . . I . . ."

"What? Speak up, Mike, I can't hear up here," Mooney called back. "Look, it's nothin', Mike. Let's just be straight with each other and then we can do business together . . . but you gotta be straight. Okay?"

"Nobody's gonna hurt you," Needles said. "Mooney just wants to know the truth."

"Okay. Okay. Maybe I been skimmin' a little extra off for a few things. But only a little. Shit, I never meant to screw you guys. You're my friends. Right? We're friends?'' He nodded and looked around the car for confirmation.

"Sure, Mike. You're among friends here,'' Mooney said, smiling.

"Yeah, we're friends. We practically grew up together. Shit, you know my family from way back . . . back in the old days in the neighborhood. Let's just get square and you guys take me back so I can get home. How much do you want?'' Mike fumbled through the pocket of his suit coat.

Mooney looked over his shoulder and fixed Fat Leonard in his gaze. Chuck recognized the look. Fat Leonard barely nodded.

"Well, I don't know. How much do you think you shorted us?'' Mooney asked.

"Uh. How's four hundred? Okay? Four hundred. No, five. Five hundred.''

Needles started to laugh. Leonard snickered.

"Mike, you're insultin' me. Five hundred dollars? You're insultin' me.'' Mooney smacked both hands on the steering wheel.

The man started to cry. "I don't have any more than that right now . . . but I will,'' he added, sniffling. "You guys are scaring me. How much do you want? Whatever you say, I'll get it. It's a promise. You have my word on my mother's grave.''

Mooney pulled the car over. Thinking he would be getting out, Mike put his hand across Needles. "Okay, we gotta deal; I'll just walk back from here.''

"You're not gettin' out,'' Needles said, pushing his arm back.

"No . . . Chuck is,'' Mooney said. "Get out, Chuck; go on home. Here's a few bucks for somethin' to eat,''

Mooney said, pressing a twenty-dollar bill in his hand. "Now, go home."

Mike started to sob. "Come on, guys. Let me out."

Chuck watched from the curb as the car sped away. The man's pleas still rang in his ears.

The next day, all he could think about was the guy from the pool hall. Mike. He had a pretty good idea nobody would ever see him again.

Chuck wasn't sure how he felt about it all; it seemed as if what Mooney did paid off. He was respected, had a nice place, a beautiful car, and women flocked to him. He had a nice wife and kids. It sure didn't look as if anybody thought what Mooney did was wrong or really bad.

The whistling man suddenly came back to Chuck. He'd heard the tune in his head as he'd walked back after they let him out. He'd been disappointed at first—not to be included in Mooney's inner circle—but he knew what Mooney's look to Leonard had meant; he'd heard what Needles had said. Yeah, it was all for keeps. It wasn't the fucking movies they were in. Mike the whiner, Mike from the pool hall was probably being picked at by some big crows out on a farm somewhere. And Chuck was glad he hadn't been there to see it happen.

A few days later, he got up the nerve to ask Mooney about the guy. He knew better and felt like a fool after he'd opened his mouth.

"Shit, you gotta remember this is fuckin' business," Mooney said over a scotch and water after dinner. "Chuck, there's nothin' personal in it . . . but you can't have bastards stealin' you blind. Let one get away with it and Christ, everything would fall fuckin' apart. Remember that. And don't ask fuckin' questions. You might get answers you don't like." That was all Mooney said. He never really answered his question and Chuck didn't ask again. Mike from the pool hall just disappeared.

Throughout the fall, there were good days and bad days when it came to his relationship with Mooney; just when he'd think maybe his brother was going to let him in—treat him like a man, not a kid brother—something would happen to screw it all up.

He knew it was his own fault; he was always letting Mooney down. Chuck still had his friends back in the Patch and more than once Mooney had caught them out at night raising hell on the street corners. It was strictly forbidden for Chuck and his brother Pepe to be out in a car with friends—which made it seem all the more racy and exciting. If he got hold of Chuck, Mooney still beat the hell out of him, slamming his fist into Chuck's jaw, punching him in the stomach or bruising a few ribs.

In spite of the certain punishment that would follow if he was caught out on the town, whenever he got the chance, Chuck hung out under the streetlights shooting craps and drinking beer. Or went over to Roosevelt and Paulina in Joe Ingolia's car to shoot the breeze with the cabdrivers, relatives of gangsters whose connections had gotten them a leg up when jobs were scarce—among them, Tony Accardo's brother-in-law "Queenie" and Rocky Potenza. The cabbies were tough guys who swore and smoked and slugged anybody who got in their way. Chuck thought they were fun to be around, so he spent a lot of time hanging out at the taxi stand trading stories.

Joe Ingolia, whose family was better off than most, was the only kid in the neighborhood who had a car. Most nights they had free, Chuck and Pepe piled into Ingolia's little two-door Model A and headed downtown for Navy Pier. They just sat out on the pier, watching the throngs of people who gathered there on warm summer nights while Joe picked out top tunes on his guitar. The boys sang and smoked cigarettes and drank beer until the wee hours, exchanging tales of sexual encounters and reading the juicier passages from *Tobacco Road* out loud. Or waxed philosophical about the meaning of life and argued about whether or not the German guy, Hitler, was really out to take over the world.

Sometimes, when Chuck knew that Mooney wasn't around town and wouldn't catch them, they'd push Joe's Model A to its limits, whipping corners and speeding down thoroughfares to the all-night bars and whorehouses or to a card game on Michigan Avenue for a few hands of poker.

But not much escaped Mooney; if he wasn't close by, it didn't seem to matter. He had eyes everywhere. And stoolies who for a dollar—or in Chuck's estimation, for a chance to get on Mooney's good side—would snitch on the boys' misadventures.

He might have been emotionless about everything else, but it riled Mooney to distraction to have his rules broken. The only reason Chuck could determine for Mooney's extreme reaction to disobedience was that he believed such flagrant disregard for his authority by some punks, his own brothers on top of it, made him look bad to his soldiers. And, if Mooney couldn't control a few rowdy kids, it might make the guys up top nervous, too. Guys like Ricca might begin to wonder how Mooney could control hundreds of men, men who would screw their own mothers for a dime.

Once this realization dawned on Chuck, he tried to keep a low profile out of respect for Mooney's position, but an opportunity would come along for a little fun out with the guys and his determination to be "good" would melt.

Once again, he'd find himself back on the streets, resenting Mooney's authority. And besides, he told himself, he was only doing what everybody else did. Hanging out was what boys his age were supposed to do.

It was the very last day of November when Mooney had had enough of his younger brother's disobedience. Late one Friday night, at around two o'clock in the morning, he calmly loaded a five-gallon can of gasoline into the trunk of his car as Ange stood in her satin nightclothes in the doorway, hands on her hips.

"Don't do something you'll regret," she called out.

He ignored her, not looking back or bothering to reply, but got in the car and drove straight to Paulina and Roosevelt, where he'd been told Chuck, Pepe, and their friends were carousing in an all-night diner.

Just as Mooney expected, Joe Ingolia's car was parked along the curb. He pretended not to see the boys—they were standing under a streetlight shooting craps but then quickly ducked around the corner.

From the safety of the shadows, Chuck couldn't really tell whether Mooney was mad; he didn't slam his car door or stomp through the street. If anything, Mooney seemed amazingly controlled. The boys watched as he soberly opened his trunk and carried the can of gasoline over to Joe's Model A. Methodically, he doused the hood and opened the car door, placing the gas can almost gently on the seat. He walked to the front of the car and leaned casually against the hood as he lit a cigar.

"What's he gonna do?" Joe whispered.

"Whatever it is" Pepe answered, "it's not gonna be good."

After a few minutes, Mooney called out at the top of his lungs, "Hey, Pepe, Chuck, I know you're out there. What did I fuckin' tell you? I know you can hear me. So listen and watch real good.'' He reached into the pocket of his coat and pulled out a box of matches. He lit one and held it up. ''Your fuckin' travels are over for good,'' he yelled. And with that, he tossed the match in the door; flames burst up with a sudden rushing hiss. Thick black smoke began pouring from the windows.

Standing back from the fire, Mooney started to laugh. ''You won't be riding around in this fuckin' heap again. Maybe now you punk bastards'll learn a thing or two about fuckin' respect.'' He threw the box of matches down and walked to his car. When the gas can exploded in a roar of metal and shrapnel, he didn't even flinch or look back. Instead, he got in his car and drove off down the street.

Within moments, Joe's car was demolished. It burned and crackled, threatening to explode, until all that remained was a large blackened cinder with rims instead of tires. There had been people along the street when it happened. Most, seeing Mooney, made themselves scarce. If Mooney Giancana wanted to burn down the entire neighborhood, no one would have lifted a finger to stop him; the backlash wasn't worth it.

The boys didn't go home that night; they sat in the alley whispering among themselves while the car glowed like an ember until sunrise. It still was smoking when the sun was straight up in the sky and they'd grown cold and tired.

They wrapped some dishrags they'd gotten from the diner's sympathetic cook around their hands and wrestled open the car's charred doors. The seats were too hot to sit on, so they squatted down. Amazingly, on the first try, the engine started and they decided to attempt to drive it back to Joe's place.

Making their way through the Patch, the rims clanged

along with an earsplitting racket. *Clang, clang, clang*— they clattered over the uneven brick streets. Foul-smelling smoke spewed from under the hood and they coughed and choked on the fumes. Shop owners came out of their shops to see what was making so much racket. Gossips on stoops paused in mid-sentence and red-faced vendors stopped haggling with choosy buyers. Even women with soapsuds on their hands rushed to poke their heads out of windows. They all wanted to see what was making so much noise, and when they did, they laughed and pointed and lined the street as if it was a parade.

The Ingolia family wasn't so jovial at the sight of what had been their pride and joy. But when told the perpetrator had been Mooney Giancana, they decided to let it pass.

Chuck couldn't get over how the Ingolias clammed up and took it—even though he'd known they wouldn't have any other choice. No matter what Mooney did, no one ever stood up to him—not when they'd heard thousands of tales of Mooney's vengeance and certainly not when a prime example of his destructive capabilities sat right outside the door. That was the bottom line. And because of that, Chuck really couldn't blame them.

CHAPTER 8

Mooney's temper, although well known from his 42 gang days in the neighborhood, had actually cooled and taken a different turn since he'd met Ange. Women, like Chuck's sisters, always tried to attribute such a change in a man's behavior to his marriage, but Chuck didn't think the change in Mooney had anything to do with Ange.

Mooney still got mad inside, but he just didn't express it the same way. "Never let anybody know what you're thinking," he told Chuck. "Don't get mad . . . get even and the other guy won't be expecting it . . . he won't know what hit him."

Somehow, people must have figured out that no matter how Mooney acted, they weren't off the hook. From Principe the tailor to Claudio the baker and everyone in between, people went out of their way to be nice to him more and more. And stories about guys like Mike or some other sap who got out of line probably helped perpetuate the fear.

In five short years, from 1933 to 1938, Mooney had become the model of composure. Chuck saw him sit at the garage for hours, totally expressionless, while guys rambled on and on. He'd lean back, arms folded, and it was hard to tell whether he was even listening. Every now and then, he'd raise one eyebrow. That was it. No other sign of reaction. He could just as quickly turn to one of his soldiers and quietly order a hit as he could order a cup of coffee. It was impossible for an outsider to tell which.

At home, however, Chuck didn't see his brother waste any time or energy controlling his temper; he exploded at Ange and the two girls whenever he felt like it. It was near Thanksgiving when Chuck got a chance to see how little Mooney's temperament had really changed and how little influence his wife exerted.

He and Mooney listened to the Charlie McCarthy radio show and talked for hours after dinner. It was probably midnight when Mooney got a call from Murray Humphreys. Chuck went in to bed.

Chuck hadn't planned to eavesdrop, but his brother and sister-in-law were making such a racket, he couldn't resist.

He knew Mooney had knocked Ange around a few times, and as he crept down the hallway, he imagined this fight was about the same thing: other women. How many women Mooney had on the line, Chuck couldn't guess, but there had to be several. There was the woman at the envelope factory, and the show girls from the nightclubs along Rush Street. Chuck's sisters knew about some of them, so he assumed Ange's friends did also. And that meant his sister-in-law knew about Mooney's infidelities, as well.

"So you're going out? Why so late? For what?" Ange yelled.

Peering around the doorway, Chuck could see her brow was pinched into a half-puzzled, half-accusing expression. She seemed ready to cry from the cracked sound in her voice.

Mooney had his coat and tie on and his hat in his hand. "For business, goddamn it. Business, Ange. Can't you stop this? You remind me of the goddamned coppers." He turned his back to her and started toward the door.

"No, I can't . . . don't go out that door without telling me who you're going to see tonight."

Chuck could hardly believe his ears; nobody ever ordered Mooney around and he knew the reaction would be swift.

Mooney spun around and threw his hat down on the sofa. His eyes were narrowed and his jaw clenched. "Or you'll do what, Ange? Do you think you can threaten me?" He stepped toward her with his hand poised to strike. Instinctively, she drew back.

"Don't you know better than to ask me about business by now?" He continued: "Jesus Christ, don't ask questions. And never, ever try to tell me what I will or won't do. You got that? Do you?" He hissed the words, edging closer to her with a cunning purposefulness. His body swayed like a fighter waiting to throw a punch. "Do you hear me, Ange?" He grabbed her by her shoulders and shook her. "Do you?"

She pulled away. "Stop. You're hurting me," she said, whimpering as she rubbed her arms beneath the soft satin robe.

"You're losin' your mind, that's what's goin' on here," Mooney exclaimed. "And I'm not seeing another woman, if that's what all this is about."

She was stunned by his directness. "That's . . . that's

exactly what I'm talking about. Why can't you admit it? Why? Can't you tell the truth?'' Her voice was getting progressively louder and more strained. ''What difference does it make? I've been humiliated enough by now. Do you think I'm one of your brainless little tramps? Do you think I'm a total fool . . . that I'm blind?''

''Oh, you want truth?'' he said, sneering. ''I'll give you the goddamned truth then. You're a goddamned pain in the neck. That's what you are. And nobody on earth would blame a man for anything he did to a naggin' woman like you.''

''How can you say that? I just want it to be like it used to be, Mooney . . . before we were married. You acted like I was the most beautiful girl in the world . . . like you loved me.''

Chuck recognized a familiar pleading in her words and thought of all the times he'd begged Mooney not to hit him; she knew what was coming, she had to.

''*Act* . . . I think I like that word. Why don't you think about that word *act* for a while. Yeah, I *acted* like I loved you. You forgot who you were dealin' with.''

''I . . . hate you. God I hate you!''

''Oh you do? Well, then, you aren't going to like this.'' He slapped her across the face and then shoved her against the wall. Placing his hands around her throat, he almost touched his lips to hers. He paused, breathing hard, and then whispered huskily, ''Goddamn it, Ange, what's wrong with you? You make me crazy. When are you gonna finally believe me? There's nobody else. I'm sorry. I didn't mean a word I said. God, I love you.'' He kissed her.

She burst into tears. ''I'm sorry. I'm sorry, too . . . but please, Mooney . . . tell me the truth.''

He looked her square in the eye. ''I'm not seeing anyone

else. And I never have. I never would." He pulled her close. "I love you, Angeline DeTolve Giancana . . . just you." He held her face in his hands and kissed her hard. When he stopped, she seemed limp and breathless, as though he'd somehow managed to drain all the anger, all the life, out of her. He put his hands on her shoulders and held her at arm's length. "Now, go ahead and go to bed. I have to go out for a while."

He turned steely again and all tenderness dropped from his face. He picked up his hat and went out the door.

After Mooney left, Ange stood there for a few minutes and then walked over and sat down. She didn't move for a long time, all alone in her beautifully furnished apartment. She started to cry.

For Chuck, what little was left of their picture-perfect life had crumbled right before his eyes. She was so alone. He suddenly wanted to hold her. He felt a kinship with this woman who was, in so many ways, a stranger to him. She hated Mooney all right. And she loved him, too. Just like every other person in his world.

That was Mooney's secret. He lured you to his snare. And he knew your weakness, what bait to use. For some, it was approval. For others, love. Or money and what it could buy. Each one ended up like some struggling, soulless animal that he hated for its weakness. But remarkably, somehow, he made you thankful in the end, made you feel guilty for hating him for hating you. It was totally insane.

Chuck didn't have the slightest idea what Ange did or what she thought about. What made her smile. Or laugh like you were supposed to at Christmas and on birthdays. Not a ghost of an idea. But he knew what she and Mooney were all about. And it made him sad. He felt a pain fill his heart. As he stood there in the darkened hallway, the sadness swept over him like the fog did in the Patch early in the morning. He wanted to cry for her; he might not know her as a real human being but neither did Mooney. And that, he thought, was the saddest thing of all. He left her to her private hell and went to bed.

The next day, Ange and Mooney smiled and went about the house as if nothing had ever happened. Mooney asked her whether she'd like to go out to see the movie *Holiday* with Cary Grant and Katharine Hepburn. She gushed and fluttered like a schoolgirl on her first date. It wasn't that they never went out; Mooney made sure they went out at least once a week. When they did, Chuck thought they looked like movie stars. Ange swept her hair high on her head, swathed herself in furs and diamonds. Mooney was perfectly groomed and dressed in a finely tailored suit. They cut an impressive figure, and when they strolled out the door arm in arm, they practically smelled of money.

The confrontation between Mooney and Ange hadn't really changed anything. Mooney just cut back a bit on his nightly outings for a while and Ange stopped whining and nagging. He bought her a new mink stole and a big diamond cocktail ring as penance. And she was satisfied.

It was a destructive cycle. Like the changing seasons, weeks would go by when everything seemed as if it was back to normal, and then, little by little, Mooney would get progressively more distant and Chuck's sister-in-law increasingly anxious and suspicious. The mood would build like a slow-gathering storm until the tension was so thick, Chuck could taste it, like a coming rain, in the air.

He could almost predict an approaching fight between the two—they had a rhythm of certainty. It was always the same. First, Ange became sullen and bitter, nagging and complaining day after day. Finally, she would burst into a torrent of tears and accusations. In response, Mooney would push her around, smack her a few times, and then Ange would cry and say she was sorry. At that, Mooney would kiss her and tell her he loved her more than anyone else in the whole wide world.

Chuck guessed it was true; Mooney did love Ange as a wife. Although, he wasn't quite sure what that meant anymore. From watching Mooney, he knew there was a difference between a wife and a girlfriend—or a friend, for that matter. A man didn't confide in his wife nor did he ever show any sign of emotional weakness; he was in control. And Mooney lived up to that description perfectly. If he ever did express any real feelings, Chuck hadn't seen them—if there was even such a thing in Mooney's personality.

Indeed, Mooney was becoming more secretive, more cautious. As his power increased, his operations became more closely veiled. People around him got little pieces of information—parts of the jigsaw puzzle. But nobody but Mooney knew how it all fit together: not Paul Ricca and the bosses, not his underlings such as Needles and Fat Leonard or Teets. Nobody. Chuck felt lucky to catch a few glimpses; he was one of the few people who'd ever followed Mooney around all day. And one thing he knew for sure was that the puzzle was getting bigger. And that Ange and Mooney's home life was just a tiny, almost remote, piece.

Mooney was basically discreet in his indiscretions. He saw women outside the "family" and made sure his outside pleasures stayed that way. His plan for a stable marriage had worked magnificently. Ange would never have considered actually leaving him—she had too much to lose. And he knew it. He'd been successful in making his wife the envy of all, and equally successful in making her relish it. As the years passed, it gave her pleasure to note that no one had a more finely furnished home, a better fur, a finer car, more stunning jewels. And no one would have dared. The men who surrounded Mooney knew better. They asked permission before they bought a home or a car. A cut beneath Mooney and Ange was all one could strive for, the only acceptable option.

Should another woman reveal, over a hand of gin rummy, her designs on a home or other luxury Ange perceived as better than her own, she told Mooney about it later during dinner, complaining bitterly. "How much do you pay your men? How can they afford to buy their wives nicer things than I have? I don't think that's the way it should be. . . . You should put a stop to it." And Mooney did. More than ever, they were the king and queen. Even if the silly, puff-brained women didn't understand how things worked, his men did. They learned quickly to stay in their place.

Of course, some people had a harder time coming to grips with Mooney's domination. His brother-in-law Tony Campo squawked a lot, but after a decade of matrimonial hell for his sister, Lena, it appeared Mooney had finally gotten Tony in line.

Campo was one of Mooney's soldiers, to Mooney a *cetriolo*, a cucumber. He told Chuck he despised Campo's weakness for gambling, the way it left Lena and the kids in near poverty and the way it fell to him to make sure his sister had enough food on the table and a nice place to live.

A snarling, dominating little man barely five feet six, Tony Campo enjoyed taking his frustrations out on his wife; it was no secret he knocked Lena around—which was one of the few things Chuck knew that still made Mooney go crazy.

Almost monthly, Mooney stormed out of the house to Lena's rescue. In December of 1938 after receiving a tearful late-night call from his sister, Mooney erupted and raced across town with Chuck by his side and a .38 in his pocket.

Lena sat huddled on the stoop, waiting for them. Up close, Chuck could see the purple bruises left by Campo's fists. Her lips were almost blue and her teeth chattered in the frigid night air as she told them through tears that Campo had thrown her out.

Mooney went into the hallway and knocked almost politely on the door. In return, Campo yelled, "Go the fuck away."

"Hey, Tony, it's me, Mooney . . . open the door and let me in. We gotta talk."

Chuck heard the door unlock and saw Campo cautiously peer out into the hall. Realizing Mooney seemed calm, Campo opened the door and said, "So how the hell are you, Mooney?" He shuffled over to pull up a chair. "Hey, come on in, have a seat."

Mooney looked back over his shoulder at Chuck and Lena. "Stay in the hall," he whispered, his thin lips hardly moving. He didn't come forward at Campo's invitation, but stood in the doorway watching his drunken brother-in-law's every move. He nodded in response to Tony's question. "I'm doin' fine, Tony, fine. What's goin' on here?"

"Hey, she's no good as a wife, as nothin'. She don't have the brains, Mooney, to do what her husband tells her. No good, she's no good."

Mooney left the door open and moved toward the table.

He took his topcoat off, draping it neatly across the chair, and then sat down.

Campo surveyed him warily. "Come on, loosen up, Mooney. You want a drink?" He put a bottle on the table.

"Yeah, don't mind if I do," Mooney replied.

Campo poured him a glass of wine.

From the hall, Chuck couldn't tell what Mooney was doing; he didn't look as if he was mad. When they'd left the house, he felt certain Mooney was going to kill his brother-in-law. Now, the two men looked more like old friends having a drink together. They sat there for a while, Tony nervously gulping down one drink after another, Mooney barely touching his.

It felt like hours before Mooney reached into his pocket and pulled out the gun. He stood up. Chuck thought Campo's eyes got the look of a cow's just before it goes to slaughter.

"Okay, motherfucker," Mooney said, never raising his voice. "Stand up." He motioned with the gun and walked around the table. Campo was frozen in his chair.

Mooney didn't say another word; instead, he pulled the man up out of the chair and then, with an animal-like growl, threw him against the wall.

"Please, Mooney. Please . . . don't do this," Campo begged.

Mooney rammed the nose of the gun in his stomach and Campo doubled over with a gasp. With one hand, he shoved him back up against the wall. "You wanna be a dead man, motherfucker?"

"No, Mooney, no. I lost my temper. It's nothin' . . . I love your sister."

Chuck heard a *click* as Mooney cocked the revolver. "Maybe I should put this gun in your mouth," he said, laughing a low, mean laugh as he pushed the gun's nose against Campo's lips, pressing it on his fleshy mouth until he cried out in pain. "Or maybe . . ." Mooney dropped his hand to his side. "Maybe . . . I should shove it up your fuckin' ass and pull the trigger."

"No, Mooney . . . no . . . please, God, please no . . ."

Mooney lifted the gun back to Campo's ear and lowered his voice. "Or maybe I shouldn't waste any more time. Maybe I should just blow your brains out and get it over with. All I have to do is pull the trigger, Tony. One . . . two . . . three. Boom. You like that? You like that, Tony? Boom. And you're a fuckin' dead man. How about it? You wanna die?"

"No, Mooney, please. I'll never hit her again. Ever. You have my word."

"Your word?" Mooney laughed. "Your word? You're a no-good motherfuckin' bum, Tony. That's what you are. Am I right? Am I? Answer me, Tony . . . am I right?"

"Yeah . . . yeah . . . you're right, Mooney, you're right."

Mooney moved in close to Campo again. "You know what would make me happy, Tony? Do you?"

Campo shook his head fearfully.

"I think I should make you eat this gun . . . that would make me happy. Yeah, I think I should stick it down your fuckin' throat and pull the trigger. That's what I think." Mooney smiled. "Open up."

"What?" Campo began sobbing now. "No, Mooney. Please, no . . . no."

Mooney pushed the man's head tight against the wall and forced the gun into his mouth. "Open wide, Tony, I might slip and then . . . boom . . . it's all over for Tony Campo."

Crying, Campo opened his mouth.

"That's more like it. Yeah, that's better. Taste it. Taste the gun, Tony. It's cold, isn't it? But it gets hot when you pull the trigger. Can you taste the lead? It's in there. Can you taste it, Tony? Can you?" Campo's eyes were wide with terror. Mooney pressed it farther and Campo started to gag.

"How's it feel? Huh? You like bein' fucked over? Naw, not much. I didn't think you would. Well, that's how my sister feels. And it's gonna stop . . . or you're gonna die."

He took the gun out of Campo's mouth. "You hear me, Campo? You hear me? I don't wanna ever hear about you layin' a hand on my sister. Got that? *Capisce*?" He pointed the gun directly at the man's head.

"Uh-huh." Campo nodded.

"Well then . . . fuckin' answer me." He moved the gun closer again.

"Yeah, I understand. I won't ever hurt Lena . . . ever."

"That's more like it. Now get the hell outta here before I change my mind and blow your goddamned head off."

Campo rushed out the door, past Chuck and Lena.

In the car later, Mooney was quiet.

"Why didn't you just kill him, Mooney? I mean, the guy deserved it," Chuck said.

"You think I'd do that in front of my sister and her children? Goddamned animals act like that. If I was gonna kill him, he'd be nowhere around them. Besides, Campo's a fool . . . he's not fuckin' worth it. And worse, he's a goddamned two-bit gambler. I got no respect for drunks or gamblers. Liquor and gambling control people, Chuck. Weak people. And when you know that about a guy, you know you've got him. And there're millions of dumb sons of bitches just like him . . . on every goddamned corner.

They're sheep. And they'll never be anything else. You can own them . . . they're weak. Remember that.''

''I still would've killed the bastard, anyway,'' Chuck said angrily.

''Oh you would?'' Mooney retorted. ''Well here, smart guy . . .'' Mooney reached in his pocket and pulled out the gun.

''No, no. That's okay, Mooney,'' Chuck quickly replied. ''I don't want the gun.''

''I didn't think so,'' Mooney said, and shoved it back in his pocket. ''Do you know what it's like . . . to kill a man?'' He laughed. ''No, you don't. It's not like you think . . . sometimes you don't even know the dumb bastard. It's not like you're mad at him or nothin'. Sometimes you know the guy like he's your own best friend.'' He lit his cigar and took a long drag. ''You stalk him, so you get to know his habits . . . where he and his wife and kids live . . . where he keeps his girlfriend. And you know who his friends are, who can beat him at poker . . . and who can't. You know everything and nothin' about the son of a bitch.''

Chuck watched the way Mooney's eyes lit up as if they suddenly had come to life. There was a pleasure in his voice, a pride in his skill.

''So you wait it out, 'til the time is right to make your move. Sometimes it's the dead of winter. You can feel the cold metal of the gun against your skin . . . your feet are cold. You can almost hear your heartbeat. You're alive, really alive. More alive than in your whole fuckin' life. You stalk him like a cat. You get so close, you can smell his cologne, and if you're out in a field somewhere . . . the air . . . well, it's cleaner. You can breathe, Chuck. And the hair sticks up on your arms and the back of your neck." He sighed. "You feel hot like you do in the backseat of a car with some bitch you've been dyin' to fuck . . . but better. Sometimes you want it to last, so you just play with a guy, toy with him a little bit. They always act the same . . . they beg you not to do it to 'em. When you finally do hit the bastard, he drops like a sack of potatoes right there at your feet. Sometimes," he said, chuckling, "you push a guy and you look down later at your new suit and see how he bled like a stuck pig all over you . . . and it makes you so mad, you wish you could fuckin' kill him all over again."

As Mooney talked, Chuck's throat went dry. His heart pounded in his chest and he felt sick to his stomach. He thought about the whistling man. When Mooney mentioned about his hair standing up on his arms, the little hairs up and down the back of Chuck's scalp had tingled with anxiety. It scared him. He was afraid all right. Of his brother, as much as his story. He knew Mooney was cold. But he'd never heard him talk about it. No thought for the other guy—it was all business. And that was what made it all right. But what about the guy's wife? What about the guy's kids? He sat in silence, stunned by the realization that, to Mooney, they didn't matter. Nothing mattered, nothing at all.

Less than a month later, on January 17, 1939, the Giancana family got some bad news. Treasury agents had raided the still in Garden Prairie and arrested Mooney along with his cohorts.

Chuck was with Ange when she got the call and he thought she might go into a swoon; her knees crumpled as she put the phone down and turned to him, sobbing. "Oh my God, what will we do without Mooney?"

He couldn't reply at first; the idea that Mooney might

be caught by the coppers and sent away to prison again hadn't crossed his mind in years. Everything had been going along so well. Mooney was starting to treat him like a man, as if he was somebody other than just a little brother. If he left, their lives and all their plans for the future—his as well as Ange's and the kids'—would be swept away. He looked at Ange slumped across the table and simply shook his head, saying, "I don't know what will happen if he goes away. I just don't know." Ange began to cry.

When the trial came up in May of 1939, the judge went light on the locals who had provided the barns and mash, but he let the wrath of the law come to bear on the Chicago punks. Convinced he would receive a lighter sentence, Mooney reversed his "not guilty" plea and was sentenced on nine counts, receiving four years, with fines and court costs of over three thousand dollars. By October 1939, Mooney was on his way to Leavenworth, Kansas.

Like Murray Humphreys, Mooney referred to his up-coming stint in prison as "school." But unlike Humphreys—who'd told reporters as he'd left for Leavenworth back in 1934, "While I'm down there, I intend to study English and maybe a little geometry"—Mooney would learn something he hadn't yet dreamed of. Something that would change the face of Chicago, and his own life, forever.

CHAPTER 9

I used to think all shines were stupid . . . stupid and
lazy, that's what I thought," Mooney said. Just a few
weeks out of prison, he breathed in the cold air with seeming relish and turned to face Chuck. "But man, oh man,
was I ever wrong." He shook his head and continued,
lowering his voice to a husky whisper, "Chuck, there're
shines on the south side . . . you wouldn't believe it . . .
shines who make millions . . . more than you can imagine. . . ." He paused as if he didn't believe what he was
saying himself.

"How?" Chuck asked. There was a light covering of
snow on the steps and it crunched under his feet as he
shifted back and forth to stay warm. He wasn't wearing a
coat, he never did; it was a habit that was a holdover
from his childhood when they couldn't afford any winter
clothes.

"Policy, Chuck, policy."

"Policy? Really?" Chuck was incredulous. "I thought

that was just nickel-and-dime shit for the colored people. . . ."

Mooney laughed and grinned. "So did I . . . but Chuck, it's more than that . . . a hell of a lot more. Dutch Schultz out of New York knew that back in the thirties. . . . The guy made a million dollars a day on policy."

"Shit, I'm not even sure how policy works, Mooney."

"It's real simple. It's a kind of lottery. You pick some numbers and bet on 'em. With a nickel bet, you could win *five* bucks . . . as much as two thousand dollars on a two-dollar bet."

"Jesus Christ. . . ." Chuck whistled, impressed. "That's a dollar on a penny."

"That's right. But the real beauty is anybody can play. Everybody's got a nickel to spare. And there isn't a soul on the south side who doesn't play. . . . They all do. It's not the big-buck, heavy-gambler shit . . . it's for the everyday people. And they've got a lot more dreams than the big guys. A nickel could buy them their dream . . . and poor people live on dreams."

Chuck knew the colored weren't alone in that; every person he'd ever met in the Patch had a dream. As a kid, he'd thought he was the only one who dreamed of being somebody, of commanding respect. But as he'd grown up, he realized everybody in the neighborhood had a dream—it's what kept people going, the reason they got out of bed in the morning.

"Policy isn't the big, one-time score . . . it's volume, Chuck, volume. Like I said, everybody plays. But the percentages are always with the house. Volume. And Chuck, pennies make nickels, nickels make dimes, and goddamn it . . . dimes make dollars. *Millions* of dollars." He paused and continued: "You'd think somebody would've heard about this before now in Chicago . . . but it belongs to the shines . . . and who the hell pays any attention to them? Even Capone didn't. Years ago, Capone had his chance and turned it down. . . . He didn't see the profit in it.''

Mooney leaned on the rail and gazed out into the street. ''Remember when they let me transfer from Leavenworth to Terre Haute?''

''Yeah, you told them you needed to be close to your family, right?'' Chuck chuckled at his brother's obvious ruse.

''Right. Well, anyway, that was probably the best thing that ever happened to me . . . besides gettin' out of 'school' a year early . . . because when I got to Terre Haute, I met Eddie Jones, a colored policy guy.''

Mooney's words took on a dreamlike quality. ''Jones says the whole thing started back in the old days. In New Orleans, back in slave times. It moved up the river and north with the shines 'til it reached Chicago. Pretty soon, everybody in the colored neighborhood played . . . washwomen, street sweepers, ministers . . . you name it.'' He paused and shivered. ''Hey, what do ya say we go have a drink?''

They headed for one of Chuck's favorite dives, the Little Wheel on California and Lexington.

''It's all so clear, Chuck,'' Mooney continued once they were in the warmth of the car and on their way. ''Nobody in the Syndicate knows. Nobody. They never dreamed the colored bosses were rakin' so much in. Nobody knows . . . but me.'' He looked over at Chuck and smiled a broad, smug smile.

''Well, what good does knowin' do us?'' Chuck asked. ''Coloreds don't let whites in on their action . . . ever.

What the hell good does it do knowin' that a handful of smart shines are makin' a killing . . . while us Italians are over here making peanuts?'' He paused for a moment and then answered his own question. ''None, huh? It wouldn't do us one damn bit of good. . . . You know I'm right about that, Mooney . . . unless one of them would let an Italian guy in.''

''Yeah.'' Mooney nodded his head in agreement. ''Well, one will. . . .''

''Who, that Eddie Jones guy?''

''Yeah, Eddie Jones.''

''Man oh man, you're fuckin' kiddin', Mooney, aren't you? He'll let you in?''

They'd reached the bar and Mooney stopped the car and turned to Chuck. ''Oh, he'll let me in all right. We've got a deal. When Eddie gets out of prison, we're partners. Meanwhile, I'm gonna work with his brother, George. Hell, it's smart business . . . good for him and good for the Italians . . . and very good for Mooney Giancana.'' He grinned and opened the door.

It was jumping in the Little Wheel. Crowded and noisy, a jukebox blared out a scratchy Jimmy Dorsey tune. The place smelled of stale beer and cheap perfume. Smoke hung in the air, casting a cold blue film over the room. As Mooney led Chuck to a booth in the back, the bartender called out a greeting. A few guys gathered around and told Mooney how glad they were he was back in town, how it hadn't been the same without him, and then respectfully went back to slouch over their red-lipped girlfriends and drinks.

They ordered scotch—''Doubles,'' Mooney said to a pock-faced waiter they called ''Goldie'' because of his gold tooth—and leaned back in their chairs.

Chuck couldn't get over the way things had changed since Mooney had gotten out of prison. Those three years at school—as Mooney and Ange referred to his prison stay—had made a hell of a difference. Chuck was twenty now and Mooney treated him like a man, an "almost-equal." When Mooney came home right before Christmas in 1942, as a result of early parole, things changed between them for the better.

All the days and nights he'd watched after Ange in Mooney's absence, carted over the envelopes stuffed with money from Guzik, Fat Leonard, and the guys for her and the kids, all the errands he'd run, all the chauffeuring to places like Marshall Field, where she continued to buy designer dress after dress—it had all paid off. He hadn't done it for any other reason than that he thought it was the right thing to do, but now he realized it had been more than that—his loyalty had earned him something he didn't think he'd ever achieve: Mooney's respect and gratitude. Mooney never said anything, but he didn't have to.

Their drinks came and Chuck's dark brown eyes searched his brother for more information about this latest venture. As if reading his mind, Mooney went on to relate the story of the Jones policy empire.

He told Chuck that by the thirties Eddie and his brothers had the most lucrative policy wheels in black Chicago. "They've got over a thousand soldiers workin' for them . . . and the money, you won't believe it . . . there's so much that they have to carry it to their headquarters over on South Michigan . . . in fuckin' bushel baskets. Over fifty thousand dollars a day. So much money, they have to divide it between twenty-five different banks."

Chuck whistled. "Wow," he said.

Not one easily satisfied with a simple gambling enterprise, Jones had invested his earnings in legitimate businesses—purchasing a Ben Franklin store, four hotels, a food market, and several apartment buildings. But of all of Jones's holdings, Mooney was most impressed with his international villas. "The guy's got a place, a fuckin' mansion, in Mexico and another one in France."

To hear Mooney talk, Eddie Jones lived like royalty. His wife was a beautiful Cotton Club queen from New York who dressed in exquisite diamonds and furs. Their home in Chicago was furnished lavishly with antique tapestries, oil paintings, and real gold fixtures in the baths. Mooney didn't have to say it; what Jones had was everything Mooney had always wanted and more. Chuck watched his brother's face in the ice blue light of the bar. It hardened with determination as his story wound down.

"So, what's next, then . . . I mean what happens with Jones and all?" Chuck asked as he leaned forward on his elbows and swished the amber liquid pensively around in his glass.

"What's next is policy, Chuck. I've got meetings with George Jones tomorrow morning at their Ben Franklin and a meeting with Paul Ricca and Jake Guzik tomorrow night. Once those guys see there's money in this . . . big money . . . well, shit, I'll have the nod. And then, I'm on my way." He smiled broadly. "Yeah, I'm on my way."

Mooney was well aware that his Chicago superiors had other, more pressing concerns to address that year—things more important, at least on the surface, than any gambling venture Mooney might propose. He told Chuck later that approaching the bosses while they were trying to finagle their way out of a federal indictment, the Browne-Bioff case, made all the sense in the world. "Maybe I should've asked for the moon . . . the guys were so distracted by this federal rap, I probably would've gotten it,'' he said, eyes twinkling.

Like most of America, Chuck had heard all about the gangland-Hollywood scandal. Three years earlier, federal agencies had begun digging into the International Alliance of Theatrical Stage Employees and Motion Picture Operators, headed by Chicago's one-time pimp and union man, Willie Bioff. What the feds unearthed was an incredible trail of corruption that led right up to—but stopped short of, for lack of evidence—Chicago's top men. Bioff and George Browne were ultimately convicted of labor racketeering. Meanwhile, their most easily nabbed partner in crime, Twentieth Century–Fox producer Joe Schenck, a man Mooney said had funneled more than ''half a million to Roosevelt's campaign for the Syndicate through Postmaster General Farley,'' was also imprisoned for not paying taxes on the four hundred thousand dollars in payoffs he received from Chicago.

According to Mooney, Roosevelt later repaid this underworld donation to his political campaign by making labor gangster and president of Amalgamated Clothing Workers, Sidney Hillman, a frequent White House guest and his most prominent labor adviser. Additionally, Roosevelt agreed to make a person whom Mooney called ''their boy''—Harry Truman—chairman of the Democratic National Committee and his vice-presidential running mate.

Mooney told Chuck that the possibility of Bioff implicating his superiors had been a legitimate concern to Ricca and the other bosses and, consequently, Bioff's life ''wasn't worth two cents''—which was probably what had led Bioff to start talking to the feds that year.

Chicago had continued to conduct their Hollywood business as usual, with Johnny Roselli at the helm after Bioff's conviction, but now Bioff's testimony would put the entire upper echelon of Chicago's Syndicate in jeopardy. Mooney seemed strangely happy about the whole affair.

"Won't it hurt the Syndicate if Ricca and the guys go off to prison?" Chuck asked. "Won't things fall apart?"

Mooney smiled secretively. "No, not if there's someone Ricca can trust to work with Guzik and Humphreys, somebody smart with the muscle to keep things in line. The guy who can step in and handle things . . . well"—he smiled again—"that guy will have it made. Shit, Ricca and those guys could be facin' ten years. That's ten years, Chuck, for another guy to get to . . . well, let's put it this way . . . to get to wherever he wants . . . to the top."

Mooney told Chuck that the studios were too lucrative to abandon. "We're not about to turn our back on so much money and power." He said relationships with men like Columbia's Harry Cohn, Warner Bros.'s Harry Warner, and Louis B. Mayer of MGM were far too important to Chicago's future. "Besides," he added, "those guys are more than business contacts . . . they're our friends now. Roselli's got them in his pocket."

With Mooney getting the go-ahead that winter to move more heavily into gambling, particularly the policy rackets, he rapidly began setting his plan in motion. He divided his territory by race and city wards; the colored section was reserved for policy—or numbers, as it came to be called by whites looking to give the game more class—while the white neighborhoods would be graced with the more traditional forms of gambling such as poker, craps, and horse racing. To oversee his little empire, Mooney bestowed the job of underboss on Fat Leonard Caifano.

Under Mooney's direction, Fat Leonard made substantial progress. In the white wards, utilizing legitimate taverns and restaurants as fronts, he set up book joints, many with back rooms for poker and the like. Any competitors were given an ultimatum: Join up with Mooney or join the other saps in the graveyard. After making good on that promise with a few guys who stood in their way, other joints fell right in line and it wasn't long before Mooney controlled no fewer than two hundred operations throughout the city of Chicago and another two dozen in the county, each averaging a healthy two thousand a month. Not one to leave any money on the table, Leonard solicited the assistance of individual bookies to work the hundreds of thriving factories and taverns.

Penetrating the colored policy rackets was another matter. Until Eddie Jones was released from prison and gave his support, progress would be slow; colored gamblers wouldn't play a white man's wheel and few colored policy men were willing to serve as front men for the cutthroat Italians, despite the monetary reward. In the white neighborhoods, Mooney's ventures fared much better; when word got out that the Syndicate was making a push into gambling and there was money to be made, the more ambitious legitimate businessmen flocked to Fat Leonard in hopes of setting up their own book joint. But, more often than not, Leonard put a trusted Italian soldier in charge as manager, with instructions to employ guys from the old neighborhood. "Take care of our people first" was Mooney's motto.

Depending on the size of the place, the manager hired one or two cashiers, several scratch-sheet writers, and a lookout for ten dollars each a day. Once business got under way, the scratch-sheet writers scurried about, receiving telephone updates continually through a wire service at local and national tracks, and revised the odds on each race. The joints hummed. All over the city, cashiers raked in the dough and lookouts stared endlessly out the door for any sign of a raid—which was highly unlikely given that Leonard had paid off the necessary coppers.

"As sure as the goddamned sun will rise tomorrow," Mooney said to Chuck one night that winter, "the captain will get his two hundred dollars for every book joint in his district." And Mooney was more than happy to pay it; he thought the Syndicate got off cheap. "If the coppers found out this operation will bring in five million this year," he said, laughing, "we'd have to make them full partners."

At the end of each month, the managers totaled the profits in order to "make books" with Leonard's bagman and then the cash was taken to Mooney. There it was counted again.

Nobody could say Mooney wasn't generous; he made sure cash bonuses were delivered each month to his managers and their men. But Mooney's bonuses could never be predicted; one month a guy might get a thousand bucks, the next, one hundred—for doing exactly the same thing. It never made any sense to his soldiers, which was exactly the way Mooney liked it. "You gotta keep 'em guessin', Chuck," he said. "Never let your men think you're completely satisfied with their job. They'll work harder when they're worried about what you're thinking . . . and what might happen if you ever got real fed up. Don't make work just a measly paycheck . . . make it life and death."

In March, while Chuck was just starting a job as a lookout at a book joint Mooney had invested in on Sixty-fifth and Cicero, news came of the indictment against Paul Ricca, Frank Nitti, Phil D'Andrea, Louis Campagna, Frank Maritote, Johnny Roselli, and Charlie Gioe. Mooney told Chuck that Ricca had instructed Nitti to take the rap for the rest of the guys, confessing he'd acted alone, "or else." Perceived as Chicago's "boss" by authorities, the ineffectual Nitti would most certainly be believed and, Ricca reasoned, considered quite a prize, practically guaranteeing the real conspirators their freedom.

Chuck secretly wondered what a confession from Nitti—and the acquittal of the other Syndicate men—would do to Mooney's plans. But Nitti, faced with Ricca's ultimatum, committed suicide, leaving Ricca and his boys to face the charges without a fall guy.

Found guilty and sentenced to ten years in prison, Ricca appointed Tony Accardo as boss of Chicago's underworld, with Humphreys and Guzik as advisers. Mooney saw the transition as his big opportunity to move up within the ranks and wasted no time solidifying his own power base.

By the time the sensationalized Browne-Bioff case was under way, Chuck was making seventy-five dollars a week in his position as a lookout. It was good money at the time, but he was still disappointed. He continued to live at home with Antonio and his brother and three sisters; his other sister, Mary, had gotten married through an Old Country arrangement and now they saw her only occasionally.

He found being at home depressing. Chuck had given up on his father ever amounting to anything more than a vegetable peddler. Antonio had opened and closed more stores than anyone could remember; living under the same roof with the man was almost more than Chuck could bear. His father's low station in life contrasted sharply with Mooney's success, offering a constant reminder of what Chuck might be if he failed to hit it with his brother.

What Chuck wanted most was some real action, a pretty wife, and some big bucks. In the past few years, he'd had his fill of whores, fast Polack broads, and penny-ante crap games. Looking at the older men—most of them old 42 members—who surrounded his brother, it seemed everybody had gotten a piece of the big-time but him. He obediently carted the small-time gamblers from Madison and Des Plaines to the book joint in Cicero that early spring in 1943 and dutifully kept his eye on the door for any sign of the coppers, but the truth was, he was bored. Worse, the other Syndicate guys who worked the place, among them Fat Leonard, were nervous around him. They thought he was a spy for his brother and it made them skittish and untalkative, always afraid they might say or do the wrong thing. The only real excitement came when there was a raid; he was always tipped off in advance, and at the sight of Chicago's finest rushing toward the door, he yelled out to the cashiers, "Clean up." In an instant, the large scratch sheets showered down from the walls like dandruff, leaving the joint's back wall as slick and shiny bare as a bald man's pate.

Nevertheless, the coppers always had a look around and then, disappointed, shrugged their blue-suited shoulders and went off on another wild-goose chase. That was Chuck's big excitement and he thought he was further than ever from big-time hoods and his brother's domain.

With the war against Japan already in full swing by the spring of 1943, Americans were asked to further tighten their belts. Consumption of sugar was limited to two pounds per month per family, and 10 million people were scraping by, in the name of patriotism, on as little as six gallons of gas a week. Ever enterprising, Mooney saw a lucrative opportunity for another racket—hustling stolen ration coupons—and busily set out to turn a profit on the nation's hardship.

As Mooney expected, there was a ready market for the

thousands of coupons his soldiers stole from Chicago's government warehouses. And like his New York counterparts—"Shit, Gambino and Luciano are makin' millions on stamps," he explained to Chuck—he found plenty of people looking to make a fast buck themselves, people willing to pay his men, who scrambled from one end of the city to the other, top dollar. From mom-and-pop neighborhood groceries and gas stations to the highfalutin' businessmen and politicians downtown, Mooney's list of contacts, and men who owed him a return favor someday, grew. Thanks to a war raging in the Pacific, business boomed for Mooney.

And while other women in the United States were learning what rivets were or struggling with hoes in tiny victory gardens, and as other women pined for the silken touch of a pair of nylons or the extravagance of chiffon and woolen yard goods, Ange began to enjoy a more lavish lifestyle. World War II brought no hardship to the Giancana household. Mooney wore trousers graced with sumptuous cuffs, and Ange's drawers and closets—as well as those of her daughters, Bonnie and Annette—were filled to overflowing with stylish leather shoes and other such black-market luxuries.

Most homemakers carted heaps of fat they'd saved for the war effort down to the corner butcher, or dreamed of the latest washer and dryer while rationing their meager supply of sugar for a few dozen holiday cookies. But Ange was a lady of privilege; she had the latest appliances and threw extravagant card and tea parties that featured linen-covered tables heaped high with cakes and confections too dear for most. Tarts, mints, and sugar-laced ladyfingers sweetened her friends' palates.

Mooney's fare, however, was beginning to leave a sour

taste in some of the more important bosses' mouths—notably Guzik's and Humphreys's. Told of Mooney's success in amassing new gambling ventures, the old guard was starting to get nervous. Word on the street was that Mooney was moving too fast, that he was an insane, cold-blooded killer—and worse, a goddamned upstart.

In April, Mooney decided to get the big boys in line and settle the score once and for all. He'd establish his supremacy by doing something so absolutely crazy that only a 42 would have thought of it. He'd kidnap Jake Guzik, his friend and mentor—the man considered the Syndicate's elder statesman, the same man who'd given Mooney his old suits for Antonio.

Mooney gave Guzik what he considered a reasonable choice: the kindly old man could either accept Mooney's "gift" of two hundred thousand dollars and support him, getting Humphreys and the rest of the Syndicate powers to do the same, or get a bullet in the brain. It was up to him. After two days in a condemned building in Cicero with a gun to his head, Guzik came to a wise decision: Mooney and his ventures had his wholehearted support. Mooney drove Jake to West Roosevelt Road and let him out. And that was that.

Already shaken by the Browne-Bioff case, the rest of the Syndicate fell right in line, just as Jake had promised.

The caper with Guzik left Mooney busier than ever before; there were new men to get on board: Jake Guzik's protégé, the Greek, Gussie Alex, who was a premier political fixer; the old-time Capone slot machine king, Eddie Vogel; and the north side's Ross Prio. He had to meet as well with longtime Capone advisers and financiers Abe Pritzker and Art Greene, and the local politico Jake Arvey.

Mooney's days and nights were filled with back-room

meetings and whispered orders to his men. He was making his move.

When he could get away from his job at the book joint, Chuck went along with Mooney on his daily rounds. Seeing Mooney hold court at Louie's gas station again, conducting business just as in the old days, made everything seem right with the world. Fat Leonard sat there as he always had, slurping down a cup of lukewarm coffee, while nearby, Needles lit cigarette after cigarette and the men—coppers, politicians, businessmen, and beggars—filed in, one by one, just to have a word with Mooney.

Occasionally, a familiar look would cross Mooney's face and Chuck knew Needles would soon be taking some poor slob for a ride out in the country; the guy would be lucky to escape with a brutal beating.

Mooney never gave a second thought to "pushing"—killing—a guy if he got in his way or if he just needed to set an example. People were like pawns to be shoved around in the context of a bigger game. It was a calculated view of life Chuck didn't like to think about—and when he did, it bothered him. But he knew damned well that if he let Mooney's tactics get under his skin, he had no place to turn. The vision of his father hawking watermelons always came to mind, quieting any misgivings.

After wrapping up at Louie's, they'd jump in Mooney's souped-up Buick and head into the heart of the city, where Mooney usually ended the day—after stopping countless times for hushed strategy sessions—at Chicago's biggest book joint.

It always amused Mooney that the Syndicate's largest operation sat directly across the street, on Canal and Van Buren, from the city's main U.S. Post Office. But he told Chuck they had the okay from the city fathers to run the joint, that the place was protected from raids thanks to a few large payoffs in the right pockets—pockets that went all the way up to the governor.

There were four large gambling joints like this one downtown, which Mooney operated with partners Gus Alex, Ross Prio, and Eddie Vogel. Proceeds averaged well over fifty grand a month at each location, with annual revenues of two to three million dollars.

At first glance, the white stone building on Canal and Van Buren didn't look like much to Chuck, but once Mooney led him up to the second floor and through the immense double doors, he discovered a gambler's paradise. There were scratch sheets on the back wall for the horses; crap tables and poker games ran twenty-four hours a day. The clientele ranged from postal workers to coppers and everything in between. There were always plenty of good-looking women roaming from table to table. And the drinks were good.

Mooney rarely had a drink, or if he ordered one, he scarcely drank it. More than once, he reminded Chuck that drinking "makes you stupid. Let the other guy get drunk and spill his guts . . . not you."

At night, the book joint was like a rowdy class reunion. Fat Leonard and his brother, Marshall, Fifi Buccieri, Needles, Teets Battaglia, Willie Potatoes—all the old 42s would gather at a table for a few hands of poker. Sometimes Gus Alex, Murray Humphreys, Jake Guzik, Eddie Vogel, and Ross Prio would join them for a game with their own entourage of underlings.

To Mooney's 42 followers and the other bosses, the gatherings at the book joint were social events; the guys laughed and gossiped like old hens. But to Mooney, the meetings were strictly business. Everything Mooney did was strictly business.

Mooney studied the way a guy laughed; the way one guy acquiesced to another—even if they were just horsing around. He paid attention to little things such as who sat where. He absorbed every last detail; nothing escaped his scrutiny. He was constantly evaluating the people around him, finding their vulnerability, assessing their worth, deciding whether they were right for the next job or if they weren't.

Chuck thought the most impressive thing about Mooney was the way he could be doing all that without anybody knowing it. The guys couldn't read Mooney, ever. It also amazed Chuck how Mooney was never wrong when he sized a guy up. The slightest move in the wrong direction and it would be all over for a guy's future; he wouldn't even be aware that Mooney had decided his fate. The guy might not lose his life, but Mooney would slowly cut him out of his. And once Mooney was done with a guy, for whatever reason, it was over; the guy would never get a break—not as long as Mooney pulled all the strings.

"Never trust anybody you didn't grow up with, Chuck," Mooney told him. "Those people you understand, you can predict. A new guy . . . you gotta fuckin' watch him. You don't know what makes him tick, if he'll be there when he's supposed to. Is a guy a coward? You don't know unless you've seen him stare down the barrel of a gun. Guys from the neighborhood . . . I know them better than their mothers . . . forget about their wives and girlfriends . . . I know them better than they know themselves. I keep a file"—he tapped his temple with one finger—"right here . . . and I remember every move a guy's ever made . . . so I always know exactly what his next move is gonna be.''

Behind his back, Mooney was called a lot of things: a ruthless bastard, a cold killer. But one thing he could never be accused of was going back on his word. Mooney believed a man's word was his bond and keeping a promise was the honorable thing to do. He told Chuck, as they drove from meeting to meeting, that that was at the heart of why he'd never liked politicians and celebrities. He said they wanted power so badly, they'd sell their souls just to get a movie contract or be elected to some lousy post—that their word wasn't worth two cents. But for the same two cents, there wasn't one he couldn't buy. Maybe it was from watching Diamond Joe or Ricca and Humphreys operate for so many years, but Mooney recognized that a guy's ego was his biggest weakness.

"They're all alike,'' he said. "Look at President Roosevelt . . . shit, he got to the White House thanks to Syndicate money. . . . We used Hollywood and Joe Schenck to funnel money to his campaign and Joe Kennedy up in Boston, too . . . he gave him millions. Roosevelt's got a lot of favors to pay back. Or look at guys like Jimmy Durante and Frank Sinatra and fighters like Graziano. They want to be big-time stars and, with us, they can. Or how about our Congressman Jimmy Adducci or Andy Akins, our friend the police captain? Why do you think they're where they are? Why do you think I can drive as fast as I want and never get a ticket? Park where the hell I please? Believe me, Chuck, they're all on the take . . . or wanna be.''

In Illinois, Mooney began fraternizing in earnest with legislators, senators, and federal judges as well as with local precinct captains, ward committeemen, and county sheriffs. He wined and dined them all at swank restaurants like Fritzel's or chic clubs like the Chez Paree. And he started traveling to Hollywood, solidifying Chicago's future while the rest of the Syndicate's top brass languished behind bars.

Mooney even took Ange along to California early in 1944. "We got the royal treatment," she gushed to friends. "A tour of the studios by all the bigwig producers . . . and we met lots of stars who acted like Mooney was their best friend. Betty Hutton was so friendly, but Ann Sothern was arrogant and rude. All in all, it was wonderful, though . . . we were treated better than the stars by the heads of all the studios."

Chuck had to smile at that. Such treatment simply meant Mooney had picked up the pieces Roselli, now in jail, had been forced to abandon. It was a thrill for Ange, but it was all business to Mooney—part of some master plan in the back of Mooney's head.

Unlike the politicians and entertainers he disdained, Mooney always kept a promise. If he said he'd give a guy a chance, he would—even if it was years later. Sitting in the Van Buren book joint one evening in late May, Chuck was reminded of that when Fat Leonard mentioned they needed two guys to run a liquor store. Mooney remembered a promise he'd made.

"Well, I said I'd give Carl Torsiello another chance if one ever came up . . . and I fuckin' meant it. If we need a couple of guys to run a liquor store, I'll put Sharkey Eulo and Carl Torsiello in. Carl's still bustin' his balls over in the rail yard. Ange tells me his family's barely gettin' by . . . and Christ, the guy's as loyal as the day is long. He's perfect to run a joint." He told Chuck to find out whether Carl wanted the job.

It had been seven years since Carl had heard from Mooney. But Chuck was sure Carl had heard all about Mooney's climb up the ladder in the Syndicate, because Carl's wife, Tillie, was a Nicastro and her brother, Pete, had been a member of the old 42 gang. Carl's sister-in-law, Rose, was friends with Ange; her husband, Sharkey, had worked for Mooney as a soldier since the old 42 days.

After the barber's union deal, Chuck imagined Carl thought he'd never get a chance again. But here it was, a chance for the guy to have an honest job running a liquor store for Mooney. When Chuck gave them the news, Carl and Tillie were elated.

Years later, Carl would tell Chuck that he and Tillie spent hours talking and dreaming about what their lives would be like with him running the liquor store. He'd anxiously awaited the go-ahead from his brother-in-law, Sharkey, and was devastated when Sharkey came by the house and delivered a less than polite reply to Mooney's offer: "Fuck that nickel-and-dime shit. You can tell Mooney to go scratch his behind. I'm not about to sit in some goddamned store all day. I don't want any part of it."

Carl and Tillie were sure Sharkey had rejected Mooney's offer more because he didn't want Carl to get a leg up than anything else. Chuck thought they were probably right; Sharkey was a small man who liked to talk big and he'd always enjoyed the fact that he was "on the inside" and Carl wasn't. "He's just jealous, Carl," Tillie had said, trying to console him.

Sharkey's decision put Carl in an awkward spot; he faced a real dilemma. He couldn't tell Mooney what Sharkey had said; the guy might be killed for his arrogance, and Carl, always wanting to do what he felt was honorable, thought telling Mooney would be wrong and vindictive.

Carl agonized for days over his decision until finally coming to what he thought was the only logical conclusion. "I couldn't tell Mooney what Sharkey had said, so I had to turn down the offer."

He admitted there'd been tears in his eyes when he wrote his reply in his best longhand. "Dear Mooney," the note read. "I regret I am unable to accept your most generous offer at this time. Please accept my humblest apologies. Sincerely, Carl Torsiello."

He gave the envelope containing the note to his thirteen-year-old daughter, Anne Marie. "Take a trolley over to Mr. Giancana's house," he instructed her. "And give him this envelope."

Chuck and Mooney had just finished dinner when Carl's daughter arrived with the message. Chuck thought the little girl pretty but timid, with the big soulful eyes of a moppet. She stood in the living room, head bowed respectfully, and awaited Mooney's response.

"Chuck, why don't you give her a ride home" was all Mooney said after he thoughtfully read the note and crumpled it in his hand. Then he surveyed Carl's daughter and added, smiling, "You're Anne Marie?"

She nodded, barely looking up.

"Chuck, on your way to the Torsiellos get a hundred-pound bag of sugar for Anne Marie's mother."

After rejecting Mooney's offer, the Torsiellos never expected to hear from him again; it was all Carl could do each morning to trudge out to his job at the rail yards. For weeks, the family mourned the loss of opportunity. Then, just as suddenly as they had heard from Mooney before, another request came. Ange had heard from Tillie's sister that their daughter Anne Marie was an excellent student. Could she be employed as a tutor for the Giancanas' girls, particularly Annette? It was a request that so honored the Torsiellos, it was unthinkable to refuse.

It was late spring when Anne Marie began her employment at the Giancana residence on Monitor Street. Watching her, Chuck could tell that the girl was enthralled by the opulence of Ange and Mooney's lifestyle. As each new luxury was revealed, her eyes grew wider. The washer and dryer, a new refrigerator, a vacuum cleaner, and the beautiful porcelain and china left the thirteen-year-old speechless with delight.

Chuck knew that in Anne Marie's home, as in most homes in the Patch, improvements came slowly; largely things had remained, with few exceptions, as they'd been decades before. The neighborhood had stood frozen in time, as well; the bustle and clamor of excitement were still in evidence on every corner; men continued to gather for a game of bocci in the evening and women still sat on stoops in their aprons, trying to catch a little sunshine and fresh air, gossiping with one another while their children played with makeshift toys.

What changes there were had been made thanks to an increase in the neighborhood's political clout and the Syndicate's pull. The streets' muddy ruts had been replaced by concrete before the war and the city sanitation department now made regular garbage pickups. Trolleys still clanged and clattered past the redbrick tenements but no longer were horse-drawn carts the norm. The vendors continued to hawk their wares, but from sagging storefronts and rusted-out trucks.

The poverty of the Patch was the same, more or less, as it had always been. But in the heart of one of the Patch's younger residents—a very serious and studious little girl named Anne Marie Torsiello—suddenly there was hope.

After school each day, she fairly rushed to her new job as tutor. It was the strong-willed little girl Annette who most needed help with her studies. Annette was smart enough, she was pretty enough, and, Anne Marie told Chuck one night as he drove her home, she thought Annette *had* enough to be the happiest girl on earth. But instead, she said, "Annette sulks through their English and history drills and refuses to do her homework. . . . She'd rather daydream about movie stars."

Worse, however, was Annette's open resentment toward her. "She hates me," she fumed. "She knows I can't make her do anything . . . and she loves to throw that up to me every chance she gets."

Listening to Anne Marie pour out her frustrations, Chuck couldn't help but feel sympathetic. Annette was an enigma, and not only to Anne Marie. No one, not Mooney, not Ange, not one person who knew her, could understand the bitterness she carried. She was never happy—no matter what her parents did to coddle her—nor did she show the slightest appreciation for the many luxuries she enjoyed. Chuck felt certain Anne Marie was angry because, like most girls from the Patch, she would have traded places with Annette, or her sister, Bonnie, in a heartbeat.

Just as she'd done with Chuck, Ange took Anne Marie under her wing and taught her how to set the table with the finest silverware, told her what was proper etiquette— and what was not. Unlike her own daughters, she found in Anne Marie a ready pupil for the social graces.

"That little girl never complains; she just thanks me over and over again," Ange remarked to Chuck and Mooney. "It can be the tiniest thing . . . a cast-off sweater, a faded ribbon, a quarter for a special treat." This was a girl who eagerly did her schoolwork and did it well; a girl who took pride in whatever she was required to do, be it washing dishes or making beds. Thus, in a few short weeks, Ange found herself lamenting to Mooney and Chuck her disappointment with Annette and Bonnie. "Why can't they be more like Anne Marie?" she asked night after night. Her comparisons fueled Annette's resentment and she soon became virtually uncontrollable at the mention of Anne Marie. Ange's slightest request was grounds for domestic warfare and fits of childish rage.

Ange and Mooney tried everything from cajoling and screaming to threats and bribery. But to no avail; nothing seemed to soothe the troubled, angry Annette. And, although Anne Marie kept her thoughts to herself, she did confide in Chuck on his evening drives to her home. "It's quite obvious to me," she said, "the Giancana girls are spoiled brats."

Chuck laughed at that. He'd known Mooney's girls all their lives and he loved them as if they were his own. He couldn't count the number of times he'd walked into their house and said, "Give me a bite," while leaning down to receive their affections. Giggling, Bonnie and Annette always complied, planting little wet kisses on his cheek.

They might be his little princesses, but he had to admit that Anne Marie was right; they were spoiled. The shy little girl, barely four feet tall, in the seat next to him was slowly gaining his respect. There was no doubt about it, Anne Marie Torsiello was a sharp little cookie.

As summer drew near, Ange decided to have Anne Marie move in, telling Mooney she thought the girl would be a help as well as a good influence. All Mooney could do was shake his head. "Well, it's worth a try," he said in uncharacteristic resignation. And then he turned to Chuck, saying, "But boarding school is where Annette and Bonnie belong."

Anne Marie quickly learned that living at the Giancana house was not the same as being their daughter. She was, for all intents and purposes, a servant. While Annette and Bonnie went out to play, she helped the cook prepare the meals and set the table. After dinner, she cleared the dishes and washed them, as well. Like Ange and Mooney, Chuck was impressed by her unswerving loyalty. Her stamina and determination were unusual for what he considered a child. She rarely smiled, going about her chores with unyielding discipline, but she positively beamed when escorting Bonnie and Annette on outings. She excitedly described her day to Chuck: the stage shows at the Oriental theater, the turquoise blue swimming pool in Forest Park, the ball games at Parichy Stadium, the beautiful clothes she saw when they went to Marshall Field's.

Chuck imagined it made Anne Marie's heart ache with desire when she went to Marshall Field's and felt the softness of a cashmere sweater or admired the sensuous luster of a satin blouse. Her station in life was sadly different from that of the Giancana girls, and on more than one occasion when he'd accompanied them to Marshall Field's, he'd heard Annette and Bonnie impudently remind her of that. "Too bad you're just hired help and can't have nice clothes," they taunted as Anne Marie watched them toss one pastel sweater set after another into the open arms of a smiling salesclerk.

Although nine years her senior, Chuck thought he and the little girl had a few things in common. It was an ultimate irony that they both were surrounded by so much and yet had so very little. As much as Ange might praise

Anne Marie's seriousness and uncommon maturity—or Mooney grant him greater status—such rewards paled next to the material world of the Giancanas.

"Someday," Anne Marie told Chuck with a fierce determination that belied her years, "someday . . . I'll have nice things, too."

Chuck often wondered whether she fell asleep with the word *someday* on her lips, just as he had so long ago. Hearing her say that made him more convinced than ever that he'd been right all along about one thing. "Hang on to your dreams," he advised her. "Because you have to have a dream to get by in the Patch."

Occasionally, Chuck thought that the lifestyle the Giancana girls led wasn't a dream come true at all but, rather, a nightmare. He believed children were like the dogs he'd seen in the Patch: They sensed a person's true feelings. Mooney rarely, if ever, expressed any warmth toward the girls. He brought them armloads of presents, things girls from the Patch like Anne Marie might give their eyeteeth for, but Chuck never heard him once say, "I love you." All the clothes and toys and fancy baubles in the world couldn't make up for that. Ange tried to compensate for Mooney's aloofness, and, in her attempt, gave in to their whims and demands, however unreasonable they might be.

Chuck saw the storm building through that summer of 1944. Annette's black mood cast a darkness over the Giancana household for weeks. In reaction, Anne Marie grew quiet and solemn, trying to be as unobtrusive as possible. Mooney had been going out of town on business to New York several times a week—something he hadn't done much of before—and Ange was left to deal with the strain of the headstrong girls alone. It almost seemed that Annette was pushing her mother purposely, seizing every available opportunity to encourage a confrontation. Ange had been almost too calm, too compliant. And then, the storm finally broke.

On a Friday night in August, Chuck was greeted at his brother's door by a tearful Anne Marie.

"Hurry, Chuck," she whispered, clearly frightened. "Please, please hurry . . . I don't know what's going to happen."

Her fear was contagious and he hesitated on the steps, afraid of what he'd find inside. A thousand horrible things ran through his mind, but he tried to look calm and nonchalant. "Now slow down," he said. "What's wrong?"

"It's, it's Ange . . . and Annette. It's terrible, Chuck. Just awful." She began to cry.

He grabbed her slender shoulders and shook her gently. "What? What's going on with Ange and Annette? Are they all right?"

Then suddenly, he knew; he heard the screams, the pleading—and with their sound, the memory of his own childhood beatings rushed on him like a tidal wave.

"Ange got real mad at Annette. Real mad," Anne Marie explained through her tears. "I'm afraid for her, Chuck . . . of what Ange might do. She got a golf club and hit Annette with it all the way to her bedroom. I didn't know what to do; I couldn't watch . . . it was awful." Chuck's breath caught in his chest; it felt just as it had when he'd gotten the wind knocked out of him as a kid, jumping off stoops. "A golf club?" He repeated her words. "A golf club?" He was incredulous; Ange had never done anything like this before; it went beyond the boundaries of discipline.

Anne Marie nodded her head. "Uh-huh . . . she got

mad at Annette and said she was going to teach her a lesson. Then she went and got one of Mooney's golf clubs. I'm afraid, Chuck. I've never seen Ange like this. She went . . . well, she went"—she lowered her voice—"crazy."

Chuck walked past the girl and toward the hallway, calling back softly, "Go to bed . . . everything will be fine. Just go to bed."

She turned and left, relieved perhaps that someone older and wiser was there. But Chuck felt neither; the closer he got to the doorway of the bedroom, the smaller and more vulnerable he felt. He talked to himself, tried to convince himself that he was an adult now, that he was in control. But Annette's cries took him back to a time and place he thought he'd left years ago.

Looking into the room, he saw Ange standing over Annette, holding the club head as the shaft blurred through the air with a silver *whoosh*; a golf club could be lethal—Ange could kill Annette.

Obviously, his sister-in-law was out of control and needed to be stopped. But, for some reason, he stood in the hallway, frozen in place, immobilized as much by the rage that reigned beyond Annette's bedroom door as by the thought of his brother's reaction if he were to intervene.

He could almost hear Mooney shouting, "Keep your eyes and ears open and your fuckin' mouth shut." Chuck took a step back; he didn't know whom he was kidding; he wouldn't go in and stop Ange; he wouldn't do anything—except turn around and leave. He wasn't sure exactly why, either. Was it fear of his brother or a desire to please him, hoping to be rewarded with his favor? Or both? He stood there in shock at the truth and then, before Ange and Annette knew he'd been witness to their madness, he silently moved down the hallway and out the door into the night.

In his car, he thought he might be sick and he rolled down the window. He didn't know whether he felt more sorry for them or himself. And why *did* he feel sorry for himself? If anything, he should feel ashamed at having turned his back on Annette. But he wasn't sure he did.

In the days and weeks that followed, not a word was said about Annette's—or Ange's—behavior. Miraculously, Annette showed no signs of abuse; but then, she never did. The headstrong girl simply nursed the bruises hidden beneath her expensive frocks and went on living in her own obstinate way. Chuck salved his conscience with that knowledge; his niece was a problem, no question about it. There wasn't a person in the family who wouldn't agree, including Mooney. No, there was no sympathy for Annette. And Chuck sure as hell wouldn't be the one to blow the whistle on his sister-in-law's treatment of the girl.

Besides, the truth was, there was nothing more important than pleasing Mooney. Nothing. He couldn't bring himself to risk his brother's disfavor. He couldn't sacrifice his own dream of being in the Syndicate for some meaningless principle or ethic or moral. Or person.

He thought that was understandable. After all, he didn't know anyone who, faced with the same choice, wouldn't do the same thing. But what he didn't understand was why he felt so angry for weeks after the incident—and so sad.

CHAPTER 10

Man oh man . . . you got so much class, you could cut it with a knife," Chuck exclaimed.

"Yeah, I think you're right," Mooney said, laughing. "But shit, for five hundred bucks, I better look good." He turned in the full-length mirror, carefully examining every detail of the double-breasted suit: the gentle drape of the soft navy wool across his chest; the wide lapels; the broad, padded shoulders. Peeking out from beneath the trousers' full cuffs, were a pair of six-hundred-dollar handmade black leather wing tips.

Jimmy Celano, the shop's plump owner, stood nearby. He pursed his rubbery lips together and softly whistled. "Mooney, you can really wear a suit," he complimented. "You're a walkin' billboard for my place here, I tell ya . . . you got a lot of style."

Throughout 1945, his brother had been spending money like water: five-hundred-dollar suits, fifty-dollar ties, seventy-five-dollar shirts, jewelry, handmade silk underwear and handkerchiefs. And though, at only twenty-three, he realized he couldn't match Mooney's image of wealth, Chuck couldn't resist gazing into the mirror and studying his own reflection. Twinkling, almost mischievous dark eyes looked back at him. Atop the thick curly black hair that framed his smooth olive face was a gray fedora. His lean, muscular frame lent nice lines to his pinstriped charcoal suit. He was head to toe a man now; he'd proven he could handle himself around his brother's late-night haunts—the lounges, whorehouses, and strip joints. And he knew what being a man was all about, too; like Mooney, he'd made plenty of women beg for more. At the thought, a feeling of pride and pleasure came over him.

He shifted his gaze to study Mooney's image. His brother wasn't just another scrawny punk anymore; he'd filled out over the past few years and his face, tanned from a recent stay in Miami, bore the tiny signs of age well and with a new sense of dignity.

There was remote coldness behind Mooney's deep-set eyes, a slight curl to his lips, which encircled a smoldering cigar, a staggering self-confidence—or was it arrogance?—in his posture. But trying to analyze what it was exactly that made Mooney so goddamned magnetic—well, it was just about impossible.

In 1946, Mooney was made underboss to Tony Accardo. The advancement in status was based as much on the success of his gambling rackets as on the ominous power base of men and muscle he'd managed to build.

Times were good for Mooney and getting better; he and Ange were wintering in Florida and had placed Bonnie and Annette in boarding school in, as Mooney explained to Chuck, a last-ditch effort to get the two rebellious girls in line. "Christ, Annette's impossible to control . . . can you believe she still wets the bed?" he complained. Anne Marie Torsiello still tutored the girls occasionally, but Chuck rarely saw her and assumed she'd gone back to her life in the Patch.

Throughout the year, Mooney traveled more frequently to Florida, California, Cuba, and New York. He'd been routinely visiting Manhattan since Lucky Luciano had entered prison ten years previously.

Luciano had appealed, unsuccessfully, for parole in 1938 and 1943. Even his assistance, at the prodding of U.S. Intelligence, in contacting the Italian Mafia kingpin Don Vizzini to request the don's aid during the U.S. invasion in World War II did nothing to convince authorities he should be released. However, Mooney confided that Luciano's ninety-thousand-dollar "campaign contribution" to Thomas Dewey, the very man responsible for putting him behind bars in the first place—coupled with Meyer Lansky's promise of part interest in a future Tampa, Florida, gambling deal in the Bahamas—was all it took to win Dewey's friendship and Luciano's subsequent release. "That's the name of the game," Mooney said, smirking. "Now we own Dewey . . . he just doesn't know it yet."

Thus, in 1945, the New York State Parole Board freed Luciano on the condition he be deported to Italy. For his part in Luciano's release, Dewey came under fire, but the crime fighter turned presidential candidate quickly pointed to Luciano's service to the United States government during World War II as reason enough for release. After his release, Luciano maintained his authority from outside the United States, living comfortably in Italy, while using Frank Costello as his overseer in New York. Costello was one of the few men Mooney obviously admired. "Costello's my kind of guy . . . smooth and smart."

Indeed, the two had much in common and Costello, eleven years Mooney's senior, stood as an example of everything Mooney was striving to achieve: Costello had the muscle, but he relied on finesse. According to Mooney, he had practically every politician on the pad—even had J. Edgar Hoover in his pocket. Costello dined with senators, was friends with George Wood of the William Morris Agency and producer Harry Cohn of Columbia, and partied with celebrities. Frank Costello, Mooney maintained, knew how to live.

Like Mooney, Costello had grown up in a teeming slum—East Harlem—and held a lifelong and deep-seated hatred for his father. He'd gotten his boost into the rackets thanks to his elder brother, Eddie, and during Prohibition, he had become fast friends with Meyer Lansky and Lucky Luciano. Collaborating with the two younger men, Costello helped develop what would become the national Syndicate. Early on, Mooney said, his path had crossed Costello's when he'd run rum and sugar shipments for Diamond Joe Esposito to Joe Kennedy's bootlegging operation. He'd liked Costello from the start.

But it wasn't until Mooney returned from Terre Haute in 1943 and made his move on gambling and Chicago's black policy wheels that their relationship blossomed. "A few drinks and we were tight," Mooney informed Chuck. "We realized we had a lot in common, our likes, dislikes. But mostly, I thought he was the smartest man I'd ever met. . . . He could tell I admired the way he could get things done and he liked that."

Mooney said Costello had style like nobody else. He

knew how to handle himself among the rich and famous, the politicians and kings. He called the judges "his boys." "Man oh man, I wanted to be as powerful as he was. . . . I watched his every move. If there ever was a guy I wanted to be like, it was Frank Costello."

Mooney's friendship with Costello had continued; they'd started working a few rackets together the year before, in 1945, when Costello needed a distribution point for his gem-smuggling operation in the Midwest. Pretty soon, Mooney was taking gems stolen in Midwest heists up to one of Costello's fences, George Unger, and returning with Costello's smuggled treasures—which Mooney turned over to his soldiers for distribution throughout the Midwest and West.

The operation was worth millions to Chicago's Syndicate, but the formation of such lucrative ties was worth far more to Mooney. He now had a powerful friend and ally in New York, something that didn't go unnoticed in his own hometown; his stature in Chicago seemed to skyrocket. Wherever he went, he got the red-carpet treatment and became a recipient of not only incredible art objects, jewelry, and other such fine luxuries—but the "smaller" things in life, as well.

In Chicago, while average citizens waited months for a car after the war, Mooney only had to visit Emil Denemark, the area's largest Cadillac dealer, to ensure that those around him were driving in style. For such treatment, he paid the dealer at cost plus cash under the table; Chevys and Fords were three hundred extra, Buicks were five hundred, and Cadillacs, a thousand. With hundreds of men to supply with automobiles, Mooney became Denemark's biggest customer and their relationship blossomed. In return, Mooney was given anything his heart desired.

When he walked into the showroom, Denemark greeted him like a long-lost friend and ushered him to his private office, where Mooney, feet up on the dealer's desk, lounged and Denemark himself sat in a chair reserved for customers. He instructed Denemark, pen and paper in hand, as to who among his lieutenants and soldiers could purchase a car—as well as what make, model, and year.

Mooney rewarded Chuck's loyalty by giving him permission to purchase an aqua-blue 1946 Buick convertible, which sported the very first whitewall tires in the country. For Ange, he bought a dark blue Fleetwood Cadillac, and for himself, a 1946 Mercury.

Mooney clearly had a love affair with cars. Although he was unimpressed by the ostentatious "luxury" models, he hadn't lost his appreciation for the low-profile getaway vehicles of the old days. These he treated as prize possessions; they were meticulously waxed and polished weekly at the dealership under Chuck's watchful eye and outfitted—in a manner that harked back to Mooney's days as a wheelman—with bulletproof steel plates and high-speed heads and cams, which allowed the cars to reach speeds of 120 miles an hour.

Mooney traveled in his souped-up cars at the speed of an ambulance, from one end of the city to the other, working deals wherever he went. But always he kept his eye on the south side colored district and its policy wheels, making what progress he could among the colored as a white Italian, until at last Eddie Jones made good his promise of partnership and financial backing.

Jones, who in 1946 still awaited parole from prison, instructed his brother, George, to proceed, bankrolling Mooney to the tune of several hundred thousand dollars that year, and, under the auspices of a partnership with the

Jones brothers, Mooney began pushing his way into colored policy wheels while simultaneously purchasing the necessary equipment for an immense jukebox, pinball, and vending-machine venture. He enlisted Chuckie English, a friend from the old 42 days, to oversee the day-to-day operation.

With the exception of the pinball machines, "illegal devices intended for the purpose of gambling," the operation was totally legitimate—until the skimming, hijacking, and shakedowns began, which was what had attracted Mooney in the first place.

Skimming—the practice of taking a percentage of income off the top before reporting it to the IRS—was especially lucrative in an all-cash business where an exact accounting of income was impossible to establish. And though jukeboxes and vending machines were seemingly only a nickel-and-dime business, they lived up to Mooney's adage, "Nickels make dimes, dimes make dollars, and dollars can make you a rich son of a bitch."

With Mooney's blessing, English recruited union guy Joey Glimco, Willie Potatoes Daddano, Joe "Gags" Gagliano, Dave Yaras, and Lenny Patrick as his territorial front men for the machines. In turn, these men brought in their own soldiers as "distributors"—in all over five hundred men—to blanket Chicago and the surrounding suburbs with what Mooney ultimately claimed were more than twelve thousand jukeboxes, cigarette, and pinball machines.

The distributors went fifty-fifty with tavern and restaurant owners on the illegal pinball machines, a small flat weekly amount on the others. An owner unwilling to allow Syndicate machines in his place of business might experience vandalism, firebombings, or worse. Once a business was infiltrated, the underworld could monitor operations, make high-interest loans to a struggling owner, or, even better, take over the business completely.

Monopolizing the city's jukeboxes also gave the Syndicate enormous clout with the entertainment industry; a new song wouldn't be a hit if it didn't receive exposure. Mooney and his associates could flood the city with a favorite entertainer's record or demand payola from a studio merely to assure placement of an aspiring new hopeful in Syndicate machines.

With an average weekly take of ten dollars per machine, the money piled up fast. Mooney and the Jones brothers split the income from the venture fifty-fifty, skimming off the lion's share of the $6 million in yearly earnings and reporting to the IRS little, if any, of the profits.

Stolen cigarettes, hijacked by Syndicate soldiers up and down the nation's highways, offered another income opportunity. Placed in Mooney's vending machines, each pack of cigarettes sold represented a clear 100 percent profit.

"This is just the tip of the iceberg," Mooney confided to Chuck. "Shit, we're goin' worldwide . . . we're settin' up a guy right now with cigarettes to move in on the Philippines. . . . The son of a bitch's practically got the fuckin' government on his payroll."

Chuck would later learn that the "guy" Mooney spoke of was a shadowy figure and ex-GI from Chicago named Harry Stonehill, whose political connections included everybody from a Philippine senator named Ferdinand Marcos and the Philippine Catholic diocese to Philippine proconsul Edward Landsdale and General Douglas MacArthur. The alliance would ultimately be worth billions, providing Chicago with an entrée into areas New York had not yet entered: Asian gambling ventures, smuggling, black markets, and narcotics.

Although Chuck's fortunes hadn't soared in 1946, Mooney's had; by spring, his personal income from the Jones deal, his book joints and gambling partnerships, as well as stolen war bonds and the numerous stolen goods from other burglaries and heists, exceeded several million dollars. And, taking Jones's lead, Mooney began to invest in legitimate enterprises, paying what was a fortune in postwar America—$65,000—for a liquor store, the R & S. Additionally, he bought an old storefront in the West Side colored district on Roosevelt near Paulina—which he planned to call the Boogie Woogie and which he promised Chuck would soon be "Chicago's version of the Cotton Club."

He also laid out $32,000 cash as down payment for a stately yellow brick home on Winonah in the suburb of Oak Park for his growing family—which now included a new baby, Francine—and gave Chuck the responsibility of supervising its renovation and delivering the monthly mortgage payment.

Chuck, who desperately wanted out of the book joint on Cicero, got his ticket with the Boogie Woogie. Mooney made him manager of the club and put him in charge of its design and remodeling—proof to Chuck that Mooney did indeed have bigger plans for his future.

Determined to gain his brother's approval, Chuck dove into the Boogie Woogie project with the tenacity of a bulldog, and, once completed, it was everything Mooney had envisioned and more.

With nightfall, the surrounding poverty-stricken neighborhood of winos and dope peddlers faded from view and the Boogie Woogie came to life, its blue and orange neon sign flashing BOOGIE and WOOGIE in alternate rhythm to the wail of jazz trumpets and saxophones playing inside. The doors of shiny black sedans and limousines, lining the street in front of the club, opened, exposing the long dark legs of beautiful Negro women dressed in slinky sequined gowns of satin and silk. Their pinstriped escorts, hair slicked back in pompadours under brimmed fedoras, were mostly Chicago's policy men or up-and-coming Negro racketeers. They lined up out front, laughing and swaggering and strutting their stuff, waiting to get inside. And once there, it all became a blur of sound and sweat and swing.

Chuck booked popular colored musicians and entertainers from all over. Some were big names like Nat King Cole, but most were local talent who packed sidearms and were just looking for a chance to make it big. Celebrities or not, as far as the throngs of Boogie Woogie patrons were concerned, this was a ''high-tone'' place. The money rolled in and Mooney was pleased; that was all that mattered to Chuck.

After Eddie Jones was released from prison in 1946, he and his dazzling wife, Lydia, frequented the club, as did one of Jones's lieutenants, Teddy Roe. Chuck had been warned about Roe; he was distrustful and suspicious of the Italians, particularly Mooney Giancana, and despite the money to be made from penetrating the Italian community, he'd vehemently disagreed with Jones's joint venture with Giancana—as had virtually all the other small-time colored wheel operators.

Chuck stood behind the bar of the club each night and listened to the policy men; he got to know how their operations worked and how the Negroes thought. More than once, he had to jump up on the bar, revolver in hand, and clear the place out amid ladies' squeals and gunfire. But that was the exception; more often than not, he discovered that the policy men settled disputes and power struggles through discussion—however heated—and he admired them for that. Their genteel cooperation was something foreign to what he'd witnessed with Mooney's gang. Mooney took care of problems in a more straightforward fashion—he killed them. Closing the Boogie Woogie each night, Chuck couldn't help but wonder what Mooney had in mind for the policy kings.

He didn't have to wait long to find out. On a warm night in late April, Mooney stopped by the club after midnight to see how things were going. Chuck poured them both a scotch and they sat at a table, watching through a cloud of smoke as glistening couples went through their bumps and grinds.

Mooney lit his cigar and leaned forward, frowning. "You might get a little trouble in here over the next few weeks," he said. "I'm gonna take 'em over . . . Roe, Jones, the whole goddamned bunch."

Chuck wasn't surprised; Mooney had just been waiting for the right time. He guessed now was as good as any and he nodded.

"I've had it with Roe; he's a no-good son of a bitch."

"And Eddie?" Chuck asked.

"Yeah, well, he's seen his day, too. Shit, I kinda like the guy. I don't wanna take him out, but he won't move over and let us in. I gotta do somethin' about him."

Chuck lit a cigarette and inhaled. "Like what?" He exhaled with the words.

Mooney smiled and pushed his chair back from the table to get up. "Don't even fuckin' worry about it, Chuck. You just run this joint like you've been doin'—you've done a great job here—and let me take care of the rest. Okay? *Capisce?*"

Mooney motioned around the room, the light catching on his diamond cuff links, and then stood up. "Just keep up the good work and"—he put his face up close to Chuck's, dropping his voice—"watch out for some pissed-off shines."

As Mooney strolled across the room toward the door, Teddy Roe walked in with an entourage of muscle and a woman on his arm. Seeing Mooney, he bristled and stood his ground. The dancers on the floor had reached a fury of movement and the noise, the music, and the crowd made it impossible to tell what was going to happen.

Chuck shot a look behind the bar at his manager, Jimmy New York, and his black bartender, Willie, and nodded in Mooney's direction. Seeing Roe, they reached under the counter for their guns. Chuck searched the pocket of his suit coat for the reassuring coldness of his own revolver and, rising quickly from the table, walked over through the dancers to his brother's side.

"Well, what the fuck is Mooney Giancana doin' in a nigger joint? Tryin' to steal more of our money? Or you think he's just here for a little taste of one of our women?" Roe said, sneering, to the two men flanking his side. They grinned arrogantly and laughed.

Mooney expressionlessly surveyed the mulatto. Chuck felt his heart skip a beat.

"I own the joint." Mooney smiled coldly. "Just like I'm gonna fuckin' own you . . . and everything else you goddamned shines got." He stared into the eyes of the sequined woman on Roe's arm. "Including her if I want." Chuck saw her red lips part. His brother was right; if he wanted her, she was his. Roe saw it, too.

"Why, you dirty motherfucker. I'll fuckin' kill you."
Roe reached for Mooney's lapels, but before he could lay
a hand on him, Chuck and Jimmy New York stepped up
and stuck their guns in his ribs.

"Forget about it, Teddy," Mooney said, never taking
his eyes from the woman. He laughed. "You're over your
head." And, without even looking back, he swaggered out
the door into the night.

On a Saturday night in May of 1946, Mooney put his
plan in action by kidnapping Eddie Jones. He and Fat
Leonard, along with Needles, Fifi, and Vincent Ioli, ab-
ducted the policy king, put him in the basement of Mooney's still-vacant house in Oak Park, and gave him a choice
similar to the one Mooney had given Guzik three years
before: Cooperate or die. Jones didn't have to be convinced. Before his release the following Friday, he came
up with $250,000 in unmarked ransom money and agreed
to turn over his entire operation. Two weeks later, Jones
and his family boarded a train to Mexico and that was the
last Mooney saw of the Jones brothers.

The colored papers called Mooney a "double-crosser,"
a convict with a record "as long as your arm." And small-
time colored policy men, among them Teddy Roe, braced
themselves for an assault. Roe brazenly suggested to his
friends and anyone else who'd listen that before the Italians
took over his wheels, he'd die first. Mooney's only response to that was, "That's not such a bad idea."

No attempt was made to kill Roe that summer. Instead,
Mooney used his political ties and police connections to
turn the heat up on Roe's operation, forcing him to shut
down his wheels.

With Roe effectively out of the way, Mooney then
turned his attention—an onslaught of intimidations, bomb-

ings, and murder—toward the less vocal policy operators. And one by one, the wheels fell under his control. By August, with the exception of Roe's wheels, Mooney owned the policy rackets "lock, stock, and barrel," as he put it.

Following the takeover, Mooney put five soldiers from the old neighborhood, the Manno brothers and Sam Pardy, in charge of policy operations. Although white Italians still referred to it as "numbers," it remained a game restricted to the colored community; the few whites wishing to play did so through one of the hundreds of bookies scattered throughout Chicago, who in turn called one of the colored policy front men with the bet.

Chuck watched the unfolding of this new enterprise with rabid interest, curious to find out whether policy, as Mooney had said, could really generate the legendary bushel baskets full of money. He began hearing tales—tall ones, he'd thought at first—of bundles of cash stacked waist-deep in the Mannos' basement. When Mooney invited him to go for a drive in late November of 1946 to Tom Manno's to see for himself, he eagerly went along. There he found money stacked from one end of the basement to the other—not waist-deep, but to the ceiling. Six years later, in 1952, three of the Manno brothers and Pardy would plead guilty and be jailed for evading over $2 million in taxes levied against their policy profits.

Still awestruck by the sight of so much money, Chuck listened during the drive home as Mooney outlined his plans for the future.

Mooney said that while he'd been getting local operations in line, Tony Accardo had instructed Jake Guzik and Murray Humphreys to work on another angle, the *national* gambling scene. Chicago was moving into Iowa, Kansas,

Indiana, and Michigan. Additionally, they were trying to set up a gambling operation in Dallas, Texas, and put the finishing touches on a takeover of Continental Press, a wire service out of Cleveland that provided national sporting-event results to bookies throughout the country.

Mooney said Guzik and Humphreys had used Pat Manno along with small-time fixers Paul Jones and Jack Nappi as their emissaries to Texas. They offered the Dallas sheriff, Steve Guthrie, $150,000 for his cooperation during their invasion of the city. "We promised the guy we'd make sure the city stays clean . . . no trouble, no drugs. Just good clean fun . . . floating crap games, bookmakin', and slot machines."

But in early November, just when Manno and Jones thought they had a deal, they discovered the sheriff had bugged their meetings. Guthrie refused the payoff and blew the whistle, resulting in Jones being charged with bribery. It put a crimp in all their plans. "But we got another card to play," Mooney told Chuck. "I'm sendin' a Jew friend of Dave Yaras's and Lenny Patrick's . . . Jack Ruby."

Chuck learned that Jack Ruby was expected to move slowly at first, opening a seedy night spot that the Chicago Syndicate would slowly transform into a jumping strip joint, offering clientele everything from bookmaking to prostitutes. Over time, if all proceeded according to plan, Ruby would bypass the sheriff, find the weak link in the area's law enforcement—there always was one, Mooney said—and begin the long process of bribery and payoffs.

According to Mooney, the other opportunity, Continental and its distributor, Midwest News Service, had fared better. Continental's predecessor, Nation-Wide, was originally owned by Moe Annenberg but was forced out of business when the publishing mogul was found guilty of tax evasion and sent to prison.

Prior to his downfall, with the backing of both the Chicago and New York crime syndicates, Annenberg had made a fortune from the gambling industry, providing racing forms and wire services to bookies throughout the country. An established wire service, with its thousands of customers, could be extremely profitable. Changing odds, results, and payoff amounts from dozens of horse tracks around the nation were continually reported over a special telephone line, or wire, to a subscribing book joint for a one-hundred-dollar-a-day fee. And without such information, a gambling operation was effectively out of business.

After Annenberg's company folded, his longtime employee Jim Ragen seized the moment and opened Continental. Mooney told Chuck that he, Guzik, and Humphreys had believed Ragen's service could give Chicago the opening they needed to move into every gambling operation in the country. "With Continental under our belt," he explained, "we could own the whole goddamned gambling business."

Earlier in the year, Mooney spearheaded a takeover of Ragen's company and, with the approval of Accardo, Humphreys, and Guzik, made the guy, as Mooney put it, "an offer he couldn't refuse." But surprisingly, Ragen *had* refused and they'd been forced to take other measures, measures that would ultimately lead to Ragen's death.

Figuring to run Ragen out of business and save themselves a bundle in the bargain, the Chicago Syndicate opened up a wire service of its own, Trans-American. The wire service's attorney, John Boyle, would go on to become the Illinois state's attorney and chief judge of criminal court. Next, to drum up customers for their new venture, Mooney and Guzik pooled a few tough guys— "Willie Potatoes, Dave Yaras . . . you know the guys," Mooney said—and sent them out to make "sales calls" on Ragen's customers. After a rash of threats and bombings, the bookmaking operations quickly moved their business from Continental to Trans-American.

The other Continental customers, most notably Bugsy Siegel out west, willingly assisted Mooney's push, moving over to Trans-American in a spirit of cooperation and national brotherhood.

"But still Ragen controlled Continental . . . until last August," Mooney stated matter-of-factly. "The guy should have just taken our offer and gotten the hell out of the wire business. But no, he had to be a big shot. So we sent Dave Yaras, Lenny Patrick, and Willie Block out to take care of things. Gussie Alex and Strongy Ferraro ran back-up. Believe it or not, with half an army, they still didn't do the job right the first time. Shot the guy and what the hell, he ended up in the fuckin' hospital. So we had to wait and see what was gonna happen . . . but those guys had to make it right, one way or another."

Chuck knew about Ragen's death, how the guy had lain in the hospital for weeks and then suddenly and mysteriously died. "They finally slipped him a few mercury cocktails in the hospital," Mooney explained.

Mooney said that thanks to the merger between Continental and Trans-American, the guys from around the country were starting to work together. "We're givin' Jack Dragna out in California fifty grand for his support and Carlos Marcello from New Orleans a piece of the action. Sort of a 'thank you' for him smoothin' our way into

Texas; at least now we've got a foothold there. Anyhow, it's only a matter of time before we've got all the gambling, everywhere, and when we do . . . I'll be right there at the top of the heap."

Chuck couldn't help thinking how casually Mooney mingled a man's murder with his own plans for success. There were times when Chuck felt sorry for some sap, even though the guy might have stepped out of line and had it coming. But not Mooney. Never. Mooney didn't have a little voice deep inside that whispered judgment on his every action. As Chuck had gotten older, he'd envied that aspect of Mooney all the more; because there was no question in his mind that what stood between him and the big time was that goddamned little voice. The only thing he could say was that he'd gotten better at ignoring it, that most things people thought were wrong—like cheating and stealing and lying to save your skin—didn't bother him anymore.

He drew the line at taking a guy out, though; he didn't want any part of murder. He knew it went on—hell, most of the guys he knew were killers—but he sure as hell didn't want to be personally involved himself. Sometimes he wasn't sure whether he was a failure or a saint—or neither. All he was sure of was that being a saint wouldn't get him where he wanted to go.

Throughout the remainder of 1946, when Mooney wasn't out of town on business, he sped up and down the side streets of Chicago putting together one deal after another.

He told Chuck that Ricca and the guys would be out "real soon," but what that meant in terms of Mooney's position in the Syndicate hierarchy was uncertain. Mooney, for his part, was highly confident that his record of the past three years, while the old guard had been in prison, was solid enough to ensure a place at the top.

"Paul knows I can make everybody a lot of money . . . that's all that matters. I've proven I've got the balls to run things with the numbers and gambling. It's only a matter of time . . . I'm gonna be boss soon, Chuck. You hear me . . . boss."

According to Mooney, the early release of Chicago's most notorious mobsters could be credited to Murray Humphreys, who'd been traveling back and forth to Washington, D.C., to work out a deal. There he'd talked to Attorney General Tom Clark about getting his assistance.

"Ricca even promised Clark a seat on the fuckin' Supreme Court if he helped get him out," Mooney said, and then, noticing the look on Chuck's face, added with a chuckle, "Chuck, what did I tell you before? Did you think I was bullshittin' you? We always own the President; it doesn't matter what the guy's name is . . . we own him. We own the White House."

Just as Mooney had predicted, Ricca and his cronies were indeed released early the next year amid public outcry. Among those in the underworld, it was claimed that Hollywood unions, still under Chicago's control, had created costly work stoppages, vandalism, and other aggravations in an effort to pressure studio moguls into coming to Ricca's aid. The tactics proved effective; according to Mooney, a personal gift of $5 million from all the major studios was made to President Truman. In exchange, Attorney General Clark granted the mobsters' parole and, as reward, was appointed by Truman to the Supreme Court.

Additionally, Truman was promised Syndicate financial

backing and the efforts of the Chicago political machine for the upcoming 1948 presidential campaign and election.

As 1946 wound down, Mooney continued to increase his holdings. He opened two more clubs, the Archer Club and the 430 Club, and a company called Windy City with his longtime associate Congressman Jimmy Adducci. Windy City was supposedly intended to set up softball leagues, but Mooney said it was just another front for book joints and a place for him to report legitimate income on his tax returns. Meanwhile, Mooney's wife and daughters strolled Michigan Avenue in postwar designer dresses, furs, and jewels and planned lavish Christmas parties.

In December 1946, Lucky Luciano, still wielding tremendous influence among bosses of the underworld since his release from prison and subsequent deportation to Italy, called a meeting of the "Commission"—the name given the national consortium of syndicates from around the country. Mooney's attendance in Havana at this meeting, which brought together the nation's thirty-six biggest gang leaders, further signaled his acceptance into the fold and was an acknowledgment of his rank in the Chicago hierarchy.

He came back from Cuba with a renewed zeal for his upward climb—"Damn, that Lansky's a fuckin' genius"—and a suitcase bulging with Havana cigars. He insisted Chuck watch the news over the coming months for a "surprise" out west. "A big guy is gonna be taken out," he said mysteriously.

By June of 1947, Mooney would be crowing, if only privately. "What did I tell ya? Somebody big? Did you hear about Bugsy Siegel out in Beverly Hills? He screwed up and it got him two of Chicago's slugs to the head."

"What the hell did he do?" Chuck asked.

"Shit, he could've had it made. . . . Lansky sent him out to Vegas five years ago to set up clubs. He started the Flamingo and right away started skimmin'. And not penny-ante shit, either . . . millions. Not only that, but he refused to give back his part of Trans-American. Siegel was a fuckin' cowboy who got too big for his own good. We voted to get him out of the way down in Havana after he had the balls to defy Lansky and the whole goddamned Commission on top of it."

"Jesus, you're really on the inside now," Chuck complimented.

"Well, let's just say I had inside information," Mooney said, smiling, and then added, "and the contract to do the job on Siegel."

Chuck was particularly intrigued by Mooney's "inside information" on the California scene and the celebrity inroads made by his brother on behalf of Ricca and Roselli.

"Hollywood is just full of guys waiting to be used, Chuck. All anybody out there cares about is whether they're gonna be a star or not. We help 'em along and we own 'em. That's how simple it is. And the broads, Chuck . . . beautiful and dumb. Shit, don't ever be star-struck by all that movie baloney . . . they're all worthless bums and whores. Hollywood is the only place I've ever been, besides Washington, D.C., where everybody—men and women—are just beggin' for you to use 'em."

After the first of the new year, Mooney and Ange again made their winter home in Miami. Mooney often left Ange in the company of her women friends and relatives while he chartered boats to Cuba for a "few days fishing with the boys" or flew off to Chicago and other parts unknown.

To Chuck, their marriage seemed happier, more settled, than it had been in years.

Mooney continued to travel that spring. But back at home in Chicago, while he busied himself opening another wire service, the Montrose Association, he relied on Chuck to escort his wife and daughters from their Oak Park home—now freshly decorated with expensive antiques and art—to posh restaurants and shops or such faraway places as New York City for a shopping spree at Saks.

Out with Ange, Chuck saw the world open up before them. The Giancana name was magical; stars in nightclubs nodded and smiled in their direction. Clerks in the finest department stores swooned with delight at the privilege of waiting on them. And out on his own, it seemed anything his heart desired—from front-row seats at the Graziano-Zale title boxing match to curvaceous show girls—could be his. All because he was Mooney's brother.

But for the rest of the Giancanas, things were hardly so rosy. Mooney was still firmly convinced that what his family possessed was only thanks to him. And they were equally convinced. In 1947, he continued to wield an iron grip over the lives of his father, brothers, and sisters and sternly dictated their futures. And yet with Chuck, he privately scorned their emotional and financial dependence. "They always have their hands out," he remarked with disgust.

But Chuck thought theirs was a condition Mooney had nurtured—had virtually demanded—as proof of their devotion and respect. They continued to grovel on Mooney's doorstep, waiting for him to toss them a bone. And they were thankful for that. Chuck found it a pitiful sight to watch his father scurry across town to get an envelope from Mooney. Antonio now sat before his eldest son each month and waited obediently while Mooney counted out a few hundred dollars from a drawer containing tens of thousands.

Antonio's children had gotten on with their own lives, albeit in Mooney's shadow. Vicki had married a factory worker in 1945; Pepe had taken a neighborhood girl as his bride and now hustled at a book joint with the rest of Mooney's soldiers. Antoinette, still unmarried and living at home at thirty-five, made belts and Paris garters at a factory. Josie, also at home and unmarried, worked at Ange's brother's company, Central Envelope. Catherine's children, the cousins, effectively had dropped out of sight.

If any of the family members resented Mooney's success, it wasn't evident. Rather, they each in their own way basked in the celebrity of the Giancana name; it gave them stature in the neighborhood. For Pepe, who, unlike Chuck, never achieved the role of confidant with his infamous brother, being a Giancana nevertheless meant the security of a good job. The sisters found it opened doors, if only briefly, to better treatment from their peers; the butcher, knowing their infamous relative, gave them the better cuts of meat; the baker, the freshest loaves.

However, other people remotely connected to the Giancana name also tried to cash in on its benefits—or attempted to gain entry, using whatever means necessary, into what they saw as the lucrative and intriguing underworld. Shortly before Christmas of 1947, a naïve yet ambitious punk, Johnny Mendolia, placed a phone call to Mooney's home with just such a scheme. He told Ange that, as the son of Mooney's sister's godmother, he believed Mooney should set him up in a book joint on Grand Avenue. Upon learning that Mooney was out, Mendolia said he'd wait at the Walgreen on Austin and Roosevelt for Mooney's call and reply.

There were some things an outsider—and in Mooney's way of thinking, most people were outsiders—never, ever did. One was call Mooney's home. Another was discuss business with Mooney's wife. Both were considered insults and demonstrated a gross lack of respect for Mooney's position. If a guy wanted to talk to Mooney, he asked another guy, such as Fat Leonard or Rocky Potenza, for a meeting. They would go to Mooney for permission and then, and only then, would the guy get to see Mooney.

As Ange relayed Mendolia's message to Mooney, Chuck concluded the guy didn't know the first thing about the Syndicate. He even started to laugh—until he looked over at Mooney, purple with rage.

"Do you know this Mendolia"—Mooney glanced at Ange and decided to temper his words—". . . this Mendolia SOB? Well do you, Chuck?"

Chuck nodded, his mirth transformed to somber acquiescence in the face of his brother's outrage. "Yeah, sure I know the Mendolias," he said. "Guy Mendolia, Johnny's brother, he's a thief. Fences his stuff through a guy on the north side. But Johnny? Jesus, Mooney, the guy doesn't know his you-know-what from a hole in the ground. He's one square John. Tell you the truth, I can't believe it was Johnny who called. He's a real greenhorn."

Mooney motioned with his cigar for Chuck to follow and turned to walk into the living room. Once alone, he whirled around and hissed through clenched teeth, "I don't fuckin' care if the little bastard is green as grass. And I sure as hell don't care who he's related to . . . nobody fuckin' calls my home . . . nobody. Ever. This little prick needs to be taught a goddamned lesson. After you're done with him, I expect he'll know a thing or two about respect. *Capisce?*"

Chuck stared into Mooney's eyes. They were as cold and dead as fish eyes. He wasn't sure exactly what Mooney was asking him to do. But he was certain, when he found out, he wouldn't want to do it. A flush of panic came over him; he hoped Mooney didn't see it. His thoughts raced. Was this his moment of truth? The moment he'd been dreading for years, hoping against hope the day would never come when Mooney demanded proof of his loyalty? Could this be it? And would it come down to something so meaningless as a guy—who just plain didn't know better—making a stupid phone call he shouldn't have? Chuck drew out a cigar and lit it. Slowly, purposefully, he walked across the room. Trying to act nonchalant, he looked back into Mooney's eyes.

"So what exactly do you want me to do to the guy?" He searched Mooney's face impassively.

"Beat his fuckin' brains in, that's what." Mooney clenched his fist. "Goddamn it, give the guy somethin' to remember."

Chuck stood there motionless, speechless.

"You got a problem with that?"

He avoided Mooney's stare and looked down at the ash on his cigar. Picking up the ashtray, he flicked it and took a long, deep breath. Before he could reply, his brother spoke.

"Forget about it," Mooney snapped. "We'll both go see the son of a bitch. I'd like to see what the guy is up to, anyhow. Go call him at the Walgreen and tell him we'll be right over."

A mixture of relief and guilt swept over Chuck as he dialed the number. He felt as if he'd let Mooney down, but he was thankful he hadn't been forced to tell Mooney yes or no. Maybe to Mooney it was the same thing; his hesitation probably said volumes. And Chuck knew there were plenty of other guys who'd have jumped at the chance to do his brother a favor—no matter what it was.

He'd heard them before. The guy who shined Mooney's shoes once offered to take out anybody Mooney wanted. And Mooney had thought it was a swell thing that the guy would offer something like that. People would do just about anything to be on the inside. And here he was, a Giancana, Mooney's own brother, and he'd hesitated.

They didn't talk much on the way to the Walgreen. Mooney coughed a couple of times and asked whether Chuck knew what Mendolia looked like. That was the extent of their conversation. Chuck still didn't know what Mooney was going to do to the guy. Or ask Chuck to do to him. His winter coat felt heavy and too warm. He rolled the window down.

"Hot?" Mooney asked sarcastically.

"No, just thought I'd let some of my cigar smoke out," Chuck replied, and rolled the window back up.

Finally, they were there. The Walgreen was crowded and Chuck spotted Mendolia in a booth near the soda fountain. With his wide brimmed fedora pulled over one eye and a trench coat with an upturned collar, Mendolia looked like a guy who'd seen one too many gangster movies. Chuck felt sure the guy had no idea how silly he looked.

They went through stilted greetings and sat down. Mooney crossed his arms and leaned back.

"So, I understand, Johnny, you wanna talk to me about openin' a joint in your neighborhood?" he said, smiling.

"That's right, Mooney."

Chuck saw his brother bristle. No one in Mendolia's position called him Mooney. No, it was Mr. Giancana.

"Mr. Giancana," Chuck corrected.

"Oh, sorry, I thought us bein' practically related and all . . . well, I thought we was like family."

Chuck wished he could talk for the guy himself, because the more Johnny said, the worse it got. He was waiting for Mooney to explode. Or worse, throw Chuck that look he'd seen him give Needles countless times before.

"Well, Johnny, we're not family. That was your first mistake," Mooney said evenly. "And we're not related in any way I know about, now are we?"

"Well, no, not really . . ."

"So you see you're off base here. In fact"—Mooney leaned forward—"you're way over your head. You could get yourself hurt real bad messin' around, shootin' off your mouth. Some guys might go pretty hard on a punk tryin' to muscle a place in the gang. Hear what I'm sayin'?"

Johnny nodded and nervously gulped his coffee.

"So let's just get a few things straight before you go home today. All right?"

Again, Johnny nodded.

When he spoke, Mooney's voice was soft and low, not at all the way Chuck had expected. "Don't ever call my home again. And don't ever talk to my wife. You aren't gonna have a fuckin' joint on Grand Avenue or anywhere else. You're gonna go back to your nice little family and get a nice fuckin' job cuttin' meat at a market or loadin' fruit on a truck somewhere. And . . . you're gonna forget about things that aren't any of your business. But you know what the best thing is?" Mooney reached across the table and patted Mendolia's hand before he could reply.

"The best thing is . . . you're gonna fuckin' stay alive."
He rose from the table. "Nice seein' you, Johnny," he
said, and, with Chuck right behind him, left the punk to
his coffee and dreams.

Figuring Mooney out, Chuck thought, was going to take
a lifetime. Sometimes he'd coil up and strike on a dime.
Or lie back real nice and let a guy off the hook. It was
hard to tell what Mooney might do. After their conversation about Mendolia in the living room, Chuck had expected the worst. And the opposite had happened; Mooney
hadn't even raised his voice to the guy. He had been in
perfect control.

There was something about the way Mooney just auto-
matically took the reins—he didn't wait to see what the
other guy would do; he just took control. And oddly,
nobody ever questioned his domination. Chuck couldn't
imagine it being any other way, and he thought it probably
had never even entered Mooney's mind, either, that he
might play second fiddle to another guy's tune.

In the latter part of 1947, Mooney gave Chuck a job
working the pinball-machine rackets in the Marquette district. It was an area where Mooney said police captain
Andy Akins would "turn his head to Syndicate goings-
on," allowing Chuck to have a "field day." And indeed,
by the following year, Chuck had managed to place over
two hundred of the illegal gambling devices without the
merest hint of difficulty from the police. From this one
operation, he grossed $120,000 a year—money he duti-
fully delivered to Mooney.

Sitting in Mooney's Oak Park basement in January of
1948, Chuck watched as Mooney counted out a thousand
for him and then bundled another six thousand for himself,

depositing it neatly alongside bundle after bundle of cash in his heavy desk drawer. He handed Chuck a cigar and sat back in his chair. "So how'd you like to go to Cuba? See some shows, win a few bucks, screw a couple of Latin broads?"

"Hey, I'd probably love it, Mooney. . . . I mean, what guy wouldn't? Right?" Chuck smiled, savoring the smooth Havana cigar. He didn't really take Mooney seriously; he thought they were just shooting the breeze and killing time.

"Well, I think you will. No point freezin' your ass off here when it's warm and sunny in Cuba. Right?"

Chuck cleared his throat; Mooney was getting at something. "Right," he replied. He leaned forward in the leather Viking chair. "So what you want me to do?"

Mooney opened the lower-right-hand drawer in the massive carved oak desk. He lifted out a small manila envelope and pushed it toward Chuck. "Take this to the Hotel Nacionale in Havana and deliver it to 'Mr. Meyer.' "

"No problem," Chuck said, smiling. He picked up the envelope. From its shape and feel, he could tell it contained money.

"Wanna know what's in there?" Mooney asked, grinning.

"Not if you don't wanna tell me."

"A half a million bucks, Chuck."

He nodded.

"In these." Mooney held up a bill.

At first, Chuck couldn't make out the numerals or the face. He'd never seen a greenback like it. He squinted across the desk.

Mooney started to laugh. "It's a fifty, Chuck."

"A fifty?" He'd never seen a fifty like it before.

"Yeah, a fifty-thousand-dollar bill."

"Oh, yeah. I see that now," Chuck said, trying to sound unimpressed. He hoped his face hadn't registered shock or amazement.

"Mr. Glass here"—Mooney tapped the face on the bill with the back of his hand—"is a world traveler. He's come in real handy in Cuba." He laughed again.

Chuck joined in the laughter and then, pausing, asked in earnest, "When do I leave?"

"Right away. Drive down to Florida and then take a plane from Miami over to Havana. Hey, take a friend if you want . . . what the hell, have a good time."

"All right. I'll leave tomorrow morning. Anything else?"

"Yeah, Chuck. There's more. Lots more action in the future. You just come along for the ride, okay?" He leaned over the desk. "Listen, we're movin' fast now. I got two points, two percent of the skim, in the Flamingo in Vegas already . . . shit, at thirty-five Gs apiece, those points were a helluva buy. And after we're done lockin' up Cuba, we're gonna look at the Arabs, the Dominican Republic. When we're done with the dictator down there in the Dominican Republic, he'll give us the whole fuckin' island . . . and if he doesn't, we'll find somebody who will." He stood up and walked around the desk.

On cue, Chuck also rose from his chair. Mooney smiled a strange, secret smile and put his arm around Chuck's shoulder. "And ya know what?" he asked.

"What?"

"You'd be fuckin' perfect to run our end down there when it opens up."

Chuck was speechless; this was the moment he'd been

waiting for, his dream come true. He wanted to say something, but everything he thought of, he quickly rejected as inappropriate or trite.

Mooney walked him to the basement's heavy steel door. "You have some fun in Cuba; take care of this for me and we'll see what happens."

Chuck's face became deadly serious as he turned to go. "You know it's gonna be handled right with me, Mooney. You can always count on me," he promised.

"I know," Mooney said softly, and with that, he closed the door.

CHAPTER 11

Chuck and his friend Sam Marcello, everybody called him "Googy Eyes," landed in Havana, Cuba, on January 18, 1948. The door of the small prop opened, revealing a cloudless azure sky—"so blue, it could make you cry," Chuck would tell his friends back home. The steamy blasts of humid tropical air swept his hair around like dry seaweed as he walked down the steps to the tarmac. He sniffed the air. "Salt," he said to his friend, and he smiled at the warmth of the Caribbean sun caressing his face. He thought he might like this place.

But his opinion soon changed. Actually, he hadn't had one, hadn't really known what to expect—a Sodom and Gomorrah? A Rush Street with palm trees? A Miami with gambling? Probably the latter, he thought to himself as their cab with its oily, torn cloth seats, stained and smelling like stale urine and cheap wine, honked and shoved its way through the crowded dusty streets, narrowed by throngs of hollow-eyed people and menacing police officers.

The poverty shocked him. It was worse than the Patch, and he'd always thought that was as bad as it could get. But no, Cuba had that beat all to hell. Here, raw sewage ran in rivulets down the twisting alleyways and blind and one-armed beggars lined each corner, hands outstretched. Hungry children, mostly boys, rushed to the cab to hawk their wares in broken English. "Want to screw, mister? My sister is very pretty," one runny-nosed kid yelled in perfect English. "Mine is prettier, mister," cried another. They pushed and elbowed their way to the cab window, pitching both shoe shines and their sisters with equal sales-manship.

As one scene melded into the next, Marcello could only shake his head and say, "Jesus, can you believe this?" Chuck patted the pocket of his linen sport coat and was relieved to find the envelope's reassuring bulge. All he cared about was making this delivery; he'd do that and then they'd get the hell out of here.

It began to feel as if they'd been driving around for hours and Chuck started to consider the fact that he had no idea where they were going; the cabbie, gabbling in Spanish, could take them anywhere he wanted and Chuck wouldn't know the difference. As the heat of the city closed in around them, he suddenly realized how dangerous this job actually was; the people here were so poor and life so cheap that two gringo *touristas* could disappear in an instant—especially two gringos with five hundred thousand American dollars. The presence of the police, their guns bristling, did nothing to reassure him.

A clammy sweat began to creep over his hands and soon spread to his clothes; beads of perspiration gleamed on his forehead. He patted the tiny bulge in his pocket more than once and silently chastised himself for being so nervous;

the last thing he wanted to do was look that way, he told himself as he struggled to maintain his composure. He lit a Cuban cigar and tried to relax and take in the "scenery."

At last, rising out of the stench of the streets, was the Hotel Nacionale. Like an island within an island, its white walls stood in green-shuttered elegance. When their driver parked the cab, Chuck threw open the door and walked hurriedly through the hotel lobby and up to the desk. More collected now, he calmly requested the manager.

Dressed in a dapper white panama suit, the small, mustached man quickly appeared. As instructed, Chuck asked for "Mr. Meyer."

Shortly thereafter, a slender Jewish man in a white short-sleeved shirt appeared. "For Mr. Meyer?" he asked. He smiled as his eyes caught sight of the envelope.

"Yes, sir," Chuck said, handing the envelope to the enigmatic man before him.

"Thank you." He tucked the envelope under one arm and then added, "Tell Mooney hello."

Chuck nodded and "Mr. Meyer" faded into the crowd. That was all there was to it and, his job for Mooney safely accomplished, Chuck loosened his tie and sighed with relief.

That night, he and Googy Eyes ventured down the shadowy streets to drink and laugh and cuddle their share of voluptuous Cuban girls. "Boy this is livin'," Googy Eyes said more times than Chuck could count. But as the night grew long, it all reminded him of a too-rich meal; the glitter was reduced to decadence and gluttony in the face of the island's poverty. And like a man who'd had more than enough, he pushed it all away and excused himself for the night.

With some relief and more guilt, he crawled into bed.

It seemed almost criminal to sleep in such affluence; somewhere outside his window, there were row upon row of tiny propped-up tin-roofed shanties with dirty floors and dirty children. If the millions Mooney and the Syndicate were pouring into Cuba was making a difference in the lives of Cubans, he hadn't seen it—unless it was to magnify their poverty. He had to believe that these people wouldn't beg in the shadow of the Syndicate's opulence forever, not without someday wanting their share. And frankly, he'd tell Mooney later, he couldn't blame them.

The next morning, Chuck awakened with one thought, and that was to get out of Cuba.

"But you must see the El Mora Castle before you leave," insisted the disappointed desk clerk as they paid their bill.

Googy Eyes wholeheartedly agreed. "We have to see somethin' besides shacks and broads," he complained.

Not in the mood to argue, Chuck acquiesced and they visited the historic site, mingling with the floral-shirted tourists in the hot midday sun.

Later, as he boarded the plane, Chuck looked up at the Cuban sky one last time and thanked God he was leaving. "A beautiful hell," he called Cuba after that. "Just one more beautiful hell."

Mooney was pleased with Chuck's performance in Cuba and dangled the Dominican Republic carrot repeatedly by commenting, twinkle in his eye, "A guy can live like a king down there."

The possibility of such a plum being bestowed on him, coupled with his renewed appreciation for the United States as a "land of opportunity," spurred him on. Chuck threw himself into his pinball-machine operation with new zeal. He held on to what Mooney had said about running Chicago's end in the Dominican Republic—although he secretly hoped it wasn't anything like Cuba. Whatever it would be like, it would signal his move up and he wanted to be ready. He was willing to work for it, to prove himself to earn Mooney's favor.

For now, he was making good money. He always had ten or twenty C notes in his pocket; sometimes he had as much as three thousand dollars. And he drove a shiny new 1948 baby blue Super Buick with a trunk chock-full of pinball-machine parts and punchboards for the book joints.

He was, for the first time in his life, on top of the world. The only thing he didn't have was a wife, which was the one thing Mooney, with increasing frequency, was quick to mention. "You're twenty-five, Chuck . . . you got money in your pocket . . . what you need now is a good Italian girl, a house in the suburbs, and some screamin' kids," he'd say, laughing.

Given Mooney's comments, Chuck might have anticipated some traditional Italian matchmaking, but he suspected nothing that April of 1948 when Ange and Mooney suggested he invite Anne Marie Torsiello to join Bonnie and Annette for an afternoon of horseback riding. Instead, he smiled at the recollection of a little thirteen-year-old girl whose common sense, resolute manner, and studious ways had once earned his respect. It didn't occur to him that Anne Marie was now seventeen—or that she'd take his breath away.

When he drove by to pick her up, he found the Torsiellos living in much the same condition as they had four years before; Carl still worked at the rail yards and Tillie still cooked big bubbling pots of sauces and smiled and laughed as though life couldn't be better. Sicilians probably would have been embittered by the turn their life had taken, he thought to himself. But the Torsiellos were Neapolitans—Italians originating from Naples—and Neapolitans were a happy people, no matter what. That was something Mooney had always liked about the Torsiellos.

But as unchanged as Carl and Tillie were, Chuck hardly recognized Anne Marie. Gone was the shy little girl he remembered and in her place was the most beautiful young woman he thought he'd ever seen. Show girls, dancers, celebrities, thousand-dollar whores—thanks to Mooney he'd had his share of women—none of them could hold a candle to this fresh-faced brunette with sparkling eyes who greeted him now. He took one look at her and fell head over heels, crazy in love.

From that moment on, nothing was the same. He could think of nothing else but the diminutive dark-eyed girl, her ruby lips, her soft dark hair that smelled of the perfume he began to lavish on her. That spring, he gave her a strand of real pearls and took her to the type of dazzling places she'd only dreamed about.

The Chez Paree became their favorite night spot with its celebrity crooners and clientele. Dave Halper, the club's smooth-talking manager—who'd later be sent by Mooney to work at the Riviera in Las Vegas—always made sure they had the best seats in the house.

"Hey, liven up . . . Mooney's brother's here," Halper whispered to the waiters after Chuck slipped him a C note. "Take care of him . . . give him whatever he wants . . . and for Christ's sake, make sure he's happy," Halper commanded.

And for the first time in his life, Chuck was. He found himself intoxicated more by the woman at his side than by the champagne that the white-coated waiters brought to their front-row table with such flourish. In the candlelight, everything paled next to his beautiful Anne Marie.

In July, Ange, flush with enthusiasm, told Chuck, "I hear Anne Marie's having the time of her life . . . and the Torsiellos are ecstatic to have their daughter courted by Mooney Giancana's brother. Everybody in the family . . . including me and Mooney . . . thinks it's a match made in heaven." Chuck was glad there was such an incredible network of gossip and support within the families, but he was disappointed nevertheless. Knowing he had Mooney's stamp of approval in this relationship was important, even critical to his future, but more than that he wanted to know that Anne Marie had fallen in love with him. And he made up his mind to ask her to marry him when he did.

On a breezy Saturday night in July as they walked from the car to the Chez Paree, he pulled her close and looked into her eyes. He wanted to make love to her more than he'd ever wanted anything in his life. "I love you, Anne Marie," he said, and kissed her with a tenderness that surprised even him.

"I love you, too," she said breathlessly, and stifled a girlish giggle. "I always have."

Perplexed, he held her at arm's length. "You always have? Since when?"

"Since I was just a little girl, when I brought the note from my father to Mooney's house. I took one look at you and, well, I fell in love . . . but you just thought I was a little kid." Her lower lip formed a tiny mocking pout.

"Well . . . you *were* just a thirteen-year-old kid. And I was twenty-one." He smiled impishly. "So you've been madly in love with me all along? I knew it, I just knew it." He laughed.

Feeling foolish, she retorted, "And you're crazy about me, too. Everybody says so . . . Ange, my Aunt Rose, my Aunt Betty . . . everybody. They say even Mooney says so."

"Is that right?" he challenged. He adored her childlike fieriness, enjoyed watching it bubble to the surface.

"Yes, that's right. That's what they say. They say Chuck Giancana is crazy in love with Anne Marie Torsiello." Her eyes brimmed with tears.

Suddenly he was afraid he'd hurt her feelings and he didn't think he could bear that. He pulled her close again. "Well . . ." He ran his fingers along her cheek until they reached her lips and then dropped his voice to a whisper, "They're *all* right. I do love you." He took her upturned chin in his hand and kissed her. "Will you marry me?" he whispered.

"Oh, yes, Chuck," she cried, throwing her arms around his neck. "A thousand times, yes!"

They laughed and hugged. Every time he touched her, he wanted her so badly, it made his heart ache. So this is what love feels like, he thought to himself when at last they stepped into the smoky darkness of the Chez Paree.

Slipping Dave Halper his customary tip, Chuck heard Halper's familiar whispered refrain, "Hey, liven up . . . Mooney's brother's here."

Mooney. All the talks they'd had over the years about what a good wife should be. And he'd never even realized that the one thing they'd never talked about was love. He thought he understood why now, too. Because he was certain Mooney had never really loved anyone in his entire life.

If Mooney and his ever-expanding circle of associates

loved anything, it was power. And it seemed, like the dope addicts loathed by the common folks of the Patch, Mooney was addicted in his own way. Certainly a desire for power didn't, in Chuck's way of thinking, qualify as a form of love—instead, it was a need. Mooney would get a piece of gambling in one state and before Chuck knew it, he'd be plotting to take over another one. His brother's hunger was an insatiable ambition that was eating him from the inside out.

Oddly, people didn't seem to find much wrong with addictions to power and wealth. Those qualities were lauded as admirable. The neighborhood saw Mooney as some kind of new hero. And politicians such as Mayor Kennelly and President Truman were esteemed as public servants—when in truth they were, if what Mooney had said was accurate, in servitude to a much higher order: their *own* need for power.

As autumn of 1948 approached, the lines between the so-called "good guys" and "bad guys" slowly began to blur. Chuck watched Chicago's well-oiled political machine spring into action in readiness for the presidential election. Mooney was unusually vocal in decrying the politicians who held out their hands for favors, and he also railed against the coppers who made more from the Syndicate than they did from the taxpayers.

This, Chuck rationalized, was just fine with him; he never knew when Mooney's clout might come in handy. The only copper Chuck always tried to avoid was Frank Pape. In fifteen years, the guy had built up quite a reputation. Chuckie Nicoletti, one of Mooney's enforcers, was always getting a shakedown from Pape and it cost him hundreds in payoffs to Pape's higher-ups. Needles had even remarked that "the motherfucker has taken out more men than all of the guys in the Syndicate put together since he joined the force in thirty-three." Of course, the difference was that Pape was applauded for his aggressiveness against the underworld—for being impossible to bribe. But Mooney found that laughable. "Did you ever notice how Pape goes after the same guys that are givin' us trouble . . . and gets them for good? Yeah, I know what I'm talkin' about . . . just think about it. You'll get the idea."

Despite Mooney's insinuations, Chuck still made a concerted effort to stay out of the copper's way. As luck would have it, though, his path did cross Pape's one September evening. Driving along Cicero and Roosevelt on his way to pick up Anne Marie, Chuck caught sight of the copper's headlights in his rearview mirror. "Goddamn it," he said aloud. Within moments, the squad car's red light began flashing ominously. "I'm gonna get fuckin' pinched," he said in exasperation. "Shit . . . this is gonna really cost me."

He wasn't so worried about paying them off; he had over two thousand dollars in his pocket. But the pinball-machine parts and punchboards in his trunk were another matter. He rolled down the window and came face-to-face with the one copper he'd hoped he'd never meet: Frank Pape.

"Get out, Giancana," the copper snarled. "Let's check you out."

Chuck readily obliged. "So what's the problem? I wasn't speedin'."

Pape turned to the other copper and said simply, "Frisk him."

"All I found was this, Frank." The officer held up a tight wad of bills.

"Give me that," Pape snapped. The other officer shrugged his shoulders and readily complied. Pape began counting. "Twenty-two hundred bucks here," he said, smirking. "Mind tellin' me where it came from, greaseball?"

"No, I don't," Chuck said, glaring. He had to think fast, and he added, "I'm a roofer and I got paid for a big job today. Nothin' to it . . . so now, can we all go on about our business?"

"A roofer?" Pape laughed and craned his wiry neck from his starched collar like a turtle about to snap. "Well, I don't believe a word of it." Bristling, he handed Chuck the money. "Leave your car here. . . . You're goin' downtown with me."

In the squad car, Chuck remembered everything Mooney had told him about shakedowns. If the cops couldn't be bought on the spot, the price went up. And once at the station house, when the coppers emptied his pockets and saw all that cash, he found out what Mooney had meant. Word got out and the coppers started coming round like vultures to a kill. They smiled and politely offered him coffee. "With cream and sugar?" they asked. He could have had a dozen cups of coffee if he'd wanted; it was amazing.

He was allowed to use the phone before they took him to the lockup. He called Tony Champagne, Mooney's attorney and old friend from the Patch—and magically, the cell door had scarcely closed before the turnkey announced Chuck was being taken back upstairs to the police commissioner's office.

A friendly face awaited him. Clearly irritated, Andy Akins sat behind his desk while Frank Pape leaned against the wall, sulking.

Akins stood up to greet him. "Chuck Giancana, good to see you, son," he said, shaking Chuck's hand.

"Good to see you, Andy," Chuck said, smiling, and couldn't resist a triumphant glance in Pape's direction.

Akins sat down. "Have a seat and let's talk a minute. Pape here thinks there was some problem tonight. So what I'm askin' you is . . . what's the problem? What was goin' on tonight?"

"I have no idea, Andy. I wasn't speedin' . . . or doin' anything else illegal. Pape here, he just pulled me over and brought me down here for no good reason . . . none at all."

"Well, where were you goin' then?" Akins asked.

"I was on my way to pick up my girlfriend for a night on the town." Chuck brushed his hand across his elegantly tailored suit. "I was all dressed up and ready to have a nice dinner, that's all. And then Officer Pape decided to go and ruin my evening."

Akins shot a hard look at Pape. "See, Frank. This man is clean. I strongly suggest you leave him alone," he reprimanded.

Pape nodded, clenching his jaw in silent anger. "Yes, sir," he said.

Akins smiled. "Well then, we'll just forget about this little mix-up and Mr. Giancana here can go home . . . with our sincerest apologies."

"Thank you," Chuck replied, finding it difficult to conceal a grin. Akins rose from his desk and walked around to the door, calling out to the men gathered in the hallway,

"Hey, one of you guys give Mr. Giancana here a ride back to his car."

That's the way it was being Mooney's brother. And according to Mooney, that's the way it was with cops in Chicago.

The graft and corruption had been going on for years. It had started way before Mooney was ever born. But he'd certainly seized on the existing machinery and used it to his best advantage. From the lowliest beat cop to the highest captain or commissioner—Mooney said they were all part of the Syndicate stable. Even Mayor Kennelly, like his predecessor Kelly, was, as Mooney put it, "our man." For Chuck, it was like walking under a constant umbrella of protection.

As the election drew closer that autumn, politics were hard to ignore; the presidential race was all Mooney talked about. Throughout October, he made his obligatory rounds of meetings and hopped from city to city, but the election was what got his blood running. Chuck didn't understand what the attraction was for his brother until he and Mooney went out to the Chez Paree one night. Mooney didn't want to sit up front at a table, so Halper placed them in a cozy nook and left them with a bottle of the house's best wine. "I'd rather have scotch," Mooney told the waiter, who wasted no time scurrying to retrieve his regular Dewar's.

"So you're gonna get married," Mooney said while lighting his cigar. "Finally gonna settle down . . . about time, too." He laughed a low, kidding kind of laugh and winked.

Chuck didn't want to talk about women or running around or any of Mooney's other philosophies of matrimony. Sure, he was in love, but he didn't want Mooney to think he was a square John. In self-defense, he changed the subject. "Yeah, married. But I'd rather talk about politics than women," he said.

Mooney's eyes narrowed. "Oh, you would?"

Chuck poured a glass of wine and nodded. "Yeah. I would."

"Politics? Politics . . . what about politics? Do I know somethin' you don't?" Mooney's face was expressionless.

Chuck wasn't sure whether Mooney was kidding or not. This wasn't a card game, yet his brother was certainly wearing his best poker face. Maybe he was venturing into territory that was off-limits. He thought about that for a moment and then decided to call Mooney's bluff. He grinned. "You might know somethin' I don't . . . like who the hell is gonna win?"

Mooney chuckled. "Yeah, you're right. I just might." He dragged on his cigar and looked at Chuck out of the corner of his eye.

Mooney would tell him; Chuck could tell he was just playing with him, wanting him to coax it out of him. He decided to play along. "So what is it?"

"Man oh man, you don't give up, do you?"

Chuck laughed. "Shit, I'm your brother, right?"

"Yeah, I guess you are. Tell you the truth, Chuck, I'm proud of you, too. You're doin' a good job over in the Marquette district. Keepin' everybody on their goddamned toes. The other districts . . . well, I wish I had a hundred men like you. We'd win the election for sure."

"Isn't it for sure that Truman will get in?"

"Well, let's put it this way . . . Dewey won't win, even if he does. Get my point?"

"Yeah." Chuck hesitated. "But really what difference does it make? . . . Like you said before, they're all alike."

"Well, not this time. Luciano still hates Dewey for puttin' him in jail in the first place. . . . Costello's worried that the self-righteous son of a bitch has a short memory, probably doesn't even know how to conduct business. We'd have to give Dewey a few lessons and I got a feelin' he's a slow learner," Mooney said, smiling. "But Truman, well, he can bullshit all he wants about bein' a common man—people eat that up—but the truth is, he grew up with our boys in Kansas City."

"Really . . . I didn't know that. How come nobody talks about it?"

"Christ, because it's just like Chicago out there. They had a mick mayor, Pendergast, on the take big time . . . loved to bet on the ponies. And they got the Italians for muscle and to make money with the rackets. So, fact is, Truman owes everything he's got to us. Pendergast made him a judge and then, with the Italian muscle behind him, got him to the Senate. When the forty-four election came up . . . Kelly here in Chicago got him on the ticket with Roosevelt. Shit, Chicago got Roosevelt and Truman nominated and elected. We were good to Roosevelt; he was good to us. He died and Truman's been our man in the White House ever since. It's smooth sailing with him there."

"I thought he was a schoolteacher or somethin'. He always seemed clean. . . . I know what you said before, but I guess I didn't know he was really connected."

Mooney sighed. "Jesus, I guess you think General Mac-Arthur was a choirboy out there fightin' for America, too? Like I always told you, 'Give me a guy who steals a little and I'll make money.' " He shook his head. "Well, there's connected, Chuck, and then there's *connected*. We pull the strings . . . so, shit, yeah . . . if they can be bought, they're connected.''

Chuck took a drink and thought for a moment. ''So Dewey would just fuck things up . . . or at least make things more''—he searched for the right word—''more uncertain?''

''Exactly. So now, think you'd like to place a bet? Truman or Dewey? Take my advice and put your money on Truman.''

Soon after, the November 3, 1948, *Chicago Daily Tribune* lying on Mooney's desk read: DEWEY DEFEATS TRUMAN. Mooney sat beaming from behind his desk, smoking a cigar triumphantly.

''What did I tell you?'' he said. ''We even made the *Tribune* look like a bunch of fuckin' idiots. Next time, they'll wait before they publish the wrong headline. I bet they learned their lesson. It ain't over 'til the bell rings. Right?''

''Hey, what can I say?'' Chuck said, grinning. ''You were right on the money.''

''Boy, does Truman owe Chicago,'' Mooney said, smiling. ''Thirty thousand votes . . . that's all he won by. Jesus, we had to beg, borrow, and steal to swing the son of a bitch. . . . No way the man doesn't know who got him elected.''

''You can be sure of that,'' Chuck agreed.

''This means the door is wide open.'' Mooney leaned back against the soft leather chair and smiled. ''Damn . . . it's all goin' our way. There's gonna be trouble out in the Pacific . . . you can bank on that. Guys found out during the war that there's money to be made if you stir up a little trouble. Government contracts, black-market shit, you name it. Truman'll play ball. And Chicago, New York . . . we got some big plans; we're gonna open up new places, like I told you . . . the Dominican Republic, for one. Remember I said we're working on the Philippines? We already got millions in Cuba. We're gettin' in with Egypt and the Arabs. The votes we bring in are worth a lot more than gettin' off on a parkin' ticket or beatin' the fuckin' IRS.'' Mooney leaned forward. ''You see, these foreign countries are funny, Chuck. They can turn in a minute. But if a President owes us, he'll make sure it's under control. He'll ship every fuckin' soldier in America out to some godforsaken hellhole if he has to . . . just to protect our interests. Because our interests are his and his buddies' interests.'' Mooney sat back and started to laugh.

''What?'' Chuck was perplexed. ''What's so goddamned funny about that?''

''Shit,'' Mooney replied, ''I just realized it. . . . Can you believe we're payin' the President for protection?''

''He's got a bigger army,'' Chuck said, joining in Mooney's laughter.

Suddenly, Mooney turned serious. ''That's right, he does. But I never met a politician yet with bigger balls than an Italian. And you know what that means?'' He raised one eyebrow.

''What?''

He leaned across the table and looked Chuck square in the eye. ''It means *we* give the order to fire.''

CHAPTER 12

The pale cheeks of his bride deepened as he sealed their future with a kiss. Afterward, she joyfully clasped a bouquet of snow white orchids to her pearl-encrusted bodice and smiled. Anne Marie Torsiello was at last a Giancana.

For months, every last detail of the lavish affair had been planned by Chuck and Ange—while Mooney had watched on the sidelines, nodding his approval. Strangely, now that his wedding day was actually here, it had taken on a dreamlike quality and Chuck felt as if he stood outside it all, moving through the motions he'd rehearsed in his mind over and over again.

The May afternoon sun cast long shadows across the wedding party standing in the doorway of Notre Dame Church. On the stairs, women dressed in stoles and crepe, with veiled hats perched stylishly atop chignons, shouted and laughed as they pelted the bride and groom with rice, nickels, dimes, and a hail of Jordan almonds. In response, the children scrambled up and down the steps, gathering as much candy and change as they could carry. Below on the sidewalk, the dark-suited men lit cigars and joked among themselves. Chuck's brother Pepe and his sisters Vicki, Antoinette, Mary, and Josie flanked a graying Antonio, now nearly seventy, while beside them stood a handsome and beaming Carl Torsiello. "Is this the happiest or saddest day of my life?" he asked Tillie, whose tear-streaked face he dabbed with a handkerchief. "The happiest," she replied.

Ange had served as Anne Marie's maid of honor and now her organza dress rustled as she gathered her daughters, Annette, Bonnie, and Francine, around her like a mother hen. Amid all the hubbub, Chuck caught sight of Mooney, standing silent and apart from the pressing crowd. In the sun, he became a silhouette of fleeting loneliness against the sleek black limousine.

The reception would be twice as large; four hundred of the city's leaders, both gang members and politicians, would attend the celebration. And all were Mooney's men—in one way or another.

But first there would be a private party for the family at Mooney's home. Petit fours and canapés catered by Gayfers: Dashing red-coated men to serve the bubbling champagne and hors d'oeuvres on sterling silver trays. And of course, Alva, Mooney's black cook, to oversee it all.

At seven o'clock that evening, they left Mooney's home and made their way to the downtown Sheraton Hotel ballroom. Forty elegantly dressed waiters stood at attention along the wall. Forty candlelit tables, seating ten guests each, surrounded a stage and dance floor. The strains of an eighteen-piece orchestra led by Lou Breeze from the

Chicago theater drifted out into the hotel lobby. Surveying the ballroom, Chuck felt a surge of pride; this was going to be the wedding reception to beat all wedding receptions.

Anne Marie gasped in stunned amazement. "It's beautiful, Chuck," she exclaimed. "Like a fairy tale."

"You like it?"

Speechless, she could only nod.

Once they were seated at the head table, he had a chance to drink it all in, to savor the luxurious drape of the crisp linen tablecloths, the lavish floral arrangements that graced each table, the monumental number of distinguished guests who, tuxedoed and bejeweled, poured through the doors.

The big guys strolled in with their wives: Paul Ricca, since his release, relegated to media figurehead; Jake Guzik, meek and mild-mannered thanks to his kidnapping; Louis Campagna, an old Capone crony who was fast becoming aligned with Mooney; Joe Fusco, the bootlegger turned liquor distributor; Tony Accardo, the current head of Chicago's Syndicate; Murray Humphreys, Mooney's political fixer; Charlie Gioe, the old Nitti crony and Hollywood extortionist—"I gotta watch him," Mooney had said; Ross Prio, police fixer and north side gambling head; Sam Golfbag Hunt, an old Capone hit man; Eddie Vogel, king of the slot machines; Phil D'Andrea, a Guzik money man and Hollywood extortionist; Gus Alex, the Greek lieutenant and political fixer; the Fischetti brothers, the Syndicate's celebrity front men and partygoers—"All for show" was how Mooney described them.

And then, as if on cue, the up-and-comers filed in— mostly members of Mooney's old gang: Fat Leonard; Needles Gianola, a smarthead from way back who would do anything Mooney asked; his sidekick, James "Mugsy" Tortorella; Rocky Potenza, the gambling lieutenant; Teets

Battaglia, Mooney's loan-shark whiz and enforcer; Frank Caruso, the south side gambling soldier; Joey DiVarco, Mooney's sometime assassin and extortionist; Willie Potatoes Daddano, the Marquis de Sade of the gang, who also handled vice rackets, cigarette, and pinball machines; Fifi Buccieri, labor-union muscle and assassin; and the brothers Butch and Chuck English, both involved in political fixes, machines, and jukeboxes. Notably absent was the crazy Mad Dog DeStefano—whom Mooney said would "just show up in his fuckin' pajamas with an ice pick in his pocket and scare the women."

Police Commissioner Andy Akins was in attendance, as well as politicians, attorneys, and union guys such as Roland Libonati, Pat Marcy, Jimmy Adducci, Joey Glimco, and John D'Arco. They were hardly through the door before they were sipping wine and slapping backs.

And there were even a few representatives from the Catholic Church among the guests, notably a priest Mooney used as a courier and bagman, "Father Cash."

It was a telling occasion; Needles was right when, at one point in the festivities, he said all a person had to do was watch the interaction between the men to know who was in control. Chuck noticed how the guys he'd thought of as the "powerhouses" fawned over Mooney. Needles described Chicago's rising star more bluntly, "They shit themselves when Mooney walks in the room."

Standing quietly by, Mooney accepted his authority with self-assurance and what Chuck thought was less than veiled pride. But Mooney had good reason to be proud; the truth was, he'd made it—and he was bringing everybody along for the ride. He'd spun the wheel and hit the jackpot and there would be no stopping him now. The whole world was Mooney's apple.

After a sumptuous meal, the entertainment began and the place took on the atmosphere of a posh nightclub. Chuck, never one to sit still for long, grew restless and excused himself. He kissed his pretty bride, and whispered into her ear, "I'll be right back."

He wanted to find Mooney, to see what he thought of it all. He edged through the tables to the back of the ballroom, where he was sure his brother would have staked out a place for whispered business discussions.

Mooney leaned casually against the wall, cigar in hand. Surprisingly, he was alone. He saw Chuck coming toward him and smiled.

"Hey, what do you think of all this?" Chuck motioned with a sweeping gesture around the room.

"Beautiful, Chuck, beautiful. You and Ange, I gotta hand it to ya . . . you sure put on a class act today. How much money you think you got? Everybody brought envelopes. Kansas City, Detroit, Tampa, New Orleans, Cleveland, New York, Boston . . . they all sent theirs." His eyes narrowed. "I think you made a killing."

Chuck nodded, lighting a cigar. "Yeah. I think you're right." He paused and added, "Listen, the entertainment's great, Mooney, thanks to you. . . . You made it all come together. When Joe E. Lewis gets up there in a minute . . . everybody's gonna go crazy."

"Yeah, he'll break 'em up all right." Mooney's face suddenly turned somber.

Just then Lewis took the microphone and began to sing "Rosie's Little Nosie."

Mooney looked at the stage and began to chuckle. "Shit, Chuck, me and Lewis . . . we go *way* back."

"You do?" Chuck said, surprised.

"Yeah, remember Jack McGurn?"

"Yeah, Machine Gun McGurn, shit, that's a name out of the past."

"Well, McGurn got pissed off at Lewis back in twenty-seven. . . . You know how entertainers are . . . always thinkin' they're big shots after you helped get 'em there. If you don't watch it, they get amnesia, forget your fuckin' name and then they get too big for their britches. Well, Lewis was gonna leave McGurn's club and go to another one because they offered him a grand a week. McGurn had a fit . . . told Lewis if he did, he'd never fuckin' live to spend it. But Lewis, the dumb jackass, went on and did it, anyway. I guess he forgot who he was fuckin' with." Mooney shook his head in disbelief. "So, always a man of his word . . . Jack sent me, Needles, and another punk over to pay him a visit. We beat him to a pulp and pistol-whipped him real good." He paused and smiled. "Shit, we cut his fuckin' throat from stem to stern. . . . His goddamned tongue was hangin' by a string out of his mouth when we got done with him. It's a fuckin' wonder the guy lived . . . let alone can sing. When he got well, let me tell you, he was as nice as pie."

Mooney grinned triumphantly and then continued, "One thing we didn't count on was how other entertainers would react. . . . The story spread like wildfire." He laughed. "Like wildfire. There isn't a star alive now who'd turn us down, especially Joe E. Lewis. He wouldn't turn me down for nothin'. He'll fuckin' croon his heart out all night if I tell him to." He looked at Chuck. "Hey forget about it. That's a long time ago; the guy's happy to be here tonight. Capone treated him real good and so have the rest of us. Now he knows his place. Nothin' personal, just business."

It *never* was personal. Chuck turned to look up at Lewis basking in the spotlight on the stage. He had to admit it was totally insane. Totally fucking crazy. Lewis and Mooney always acted like the best of friends; he would never have imagined such a thing and he wished Mooney hadn't told him tonight. Here Lewis was entertaining the man who'd dealt a nearly fatal blow to his career.

Chuck looked on as the crowd cheered and Lewis smiled and began a string of one-liners. He wondered how a person could want their name in lights so much? How could anyone let bygones be bygones after practically having their tongue cut out?

He had to admit Mooney sure had figured out all the angles. He knew weakness when he saw it. Knew who could be manipulated, sucked clean dry—as long as he made them a star. Lewis and the rest of Hollywood might even hate Mooney. But it didn't matter—because they feared and respected him more.

It was just midnight when Chuck and Anne Marie finally left for their honeymoon in Los Angeles. As he put his arm around his new wife, whom he'd recently and affectionately nicknamed "Babe," and escorted her to the car, he turned, taking one last look at the hotel looming behind him, and silently vowed never to forget May 7, 1949. Today, he'd come of age. It wasn't just that once a guy got married, he had certain responsibilities to fulfill. Certainly, he wanted to give Anne Marie a beautiful home, wanted to drape her in furs and diamonds. But the day had been more than that.

It wasn't often all the guys came together—unless somebody had died or gotten married—and today he'd finally seen with his own eyes the amount of control and power Mooney wielded. What Mooney had been telling him for years was true: "Get to the top, and don't get caught along the way, and you'll not only be a good husband and provider . . . you'll be a hero, too.''

California was ritzy enough, but in no time at all, Chuck tired of tropical drinks and sunshine. He was eager to get back to Chicago and even more eager to get on with his life. Now wasn't the time to be lounging around, he explained to Anne Marie. And they checked out of their hotel.

Mooney had told him to come over when he got back into town, and after depositing his new bride in a spacious apartment he'd rented from Mooney's friend ''Tough Tony'' Capezio, Chuck drove right over to Oak Park. He envisioned Mooney announcing that he and Anne Marie would be moving to the Dominican Republic or that he had a new, more important and lucrative job or was being given more territory as reward for his loyal service. Instead, Mooney had some bad news.

''You gotta pull in your machines, Chuck. Shit . . . put 'em in storage or somethin' . . . but pull 'em out. There's gonna be trouble over in the district. In the meantime, go over to the union and get a job as a motion-picture operator. Okay?''

Chuck surveyed Mooney's face. He could tell Mooney was only mildly disturbed by the momentary glitch in business. To his brother, the ten grand a month was a drop in the bucket; to Chuck, a lifeline. He found himself resenting Mooney's apparent lack of concern. Shit, Chuck thought to himself, Mooney probably orchestrated the ''trouble'' he was talking about with Commissioner Andy Akins. As his heart sank, he realized the last time he'd been this disappointed was when Mooney brought him that fucking clarinet when he was a kid. He guessed he was just supposed to lie down and play dead for who knew how long.

"So what's happened with the Dominican Republic? I was kinda hopin' that maybe that was gonna come through," Chuck said. He felt as though he sounded desperate, as if he was grasping at straws.

Mooney studied him from across his desk before replying. "Shit, right now the fuckin' dictator down there is causin' problems. We can't move in 'til somethin' breaks, but Humphreys tells me the government's workin' on it." He shrugged his shoulders. "These things take time."

"I understand that . . . but Mooney, I just got married. I got a wife who likes nice things and a new place now. Bills, you know—"

Mooney cut him off. "Yeah, you like the place? Pretty nice, huh? See how I take care of you? Pretty good."

"Yeah, it's nice. We appreciate everything you've done for us." He checked himself; he didn't want to raise Mooney's ire or make him think he was ungrateful—or worse, make him think he was just like all the rest of the family, with his hand always out. "Really nice . . . My wife loves it." He tried to sound appreciative.

"I guess she'll be comin' over to play cards with Ange and the other women now. She'll get to know the rest of the family."

Chuck knew Mooney meant "family" in its larger sense. The Syndicate guys' wives all played cards together each week. It kept the wives busy and gave them friends who understood the business. Having his wife join them was a big step; it signified his own acceptance as one of the men who belonged. He tried to salve his discouragement with that knowledge. And although he had no idea how they would make it on a motion-picture operator's salary, he brightened at the thought of being included in the inner circle. On later reflection, he realized that was precisely why Mooney had mentioned it in the first place. But comforted for now, he changed the subject. "So what else has been goin' on since we left for California?"

Mooney frowned. "The usual shit. Ange has been spendin' money like water. The girls . . . what can I fuckin' say?" He raised his hands in mock despair. "Annette is drivin' me nuts. Jesus, all she talks about is Hollywood and boys. Bonnie's doin' all right. And Francine, now she's a sweetheart. But kids . . . well, all I can say is you need a few to know what I'm talkin' about." He paused and lit a cigar before adding, "Besides that, it's always the fuckin' same. Everybody's always got their hands out. . . . Pa, he always wants somethin'. Ange's folks . . . boy, their stripes sure changed when the money started rollin' in. Now I'm their precious fuckin' son-in-law. Fat Leonard and the rest of the guys . . . they all got their hands in my pocket."

"Don't forget the Church," Chuck added.

If it wasn't a raffle or some piece of real estate, it was a car or contribution for some camp the diocese was building. And Cardinal Stritch always went to Mooney. Chuck suspected there was more to Mooney's religious affiliations and philanthropy than met the eye. None of the Giancanas had been "good" Catholics. Growing up in Antonio's household, salvation meant making it through the week. Forget about heaven. Ange, like his own wife, was deeply religious, and he knew much of Mooney's generosity had been thanks to her constant prodding. But aside from a few raffles, if Mooney was more deeply involved with Cardinal Stritch, there had to be something in it for Mooney.

"Yeah, the Church," Mooney growled. "Ange is comin' in here practically every goddamned day for some fuckin' charity." He softened momentarily and added, "But it makes her happy." He shrugged his shoulders and leaned back in his chair, curling his lip around his cigar. "You know, Chuck, these priests remind me of the old neighborhood. They got some Chicago guys workin' in the diocese who Stritch says will make it to the top . . . all the way to the Vatican. Let me tell you, Stritch is one ambitious bastard. And the Church is just like any other political game. There's a racket behind every altar when you got a guy like Stritch runnin' the show." Mooney chuckled. "Or as Stritch says, 'Doin' God's work.' "

At the time, it all went over Chuck's head. Years later, Mooney would confide that Father Cash, the young priest Mooney used as a courier around Chicago, also served in that capacity for an enormous international money-laundering venture that funneled money all the way to the Vatican. But it was another ambitious young priest, Paul Marcinkus, a big ape of a man born and raised in Capone's Cicero, whom Mooney had referred to when he spoke of "Chicago guys workin' in the diocese." In 1952, Stritch would recommend that Marcinkus be sent to the Vatican, where he would eventually rise to bishop and secretary of the Vatican bank, reaching the highest position of any American in the Church's history. At that pinnacle, Marcinkus would be accused of international money laundering and suspected of involvement in the murder of at least one uncooperative man, Pope John Paul I.

Chuck stood up to leave. Like everyone else surrounding

Mooney, he would do exactly as he was told—and he wouldn't complain or ask too many questions. He left Mooney's office that day, unhappy with Mooney's order to go to work as a projectionist, but if that's what Mooney wanted, he'd close down his machines. He had to believe that he'd get his chance sooner or later.

For the remainder of 1949 and throughout 1950, Chuck went to work like most normal people. He missed the action, the hustle of the streets. And it perpetually worried him that the job of motion-picture operator was known to be the final resting place for Syndicate guys' relatives. "Once a guy gets in the booth, it's like a fuckin' coffin— he never gets out," Chuckie Nicoletti teased.

Fortunately, Mooney gave him a job now and then. The phone would ring and Mooney would deliver a cryptic message: "Go by the Fat Boy's place and pick up six loaves. Take a short one to the guy out west, a long one to the guy downtown, and bring the other four to me."

Such coded messages were second nature to a kid from the Patch like Chuck. Anybody who'd grown up on the streets knew that all the gang members talked that way. It wasn't so much that they were paranoid about phone conversations—often they talked in riddles face-to-face. If you didn't belong, you didn't understand.

There were rules, too. You never mentioned a guy's real name. Instead, you said "that guy out west" or used a nickname. Tony Accardo's was "J.B.," Murray Humphreys was Curly, or the Camel. Mooney's was everything from Mo to "the Cigar" and "the Hoop"—identifying him as the Syndicate's big wheel. Every place or thing of any importance at all had some sort of code name.

Amused by his young wife's naïveté, Chuck would repeat it all to her—she had no idea what it meant. "Loaves are money, Babe,'' he'd tease. ''Short ones are light . . . you know, less. Long ones are nice and fat . . . stacks of cash. The Fat Boy is Fat Leonard and he'll have it all divided out for me when I get there. So now, all I have to do is deliver.''

He'd pick up a few C notes from Mooney when he made the delivery, and it kept them going. But it was penny-ante stuff. Chuck lay awake nights thinking about how he could possibly provide all the things he wanted for his family. Mooney seemed unconcerned, as if he thought Chuck had a gold mine stashed away somewhere. But the truth was, Chuck had no idea what the hell to do. All he knew was the street, the Syndicate, Mooney's world. He hated himself for being so dependent on Mooney; it made him just like any other common greaseball soldier.

When Chuck learned they were expecting their first child in the spring, he nearly panicked. His life had become tedious, no longer filled with nightly soirees in ritzy clubs. And when Christmas rolled around, it nearly killed him to tell Anne Marie that they would have to tighten their belts. From Chuck's perspective, the gin rummy parties at Ange's that meant their acceptance into the inner circle were a two-edged sword. The women Anne Marie now associated with sported full-length furs and five-carat diamonds. His little Babe probably had expected she'd have the same, which made their financial situation all the more demoralizing.

Anne Marie, too, saw her relationship with the inner circle of Outfit wives as a mixed blessing. She was young enough to be any one of their daughters—her aunts regularly played cards with Ange—which meant she always had to demonstrate respect for their stature and experience.

Because of that, she knew she never would be accepted as "one of the girls."

And she couldn't turn to the younger Bonnie and Annette for friendship. It had become clear shortly after her marriage to Chuck that Mooney's daughters would always think of her as the family servant of their childhood; they would always hold her in disdain.

Interestingly, the other Giancana women were not a part of Ange's exclusive club. Ange was polite but avoided socializing with Josie, Mary, Vicki, Antoinette, and Pepe's wife, Marie. Accordingly, Anne Marie had felt an initial surge of pride at being singled out by Ange. However, pride soon turned to nagging guilt whenever she found herself faced with Chuck's sisters. Ange had placed a wall between them that would always serve to separate.

Ironically, even as Anne Marie recognized that her relationship with Ange was the alienating factor in her relationship with Chuck's sisters, she realized that Ange regularly condescended to her. The condescension made its presence felt in typical female fashion: in a haughty downward glance at Anne Marie's less expensive dress, in a tiny sniff of amusement at Anne Marie's youthful faux pas, in the slightly raised eyebrow women use to demonstrate their superiority.

Chuck and Anne Marie were staggeringly well off compared with other American couples in 1949. Still, they both knew that what they had was paltry next to the luxuries enjoyed by other gang members and their wives.

As the holidays drew near, Chuck's heart sank as he listened to Anne recount stories of her shopping trips with Ange, how Ange was having this dress or that coat specially designed by Georgianna Jordan, Chicago's reigning fashion maven. He saw her youthful desire for life's finer things kindled and he couldn't fault her for thinking she should have the same. After all, he was Mooney's brother.

The clock was ticking on his life—he forgot the illusion of ever equaling Mooney's stature in the Syndicate. Now, he only wanted to bask in it, share in the opportunity his brother's contacts provided. "I think I'll go into business for myself," he told Anne Marie. "Maybe Mooney can open a few doors. Maybe I'll build some six-flat apartments." It was his secret dream to be a builder and run his own show.

Anne could tell he was discouraged. "Well then, ask Mooney . . . he'll help . . . your chance will come, Chuck, I'm sure of it," she'd say cheerfully, still exuberant with the possibilities the future held. Determined to change his situation, he paid his brother a visit.

Mooney's house was adorned in all its finery for Christmas. A lush, elegantly decorated tree twinkled invitingly in the living room; wreaths of fresh-scented pine sprinkled with sprigs of mistletoe and holly graced the doorways. Mooney greeted him; he was in an unusually festive mood and led him down to the basement, glass of eggnog in hand.

"So, how's it goin'? Theater job doin' all right?" he asked as he sat down behind his desk.

"Well," Chuck began almost haltingly. "That's why I came over. I'd like to take a shot at starting my own business. Go into construction, build a few apartments, some stores . . . somethin' like that." He smiled. "Besides, you always said I did a hell of a job remodeling this house."

"Yeah, I did say that. You know how to get a job done

From left to right: the infant Mooney (Salvatore Momo) with his mother, Antonia, elder sister Lena, and father, Antonino Giangana (later Americanized to Antonio Giancana) in Chicago, 1908.

Mooney had assumed dominance over the family by the time this only known Giancana family portrait was taken at his sister Lena's wedding in 1927. *From left to right:* Joseph "Pepe," Josephine, Antonino, Lena, Mooney, Mary, Antoinette, Vicki, and Chuck.

Six of the men who were shot as part of the infamous St. Valentine's Day Massacre, February 14, 1929. *(AP/Wide World)*

Anne Marie Torsiello *(fourth from left),* enjoying dinner at Chicago's swank Boulevard Room in the Stevens Hotel, 1946. *From left to right,* the Giancana family: Ange, Bonnie, Mooney, and Annette.

Preparing to attend Lena's funeral in Chicago, 1941, nineteen-year-old Chuck stands with his sister Vicki *(far left)* and their Aunt Josephine DeMarco.

Mooney cradles his namesake and godson, Samuel "Little Mooney" Giancana, at a family gathering, 1954.

Chuckie and Little Mooney, 1957.

Mooney and his wife, Ange, 1949.

Newlyweds Chuck and Anne Marie Giancana, May 7, 1949.

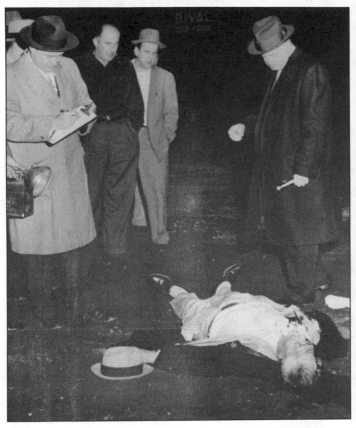

One of Mooney's victims, banker Leon Marcus, April 1, 1957.
(AP/Wide World)

Hollywood's famous "Rat Pack" in rehearsal, January 20, 1960. *From left to right*: Peter Lawford, Frank Sinatra, Dean Martin, Sammy Davis, Jr., and Joey Bishop. (*AP/Wide World*)

Paul Ricca. *(AP/Wide World)*

Murray Humphreys. *(AP/Wide World)*

Frank Costello. *(AP/Wide World)*

Gus Greenbaum. *(AP/Wide World)*

Tony Accardo. *(AP/Wide World)*

Jimmy Hoffa. *(AP/Wide World)*

Carlos Marcello. *(AP/Wide World)*

Johnny Roselli. *(AP/Wide World)*

Santo Trafficante, Jr. *(AP/Wide World)*

Chuck Nicoletti. *(AP/Wide World)*

Felix "Milwaukee Phil" Alderisio. *(AP/Wide World)*

Richard Cain. *(AP/Wide World)*

Hearse transports Marilyn Monroe's body from the star's home, August 5, 1962. *(AP/Wide World)*

Photograph taken moments after President John F. Kennedy was shot, November 22, 1963. White arrow points to Kennedy's foot protruding over side of car. Black arrow points to Mrs. John Connally, wife of Texas' governor, ducking bullets. Connally is visible just to the right of the secret serviceman leaning over back. *(AP/Wide World)*

Nightclub owner Jack Ruby steps forward and levels a revolver at Lee Harvey Oswald, who is in custody for killing the President. A second later, Ruby pumped a bullet into Oswald's stomach from which he died several hours later. (AP/*Wide World*)

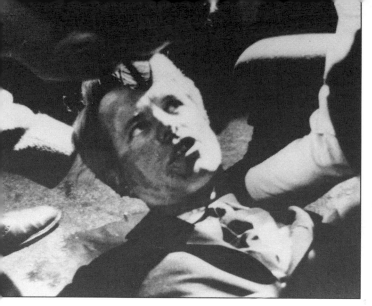

Senator Robert F. Kennedy lies gravely wounded on the floor at the Ambassador Hotel in Los Angeles, moments after he was shot during a celebration of his victory in California's primary election. *(AP/Wide World)*

Sam "'Mooney" Giancana's body lies on a stretcher in the Cook County morgue. *(AP/Wide World)*

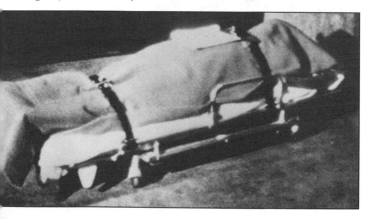

Chuck and Anne Marie Giancana today.

Sam Giancana, godson of Sam "Mooney" Giancana, today.

right. No question about that." Mooney gazed past him in momentary thought. "I think you're on to somethin'. It's a damn good idea for you to be in business." He rose from his chair. "I'll keep my eyes and ears open. If somethin' comes up"—he rounded the desk and put his arm around Chuck, now standing—"I'll let you know. For now, keep up the good work at the theater."

Within moments, Chuck found himself driving back home. He didn't know what he'd expected, but "keep up the good work" wasn't it. Mooney obviously wanted him right where he was for now—and had no intention of making a change. If he struck out on his own, without his brother's permission, he was afraid it would be all over between them. He'd be on his own all right—*totally* on his own. He guessed nobody in the family or the gang had ever done that. If one of the guys had, he was now safely buried out in the county. As Mooney's brother, it was unthinkable. It would be a sign of blatant disrespect. But now, the thought fleetingly crossed his mind. He pushed it away; being Mooney's brother gave him an added responsibility; maybe it was an honor. But whatever it was, it left him with no choice other than to bide his time.

During the winter of 1950, Chuck tried to be patient. He made a point of dropping by to see Mooney two and three times a week. Occasionally, he made some extra money making deliveries for him. And he stopped by the Syndicate bars for a drink every day, knowing it was important to stay on the grapevine. Besides, he didn't know where else to go, or what else to do. His world revolved around Mooney.

In February, while Chuck was wasting away at the Cosmo theater in a darkened booth, the world continued to turn. People were talking about a Commie-chasing senator named McCarthy, who had put together a list of subversives. Chuck almost gleefully announced to Mooney one day, "Well, I bet McCarthy's a guy who can't be bought."

Mooney snorted and replied, "He sure as hell can be used, though."

"Used?" Chuck was incredulous. "How can a hardass like McCarthy be used by anybody but Commie-haters?"

"Chuck, nothin's ever what it seems. Chiang Kai-shek? He's mob. Chinese mob. Goes back to General MacArthur. See, these guys up top know that, in the name of patriotism, Americans will do anything, go anywhere . . . they just gotta have an enemy. Shit, the guys up top'll make one up if they have to. So now the enemy is communism. This McCarthy guy gets people riled up while our country's secret agents stir up a supposed Commie threat, people read about it in the newspapers . . . and boom . . . they'll back a war one hundred percent. Murray Humphreys tells me things you wouldn't believe." Mooney was adamant. "Chuck, don't be a fuckin' patsy . . . the politicians know what's goin' on . . . mostly because half of 'em have some investment, just like we do, in countries with names you've never even heard of. You watch, this Commie crap will get people up in arms. . . . If anything threatens business as usual over there . . . well, our great and powerful President will do somethin' about it. All he's gotta do is yell 'Commie' and every red-blooded American will lay down their lives . . . and for what? So a few fat-cat politicians and businessmen . . . and a few guys like me can make a killin'. We all have too big an investment to let some rum-dum slant-eyed bastard overthrow the government and screw it up. And it's gettin' to the point that if the guy is already in power and we want him out, we'll take care of him . . . one way or another. There's too big an investment.''

''What kind of investment?'' Chuck had lost his initial bravado and was now captivated by Mooney's story.

''Well it isn't fuckin' steel mills, I'll tell you that. For some investors, it's the cheap''—he hesitated—''well, I call it *slave* labor. For other guys, it's real estate.'' He opened his desk drawer. ''See this?''

Chuck nodded. It was the most beautiful square-cut emerald pinky ring he'd ever seen. The stone was huge.

''Twenty-two carats. This could buy a house . . . forty Gs.''

''Jesus Christ.'' Chuck whistled. ''Forty thousand dollars.''

''Now, this is what I call a fuckin' present. A real beauty. And you know who gave it to me?''

''No.''

''King Farouk, that's who. I'm workin' with him.'' He paused to let the implications sink in. ''Chuck, all these foreign bastards that are our fuckin' U.S. allies . . . all they care about is linin' their own pockets. They get paid off and they make sure things stay nice and quiet. All over the world it's like that.''

''What about communism? They gotta care about that. I mean, about their people. Right?''

Mooney broke out laughing. ''You're readin' too many newspapers,'' he taunted. ''That's what you're supposed to think. Nobody in the Syndicate or the government cares what the guy in charge really believes or how oppressed the people there are. Nobody cares about whether or not the people are living in some democracy. The bottom line is money and power. Just like it is here in this country.''

Chuck shook his head.

"Hey, this is business, Chuck. With Farouk, it's business. There's oil in the Middle East; I got a piece myself. There're gambling opportunities in Iran. In Beirut. We keep Farouk happy and he'll make sure his friends around the desert do the same. Remember the guy I told you about with cigarettes in the Philippines? Well, he's got a string of contacts lined up for all kinds of shit . . . opium, for one. New York is probably gonna go in on it. Hell, they got more dope-usin' shines up there than we do in Chicago."

"Opium? I thought all the guys were against narcotics?"

"In our neighborhoods, sure . . . but shines want it and somebody's gotta supply it. So it might as well be us. But that's nothin'. There's shit they do over in Asia that would make your hair stand on end. Our guy in the Philippines was tellin' me that in Manila a dollar buys you a blowjob from a two-year-old. Christ Almighty, there are even babies you can screw. Can you believe it? Orientals are fuckin' animals. Shit, you can buy a girl there and do anything you want with her . . . kill her if you want. . . . Nobody cares in those fuckin' hellholes. Life is cheap. And where life is cheap, politicians are cheap."

The image of Cuba flashed through Chuck's mind. "It sounds worse than Cuba."

"Cuba?" Mooney cackled. "Things are straight down there. Cuba is heaven compared to some of these other places. You got people eatin' raw monkey brains and drinkin' snake blood in Asia. They screw dogs and babies over there. They got a mob, mostly out of Japan, the Yakuza . . . that are some of the meanest motherfuckers I've ever seen. They'll do anything for a buck and they control the governments."

Mooney sighed; he was obviously tiring of the conversation, but he brightened suddenly and decided to continue. "We've got some pretty high hopes for those slant-eyed bastards. If the governments there play ball with our government—and why shouldn't they?—then we're in."

From that point forward, Chuck noticed when Mooney went out of town to Europe or the Middle East. Over the coming years, his sojourns would become more frequent and, Mooney would boast, more profitable than he'd ever dreamed.

The spring and summer of 1950 would prove eventful for Chuck and Anne Marie, as well as the rest of the world. In April, Chuck's first son was born. They named the frail four-pound premature infant Charles Joseph.

In May, a government committee was formed by a Tennessee upstart senator named Kefauver to investigate organized crime—but Mooney insisted that no matter what the rest of America believed, the guy was still crooked. And sure enough, a little over a year later, it turned out the senator had accepted campaign contributions from a numbers racketeer back in his own hometown. That same May, when the secretary of state announced the United States would back the French in Indochina, Mooney gloated and Chuck was hardly surprised.

When President Truman announced in June that the United States would provide military aid to assist South Korea in their bid for democracy to defeat North Korean Communists, Mooney commented matter-of-factly, "The guy runnin' the show in South Korea is part of the Oriental mob."

Thus, Chuck wasn't amazed when Truman placed "the nation's most esteemed military hero," General MacArthur, in charge of the whole mess and it was reported that MacArthur was conferring with Mooney's Chinese mobster associate, Chiang Kai-shek. Instead, Chuck started to believe Mooney knew what he was talking about.

But the war in Southeast Asia was eclipsed in Chuck's world by the Kefauver hearings that fall. No matter where he went, the guys were talking about them. And somewhere about this time, they all stopped calling the Syndicate the Syndicate and started calling it the Outfit. It had a nice ring to it.

Mooney told him that Meyer Lansky had suggested everybody give their organization a name, that it would improve cooperation and boost morale. The national alliance was called the Combination or Commission. In New York, it was the Mob, in Chicago, the Outfit. New Orleans liked the sound of the Combine or the Mafia.

No wonder Kefauver was so damned confused. Chuck laughed to himself as he watched the hearings on their new RCA television each night before going to work at the theater.

The Kefauver hearings were no laughing matter to New York's mobsters. Labeled the "prime minister" of organized crime, Mooney's friend Frank Costello was particularly displeased. His lifestyle, filled with prominent businessmen and political leaders, was laid bare before the American public. And although he gave the committee members no information, the publicity provided his enemies with an opening. The scheming Vito Genovese had especially coveted Luciano's power, and while Costello's hands fidgeted on camera during his testimony, the world and Vito Genovese watched. The word in New York was direct and to the point: Costello's term as boss would soon be over.

Like Costello, Mooney had his share of headaches in

1951. In March, the IRS started nosing around, questioning his income. Additionally, he was indicted on sixty-seven counts of gambling. Shortly thereafter, he had a run-in with his old nemesis Teddy Roe, who continued running his wheels on the south side, in spite of Mooney's constant threats. Meanwhile, rumors began to fly about his love life. People said he'd gotten a secretary at the Envelope Factory pregnant, which did nothing to help temper Ange's simmering jealousies.

But through it all, Mooney remained undaunted. He never faced trial on the indictments, was never served with so much as a subpoena. He explained that twist of fate thusly, "I may not be able to control a jig policy king . . . yet . . . but I have most of the cops and politicians around the country in my pocket."

He also managed to prove in May of 1951 that he had a number of big-name celebrities in his pocket, as well, with an event called "Night of Stars." This extravaganza was sponsored by the Italian Welfare Council—one of Ange and Mooney's only real charities—and was an effort to raise money for poor Italian children.

Years later, Chuck would hear people claim that Night of Stars had been Ange's brainchild, that she'd manipulated Mooney, using her feminine guile, into participating, and that she'd personally worked long hours promoting the event.

On the contrary, Night of Stars hadn't been Ange's idea, nor did she exert herself promoting the community charity. Not because she was ill or frail—as she was so often portrayed—but because as Mooney's wife she was "above all that." Indeed, Mooney had been more than willing, without his wife's prodding, to provide the underworld leverage necessary to assure the success of Night of Stars.

Whether it was a charity or a union Outfit guys wished to promote, they always used the same tactics: muscle and men. And in this case, Mooney put his men to work promoting Night of Stars, directing them to "encourage" customers to purchase tickets to the event. As Chuck quickly found out, if a guy didn't manage to unload his share of tickets, well, he was stuck buying them all himself—which was good incentive to turn to muscling other guys into taking them off your hands.

Chuck would never be able to say whether all the effort had paid off for the poor children of the Italian neighborhood—he never saw the final tally for Night of Stars—but three years later, Mooney would confide he'd grown tired of carrying the neighborhood, growling, "Hey, why the hell should my men pick up the tab and buy all the goddamned tickets? If the Italians in the neighborhood don't give a damn about their own people, then fuck 'em."

Mooney stopped supporting the event after that and that was the end of Night of Stars. Each spring, Chuck couldn't help missing the lineup of celebrities his brother always managed to assemble—entertainers such as Bob Hope, Dean Martin, Jerry Lewis, Jimmy Durante, and Frank Sinatra. Such a public demonstration of his brother's power made Chuck proud to be a Giancana—which was the real reason why, he guessed, he'd always miss Night of Stars.

Like his role model, Mooney, Chuck spent more time away from home than not. He insisted that dinner be served at five-thirty each night, and after eating one of Anne Marie's painstakingly prepared dinners, he either made his way to the Cosmos theater for work or dropped by an Outfit bar to talk to the guys. Late one night in June, he was shooting the breeze with Needles and Fat Leonard, and they started reminiscing about the good old days at the Boogie Woogie.

"Man oh man, the shine broads in there were class, real class," Leonard remarked.

"And what about the music?" added Needles. "That joint was really hoppin'. I never seen so many hot colored packed together."

"Hey, remember when Mooney and Teddy Roe ran into each other?" Leonard said. "Boy, was that shine burned up." He began to snicker. "He coulda killed Mooney, for sure."

"I bet he would still now, if he could," Chuck remarked.

"Yeah, well the guy's number's up. I can promise you that. Mooney's had it with the little fuck. He'll be gone with the wind," Leonard said, chuckling.

Needles laughed. "Hey, I like that one . . . gone with the wind . . . just like the movie. Send Roe back to a plantation somewhere and let him fertilize some fuckin' cotton."

"Or back to hell, where the nigger bastard came from to begin with," Leonard added, picking up his drink in a gesture of mock toast. "Here's to Teddy Roe, may the sorry motherfucker soon rest in peace." Leonard shot a look at Needles, who couldn't contain a smirk.

About that time, Milwaukee Phil walked in with Chuckie Nicoletti. They pulled up chairs and ordered drinks.

"Hey, where's Mad Dog? I thought he was comin' over," Needles said.

They groaned collectively.

"He'll be here. He stopped who the fuck knows where. But, if he said he was droppin' by, he'll be here," Phil said, taking a sip of his drink. "So I hear Teddy Roe's ship has come in," he added, and raised one eyebrow. The group began laughing.

"Yeah, that's what we were just talkin' about. . . . That's one shine Mooney's gonna give a one-way ticket," Needles said.

"Ain't life shit?" Leonard said, and then burst out laughing.

They all joined in and Chuck noticed Mad Dog come in the door. The guy was a lunatic; they didn't call him Mad Dog for nothing. Mad Dog DeStefano was crazy, totally nuts. He'd be in a rage one minute and the next, laughing like a loony. He usually wore pajamas, fly open, wherever he went, and looked as if he'd just crawled out of bed. He got off on killing. It was almost funny the way everybody gave Mad Dog wide berth. Cold-blooded killers didn't want to cross him. Chuck always tried to avoid him. De-Stefano spotted their table and made his way along the bar. He sat down and, amid roars of laughter, immediately launched into a graphic description of his latest torture technique. He loved ice picks, but he loved to talk about them more.

Chuck scanned the faces of the men seated alongside him. There wasn't a man sitting at the table who hadn't taken a guy out, except him. And, with the exception of DeStefano, they were really nice guys. They didn't act like people might think killers would act. They acted like normal guys. The wives would never have guessed that any one of them could slit a man's throat without blinking an eye. But they'd all done that and a lot worse. All for Mooney.

Which made it okay, Chuck guessed. Whether it was

gambling, burglary, or murder, it was all the same. Everybody had a job to do in the organization. And they did it for Mooney. Although sometimes he wondered whether Mooney was just an excuse. Like fear. How many times had he heard somebody say they were afraid of Mooney. Afraid they would be killed if they didn't do exactly what Mooney wanted—from buying the right model car to making an appearance at a family wedding. To hear people associated with the Outfit talk, they were always afraid. But looking around the table now, he didn't think any of the guys looked afraid of anything. Actually, they all looked as if they thought they had it made.

The question of whether something was right or wrong never entered a guy's mind. That question got buried early on. And out of a desire to get ahead, it stayed buried. Should it surface by some strange chance, it was fear that pushed it down again into the backwaters of the guy's conscience.

Chuck tried not to think about those kinds of things—never discussed them with anybody, not even Anne Marie, most of all not with her. But sometimes he thought the honest-to-God truth was that it was all just an excuse. It wasn't because of Mooney—or fear—that he and the rest of the guys worked for the Outfit. Anybody who worked for the Outfit did it because they liked the money. It didn't matter whether it was all stolen; it didn't matter whether a guy had to kill for the privilege of being in the Outfit. What did matter was that you had five hundred a week when other saps had fifty. And you were respected, treated as if you were special. People knew your name—you got the best seat in a restaurant, the best cut at the butcher's.

He and the rest of the guys who worked for the Outfit

might tell themselves they did it for Mooney or that they didn't have a choice, but that was all just bullshit. You did it for yourself.

Later, Chuck would chide himself for not realizing what Fat Leonard and Needles had been getting at with all the talk about Teddy Roe. But that night, he didn't take it too seriously. He always knew Mooney would go after the guy sooner or later—which made Chuck no different from any other person familiar with the law of the street. He just didn't know how soon.

CHAPTER 13

What happened on June 19, 1951, was almost, to the letter, a repeat performance: a darkened street; a sleek sedan stealthily stalking its intended victim; its passengers, three fedora-hatted men in silk suits, toting guns. The moment Teddy Roe looked into his rearview mirror and spotted the bright headlights flashing behind him, he probably knew. It had Mooney Giancana written all over it.

Roe had prepared himself for just such an inevitability. After a series of run-ins with Mooney, he'd hired off-duty coppers as bodyguards. In the five years since Eddie Jones's abduction, the black policy king and his family had lived with the constant threat of death. Mooney had once said that fear wore a man down—made him tired and careless—and that living in fear was worse than death itself. But Mooney hadn't yet locked horns with the likes of Teddy Roe. Roe had become a hero in the colored neighborhood because he hadn't knuckled under to the dago mobsters. He'd stood up to the man the colored papers called "the meanest of them all," Mooney Giancana, and lived to tell about it. That alone won him their adulation and the nickname the "Robin Hood of Policy."

With Roe alive and flourishing, Mooney had yet to gain control of all south side policy wheels. Teddy Roe was the last holdout, and for that he was a hero.

After the heat died down following the Jones incident, Roe's business thrived instead of folding. It grated Mooney to know that his policy takeover was incomplete, that Roe's loyal gamblers flooded his wheels in record numbers, making him richer than ever.

Mooney had tried a number of tactics to pry Roe out of operation. His soldiers bombed Roe's home and threatened his family. Meanwhile, Mooney offered the cocky mulatto $250,000 to leave town, to which Roe had sneered, "I'll die first." It was a surprise to those who worked for Mooney that he hadn't taken Roe up on it. Why he'd waited so long to move against Roe was a mystery—because he plainly hated the guy.

Chuck, however, theorized that Roe struck a chord somewhere in his brother. There had never before been a man or woman Mooney couldn't have. Nor had there been, to Chuck's knowledge, anyone who stood up to Mooney in his forty-three years as Roe had. In some twisted way, Chuck knew Mooney admired that. It was the same with a broad. As long as she played hard to get, Mooney was up for the challenge. He'd try everything—money, gifts, introductions to his celebrity friends—because, as he put it, "There's always somethin' a broad wants more than her fuckin' virtue."

Perhaps what Mooney wanted most was to find the one person who didn't have a price. Someone to restore his faith in humanity—a faith that had been lost as a child while chained to the tree on Van Buren. Significantly, he'd often told Chuck that, "unlike those whores they call politicians," once he'd made up his mind about something, "nobody can buy me or fuckin' scare me into anything."

Mooney's was a hardheaded stubbornness that struck Chuck as a trait more Irish than Italian. But Mooney had his own unswerving brand of principles and for better or worse—legal or illegal, immoral or moral—he held to them with uncommon tenacity. Somewhere there existed his equal. Chuck had to believe that so far, the stubborn, snarling, self-assured policy king was as close as Mooney had ever gotten to that man.

Roe must have thought it was the end when he curbed his Lincoln; but unbeknown to his assassins, his off-duty bodyguards were shadowing him. With customary confidence, and not a small amount of courage, Roe got out of his car to face whoever was tailing him.

Fat Leonard, Jimmy New York, and Vincent Ioli watched the man bravely walk toward them. They smiled at one another and snuffed out their cigarettes.

"It's time," Leonard said softly, and opened the door. Those would be his last words.

The three Italians were caught completely off guard for perhaps the first time in their lives. A hail of bullets, from both Roe and his bodyguards, greeted them the minute their feet hit the pavement.

Leonard managed to get off one shot before Jimmy New York heard the sickening crack of bone and saw his friend's skull pop open at the temple with a snap, gushing blood and brains. From the other side of the car, Ioli screamed he'd also been hit. Instinctively, they scrambled back into the safety of their car and sped off into the night, leaving Fat Leonard behind to die in a pulsing pool of blood.

The 42s had a rule in the old days; Joey Colaro had passed it down when Mooney and the rest of them were nothing more than crazy punks in the Patch: "Never, ever, leave one of your own behind." Mooney remembered it clearly—just as if it were yesterday, he told Chuck. And he would never forgive the two men who didn't. "When push comes to shove, when a guy's got a gun to his head, that's when you know what he's made of," he said at the news of the bungled job. The two men might have saved their own skins, but they lost Mooney's trust in the process. Chuck knew Mooney would never allow them to rise in the organization after such a transgression.

Chuck was sobered by the news of Fat Leonard's demise. "Live by the sword, die by the sword," Mooney said all the time. Chuck guessed that justice had just come to Fat Leonard Caifano sooner than most.

Roe was initially charged with Fat Leonard's murder, but predictably, the charges were dropped and he was hailed in the colored papers once again for his courage in the face of the Italians. Chuck imagined Mooney probably had never wanted to defeat an adversary more than he wanted to defeat Roe. But, leaving Fat Leonard's funeral, Mooney's only comment about the entire affair was characteristically succinct: "Roe's a fuckin' dead man."

For the rest of the summer, Mooney traveled from city to city. He went to Miami and Cuba all the time now, sometimes as often as once a week. Las Vegas had also become a frequent stopover point during his trips to California. His touch points were largely gambling enterprises and they now stretched west from Chicago to Kansas City, Las Vegas, and Hollywood; north to Detroit and Canada; and south to Miami, Louisiana, and Texas. Nicoletti and Needles told Chuck, "Your brother's the only guy the other bosses will even let come in to their town. There're only two guys Marcello will do business with . . . Mooney and Costello. But Mooney's gonna sew up the whole fuckin' country before it's over with.''

Mooney was also making frequent jaunts to Mexico, the Middle East, and Europe—solidifying, Chuck imagined, the international contacts about which he'd spoken. For most people, such treks would have been part business, part vacation. For Mooney, it was always all business. Not that he didn't come across some good-looking woman and have a little extracurricular fun in the sack, or roll a few dice in a swank casino somewhere. But the points of interest—the famous museums, the ancient ruins, the grand architecture to be found in the cities he visited—all left him cold. If Mooney wasn't cutting a deal or planning one, he was bored. That was a Giancana trait. And it told Chuck that Mooney was not out on a lark in a sunny resort somewhere. Mooney was moving up and moving up fast.

The guys Chuck talked to all agreed. That fall, Chuck sat down in the Armory Lounge, a favorite hangout among Outfit lieutenants, with Chuckie English, one of Mooney's right-hand men.

''Mooney's taken over Chicago,'' English stated matter-of-factly. ''Nobody here is gonna stand in his way.''

''Why do you say that?''

''Two reasons, Chuck, two simple reasons.'' English held up two fingers as he spoke. ''First, your brother is a genius at makin' money. Meyer Lansky says he's the only Italian he's ever met who handles money like a Jew—and better than most Jews, at that. And when Mooney makes money, everybody makes money . . . that's the first thing.''

''And?''

"The second thing is real simple. If the guys in Chicago don't fall in line, they're gonna be pushed. And they know it. So"—English laughed—"it's an easy choice. Die or be rich. Mooney doesn't fuck around."

The two sat in silence before English continued. "You know I've gone with Mooney to New York, Cuba, Vegas. He's cuttin' these guys in on deals he's put together all over the country . . . hell, all over the world. It's usually gambling that opens the door, but now it might be guns or jewelry, opium or oil or cigarettes, you name it. And it's the same all over. Word gets around. You know, he's the only guy who goes to meet with the families in New York or to see Marcello in New Orleans who doesn't take a bodyguard. That's how confident he is. Nobody would dare hit Mooney Giancana. He's worth too much alive."

As Mooney's influence within the national Commission soared, so, too, did his political clout. Murray Humphreys continued regularly to shuttle back and forth to Washington, making "social calls," and recently he had added California to his list. Meanwhile, Chicago political leaders such as Jake Arvey worked on the inside, greasing palms and trading favors. Considered a "kingmaker," Arvey was particularly busy now, working on the upcoming presidential election.

As Mooney said was typical, New York was again rumbling under the greed that had become its heritage. Since his Kefauver testimony, Frank Costello had been targeted by Vito Genovese. To get to Costello, however, required the removal of Costello's longtime ally, Willie Moretti. Moretti had been partners with Longy Zwillman in New Jersey and was rumored to have acted as Frank Sinatra's "godfather" by helping to break the singer's ironclad contract with the Tommy Dorsey band in 1939. Recently, he'd begun showing signs of advanced syphilis, shooting off his mouth about family business. Genovese leapt on this excuse to eliminate Moretti and insisted he be hit. Costello, who had served as best man at Moretti's wedding, sought to protect his friend, hiding him in California until Moretti was brought back to New York prior to the Kefauver hearings.

Although Moretti behaved himself during testimony before the committee in early 1951, shortly thereafter, he began granting interviews with reporters. Again Genovese, with secret hopes of taking over Moretti's operations in New Jersey and further weakening Frank Costello, insisted Moretti be taken out.

Recognizing that Moretti offered him little protection from Genovese, Costello looked to Albert Anastasia, head of New York's Murder, Inc., for support. He told Anastasia that he'd back a hit on Anastasia's boss, Vincent Mangano, and push for Anastasia as Mangano's replacement. In April, Vince Mangano disappeared and was assumed murdered. Anastasia was made boss, giving his full support privately to Costello.

Not to be outdone, Genovese cried for Moretti's death once more. Terming it "mercy killing," Genovese convinced Anastasia to do the job, and on October 4, 1951, while dining on pasta in a New Jersey Italian diner, Willie Moretti was shot to death. The murder cast uncertainty over Costello's future; not only was Costello's lifetime friend now dead, but the man he'd helped make boss of the Mangano family had carried out the execution. Mooney watched warily from Chicago as word spread that Vito Genovese was one step closer to power.

In spite of the upheaval in New York, the wheels of enterprise continued to turn in Chicago and, with the exception of the Teddy Roe incident, things were relatively quiet.

Until March of 1952, Mooney's goings-on had been low-profile—and he liked it that way. But that March, perhaps in an attempt to find a replacement for the gregarious Al Capone, the *Chicago Tribune* published a list they called the "Bad 19." There was little in the collection of leering mug shots to fire the public imagination. Most of the shots were of old-timers such as Ricca, Guzik, and Humphreys, whose charisma was minimal. However, there were a few new faces, most notably, Mooney Giancana's.

Anne Marie gasped as Chuck handed her the paper. "Oh my God, Mooney's picture is here," she exclaimed.

Her reaction was echoed in most Italian homes where Mooney had already become a household name. His appearance among the hoodlums was met in the old neighborhood with a mixture of pride and indignation. On the one hand, one of their own had made it to the big time. On the other, most found the label *bad* too strong a word.

"Mooney isn't really bad," Anne Marie commented. "Not really. He can be so nice. And there isn't a person I can think of who wouldn't say the same thing, too."

Of course, all of her acquaintances were people in the Outfit. Saturday nights out at the Chez Paree had become a sort of an Outfit get-together. She played gin rummy with the wives, shopped with Ange, had coffee with Mary and Laura English, and lunch with aunts whose husbands worked as soldiers for Mooney.

For the most part, she found the men in Mooney's entourage handsome and well bred. They behaved politely and never swore in front of the women. And if they were unfaithful, their indiscretion was discreet and always—an unspoken rule among the men—outside the "family." The women never discussed their husbands' "business," nor did they ask questions.

Chuck and Anne Marie's life had become typical of others in Mooney's world. Not only did he control their employment—and therefore their financial status—but their day-to-day decisions, as well. They asked for permission to move into a new, more spacious apartment. Asked for permission to buy a new car. They went out to the restaurants, clubs, and events Mooney supported. They contributed to charities Mooney sponsored. They used the physicians and attorneys Mooney and Ange "strongly recommended." And they did these things without question—not necessarily out of fear, but out of what they termed "respect" for Mooney's position.

Chuck occasionally recalled old conversations he and Mooney had had about wives and marriage. Older and now married himself, he'd come to think that Mooney had been right. In organizing one's life and family around a tight-knit, structure like the Outfit, things became predictable; your home life stayed nice and neat. The people connected to the Outfit became your friends, your wife's friends, your children's friends. It would be more than a decade before Chuck would recognize the fatal flaw in this arrangement: Outfit members became your only friends and, as such, your only contact with reality. And Outfit reality was quite different from that of the rest of the world's.

Mooney didn't wrestle with such complex philosophical or moral issues when he ordered Teddy Roe's execution on the night of August 4, 1952. This time, his men were successful and their shotguns blasted Roe five times as he walked from his home to his car.

Not much attention was given to Roe's untimely end.

The police displayed their usual apathy regarding gangland slayings. With the exception of an outcry from the colored alderman, Archibald Carey, directed at Chicago's Mayor Kennelly, and a postfuneral skirmish between a colored contingent and the authorities, Roe's legacy was quickly and effectively buried.

In late August, Chuck found himself in Mooney's Oak Park backyard, watching as his brother sharpened his golfing abilities. It was warm and Mooney's putting green was a lush velvet carpet of perfectly manicured grass.

An avid golfer who excelled at chipping and putting, Mooney took his game seriously—too seriously, Chuck believed. He stood by silently as his brother frowned with determined concentration. After he made the shot, Mooney turned and said hello with what had become a characteristic growl.

"You had enough of layin' around on your ass at the theater?" he queried.

Chuck's heart leapt and, though slightly offended by Mooney's insinuation that he'd been lazing merrily along for the past two years, he replied with enthusiasm, "You're goddamned right I have."

Mooney put his club in his golf bag and smiled. "That's good, because I got an opportunity I think you're gonna like."

Chuck's mind raced.

Mooney grinned, adding, "But you'll never guess what it is . . . not in a million years."

"Well, tell me then," Chuck countered.

"I will, but let's sit down first and have a drink."

They sat in the warm sunshine at a wrought-iron table

on the patio. Alva, Mooney and Ange's faithful cook, promptly appeared to serve coffee.

"Plastics, Chuck. What do you think of plastics?"

"Plastics? I don't know . . . what about them?"

"Well, I'm told by people who should know that plastic is the material of the future. That someday, just about everything will be plastic."

"Yeah, I see." There was doubt in his voice.

"Well, I want you to go to see Joe Esposito over on Milwaukee Avenue. He's startin' a plastics factory, gonna make vinyl bags, stuff like that. Someday, who knows, the Outfit might be a giant in a new industry." He chuckled and reached over to smack Chuck's hand playfully.

Joe and his brother, Chuck, were the sons of a man with an infamous history in Chicago's Patch: Diamond Joe Esposito. Chuck remembered the brothers from the streets of his childhood, recalled hearing stories about the hit on their father.

"You really think this thing will fly?" Chuck asked hesitantly.

"Yeah, and I want you to help pilot the ship. You said you wanted to run a business . . . now here's your chance."

"What made you decide on plastics? I mean, there're lots of opportunities out there."

"Yeah, and most of them I've already got a piece of. I got Willie Potatoes workin' on the sanitation business. There's big money in garbage. And the more people there are in the world, the more garbage there's gonna be. I got a shrimp business in Cuba, oil wells in Texas, and gas in Louisiana. Besides that, there's so much shit, you have to be a Hebe accountant to keep track of it."

"How's your partner, King Farouk?" Chuck said, smiling.

"Happy as a fuckin' clam for now. But there're problems over there. Hey, like I've said before, these foreign countries are always on the verge of war. Look at Korea. Look at China and Taiwan. My guy in Manila told me that if it weren't for the CIA and the Outfit, the whole fuckin' place would blow up. They're already gettin' nervous about Cuba."

"Nervous? I can't understand what the fuck for," Chuck said, sarcasm lacing his voice. "Unless it's the thousands of Cubans who'd like to overthrow the Cuban government. Frankly, after goin' down there myself, I can't fuckin' blame them. While Batista's gettin' fat off payoffs, they're all starvin' and sellin' their sisters for a buck."

A scowl formed on Mooney's face. "Hey, goddamn it. That's some of my fuckin' money the cocksucker is gettin' fat on. If he's out . . . we could all be out." He paused. "But we're hedgin' our bets. Politics are politics . . . forget about the country. It's all the fuckin' same. You gotta protect your interests by playin' both sides."

"Both sides?"

"Yeah," Mooney said, grinning. "Now, instead of one bag of money"—he shrugged his shoulders—"what the fuck, we send two."

"One to Batista and—"

"One to the rebels."

"That's pretty good. I guess I can hope the rebels win, then."

"What the hell are you talkin' about?" Mooney snapped. "You sound like the fuckin' government, some *cetriolo* agent. What we want is to keep things the same if we can. We stand to lose a lot of money . . . the other money is just insurance 'til we see how things go." His voice trembled in anger. *"Capisce?"* He raised his clenched fist and slammed it on the table. "I don't ever want to hear you say that again. *Capisce?* Never."

Realizing he'd made a serious error in judgment, Chuck tried to backpedal. "Hey, sorry. Just an opinion, that's all. You don't need to go gettin' burned up at me about it."

Still angry, Mooney stood up and looked at his gold Patek Philippe watch. "Hey, why don't you just fuckin' go to your new job and get the hell outta here."

"Hey fine, fine. You don't have to fuckin' tell me twice." Chuck turned to leave.

"Goddamn it. Come back here, you lousy son of a bitch. Just forget about it. Okay?"

Chuck nodded uncertainly.

Mooney, ever the enigma, suddenly smiled. "You got me so fired up . . . shit . . . I forgot this." He pulled an emerald and diamond bracelet from his pocket and held it up in the sunlight. "Give this to Anne Marie. You don't have to say I gave it to you. Just give it to her. Part of a celebration for your new job. And while you're at it, go buy a few new suits over at Celano's for yourself." He handed Chuck a roll of cash. It was all hundreds. "If you're gonna run a business, you gotta look like a fuckin' businessman. Right?"

"Right," Chuck agreed, nodding. He thanked Mooney profusely and left hurriedly for home.

Mooney did crazy shit like that all the time. One minute he'd be so pissed off, a guy might think Mooney was gonna kill him—a mood of his that came to be known as "tight shoes"—and the next, he'd be all smiles, putting a wad of bills in the guy's hand.

Mooney came by their house now and then for breakfast and always brought Anne Marie some Danish. Once, he'd even brought a mink coat along as an added surprise. He was always doing things like that for people. It could be a car for a politican's wife, whom he was screwing at the time right under the man's nose; a diamond friendship ring for a celebrity; or a playground full of equipment for the Church children's camp. You never knew what Mooney would do next, whether he'd be in a good mood or have "tight shoes." His unpredictability was a strength; it kept everybody around him on their toes, whether they were soldiers or women or family. And it made them eager to please the man who could pass out expensive baubles as if they were candy.

On his way home from Mooney's, Chuck stopped by a jeweler and got a black velvet presentation case for the bracelet. He had a chance to examine it more closely as he placed it in the case. There were eight perfect square-cut emeralds, five carats each. These, in turn, were linked by a dazzling chain of sixteen diamonds set in platinum. It was a stunning gift and he could hardly wait to see his little Babe's face when she first laid eyes on it.

He wasn't disappointed. Anne Marie's reaction was a combination of ecstasy and tears.

"Oh, Chuck, it's so beautiful," she cried. "Look at the diamonds, the emeralds." Hugging his neck, she started to laugh and then her eyes twinkled mischievously. "Well, I know one thing . . . I need a new dress to wear with this bracelet."

"Well, go get one, get two. I've got some good news."

"There's more?"

"Yeah." He smiled broadly. "I got a new job."

"Really? You mean it? Oh, Chuck, that's wonderful."

If he hadn't wanted to tell her what he was doing, the conversation would have ended right there. She never would have asked; a good wife never did. But he wasn't going to be secretive about something so legitimate as running a plastics factory, so he continued. "Yeah, I think it's pretty exciting. Mooney is sending me over to run a plastics factory with Joe and Chuck Esposito."

"Plastic? What is that for?"

"I'm not sure yet, but Mooney kept tellin' me over and over how it's the thing of the future. He thinks we can all get rich in the plastics business. I guess we'll just have to wait and see."

The fall of 1952 marked the presidential elections and again, as in 1948, Mooney was more than mildly interested. In fact, to Chuck, who'd never been politically inclined, Mooney seemed something of a scholar on the subject, aware of things going on in the government Chuck felt sure most people knew nothing about.

To his surprise, though, when asked if he was supporting Illinois's favorite son, Adalai Stevenson, Mooney laughed. "I like a winner. I like Ike. But Hump and I like his running mate, Nixon, even better. You can be sure he'll be on our side."

"But isn't Jake Arvey supporting Stevenson? Didn't he help make sure Kefauver wasn't nominated?" Chuck asked, referring to the genius political-machine organizer who'd been instrumental in Truman's 1948 election, and who'd ascended to national attention months before with his behind-the-scenes defeat of crime-busting Senator Estes Kefauver at the Democratic convention.

"Yeah. We had to get Kefauver off the ticket. But Arvey knew all along that Ike was the one."

Mooney must have noticed the blank look on Chuck's face; what he was saying wasn't registering. He decided to elaborate. "Listen, it's just the way it's supposed to be. Any way this one goes, we win. I'm hedging my bets. We got campaign contributions to both sides: Our guys out in California are helping Nixon, and Arvey's handling Stevenson. Can you beat those odds?"

Chuck had to admit things looked pretty good for the Outfit. And when Ike eventually won, all Mooney did was wink and say, "What did I tell you?"

By 1953, Chuck was firmly entrenched in the plastics business. Mooney had been right; the more Chuck read about the industry, the more convinced he was that it was the wave of the future. But the operation he was running with the Espositos wasn't taking off; Chuck thought it might not make it through the end of the year. The problem was that the rest of Chicago—or the United States, for that matter—didn't have the same vision. Nevertheless, he plunged into his new job, determined to make *plastic* a household word.

"It'll happen. I told you plastic is gonna be big," Mooney insisted. "But if it doesn't," he said, shrugging, "who the hell cares?"

Chuck kept it to himself, tried to play nonchalant, but the truth was, he cared. He wanted more than anything to prove to Mooney he could make it work. That way, when Mooney wanted someone to run another, more elaborate business, he'd turn to Chuck. That was the real reward Chuck was waiting for—the chance to move up in the organization.

Chuck wasn't the only person Mooney rewarded with a

new job. With Accardo's and Ricca's agreement, Mooney sent Marshall Caifano to Las Vegas as Chicago's casino watchdog; it was considered a "cush" assignment.

To make way for Marshall, Johnny Roselli—considered Chicago's "rep" in Vegas—began to spend even more time in Hollywood and Los Angeles. Since his release from prison in 1947 for the Browne-Bioff extortion scam, Roselli had divided his attentions between Los Angeles— where he had the impotent local boss, Jack Dragna, acting as Chicago's virtual lackey—and Vegas, watchdogging the casinos. But his first love would always be Hollywood; he produced a few films, became a member of the Friar's Club, where he rubbed elbows with some of the day's biggest stars. There was nothing Johnny Roselli loved more than playing footsie with celebrities and the studios.

"He's perfect for Hollywood," Mooney said of Roselli. "The Screen Actors Guild isn't like the other fuckin' unions—the others are animals—out there you gotta have class. And Roselli's smooth as fuckin' silk."

Chuck heard that Roselli was also supposed to be on the lookout for rising stars who might come in handy someday. "They make great bagmen," Mooney commented. "Everybody's too busy bein' dazzled by a star and askin' for their autograph to ask what's in a briefcase."

If Roselli spotted a promising talent, he called Mooney. Mooney would help the fledgling star's career—whether through an engagement at Vegas, a part in a movie, or a recording contract. And if the individual was genuinely talented, it was all the break he or she needed. But it was clearly understood that when Mooney needed a favor, the star would reciprocate. The bigger the star became, the bigger the debt to Chicago.

According to Mooney, Chicago used its money and influence to help everybody from Ronald Reagan to Ed Sullivan. And there were the others, old-timers by now to the Outfit's many fringe benefits: Sammy Davis, Jr.—"a nigger weasel," Mooney called him; Dean Martin and Jerry Lewis—"fuckin' prima donnas"; Frank Sinatra— "a real stand-up guy . . . he's too good for those bums in Hollywood."

Mooney's influence was also spreading rapidly into the sporting arena—something that came as no shock to Chuck; he himself had been the recipient of the best seats in the joint at enough fights, ball games, and tracks to know the power Chicago wielded with athletes and promoters. And besides, sports were a logical extension of Mooney's gambling enterprises.

According to Mooney, the underworld's interest in big-league sports went back to a New York guy named Louie Jacobs, who got his start running rum with Costello and the guys during the Depression. He later parlayed his earnings into the world's largest sports concession-stand business, handling even the 1960 Olympics in Rome. Jacobs had been instrumental, thanks to his connections, in putting the money together for three major league baseball teams owned by Chicagoan Bill Veeck.

But that was only one example of Jacobs's abilities as a matchmaker, Mooney told Chuck. "Our name might not be on the dotted line as owners of the all-American pastime," Mooney said, "but the money came from us. Having Jacobs operating at the parks is like having jukeboxes in a joint . . . we know what's goin' on all the time. We know if an owner is in financial trouble. Jacobs lets us know, and we bail 'em out. It's like points in Vegas. Eventually, we get a piece of the pie—football, baseball, boxers, horses, jai alai, dogs, even fuckin' golf tournaments, you name it.''

As happened with the entertainment industry, word got out under Mooney's reign that if an athlete would cooperate with the Outfit, his career would soar. He'd get the publicity—''We pay off the sportswriters,'' Mooney said. He'd get the right fights or be placed on a big-name team; he'd get everything he needed to make it to the top. The only catch was simple and understood up front: When Sam Giancana said, ''Fall down in the third round'' or ''Drop the ball,'' the guy had better do it.

By mid-1953, Mooney's circle of athletes—most of whom he thought of as ''friends,'' if there really was such a thing with Mooney—had grown to include the nation's greats, including American baseball idols such as Joe Di-Maggio, Mickey Mantle, and Willie Mays. Mooney never claimed the trio actually did anything out of the way, nor did he insinuate they'd thrown their share of games, but he did make it perfectly clear that these three players routinely enjoyed a ''good time'' at Outfit expense and that the Outfit guys, in turn, enjoyed their company: ''Those guys should just move in to Frank Costello's seventh-floor suite at the Washington Hotel. They're there all the time . . . we give 'em broads, whatever they want.''

In boxing, Mooney's acquaintances included Rocky Marciano, Jake LaMotta, Rocky Graziano, and Sugar Ray Robinson, the latter of whom he'd called a meeting with to get him to throw a fight with Graziano. ''I offered him a million bucks and the promise that he'd win the next match,'' Mooney said. ''Can you believe the guy turned it down? Robinson's got balls.''

Mooney's world was fast becoming one of glitz, glamour, and greed—a place where nothing was out of reach. Listening to Mooney recount his wanderings and his conquests, Chuck thought he also caught a glimpse of his brother's dreams. But where could Mooney go from here, Chuck wondered. Where?

CHAPTER 14

Union problems were probably the only difficulties Chuck hadn't encountered with the plastics factory. Mooney's union muscle man Joey Glimco would have had a hundred Teamsters lined up every day outside the factory had Mooney ordered it and Chuck could have shipped his product all day long—if only he'd had someplace to ship it to. But the truth was, there just weren't any customers interested in harebrained items like plastic bags. Chuck had dreaded telling Mooney what was coming, but when he warned his brother in the spring that the business might go under, Mooney hardly responded. "Win a few, lose a few," he commented offhandedly, shrugging his shoulders.

Reluctantly, in June of 1953, Chuck and his two partners filed for bankruptcy. And Chuck, who'd put up ten thousand dollars of his own money and struggled for months to make it work, was finally defeated.

Anne Marie stood by helplessly while Chuck twiddled

his thumbs through the summer. Out of work, he became moody—a growling tyrant. Mooney had promised him that a job would turn up, but as the weeks passed, he heard nothing from his brother.

What bothered Chuck most about this job situation was that deep down he knew if Mooney had wanted to give him a job, he could have. Like a fairy godmother, his brother could have simply waved his hand and solved all Chuck's problems—overnight, Mooney could have made sure Chuck was worth millions, could have set him up in Vegas or Cuba or some other glitzy spot. But it looked as if that wasn't in the cards, and Chuck sat up nights that summer trying to figure out if Mooney didn't think he could cut it or if he just didn't give a goddamned whether Chuck and his family starved to death.

Sometimes, when he felt the hurt most acutely, Chuck rationalized Mooney's lack of assistance by telling himself that his brother didn't realize how close to the edge he was financially, that he was too busy with more important things. But secretly, he knew the truth: Mooney didn't believe he had what it took to be in the Outfit. The realization was so deflating, Chuck found himself incapable of striking out on his own. If Mooney didn't believe he could cut it, why should anyone else?

Over the following weeks, he stubbornly refused to make his weekly visits to Mooney's Oak Park home. "I don't want him to think I need a handout," he insisted. But at last, his pride succumbed to desperation.

"Shit, I don't care what it is, Mooney," he said to the impassive face across the desk. "Just give me somethin' to do. I gotta work. I got a wife and kid to feed."

"Hey, relax. There's nothin' right now. But somethin' will break, and when it does, Christ Almighty, Chuck, you know I'll give you a call. In the meantime, let me help you out.'' Mooney opened his desk drawer and motioned around the desk with one slender diamond-ringed hand. "C'mon over here," he said, "I want you to see somethin'."

Chuck edged around the massive oak desk to Mooney's side. The open drawer revealed tightly bundled stacks of cash.

"See this?" Mooney pointed downward. "There's over half a million bucks here. And there's plenty more where that came from in a hundred bank accounts from the Bahamas to Switzerland." He looked up, his eyebrows knitted into a scowl. "So do you think you should worry about a few measly bucks? Do you?"

Sheepishly, Chuck shook his head and put his hands in his pockets. He didn't want Mooney to think he was being silly about it all. "No, I guess not," he said, and then feeling his pride surge up within him, he suddenly burst out, "But damn it, Mooney, this is your money, not mine." His hands were out of his pockets now and he was flailing them around. He shook his head. "Goddamn it, I'm not asking for a handout. I came over here to ask for a job."

Mooney remained calm and smiled. He casually lifted one bundle from the drawer and peeled off twenty bills. "Here, here's two thousand dollars," he said softly. "Now, go home and relax. When a job comes up, it's yours."

Chuck hesitated, but he didn't want to insult Mooney and, besides, his family needed the money. "Okay, I'll try to be patient," he said, taking the cash from Mooney's outstretched hand. "But I'm not very good at it."

Mooney laughed. "No kiddin'?"

Chuck didn't join him in his joke. "Hey, I'm serious here. Just remember, I don't want a free ride, I want a fuckin' job."

He left, dissatisfied with the outcome of the meeting but somewhat relieved. He hadn't really thought about what type of job Mooney might come up with, but the truth was, it didn't matter. He just wanted another chance to prove to Mooney he could do it. More than an income, more than anything he could think of, Chuck wanted to be a part of the Outfit, wanted his brother's respect.

When he didn't have a job by August, Chuck was beside himself. Each week, he saw Mooney and each week was the same. "Nothin' yet," Mooney would say, shaking his head.

Chuck's money ran out and once again he was desperate. For her part, Anne Marie was confused, unable to understand why Chuck couldn't go out and get another job, outside the Outfit. "If Mooney won't give you a job, then why should he mind if you find one yourself? After all, a man has to work," she said over and over. Chuck knew she didn't understand how much their lives were controlled by Mooney. It would never change, and he wasn't convinced he wanted it to. If he went out and got a regular job like other people . . . well, the truth was, that was out of the question. He had to have Mooney's permission to do that. And Mooney would never in a million years give him permission to leave the family. Besides, he had something to prove and he couldn't do that working for some sap in a factory. He had to work for Mooney.

"You can't have your cake and eat it," Chuck railed at Anne Marie. "If we want nice things"—he pointed around the house—"if we want nice clothes, a new car anytime we want one . . . if we want Mooney's confidence . . .

well, then we have to stay in line. We have to do what Mooney wants." He didn't think that's what she wanted to hear, but it was the truth. And he would hear of nothing else.

On a Thursday evening, Chuck went by Mooney's home again. This time, he was determined he wouldn't leave without a job.

"Goddamn it, Chuck, quit bustin' my balls. I don't have a fuckin' job for you right now," Mooney snapped.

Momentarily, Chuck recoiled, but he quickly decided to plunge ahead. "Well, then, Jesus Christ"—there was frustration in his tone—"what do you expect me to do about not bein' able to make a living? What?" He raised his hands heavenward. "Pray? Go play fuckin' pool with the guys? Or just sit around, starin' out the goddamned window? What?" Chuck's face turned flush, his jaw clenched, and his hands began to tremble—he felt himself losing control. Mooney, however, looked as calm and collected as ever. "Mooney, what the fuck am I supposed to do? What? Just fuckin' tell me," he pleaded, screaming the words. He'd never screamed at Mooney in his whole life.

"Okay, okay. Don't go fuckin' crazy," Mooney said, shaking his head. "Jesus . . . here . . ." He reached for the drawer.

Chuck saw his brother move for the bundles of cash and felt his blood pressure soar. "Don't even fuckin' think about it," he screamed. "I don't want one red cent."

Mooney pulled out a thick stack of bills and softly, almost seductively, said, "Hey, come on, it's the least I can do, for now. Come on take it . . . there's ten grand here." He held the money out. "Take this and go have a drink at the Armory and calm down."

Mooney's smile oozed like warm honey and Chuck felt it envelop him. He struggled against the temptation, against being bribed by his brother, and suddenly he was enraged; he wasn't going to be appeased or patronized.

Later he would say he didn't know what came over him—but he knew at the time he'd snapped. With one quick stroke, he knocked the money from Mooney's hand. "You can keep your goddamned money," he yelled. "I don't want one . . . do you hear me? Not one . . . goddamned motherfuckin' dime." Chuck leaned over to pick up the bundle and then threw it back on the desk. "Keep it," he said, and turned on his heel. "And fuck you."

"Fine then, fuck you," Mooney yelled back.

Chuck marched out of the house, slamming the door behind him. He drove around for a while to try to cool off. It was the first time he'd ever stood up to his brother like that. Now, not only was he mad at Mooney, he was furious with himself, as well. Mooney wouldn't stand for that kind of thing—thank God no one else had seen it all. His behavior had been inexcusable. He didn't know what had come over him. But there wasn't anyplace else to turn. If he didn't get a job, he thought he'd go crazy. Mooney obviously didn't think he had what it took. And he wasn't going to be one of the freeloaders his brother despised and lower Mooney's opinion of him further. If he couldn't work, then he wasn't asking him for money. No way.

When Chuck got home, he was still upset. He screamed and stormed through the house and finally left for the Armory.

Later that night, he waited until he was sure Anne Marie would be in bed asleep before going home. He'd tried to get drunk and even that hadn't worked; he was still sober and miserable. He lay awake, hating Mooney, thinking about all the times as a kid Mooney had kicked his ass, had held authority over him. At the same time, he couldn't deny that he loved Mooney—all his life, he'd only wanted to please him. He wanted to make him proud, wanted to be accepted as his equal. He thought he'd probably do anything to gain Mooney's acceptance. And worst of all, Mooney wouldn't even give him the chance.

Now that the other guys in the Outfit were on easy street, they all thought that since he was Mooney's brother, he, too, should be rolling in the dough. He didn't know how many invitations he and Anne had turned down for a night at the Chez Paree that summer—all because they couldn't afford it. Of course he didn't tell anybody that; he had an image to uphold. He'd die before he let anyone know that Mooney was dangling him on a fucking string.

Image was everything, and with that in mind, Chuck got up each morning over the following weeks and donned a suit and tie, just as if he was going to work. Anne Marie fixed him breakfast and coffee and he read the paper. Then he kissed her good-bye and got in the car. It was a strange charade and they didn't discuss it.

He wanted to stay on the grapevine, so he stumbled around town, dropping by the Armory lounge for a few drinks, lunching on what money he had at Fritzel's with the guys, pretending as if things couldn't be better. As each day passed, he hated himself more and felt increasingly alienated from Mooney—the only person in the entire world who really mattered.

By September, Anne Marie had had enough. She decided to take matters into her own hands, to go see Mooney herself. After Chuck left one morning, she packed up her three-year-old and drove over to Mooney's.

It was the first time Anne Marie had been across the

desk from Mooney. Their relationship had been cordial and friendly; he was the giver of expensive gifts and theater tickets. He was a man whom people respected and feared, loved and hated. She viewed him as a kindly, but unyielding, force in their lives. Now, sitting in front of him, she realized it would take all the courage she could muster even to speak. Always shy, she found herself awed in Mooney's presence.

Her black curls fell across her eyes as she lowered her head, collecting her thoughts. "Thank you for seeing me today, Mooney," she said in a soft, whispery voice. "I can't tell you how much I appreciate it"—she looked up to meet him squarely in the eye—"but I had to talk to you."

Mooney sat silent and she felt his eyes brush over her; the power he exuded ran through her like an electric current.

"About what?" he asked gently.

She cleared her throat and felt her heart skip. "About you and Chuck," she said with all the bravado she possessed.

He seemed to soften, the hard lines that traced his face blurred. He nodded and lit a cigar. "Go on."

"Well, Chuck . . . Chuck is so disappointed. All he wants to do is please you. I know that because ever since I met him when I was a little kid, well . . . he's idolized you. Your opinion is all that matters to him, Mooney. There isn't anything else. But Mooney, he's proud. And he won't come to you and ask for anything again. I know that. He won't. He doesn't want to lose your respect . . . because that's what he wants more than anything else in the world."

"I see," he said as he thoughtfully puffed on the cigar.

"I'm glad you do. I knew you would. The truth is, Chuck would kill me if he knew I'd come over to see you myself. But I had to. I love him and I hate to see you two like this. I want him to be happy. And he's not, because deep down he doesn't think he has your respect and confidence."

"I could sure tell that," Mooney replied, grinning.

"I was hoping you could *change* that." Her voice shook and tears filled her eyes.

"How?"

"By giving Chuck a job."

Bemused, Mooney shook his head and leaned forward. "You really love him, don't you?"

She nodded.

Mooney slouched back in his chair and exhaled. Spirals of cigar smoke enveloped him. In the shadow of the lamp, she thought he looked tired, like a man who'd been working too hard. After a moment, he sighed and said, "I'll find him somethin', Anne Marie." He sat up, flicked the ash from his cigar, and put his elbows on the desk. "You know, there're a couple of things I've been thinkin' of doin' anyway and I know he'd do a good job handlin' them for me." He smiled again and added, "I'll call him." He snuffed out his cigar and got up.

"Oh, that would be wonderful," she cried, clasping her hands together with delight.

As he came around the desk, she stood up.

"Listen," he said, putting his arm around her as he escorted her to the door, "everything will be just fine."

When he said that, there was an assurance in his voice, a soothing, hypnotic quality in the way his words flowed as he spoke. She looked up into his dark eyes. When he looked back, she felt as if he'd penetrated her soul, as if he could read her mind—and it made her uneasy. Almost instantly, she felt vulnerable, naked, stripped of any secrets she might have. She imagined Mooney had the same effect on other people. Yet there was something else, too. An amazing warmth. And just as quickly as she'd felt unsure, a sudden calm came over her. Just Mooney's voice, his gesture, and manner countered any fears or doubts she might have had. Paradoxically, she felt safe, totally safe. She was perplexed, like a deer that had been in the hunter's sights and then realized the hunter wasn't going to fire— but could have at any moment, if only he'd wanted.

She understood Mooney's power; somehow, he made people willing to be his prey. And it didn't matter what he did to them—they were just grateful that they could be in his world at all. He made you feel happy to be at his mercy. It was crazy and she felt dizzy from it all; she wanted to go.

"I'll take care of everything," he repeated. "Chuck'll get back to work and everything will be fine. In the meantime, take this," he said, handing her an envelope.

She averted his gaze and shook her head. "Oh no, Mooney, I can't take that. You'll have to give that to Chuck yourself. I can't take it. Thank you, but I just can't."

"Now, come on, put it aside for household expenses. . . . It can be just between us," he goaded.

"Oh, I've already done enough just coming over here on my own."

"All right. But for now, we'll keep our talk a secret."

"I probably should tell him . . . that wouldn't be right. But I don't want Chuck to think I got him the job."

"You didn't . . . I did. And I'll make sure he understands that.'' He walked her to the door. ''Don't stay away so long. It's nice to see a pretty face.''

Two days later, the phone rang. Chuck was going back to work.

Chuck didn't know what the job was, but it didn't matter to him anymore what it might entail; he'd decided over the past months that anything Mooney asked of him he would do. He hoped his brother wouldn't demand he cross over the line into a murky world of hits and muscle, but it was only a hope. He had to be realistic, he told himself; if he wanted to be with Mooney, he had to be like the rest of the guys. He had to offer his brother his unswerving, unquestionable loyalty. He had to be willing to do whatever Mooney asked of him. If he didn't, it was over. He felt he was at a crossroad in his life; he'd had enough time to consider what it meant to be outside the Outfit, to be cut off from Mooney, not to see him or talk to him. To be denied his approval and its benefits. Forget morals. Forget right and wrong. He'd come to the conclusion that he couldn't fathom living like that for the rest of his life; he wanted his piece of the pie and, whatever the price, he would pay it.

Mooney was standing in the backyard, practicing on his putting green when Chuck drove up. He waved.

''Let's have a seat and talk,'' Mooney offered.

They walked over to the patio, where Alva promptly appeared with iced tea.

''Hey, like I said on the phone, I got a job for you, Chuck. You're the best guy for it. You know the joint Willie Potatoes has been runnin' whores out of in Rosemont? The River Road Motel?''

''Yeah,'' Chuck said cautiously, hoping Mooney wasn't

going to ask him to work the prostitution rackets, but ready to swallow his reservations if that was what was required.

"Well, we're gonna turn it legitimate."

Chuck felt a wave of relief sweep over him.

"Yeah, no more whores," Mooney continued. "Willie's got to handle some shit with Tampa and New Orleans . . . and I don't want him messin' around with the place. You made the Boogie Woogie a real class joint and that's what I want this place to be. It's got a lounge . . . get it hoppin' . . . it's gonna have a restaurant, fifty-two rooms, a pool. Get it goin' like a normal motel. And then hire a manager to take care of the day-to-day shit. Maybe drop in an hour a day. I want you to be free to handle somethin' else at the same time. Salary's two hundred a week and I'll give you a five-grand bonus at the end of the year. Okay?"

"It sounds great, Mooney, great. When do you want me to start?"

"Tomorrow. Get it turned around. I want the place cleaned up . . . so clean, it squeaks."

"Hey, no problem. You know I always said you can count on me."

"I know. You think I forget anything? You said that when I sent you down to Cuba to see 'Mr. Meyer.' You handled that real nice. Well, that's what made me think of you for this other job. . . . I'm gonna have some regular deliveries and pickups."

"In Cuba?"

"No . . . not Cuba. Jesus, you sure as hell don't like Cuba, do you? Nope, not Cuba. It's a three-day swing. . . . You'd go every week. Wednesday, Thursday, Friday."

''To where?''

''Tampa, New Orleans, Vegas, and back to Chicago to me. I'm gettin' it all lined up and by the time you've got the motel on the right track . . . you can ease up and do a little plane hoppin'.''

Later, Chuck picked up from the grapevine that Willie Potatoes was working a deal for Mooney with New York. The guys said it was drugs out of Central America and Asia.

''Trafficante and Marcello have it all lined up,'' Chuckie Nicoletti told him. ''Lined up real nice. It goes mostly to New York and Costello and Gambino. But now that Mooney's got Tampa and New Orleans workin' real good with us, well, Chicago's cut in on everything that comes through down there. We already got the gambling partnerships with those guys. . . . We get a piece of Miami and Dallas . . . all over down south. Mooney is gonna be fuckin' king of the world before it's over with. King of the world.''

Once he got involved with the River Road Motel, Chuck launched a grueling around-the-clock vigil, determined to prove himself to Mooney once and for all. Willie Potatoes cleared out the whores and Chuck hired a housekeeping staff, brought in new entertainers for the lounge, and the place really began to shape up. More than once, he'd had to tell the Outfit guys, whom the place drew like flies, that the place was clean. ''Don't be bringing any whores or games in here. This place is gonna stay clean just the way Mooney wants it. *Capisce?*''

Nevertheless, the gang still hung out in the lounge and managed to bring in more than a few busty broads with peroxided hair for their afternoon trysts. As long as they weren't whores, but unpaid girlfriends, there wasn't much Chuck could say—after all, Mooney did that himself all the time.

Chuck couldn't get over Mooney's way with women. He could have any girl he wanted. It was every man's dream come true. The women Mooney brought in were all knockouts. Most were blondes. But he liked a redhead now and then. If they were whores, they were the best. If they were girls from the Chez Paree Adorables—the club's chorus girls—they were the prettiest and most voluptuous of the lot. The Adorables were the hottest item in town and guys from all over were knocking their doors down trying to make time. Mooney said Kirk Douglas, Dean Martin, Frank Sinatra—they all had a Chez Paree Adorable on the side. There wasn't much question about it, Mooney had it made.

The rest of the Outfit guys all liked the fact that the motel was located in the less tightly controlled Cook County. It meant they could rendezvous with a current mistress and draw little or no attention from the authorities. They all had a thing about being discreet, but some afternoons the place was like a turnstile. As long as they were consenting adults, Chuck turned his head. When he changed the name to the Thunderbolt in October, Nicoletti said kiddingly that he should have called it the Mistress Motel. No whores, just girlfriends—that was the rule. And it seemed to suit the guys just fine.

By Thanksgiving, Chuck had the motel running smoothly and, he asserted with pride to Mooney, "so clean, it squeaks."

The entire Giancana family was invited to Ange and Mooney's for Thanksgiving dinner that year. Chuck knew it was not an event to which Ange looked forward. His sisters—Josie, Antoinette, and Vicki—almost invariably ended up in an argument. And Antonio, who still could barely speak a word of English, was gruff and defensive about his continuing relationship with their Aunt Catherine. But nevertheless, Chuck imagined, as he pulled in the drive with Anne Marie and little Chuckie, that everyone would be on their best behavior for Thanksgiving dinner at Mooney's house.

The only thing that worried Chuck was the kids; he hoped his little boy would behave himself. Mooney was funny about kids—he really didn't know what to do with one. And he definitely didn't know how to play with them—or talk to them, for that matter. In all the years Chuck had known him, Mooney never had held or cuddled a child—not even his own daughters. Instead, he taunted and teased them, testing to see what they were made of. And in so doing, he came off as gruff and frightening. In fact, he seemed to get a kick out of scaring the smaller children.

This Thanksgiving would be no exception; the minute all of the children were present, Mooney took off his belt.

"What the hell do you kids think you're doin'?" he growled.

The four little boys froze in their Eton suits.

"Come with me. Right now," he snapped.

The children stood there, motionless. Chuck saw their chins begin to quiver.

Mooney raised his voice to a shrill hiss, "I said . . . now."

None of the parents intervened, afraid themselves to interfere with Mooney's little game. But mostly, it didn't even occur to them to object to Mooney's behavior; they never had before—ever.

The children sniveled and obeyed, corralled by Mooney into the living room like wild-eyed calves going to slaughter.

"You kids see this?" He feigned anger and waved his belt. "I'm gonna let you have it if you don't do what I tell you. You hear me?"

They nodded fearfully.

"Sit right here," he ordered, pointing to the sofa. "Right here. Don't you even move a muscle." He swung the belt against his silk trousers and it made an agonizing crack.

They burst into tears. "Please, no, Uncle Mooney, we'll be good. We promise," Chuckie begged. The rest nodded in silent agreement.

To their credit, Mooney said later, the children tried not to cry. But there was disappointment in his voice when he told Chuck, "I'm waitin' for somebody to bring in a little man . . . a kid with some guts. None of that crybaby shit. I'm waitin' to see that kid. When I do, I'll know we have a new generation that can handle things after we're gone. I'm waitin'."

The Thunderbolt started making a profit in December. Mooney and the guys rolled in for a few drinks at the end of the day. They all sat around a table telling jokes and inventing stories about broads—Chuck believed only about half of what he heard. One evening, Needles came in with another guy from the old neighborhood, Nicky Visco. He was carrying the first issue of *Playboy* magazine.

"Hey guys, get over here and feast your eyes on some real fine pussy," Needles called out, pointing to the magazine's centerfold of Marilyn Monroe.

They all gathered around to see the scandalous maga-

zine—Willie Potatoes, Fifi, Chuckie Nicoletti, and even
Mooney came over to get a look at the magazine that was
supposed to be the most daring, racy thing ever to hit
American newsstands.

"She can cock my joint, all right," Nicoletti commented.

"Yeah, you got that right. Look at that mouth . . . bet
she gives good head," Willie said, laughing.

"Hell, yes, she does. I'd like to give it to her," said
Needles.

"Only in your dreams," Mooney taunted. Chuck could
tell he was in an unusually good mood.

"Oh, so you got an in we don't know about?" Nicoletti
teased.

They all broke up at the pun.

"I might," Mooney said, smiling.

"Hey, if anybody nails this broad, it'll be Mooney,"
Needles spoke up.

"Well, he already knows her," Nicoletti said. "Besides, if the Outfit can get Sinatra a part in *From Here to
Eternity* . . . anything's possible."

They all laughed.

"Hey, we just protect our investments," Mooney retorted, grinning.

"Yeah, what about this one, huh?" Fifi cracked.

"I promise to let you all know when I fuck her. She's
on my list, right after Mamie Eisenhower," Mooney said.

They roared at that one.

Mooney picked up the magazine and took a hard look
at the voluptuous blonde staring invitingly back at him.
"Yeah, I'll fuck her," he said, sneering, and threw the
magazine down. "So what else is new?"

In February of the following year, Anne Marie announced they were expecting another child in October. Chuck recalled what Mooney had said on Thanksgiving; he secretly hoped they would have a boy and found himself daydreaming about walking the kid in to Mooney and saying, "Here, here he is, the one you've been waitin' for." He knew it was a crazy fantasy, but somehow he believed that if his son measured up to Mooney's test, he'd finally measure up, too.

The winter of 1954 was a cold one, at least that's what everybody told Chuck, but he was too busy to notice. He was at the motel from seven-thirty in the morning until right before five-thirty, when Anne Marie served dinner. After dinner, he'd do chores around the house until nine and then rush back to the motel to oversee the lounge. By 3:00 A.M., he was back home to catch a few hours of sleep. It was a grueling routine that left little time for much else, but he was happier than he'd ever been in his life.

Chuck's efforts were rewarded by the fact that he saw Mooney practically every day; his brother dropped by for a drink and they'd shoot the breeze for hours. At noon, Chuck never knew which members of the old gang would show up for lunch: Willie Potatoes, Paul Ricca, Chuck and Butch English, Rocky Potenza, Needles Gianola, Murray Humphreys, Tony Accardo, Joey Glimco, Frank Ferraro, Milwaukee Phil, Joe Amato, Eddie Vogel, Chuckie Nicoletti, Ross Prio, Gussie Alex, Fifi Buccieri.

There were a few new faces as well, guys who were starting to move up in the ranks: Johnny Matessa, Dave Yaras, Lenny Patrick, Butch Blasi, Ralph Pierce. Every day at noon, the joint was jumping; Chuck thought it was the best part of the job.

Chuck usually joined the group for a corned beef sandwich or hot roast beef and a beer. Instead of talking, he preferred to sit back and listen or just watch Mooney. Mostly, Mooney sat back and watched the other men. He still was sizing them up, just as he always had, trying to decide whether a guy could be trusted, whether he was right for a job.

The other thing Chuck found especially interesting was the other guys' reactions to Mooney. It reminded him of a game of Simon Says. He started to think that if Mooney said, "Roll over," they would. His brother was like a god. Even an elder statesman like Paul Ricca now deferred to Mooney, asking what Mooney thought about this or that. "Find out what Mooney thinks," Paul advised one of the younger men. It was a landmark realization for Chuck; Mooney's authority was now undeniable. His admiration for his brother grew with each passing day.

In late March, Mooney came by for lunch, but rather than sitting down, he waved Chuck toward the motel office. "Let's talk," he said.

Mooney took the chair behind the desk. It was stacked with papers and he leafed through them as though he was looking for something. Finally in exasperation, he pushed the papers aside and said, "Jesus, where's the fuckin' ashtray? What the hell is all this shit? Paperwork?"

"Yeah, paperwork. Here's one. . . ." Chuck sighed and handed Mooney a brass ashtray, then continued. "I guess if you have a business, you gotta do this fuckin' shit. There're mountains of it and it's never done. I'm doin' paperwork 'til three o'clock in the morning."

"Well, that's what I want to talk to you about . . . you're gettin' too fuckin' busy. Shit, make the manager do this crap. You're supposed to drop in for an hour for lunch . . . not live here. Besides, I got that job goin'."

"You mean the deliveries?" Chuck asked; he'd all but forgotten about the other job Mooney had mentioned.

"Yeah. I got the whole thing worked out. Goddamn it, Chuck, I think I'm gonna have to pat myself on the back for this one. I've finally done it." It was unusual for Mooney to be so high; he was acting like a schoolboy, grinning like the proverbial cat who swallowed the canary.

Chuck knew Mooney wanted him to ask, so he did. "So what did you do? You're pretty happy with yourself."

"Well," Mooney said proudly, "I should be . . . I've got all ins and no outs, that's what."

"*All* ins and no outs?"

"Uh-huh. Well, maybe not *all* my way, but the gravy is mine. In Tampa, I got Santo Junior takin' over. I talked to Lansky and the rest of the Commission. He'll be boss now. I got Marcello workin' with me . . . just me and Costello . . . Chicago's the only city Marcello's gonna let into Texas unless he talks to me first. And there's some rich motherfuckers down in the Lone Star State, let me tell you . . . big oilmen who can't have enough . . . always lookin' for more. And have I got a few deals for them." He chuckled. "I got Murray goin' around right now workin' the politicians down there."

"So what about Vegas?"

"Hey, let me finish, will you? I'm gettin' to Vegas."

"Okay, okay." Chuck lifted both hands, palms facing Mooney, in mock retreat.

"Vegas is set. I mean set. I got everything covered from Vegas to Los Angeles. I figure the other key cities are Tampa and New Orleans; they're good low-profile entry points for any imports or exports we might have. I'll send out our men to cover everything in between . . . and then, it's all as good as mine."

"And you got your points in Vegas," Chuck said. It was a rhetorical statement. He knew the Outfit had penetrated the Flamingo, Thunderbird, and Desert Inn—as well as the Sands. Mooney had confided previously that his take was well over 3 million a year. But knowing the answer to his question didn't lessen Chuck's interest in Mooney's reply.

"Yeah and I'm gonna give Santo and Marcello a little gift each month from the skim there to keep 'em happy. It's smart business. But there's another guy. Remember the Spruce Goose?

"Howard Hughes. Yeah, I remember him from the papers."

"Roselli's been talkin' with him. He's one rich cocksucker. He knows how to play the game. . . . He says he's got Vice President Nixon eatin' out of his hand. Military contracts, shit . . . the guy's got Washington all paid off. And he knows how to make a buck. He likes Vegas . . . likes the tables. I got a feelin' we can work together real nice."

"This is gettin' to be pretty big stuff, Mooney. What about the coppers? The IRS? You're talkin' about transportin' a lot of dough. Won't so much activity bring them down on the whole operation?"

"Fuck them. . . . You know Banister here, the Chicago FBI guy? And Bob Maheu? We know those guys . . . real well. Hughes knows all the feds. Murray Humphreys does, too. Roselli knows the government guys who work over in Asia. . . . We've been workin' with them in the Philippines for years now. Over the years, we've helped Banister and Maheu on a few deals, tippin' them off to car thieves and musclin' their favorite enemy"—Mooney laughed— "Commies." He leaned forward and lowered his voice,

"The Outfit's gonna work with the FBI stateside, and outside of the country with the CIA. You can be sure they'll be on our side."

"So what you need then is a good courier?"

"Exactly."

"Well, Mooney, you think this place would go to hell?" The last thing Chuck wanted was for the motel to fail.

Mooney studied him for a moment. "I doubt it. But you're doin' a good job here." He looked around the room and absentmindedly leafed through the mounds of papers on the desk. "But it's good money, Chuck. Damn good money. Let's talk more about it tomorrow."

That night, Chuck lay awake thinking about the opportunity Mooney had offered. It did sound great—but he was afraid the motel might fold if he didn't keep a tight rein on the business. He couldn't stand letting Mooney down again. If the motel folded, he'd be out on the street again, without a steady job. The motel was a sure thing.

On the other hand, Mooney's couriers made big money. Five, ten thousand a job. One guy he knew was going back and forth to New York and clearing more than that each trip, and it was pretty simple, too. According to Mooney, the courier delivered diamonds and jewelry to George Unger, the fence, in exchange for cash. Nice and neat. Nothing to it really. For his trouble, the courier was making over a hundred thousand a year. Of course, if the guy ever got caught with all that stolen merchandise, he'd be sent up the river forever.

Using this same routine for Tampa, New Orleans, and Vegas would probably work—if anybody could pull it off, Mooney had the connections to do it, but it was a lot bigger than the New York deal. Chuck thought it might be too big. The money would be even greater—his mind raced, thinking about making a couple hundred thousand a year—but so was the risk.

He looked over at Anne Marie, sleeping next to him, and quietly got out of bed. He lit a cigar and ventured out into the comforting stillness of the living room.

Mooney had never failed at anything. Chuck couldn't think of a thing, not one. But this national deal—and with Asia and Cuba and God knows what on top of it—Chuck could hardly conceive of such an operation. He even wondered whether Mooney was in over his head, but he quickly dismissed that as counter to everything he knew about his brother. He could only assume that the deals overseas were related to drugs and gambling, maybe politics, maybe some secret spy shit.

One thing that troubled him was that Mooney actually thought he could control the United States government, actually work with the guys like undercover partners. Chuck thought Mooney was either crazy or he was really on to something. And at four o'clock in the morning, Chuck was too foggy-headed to know which. He turned it over again and again in his mind and finally came to the only logical conclusion: Mooney wasn't crazy; he had a tiger by the tail. And he had to know a lot more than he was telling. God knows, he could be vague sometimes. The Outfit, Howard Hughes, Vice President Nixon, the FBI, secret agents—it all sounded like some fucking spy story. And Chuck had a feeling the stakes were high, that a guy could pay with his life in a deal like this.

He looked around the darkened room. He and Babe were really beginning to get on their feet. So far, he'd managed to make a good living with Mooney without crossing the line; recently, he'd even come to believe it was possible. But if he agreed to take on this other job, he felt it would be like cliff diving—there was no telling how deep he'd get in and no telling what was beneath the surface. He could be jeopardizing everything: his wife, his family—his life. "If you do crime, you gotta be ready to do time," Mooney used to bark at him as a little punk. Was a couple hundred grand worth it? He thought for a while about what it would mean to lose everything he had with his little Babe. They had one little boy and a baby on the way. He lit another cigar.

Chuck was still sitting up when the sun spilled through the lace curtains and the birds began to sing outside the window.

"What on earth, Chuck?" Anne Marie exclaimed when she saw him sitting bleary-eyed in the chair.

He thought she always looked so beautiful first thing in the morning, like a new rosebud, all fresh and pink.

She tied her terry-cloth robe and smiled sympathetically. "You want a cup of coffee?"

He held one up. "Already made it."

"My God, you look exhausted . . . what's wrong?" She sat down on the French provincial sofa across from him and, ready to listen, folded her hands in her lap expectantly.

But he'd already made up his mind that he wouldn't discuss this with her; what she didn't know wouldn't hurt her—that was a rule everybody learned to live by. You didn't tell your wife anything, ever.

"Nothin', I just couldn't sleep."

"Chuck, look who you're talking to. . . . I find that hard to believe. Is everything all right at the motel? Are you and Mooney all right?"

"Yeah, the motel's fine . . . Mooney's fine. Hey, everything's fine. Okay?'' Irritation was creeping into his voice. He wasn't in the mood to be interrogated or pushed. ''Like I said, everything's fine.''

She knew him pretty well, Chuck thought. There wasn't much that would leave him sleepless except Mooney. It had always been like that—from the time he used to lie awake thinking about Mooney's escapades as a kid.

Anne Marie suddenly giggled and stood up. ''I'm starving,'' she said, placing one delicate hand on her rounded stomach. ''And you know what?''

''What?''

''This baby is hungry, too. . . . Are you? You want breakfast? Maybe you'll feel better.''

He took one look at her smiling down at him and wondered whether he could go through with it; it meant risking everything. In the final analysis, that was what Mooney was asking him to do. Still, as much as he loved Anne Marie, as much as he loved his kid and the one on the way, he knew what his decision would be. He would do whatever Mooney asked. Sighing, he got up to get ready for work.

Chuck was caught off guard when Mooney sat down in the motel office later that morning and said, ''I got another guy to handle that job.''

''You did?'' Chuck's heart sank—he hadn't been totally convinced he wanted the job, but not getting it was worse. Mooney must have thought he couldn't handle it; his decision to use someone else could only mean that. He tried his best not to show his disappointment and said, ''Well good, I'm sure it'll go fine with somebody else, right? Who'd you get?''

"Father Cash. He's perfect . . . nobody'll ever think twice about a priest carryin' dough."

"A priest? Isn't this pretty big for a priest?"

"Pretty big? Pretty big? Chuck, you have no idea. Chicago's gonna go international in a big way. Man oh man. Pretty big? I started thinkin' about how the Church has its fingers in all the same pies"—he laughed—"or should I say, countries, that we do. The Philippines, Mexico, all over the world—"

"Except the Arabs," Chuck interrupted.

"Hey, I got this all handled, includin' the Arabs. Listen, the U.S. government is gonna help us and we're gonna help them."

"Help how? And besides, even if they do help . . . how can you be sure of that?"

His brother sighed and reached his hand into his trouser pocket, emerging with a small coin. He held it up between two fingers and said, "See this?"

"Yeah."

"Here, take a good look." He tossed it across the desk.

Chuck caught the coin and instantly realized it was old, ancient in fact. Mooney was always buying antiquities. He'd become quite a connoisseur of rare books, Dresden porcelain, and the like, so Chuck was only mildly intrigued. "Yeah, what's this supposed to be?"

"It's an old Roman coin, Chuck."

Chuck fingered the coin, turning it over again and again, and then tossed it back to his brother. "That's real nice, Mooney, but what the hell does it have to do with what we're talkin' about?"

Mooney leaned forward. "Look, this is one of the Roman gods. This one has two faces . . . two sides. That's what we are, the Outfit and the CIA . . . two sides of the same coin. Sometimes our government can't do shit on the up-and-up. Sometimes they need a little trouble somewhere or maybe they need some bastard taken care of. . . . Jesus, they can't get caught doin' shit like that. What if people found out? But we can. Guns, a hit, muscle . . . whatever dirty work needs to be done. We're on the same side, we're workin' for the same things . . . we just look different. So . . . we're two sides of the same coin. Right now we're workin' on Asia, Iran, and Latin America. Someday, Chuck, we'll be partners on everything. If you think we had Truman . . . let me tell you . . . we got this deal sewn up. Ike, all he does is play golf.''

"So that's what you like about the guy," Chuck teased.

"Shit, he's a pigeon . . . it's Nixon that's got the power. He's the one with the backing of the big money, like Hughes and the guys in California and the oilmen in Texas. . . . Hump says Nixon's gonna call us if he needs a little hardball behind the scenes.''

"Really?"

"Really. From now on, you can call me Sam Giancana, civil servant.'' He chuckled with pleasure and leaned back in the chair, putting his feet up on the desk. "We've got it made, Chuck.''

"Maybe you should see if you can get a government pension?'' Chuck said, grinning.

"You think so?'' he replied, and they both laughed. "Yeah, I like that idea. . . . I'll have to check on that.'' Mooney stood up to leave. "I got an Adorable friend comin' over in a while. Same room all ready?''

"Yeah . . . it's all yours. But listen, would you do me a favor? Tell the other guys to stop usin' so many towels when they come over here . . . the laundry bill is through the roof. What the hell does a guy need five towels for, anyhow?''

Mooney smiled. "You really like workin' this place, don't you?''

"Yeah.''

"Well, you're doin' a good job. Don't worry about the other deal . . . you just take care of this joint." He handed him a roll of bills. "Here, go celebrate. And tell Anne Marie she'd better have a boy for me. Okay?''

"Okay.''

Over the next weeks, Chuck wrestled with his conflicting feelings about losing the other job. He had to admit it was nice being off the hook. The risk involved would have been more than he would have liked. But he couldn't help feeling that for some reason he hadn't cut it in Mooney's eyes. He wasn't sure what it was or what he had or hadn't done. But he was certain of one thing: His dream of ever becoming Mooney's equal was getting further and further away.

That spring, the government appeared to be moving in exactly the direction Mooney had indicated. There was a Latin American meeting in March about the communist threat in Guatemala. "We're gonna take care of that,'' Mooney said, tipping his scotch with a knowing smile.

In April, Ike made a speech about dominoes, comparing them to the tenuous political situation that existed in the Southeast Asian countries and saying that if the United States allowed even one country in Asia to fall to communism, the rest were sure to follow. Hearing that, Chuck jokingly asked Mooney whether he'd been playing golf with the President again.

"No, I don't have to," Mooney said with a bit of a swagger in his step. And then, suddenly serious, he remarked, "You don't believe that bullshit do you? I mean about communism? The CIA stirred up some shit to give us an excuse to go in and take over, that's all. People sure eat that up, though, don't they?"

"Well, there is such a thing as communism," Chuck retorted. "And Communists do want to take over the world. That's a fact."

"Watchin' your RCA again, huh?" Mooney cracked. "Wise up, will you? The United States wants to take over everything, too. And it's not to sell apple pies and flags to a bunch of fuckin' slant-eyed bastards or Mexicans, either. Our guys in charge don't give a fuck about the people in those countries; all they want is to line their pockets. Shit, I can be a millionaire just off the mess in Guatemala."

"Okay, then, so what do you know about Guatemala? Don't go bullshittin' me, now, just to make a fuckin' point. Okay?"

Mooney laughed. "You're gettin to be a regular doubtin' Thomas, aren't you? How fuckin' long have you known me? Huh? How long? I just know how the real world works, that's all." He grinned sheepishly. "Well, maybe I do have an inside track on a few things." He leaned forward and lowered his voice. "Our government wants an uprising in Guatemala . . . but they need guns for a rebellion. And we supply 'em out of our guys down south."

"Why don't they just get the army to do that?"

A mortified look crossed Mooney's face. "Because then everybody would know what they're plannin' . . . that's

why. This shit is top secret, Chuck. You hear what I'm
sayin'? *Top secret*.''

Chuck couldn't think of anything to say to that. He
didn't know where the hell it was all going, but he had to
believe this was all part of Mooney's plan. He was getting
it all wired. Whatever it was.

CHAPTER 15

There are some moments that hang forever suspended in time. Chuck thought the day of Angeline DeTolve Giancana's funeral was certainly one of those. Two weeks before, on April 10, 1954, she'd suffered a cerebral embolism while in Florida, and now the woman who'd introduced him to the finer things in life, to what was right and proper, lay cold and pale before him.

Swathed in a cherry red organza dress—they said the fashion designer Georgianna Jordan had been up all night personally hand-rolling and stitching its delicate layered hems—Ange reminded Chuck of a hothouse blossom that had closed its petals too soon.

Her death had been totally unexpected, although some said inevitable, because she'd suffered from rheumatic fever as a child and doctors had warned that her heart had been weakened by the illness. But for all practical purposes, as long as Chuck had known her, she'd lived her life normally—dancing, swimming, doing whatever her whims told her.

Years later, when people related stories of Ange's frailty and domestic suffering, Chuck would angrily dismiss them. On the contrary, he insisted, his sister-in-law had lived a charmed life, saved from the difficulties of housework and cooking, thanks to an endless string of maids, housekeepers, and cooks. She'd been graced with a lifestyle enjoyed only by the truly wealthy, albeit one that was, out of necessity, low-profile. Perhaps the only thing she hadn't been was loved.

But if asked, Chuck believed there wasn't a person present who wouldn't say with all sincerity that Mooney had treasured Ange more than any other woman. He had given her everything a woman could ask for and more—in her closets hung rows of furs; in her jewelry boxes rested hundreds of precious gems. She'd wanted for nothing because, Chuck thought, she'd settled for second best.

The tentacles of the thousands of glittering objects his brother had placed before her over the years, just like the diamond collar now sparkling around her throat, had slowly entwined her, choking out all youthful desire for romantic love, and left her satisfied with a Porthault linen as her bedmate. It had all worked out just as Mooney had planned. Except she had died.

He looked over at his brother's face; it was properly drawn and stoic. Even if Mooney wanted to cry, he wouldn't; there were too many men who now waited in his shadow, hoping for some sign of weakness. He would be anything but weak. But then, Chuck wondered, what was his brother feeling? Thinking? Had he loved Ange and just not been able to express it with anything other than material gifts? Or had she simply served as a necessary fixture, a dutiful and proper wife who was little more than one rung on the ladder of his goals? It was possible even Mooney didn't know the answer to that question.

Throughout their marriage, his brother had knocked Ange around if she got out of bounds, had romped with countless other women—all more physically beautiful than his wife. In truth, although he'd been discreet, she'd known about Mooney's philandering right from the beginning; she'd had a choice, although Chuck doubted she ever realized it. She could have left. A part of him wondered why anyone would leave such material wealth. But another part of him questioned the logic of such an existence. He had to believe Ange had resigned herself to a marriage of image and convenience—while Mooney did as he pleased. It was a trade-off. Usually, Chuck thought it was a fair one. But seeing her in death, he found himself wondering whether, despite all appearances of marital bliss and material prosperity, his sister-in-law hadn't lived a life as hollow as the priest's voice that echoed throughout St. Bernadine's Church at that very moment. And then, at only forty-three, that life was over.

The weeks following Ange's burial were solemn, and spring came and went without much notice. In his wife's memory, Mooney donated a marble and mahogany communion rail to the church and announced he was building a mausoleum. Out of respect, the guys maintained a somber facade in his presence, waiting for some cue that said things could return to normal.

It didn't take Mooney long to get back to work; there were too many deals to be cut, too many deals to be closed. In life, Ange hadn't curbed his cross-country travels, nor would she in death. To assure the freedom he needed to maintain his business, he turned over all household duties to Ange's sister Anna Tuminello and her daughter and husband, Marie and Jim Perno. By June, he'd detached himself completely from any familial obligation regarding his daughters, entrusting the Pernos to oversee their upbringing.

Doing so caused Mooney little regret; he'd all but given up on the rebellious nineteen-year-old Annette, who now, to his dismay, called herself Toni and wanted to be a movie star. He found her spoiled, confiding to Chuck, "I guess I gave her too much. She's selfish and sneaky. . . . She lies all the time. Really, she's an embarrassment, because I never know what she's gonna do or say." Bonnie and Francine, however, continued to be his obedient and loving daughters and, consequently, he rarely spoke of them at all. "Women and children should be seen and not heard," he'd often say. "That's what's right about Bonnie and Francine and wrong about Annette."

Just when things seemed to be returning to normal and Mooney was back in the swing of things, seventy-three-year-old Antonio suddenly died. And on July 27, Chuck found himself attending his father's funeral.

Like Ange's funeral, all the big guys were there and many came in from out of town to pay their respects. There were the assistants to the mayor; city councilmen and aldermen; state congressmen and senators. If anything, their presence demonstrated his brother's increasing national power; if Outfit guys didn't fly in, they sent flowers. Chuck thought it was quite a tribute to a man who'd risen up from poverty as the son of an immigrant street vendor. Respect—and demonstrating it—was a funny thing with Outfit guys. It was a code they lived by.

Mooney had announced he would be placing Antonio's remains in the mausoleum, still under construction. Chuck wondered whether this tribute was a concrete demonstration of Mooney's remorse—whether it was rooted in love. But out of respect, he didn't ask his brother.

In September, Chuck decided to drive by the cemetery and check on the mausoleum's progress. To his surprise, he found Mooney there, standing alone under a tree. In the bright sun of the late afternoon, the tombstones cast long shadows on the grass. His brother turned and shaded his eyes with one hand when he heard the car. Seeing that it was Chuck, he waved.

"Hey, we both must have been thinking about Pa, huh?" Chuck said. It was more a statement than a question.

"Yeah, I was . . . I guess . . ." Mooney's voice trailed off. "I wanted to see how this was comin' along." He pointed to the impressive granite structure. "Pretty nice, don't you think?"

"Yeah, beautiful. It's"—he searched for a word—"magnificent . . . really magnificent. You know, Ange and Pa would be so proud."

"Yeah, I guess they would." Chuck noticed that Mooney seemed distracted as he shook his head and then cupped his hands over his cigar to light it. A fleeting smile passed over his face. Then suddenly somber again, he sighed and stared out across the graves. "Ever notice how the sunlight and the shadows make a cemetery look like rows of piano keys?"

"Why, no. I guess I never did." Mooney's comment startled Chuck; he had no idea what his brother was talking about. He studied the contrast of dark and light that alternated between each row of tombstones and then nodded in agreement. "You know, you're right; they do, don't they?"

"Yeah, I noticed it when I first came out here. It's

funny, but when I did, well, I kinda realized somethin'." He paused and there was a mournful look in his eyes Chuck hadn't seen before. "It's all one big fuckin' game, Chuck. No matter what tune you play . . . this . . ." He motioned to the graves. "This is where you end up. Death . . . it's the great equalizer." He started to laugh. "It's almost funny, isn't it? Because in the end, nothin' really matters, after all. Not one fuckin' thing." He sighed and threw his cigar into the fresh dirt at his feet. "So you like the mausoleum?"

"Yeah."

"Me, too," he said, and without another word, he turned and walked to his car.

Chuck thought about his conversation with Mooney for several days. The last time he'd seen his brother so morose was when he was going to Joliet back in 1929. Certainly in the days after the funeral, Mooney'd put on a damned good show; to see him around the guys, you'd never have known there was anything wrong. But that day at the cemetery, Chuck thought he'd seen a lonely man. One who'd locked himself away from human emotion. Mooney was slowly becoming entombed by a living mausoleum of his own making.

Chuck believed death was a funny thing; right out of its shadow, life always creeps in. It was as if God didn't want people to dwell on their own mortality for very long—and to make sure they didn't, He always sent a new life. At least, that's how Chuck felt when their baby was born on October 28, 1954.

It was a boy and he thought he'd never been so excited in his life. He loved his other son, little Chuckie, with all his heart and soul, but there was something about the birth of this baby—maybe it was the timing—that was special.

He wasn't sure when he'd had the idea; perhaps it was when he'd been daydreaming about taking a kid in to Mooney and saying, "Here he is . . . this is the one you've been waiting for." But at some point over the past months, he'd decided he wanted to name the baby, if it was a boy, Samuel Mooney Giancana. It would be the ultimate tribute to his brother. And it might do more to lift Mooney's spirits than anything else.

There were only two problems with his idea. First, Anne Marie had long ago decided she wanted to name the baby Ricky. And second, Chuck knew he had to have Mooney's permission to do something so extraordinary.

He imagined Anne Marie would be more difficult to convince than Mooney. Mooney would be pleased, perhaps even genuinely thrilled, to have a male child named in his honor. Conversely, Anne Marie would be disappointed.

"Oh, Chuck," she said, sighing from her hospital bed. "Does Mooney have to be a part of our lives to the extent that we name our son after him? I wanted to name him Ricky . . . you've known that for months." She looked down at the gurgling pink-faced infant swaddled in her arms. Chuck sensed the bitterness in her voice. "Why? I don't think it's so important to name him after Mooney." Her dark eyes suddenly grew fierce. "And I don't want to. I really don't." She glared back at him. "Furthermore, I won't."

He sat down on the bed. "Please. It would mean so much to my brother. I know it would. And, Babe, it would mean so much to me. Please." He took her hand.

"I don't think so." She pulled her hand away. "I just don't want to, Chuck. No."

"Babe, I don't ask you for so much. Do I?" He tried

to fix her eyes in his. He wanted her to see, to understand why this meant so much to him.

"Well, this is asking too much. I won't do it. I won't have Mooney be a part of our lives like that. . . . He's already more important than anything else in the world to you. He already rules our lives as it is. And that's fine . . . I knew that when we got married. But no more. Please, no. No more. It's not fair."

"But you don't understand. Mooney doesn't have a boy to carry on his name. This would be so special. And an honor. We would be thanking him, too."

"Well, didn't I hear that some girl at the envelope factory had a boy by him? Why can't she name her baby after him?"

"Babe, stop it. . . . You know that can't happen. Listen to me, please, Babe. This is more important than anything I've ever asked. Please, I'm begging you now," he said, his voice tremulous. Tears filled his eyes. "Please."

She looked away and then down at the baby sleeping in her arms.

"Well, at least tell me you'll think about it," he pleaded.

She was silent. "All right. All right. I'll think about it . . . but that's all . . . I'm not promising anything. You understand?"

He was elated; she was weakening. "That's all I ask," he said, and kissed her.

Two days later, Chuck went by Mooney's house. In the basement kitchen, Mooney fried some sausages and green peppers for lunch and they sat down at the long carved oak table with their meal and a bottle of wine.

Chuck had waited anxiously for this moment and his words spilled out in breathless, rapid fire. "Mooney, I had a special reason for comin' over. . . . I've come to ask your permission for somethin'. Somethin' I hope you'll be pleased about.''

"Yeah? What's that?" Mooney set his glass down and gave Chuck his full attention.

"We want to name our new son after you . . . Samuel Mooney Giancana. It's our way of makin' a lasting tribute to you. A way to show our respect"—his voice grew soft as he continued—"and love for you." Chuck took a deep breath; he'd never said anything like that to Mooney before.

Mooney stared into his eyes for what felt like forever before speaking. "After me? A little kid named after me?"

Chuck thought he detected a mist come over Mooney's eyes. He held his breath, waiting for his brother's reply.

A broad smile spread across Mooney's face. "Of course, Chuck. Of course . . . I'm honored." He reached over to grasp Chuck's hand in his.

"No," Chuck corrected. "We are."

Mooney grinned and said, "Hey, you think he'll be the one?"

"The one?"

"Yeah, the kid I'm waitin' to see. The one who can measure up. The one who will go to college and be smarter than the rest of us assholes? You think?"

"Hell, maybe he'll be President," Chuck said, laughing.

Mooney laughed, too. "No, we want him to be the dog . . . not the tail. We want him to be in control."

"Yeah, you're right about that. You can be sure Anne Marie and I will do everything within our power to make certain this little boy grows up to make you proud . . . everything to make sure he honors your name."

"I know you will, Chuck . . . that's why I'm givin'

you my blessing. I trust you. Shit, you know what that means?''

Chuck nodded. ''I think so.''

''It means that there're not too many people I can trust. But you've never let me down.'' He lifted his wineglass. ''Here's to the future . . . the future of Sam Giancana . . . my godson. *Salud*.''

''*Salud* . . . and here's to my son's godfather.'' Chuck raised his glass. ''The most powerful man the Outfit has ever known.''

''I'll drink to that,'' Mooney said, filling their glasses again.

Chuck left his brother's home that day happier than he'd ever been in his life; his son would make Mooney proud someday.

They called the little boy Mooney from the start, and it didn't seem to take Anne Marie long to adjust to the idea. In fact, she now seemed proud that his brother had been so pleased.

It was a year of contrasts they wouldn't forget, and as it drew to a close, Chuck often thought of the tombstones, Mooney's ''piano keys,'' the light and dark. In Chuck's way of thinking, they'd come out into the light; he didn't think his brother was right about it not mattering which tune you played—it did matter. He hardly ever thought about the whistling man of his childhood anymore; his dreams were no longer haunted by the eerie tune or Mooney's face staring from within the crowd, his whispered ''*omertà*.'' Chuck had come to the conclusion that it wasn't death that was the equalizer, as Mooney had said; no, it was life. And he wanted to make sure they lived it to its fullest.

Mooney's thoughts were fixed on death, however, when he sent Chuckie Nicoletti and Milwaukee Phil to eliminate his last few local stumbling blocks to personal power in 1955: Charlie Cherry Nose Gioe, Frank Maritote, and Louis Greenburg. They'd been old-timers, Capone men, whose grumblings represented an affront to Mooney and his control. Others, like Louis Campagna, Charlie Fischetti, Jake Guzik, Claude Maddox, and Sam Golf bag Hunt were aging rapidly or were by now largely impotent members of the Outfit.

By mid-1955, Tony Accardo and Paul Ricca were being scrutinized by the IRS. Accardo, in particular, was nervous and anxious to drop out of sight. Just as the Browne-Bioff scandal had been a godsend to Mooney more than a decade earlier—resulting in the imprisonment of his superiors and freeing his way to power—now the heat on Accardo and Ricca gave him the last nudge he needed to assume absolute control. Accardo stepped aside and, at a private Outfit gathering held at the Tam O'Shanter Country Club in north Chicago, Mooney was formally made boss of Chicago's Outfit.

In November, Chuck heard that Marshall Caifano, still working Las Vegas, had stumbled across a name from the past: Willie Bioff.

Since turning on his friends during the notorious Browne-Bioff case in 1941, an act that led to many of Chicago's top mobsters being convicted and imprisoned, Bioff had fled to Phoenix and lived under the name William Nelson. He'd become close friends with Republican Barry Goldwater, supporting Goldwater's campaign and jaunting around the country in the senator's private plane. In 1952, perhaps in a fit of overconfidence, he'd taken a job at the

Las Vegas Riviera under its manager, Gus Greenbaum. Once in town, it didn't take Marshall Caifano long to spot the traitor—the Riviera was backed by Chicago.

At the news of Caifano's discovery, Mooney reverted to the tried and true. On November 4, 1955, Bioff turned the key in the ignition of his truck and was scattered like so many leaves in the wind. The explosion was heard for miles.

It was typical Chicago, typical Mooney. Bioff had probably grown tired of the day-in, day-out fear and lost his edge. That's the way it always happened; just when a guy let his guard down, the hammer would fall.

By 1956, Mooney was publicly known as "the man" in Chicago—and Chuck's admiration for his brother's power, savvy, and style grew. The Outfit was rapidly expanding its geographic territory under Mooney's iron fist to include towns, both large and small, scattered throughout the nation's midsection. Communities as seemingly diverse and inconsequential as Paducah, Kentucky, and Ames, Iowa—and hundreds in between—now had something in common: They all felt the force of Chicago, all had one of Mooney's lieutenants in their midst, running games and whores. In every instance, the lion's share went back to Mooney; if it didn't, the sleepy little towns were awakened to Chicago's presence by the stench of decaying flesh on one of their deserted country roads.

Over thousands of miles, Mooney Giancana—or Sam, as he was being respectfully called more and more—held the fate of two-bit hustlers, whores, bookies, and loan sharks in his hand. And anybody who was anybody knew it.

The sheer expanse of territory he controlled gave him

the instant respect of the Commission, and it was this power that Joe Kennedy was counting on when he instructed Chicago's Mayor Daley, who owed Kennedy several favors, to "contact Sam Giancana" in May of 1956.

Kennedy was at the end of his rope; he'd erred in judgment, Daley relayed to Mooney, and now he needed help. Could they meet on the East Coast? To that question, Mooney responded with a resounding no. If Joe Kennedy wanted to talk, he'd have to come to Chicago. After all, Mooney protested, Kennedy had been conducting business in Chicago for years; he'd owned the Merchandise Mart since 1945 and maintained an office in the city. If there was a meeting, it would be in Chicago or not at all.

In Chicago, three days later, he met with "old man Kennedy" in a suite at the Ambassador East.

The meeting with Joe Kennedy intrigued Mooney for several reasons. Although most closely tied to Costello and the New York gang, Kennedy was no stranger to Chicago. Mooney had known the scheming Irish bootlegger for over twenty-five years, a relationship that hailed back to the days of Diamond Joe Esposito and Mooney's sugar runs to Boston during Prohibition's heyday. Nor had he forgotten the scrape Kennedy had had with Detroit's Purple gang; Chicago had bailed the arrogant mick's ass out of a sure hit back then.

Kennedy's ties to the underworld intersected at a hundred points. Besides making a fortune in bootlegging, Kennedy had made a financial killing in Hollywood in the twenties—with the help of persuasive behind-the-scenes New York and Chicago muscle. When Prohibition came to a close, as part of a national agreement between the various bootleggers, Kennedy held on to three of the most lucrative booze distributorships in the country—Gordon's gin, Dewar's, and Haig & Haig—through his company Somerset Imports.

It was also no secret, according to Mooney, that Joe Kennedy—along with such industrialists as General Motors's founder William Crapo Durant, and John David Rockefeller, Jr.—had been given prior knowledge of the coming stock market crash in 1929. "In fact," Mooney told Chuck, "they *made* it happen. They figured out how they could get even richer. Shit, old man Kennedy made over a million bucks sellin' the market short before it fell. They manipulated the whole fuckin' thing."

The thirties were good to Kennedy. Mooney said Joe used the leverage gained from obtaining campaign contributions for FDR—one hundred thousand dollars from Chicago and New York alone—to win an appointment from Roosevelt as chairman of the Securities and Exchange Commission. And four years later, in 1938, FDR gave him the coveted ambassadorship to England in exchange for a similar amount.

According to Mooney, as the forties gave way to the fifties, Kennedy tried to distance himself from his old cronies by selling Somerset Imports and his interest in the racetrack at Hialeah. Initially, Mooney said, that had been fine. "We liked it that way. He was a guy on the inside and he owed us big. We didn't care if he wanted to play high-and-mighty . . . as long as we could work with the guy . . . because if there ever was a crook, it's Joe Kennedy."

Joe had called on Mooney once before, regarding a distasteful little problem his son Jack had gotten into. A marriage needed to be annulled and Joe didn't want any publicity—in fact, not only did he want the marriage annulled, he also wanted any record of it completely removed from all legal documents. Once this was accomplished, Jack—his slate clean once more—could get on with his father's political agenda.

The job required discretion and a man who knew how to get things done. Mooney directed Johnny Roselli to handle the legalities for Kennedy, and that was the end of that.

Most recently, Mooney's friend and longtime Kennedy mentor Frank Costello had had a major falling-out with the Irishman. The rupture had been building due to Joe's increasingly fierce reluctance to return favors to his former pals. Costello rightfully believed the Mob had helped make Kennedy a rich and powerful man, and now when he'd called in a marker, the Irish bastard had not only balked, he'd ignored him. It was easy to understand why there was a contract out on Joe Kennedy.

Surveying the gnarled face of the aging bootlegger, which was how Chuck's brother insisted on describing Joe Kennedy, Mooney felt a twinge of admiration. The guy was taking his life into his hands coming to Chicago like this; he couldn't be sure Mooney wouldn't make good Costello's contract. But here he was.

Mooney looked distractedly around the suite. He'd take his time, make the guy sweat a little. He finally lit a cigar and met Joe's eyes. "So, what can I do for you, Joe?" He tapped his cigar on the ashtray.

"I need your help."

"My help?" He placed one hand over his heart in mock innocence. "Why *my* help?"

Kennedy cleared his throat. Mooney knew it was tough

for the old bird to come crawling to Chicago, and he watched with some pleasure as the man's hands twisted in his lap; they were the only outward sign of his anxiety.

"Sam, I know you're close with Frank Costello . . . and I have a problem . . . a misunderstanding, really, with him."

Still playing naïve, Mooney replied, "What kind of problem?"

"Well, there's a misunderstanding between Costello and me concerning some property. It's gotten blown all out of proportion."

"Misunderstanding?" Mooney raised one eyebrow.

"Yeah, you see, he wants me to be the front man on a piece of property and—"

Mooney cut him off. "Well, can't you do that?"

Kennedy's hands clenched into fists and, suddenly defensive, he retorted indignantly, "Look, I'm in a sensitive position given my son's political career. You understand?"

"You owe Costello, don't you?"

"Hell no," Kennedy snapped.

Mooney's eyes narrowed and a scowl crossed his face. He waited to speak, puffing on his cigar for a moment. "Hell no?" He leaned forward. "Joe, what exactly does that mean, 'Hell no'?" He shook his head. He wanted to laugh at the man's arrogance but didn't. "You made money with Costello, didn't you?"

Kennedy sat upright in his chair and said sarcastically, "Hey, Sam . . . I was there at the beginning. They rode my coattails."

"Yeah, and I know whose coattail you rode." Mooney chuckled at the sheer audacity of Kennedy's statement.

"Well, anyway," Kennedy continued, his hands now

twisting in his lap again, "I haven't talked to him, hoping he would go away."

Mooney laughed outright. "Go away? You ignored the man?"

"Hey, like I said . . . I can't afford the association right now. And my son Jack can't afford the association right now, either."

"That's an insult, Joe." Mooney stood up and stared down at the man. Kennedy made a move to stand. "Sit down," Mooney barked. "What the fuck were you thinkin'? Huh? You've insulted Frank Costello. How do you think he's gonna react?"

"I already know. He has a contract out on me."

"Well, what makes you think I could do anything about it? Or for that matter . . . would want to?" He glared down at the Irishman.

Kennedy's demeanor softened. "Hey, Sam. Everybody knows you're the power outside New York. You're the only one who can get Costello off my back. He doesn't understand . . . not at all." He shook his head.

"And how is that?"

"Well, my son Jack is moving up in politics. . . . I'm hoping he'll be President someday. Now, I can't jeopardize that, can I?" He looked up at Mooney and shrugged his shoulders. "Can I?"

"I noticed your kid's been makin' quite a name for himself." Mooney turned to look out the window.

"He has." Kennedy rose from his chair and walked across the room to Mooney's side. "He has . . . and he'll continue to . . . as long as some ugly skeleton doesn't pop out of a closet. That, my friend, would be political suicide."

Mooney spun around. "So what do you want me to do about it?"

"Talk to Frank . . . make him understand. I'm a marked man if you don't get this contract called off." He placed one bony hand on Mooney's shoulder and lowered his voice to a nasally whisper. "But if I live . . . I can help my son get to the White House. Isn't that what we've all wanted all along? A guy on the inside?"

Mooney turned his back to Kennedy to face the window once again. "So let's assume I talk to Frank. . . . I see no benefit to Chicago, here. I've heard nothing today that leads me to think that . . . that you can promise me anything in return for my assistance."

"I can. And I will. You help me now, Sam, and I'll see to it that Chicago . . . that you . . . can sit in the goddamned Oval Office if you want. That you'll have the President's ear. But I just need time." There was an urgency in his tone. "I get pushed and I don't think my son has the experience, or the contacts, to see him through a presidential race. Do you understand now why I want you to talk to Costello?"

Mooney turned to look him square in the eye. "Let me see what I can do. But I want your word that the day your son is elected . . . that's the day that—"

Kennedy interrupted: "That Sam Giancana is elected, too. He'll be your man. I swear to that. My son . . . the President of the United States . . . will owe you his father's life. He won't refuse you, ever. You have my word."

That afternoon at the Thunderbolt Motel, a fan on the bar whirred in the background as Mooney recounted the story to Chuck. It was an unusually warm day and beads of perspiration glistened among the lines, slowly deepening with time, on Mooney's tanned face.

Certainly the fact that Joe's son Jack was now in his second term as senator hadn't escaped Mooney; he was being groomed for the White House. And the prospect of having such power—a man so tied to him in the Oval Office—was a temptation greater than anything he'd ever experienced. He told Chuck they'd play it safe in 1956 right up to the end—they'd play both sides, make contributions to each candidate, and then he'd simply sit back and wait.

He broke into a broad smile when he'd finished. "Hey, give me a Gordon's on the rocks," he cried to the bartender from his perch on the stool next to Chuck.

"Gordon's? Since when did you start drinkin' gin?"

Mooney picked up the glass and took a sip, then smacked his lips dramatically. "Right now, that's when." He grinned. "From now on when I have a gin, it's Gordon's . . . to remind me that Joe Kennedy will sell anything to save his own skin. His liquor business, the Senate, the presidency . . . the White House . . ." He lifted the glass and tipped it toward Chuck. "Even his own son."

That night, Mooney put in a call to New York. The contract was off on Joe Kennedy.

CHAPTER 16

I'm a very patient man," Mooney said, smiling. He laid the newspaper, dated November 3, 1956, down on the bar. "Besides, right now it's all the same . . . Nixon's been good to us." He shrugged his shoulders. "Shit, there're already rumors goin' around that it'll be Jack Kennedy versus Nixon in sixty. We can't lose with two candidates for President like that." He sipped his coffee and looked over the cup's rim, eyes twinkling. "Or should I say, I can't lose?"

Mooney was unconcerned in early December when another of Joe Kennedy's kids, Bobby, visited Chicago for a little snooping into labor racketeering. But, as chief counsel to the Senate Select Committee on Improper Activities in the Labor or Management Field, the thirty-one-year-old left the Midwest having reached a disturbing conclusion: Corruption and organized crime were rampant among the nation's labor unions, particularly within the Teamsters. And with that in mind, Bobby Kennedy vowed to bear down on Teamsters International president Dave Beck, Detroit's Jimmy Hoffa, and Chicago's Joey Glimco.

"Old man Kennedy'll set him straight," Mooney said, sneering. "This country's got bigger problems than labor unions. He should be down in Alabama doin' somethin' about Martin Luther King and all the trouble he's stirrin' up. Marcello tells me King's a Communist . . . wants the colored to take over the whole fuckin' country. Bobby better get his little East Coast ass down south if he wants to do somethin' useful."

Inexplicably for a man who was counting on the labor vote for the 1960 race, Joe Kennedy didn't deter his ambitious son. And on January 30, 1957, at Bobby Kennedy's recommendation and urging, the McClellan committee was formed.

The word back to Chicago through Murray Humphreys was, "Don't worry . . . Joe Kennedy promises he has everything under control." Taking Kennedy at his word, Mooney went about conducting business as usual, traveling to inspect his interests in Florida, Cuba, Central America, and Las Vegas.

Since taking over the motel, Chuck's life had swung into high gear. He'd bought a six-flat apartment building in Berwyn, and purchased a lot in Inverness, an elite suburb of Barrington, on which he planned to build a sprawling three-bedroom home. He drove a snazzy little red 1957 T-bird, which sat next to the family's luxurious black Oldsmobile, took his beautiful dark-eyed wife on weekly whirlwinds of Chicago's downtown nightclubs, and wintered in Miami at the Fontainebleau.

Unfortunately, the rewards that came with being a Giancana were often overshadowed by Mooney's snarling temper or icy aloofness; Chuck still couldn't predict his brother, even after all these years. In the afternoon, Mooney might drop by the Thunderbolt Motel sporting his legendary "tight shoes" and grumpily order a drink—and by nightfall, he might be on Chuck's doorstep in Berwyn holding a gift box.

Often he called Chuck at home to make amends after an unusually nasty outburst. He never said that was why he was calling or that he was sorry—a word Chuck didn't think existed in Mooney's vocabulary—but nevertheless, his motives were obvious when he said, "I got somethin' for you, Chuck . . . get over here."

One such event in February 1957 stuck in Chuck's mind because it was so extraordinary. Mooney had been especially irritable earlier in the day, scowling and swearing at anyone within range of his bar stool. But, true to form, later that night he called Chuck at the lounge, barking his order like a drill sergeant. "Get over here," he said. "I'm tired."

No wonder Mooney was tired, Chuck grumbled to himself; it was after one in the morning. But he'd do as he was told. He would have preferred going home to bed rather than playing audience to one of Mooney's monologues. But Mooney couldn't wait until morning, Chuck reminded himself as he gulped down a cup of coffee on the way out the door.

Secretly, Chuck aspired to greater things; he'd made up his mind that when the time was right, he'd go into building and become a full-fledged contractor. The thought of losing the chance by insulting Mooney was enough to start the adrenaline pumping through his veins.

By 2:00 A.M., he was wide awake, sitting across from his brother at his desk in Oak Park. Mooney, dressed in a gray silk robe and slippers, smiled back at him mischievously. Then with a look of casual arrogance, he lifted a large brown paper bag from the drawer.

"Here, take a look," he invited, tossing the bag at Chuck. It landed with the heavy thud of metal.

Chuck peered in and squinted.

Mooney laughed and took the bag. "Here, get a good look," he said, dumping a mound of tangled gold and silver and sparkling stones on the desktop.

"That's real nice," Chuck commented, nodding. Actually, he thought the stones were gaudy and garish—the emeralds too big, the diamonds ostentatious and gargantuan. Costume jewelry, he thought to himself, and he wondered why Mooney would make him come all the way over at this hour of the night to look at such obvious junk.

"Take one," Mooney offered. "Here, look at this one . . . a canary, seven carats . . . it's the smallest of the bunch." He held out a ring.

Chuck inspected it closely and then handed it back with a smile. "They sure are big," he said, motioning to the jewelry Mooney was spreading out on the desktop before them. "Why'd you get costume jewelry?"

Mooney raised his eyebrows and let out a howl. "Costume jewelry? Costume jewelry? Is that what you think?" He doubled over with gales of laughter.

"Well, yeah . . . isn't it?" Chuck said, feeling like an idiot. He hated it when Mooney did that. "Shit, the stones are so big . . . I thought—"

"You thought this stuff was fake?" Mooney wiped his eyes and leaned forward, with the ring in his open palm. "This is the real fuckin' McCoy, Chuck." He waved at the jewelry with his smoldering cigar. "All of it."

Chuck didn't know what to say. He felt like a fool, but it was an honest mistake; he'd never seen diamonds and emeralds so mammoth and he doubted whether most of America had, either. "Jesus, I had no idea. It's real, huh?" He took the ring from Mooney and examined it with renewed appreciation, turning the glittering golden diamond in the light. "It's beautiful. Beautiful." He handed the ring back, adding, "But Mooney, what the hell are you gonna do with this stuff? Some of these stones must be over fifteen carats."

"Yeah, they are." He paused and added, "Think these'll make a woman happy? There's over five million in jewelry right here."

"She's gonna be a lucky lady, whoever she is, that's for sure," Chuck said, whistling.

"Yeah, but you get first pick . . . take one."

Chuck surveyed the table thoughtfully. He was hesitant; he didn't want to insult his brother, but he also didn't want to appear greedy, and therefore he chose the smallest, least impressive of the lot. "The canary diamond," he said. "Anne Marie will love it."

"It's all yours," Mooney said, grinning, and put it in his hand.

That was the last time Chuck saw or spoke of the fabulous cache until four years later, when singer Phyllis McGuire turned Mooney's head and his brother confided, "Remember all those twenty-carat rocks I showed you? I gave Phyllis every fuckin' one . . . and more."

Mooney's generosity knew no bounds. He was on top and he was enjoying the hell out of it. "Spread the wealth, that's my philosophy," he'd say with a wink. When he was in one of his better moods, he'd tell Chuck, "Hell, you can't take it with you."

Scarcely three weeks after Chuck had walked in the house with the canary diamond ring, Mooney called with a mysterious request: "Pack up Anne Marie right away and bring her over to Dago Frank's . . . there's a surprise for her there."

"Surprise?" Anne Marie's eyes lit up like a little girl on Christmas morning. "What could it be? What's Mooney up to now?"

Chuck had no idea, but he obeyed Mooney's directive without question. They called a sitter for the children and in less than an hour were comfortably sequestered—along with a half dozen other Outfit wives—in Dago Frank's living room.

Dago Frank was well known among the Outfit guys for his high-quality trove of stolen goods. He was a jovial Italian who'd become Mooney's favorite Chicago fence. "If you want it, Dago Frank either has it . . . or he can get it."

Oddly, it didn't bother the women that the gifts of jewelry and furs that found their way into their hands were mostly hot—stolen from other women's closets. They learned to take without asking where it all came from; that was the mark of a good wife. The gifts were simply their reward for silence and obedience. Should a twinge of guilt assault their sensibilities, it was quickly salved, lost amid so much glitter. "A diamond's sparkle can blind a woman to a lot of things," Mooney was fond of saying.

Full of anticipation, the women looked on as Frank strode over to a large, round Queen Anne table placed in the center of the room. He smiled a broad, toothy smile, and with one slender ringed hand, he ceremoniously removed a linen tablecloth, revealing a virtual treasure of gold and silver studded with every imaginable gemstone.

A gasp went around the room. There were hundreds, perhaps thousands, of gold and silver trinkets: rings, charms, bracelets, earrings, necklaces. It was like a pirate's chest had been opened before them.

No one moved from their chairs; everyone was speechless.

"Well, what are you waitin' for? Take what you like," Frank admonished, chuckling. Mooney's gift was having precisely the desired effect. "Get up, will you all . . . and try some on. Take whatever you want . . . it's Mooney's gift."

A flurry of thank-yous crisscrossed the room for the next hour as the women oohed and aahed and sorted and traded among themselves.

When at last they were finished, Dago Frank smiled and said, "Hey, now that you ladies have gone through the jewelry, how'd you like to see some other merchandise? It's for sale, but you know I'll treat you right." Without further comment, Frank pressed an unseen lever and the wall swung open, revealing a well-lit hidden room.

"Oh, my, look at that," Anne Marie exclaimed. She'd never seen so many gorgeous furs in all her life. There were dozens upon dozens of stoles, capes, and full-length coats and wraps hanging on rack after rack.

The other women gushed over the coats but decided to leave without a new fur for warmth that night. Anne Marie, however, spotted a lynx walking coat that was the most beautiful fur she'd ever seen."

"Oh, Chuck, can we buy it? Please?" she pleaded.

He never could resist his little Babe and he certainly wouldn't deny her something so magnificent; she wore it home that night.

"Wait 'til all your friends see you in this." Chuck whistled admiringly as she snuggled into its deep softness.

Like her other friends, Anne Marie had her nails and hair done weekly, dressed her two little boys in Eton suits and matching playsuits, enjoyed facials, pedicures, and frequent jaunts to Neiman Marcus, Marshall Field's, and her own dressmaker.

Her drawers were filled with Chanel sachets, dainty lace peignoirs, lingerie sets, silken hosiery, and dozens of stylish gloves. Her shelves held row upon row of the finest shoes, boots, and handbags, as well as beautiful hats of all sizes and descriptions. The latest fashions—from trapeze dresses, sheaths, chemises, bubbles, and Chanel Italian knit suits to cashmere Givenchy cowl-neck sweaters, car coats, tapered slacks, and toreadors—hung in her closets.

A collection of gems filled her jewelry boxes. There were glittering cocktail rings, bracelets, earrings, brooches, and necklaces. And there were her treasured fur coats of lynx, beaver, mink, and lamb.

Likewise, Chuck had only the finest money could by: elegant Douppioni silk suits, Ivy League blazers, dozens of trousers and fashionable narrow silk ties, madras sport shirts, cashmere sweaters, fedoras, Italian leather boots and loafers. Following Mooney's lead, he possessed count-less diamond and gem-studded tie tacks, cuff links, watches, and rings.

Chuck and Anne Marie both agreed life could only get better. They were young and on their way up, with two beautiful children. They were going to build a brand-new home in a posh section of town. They had money to spend on nightclubs and trips. Occasionally, Chuck might day-dream about being a contractor or stop to think about where he was headed, but largely he believed he was already there. The American dream, complete with a fluffy white toy poodle, lived at his house. "What more can a guy ask for?" he exclaimed to Anne Marie one day as he turned a hamburger on their backyard grill.

On Sunday, March 31, 1957, everything changed.

Leon Marcus had been a conniving, crooked banker who was involved in more shady deals than a fast-talking Chicago prosecutor could shake a stick at. He'd been indicted, along with his son-in-law and brother, earlier that year on misappropriation of bank funds for his Chicago Southmoor Bank. By the end of March, he was yet to go to trial.

Ever since he'd been charged, the foolhardy Marcus had attempted to blackmail Mooney, hoping some pressure on the Outfit boss would result in his acquittal. He had the information that could send Sam Giancana up the river for life, he boasted to fellow gangsters, waving his wallet.

Chuck believed Marcus had seriously underestimated his brother. The decision for Mooney would be a simple one.

Months later, Chuck would learn that Mooney had given the order to Willie Potatoes, who'd then selected his own soldier, a copper-turned-mobster hit man—Sal Moretti—to take care of the job. In turn, Moretti invited three of his aspiring flunkies along for the ride. They weren't there for added backup; Sal was to handle Marcus on his own. Rather, they came for the sheer entertainment.

Moretti nabbed Marcus in front of Chicago developer Alfred Rado's home on Sunday, March 31. Willie Potatoes had instructed him to kill Marcus and retrieve from his wallet a particularly damning document, a receipt for a one-hundred-thousand-dollar cash payment made by Mooney on the Thunderbolt Motel.

Within blocks of the Rados' home, Moretti shot Marcus

in the head, threw him in a vacant lot, and drove away. In so doing, Moretti made a fatal mistake; he left the receipt on the body of Leon Marcus.

The gangland-style execution was sensationalized on television, detailed in all the papers. And thanks to the incriminating receipt, Mooney was apprehended for questioning. He was released, but not before receiving more press coverage than the crowning of Queen Elizabeth II. A court date was set for the all-but-forgotten sixty-seven-count indictment against his suburban gambling-joint, the Wagon Wheel, dating back to 1951.

"It'll all blow over," Chuck consoled his wife. But he found himself recanting when, on Thursday of that week, Sal Moretti's tortured and bloated body was discovered crammed into the trunk of a Chevy on Caton Farm Road, southwest of Chicago. From the description the papers gave, it sounded as if Willie Potatoes had taken care of his bumbling soldier. Moretti's pockets had been emptied and turned inside out, his labels torn from his clothes. All that remained was an aluminum comb—a symbol and warning to every soldier in Chicago. Like the infamous nickel in the hand of an executed stool pigeon—meaning the man's life wasn't worth a plug nickel because he'd violated the code of *omertà*—the comb told one and all to do a job right, to go over every detail with a fine-tooth comb. Or end up like Sal Moretti.

The incident sent an icy chill through the guys in the Outfit, mostly because the man who took care of Sal was a person none of them wanted to cross, ever. And because of that, nobody ever talked about who did the job on Moretti.

But there wasn't a guy in the Outfit who didn't think that Willie Potatoes, the quiet, unassuming man with a

houseful of children and an eternally pregnant wife, had
hit Moretti. Moretti was Willie's soldier and Willie had to
make things right—it was his responsibility to square
things. Willie was well known for his torture tactics, and
Sal's murder had his name written all over it. Moretti had
been tied on his knees and pistol-whipped; Willie loved to
get a guy on his knees, begging for his life. Moretti's skull
had been mashed and dented by a club and then he had
been strangled with a rope; Willie liked to use ropes. And
after Moretti's executioner threw him in the trunk, he fired
four shots into the soldier's battered head; Willie always
made sure any guy he took out was good and dead.

It also was common knowledge that Willie got turned
on doing jobs like the one on Moretti. So did Fifi Buccier
and Mad Dog DeStefano and Teets Battaglia. But Willie
would go those henchmen one better, giving guys lie-
detector tests if he didn't trust their loyalty. If they failed
they were goners; Willie tortured and murdered them on
the spot.

The way the Outfit ran, Mooney was always insulated
from a murder charge. He never killed anyone himself
anymore; he didn't actually even have to say the words.
All he had to do was give one of his trusted henchmen a
look. They knew and they took care of it. The guys would
go to any lengths and do whatever was asked of them. I
could be an enemy or a best friend. It made no difference.
Usually, a guy let his guard down if he was a friend. And
that was ideal.

To further insulate himself, Mooney might have one of
his lieutenants bring in one of his own soldiers for a job
Moretti had been working for Willie Potatoes. Often, Mooney might not even know who performed a hit—it was an

insignificant occurrence in his busy world of deals and international intrigue. And besides, it didn't matter to Mooney as long as it was done right. Obviously, the Marcus fiasco had gotten his attention after the fact, if it hadn't before.

Knowing how Mooney excelled at manipulating the authorities, no one was surprised when the Marcus-Moretti affair blew over in a matter of weeks. Chuck and Anne Marie couldn't as easily wish problems away. On the Friday following Moretti's death, along with the morning paper that blazed with the name Giancana, Chuck received an ominous phone call from McIntosh Developers at Inverness. They wanted to see him right away.

"Quite simply, Mr. Giancana, we don't want you . . . or your family here at Inverness," the gray-suited executive told Chuck when he arrived at the developer's office.

His cohort, a bespectacled man in his forties, nodded in tense agreement.

"And why is that?" Chuck demanded.

The executive pointed to a large map of the development on the wall. Property owners' names were prominently highlighted and Chuck noticed that theirs had been recently removed.

"You see that? Well, you're not wanted here. I suggest you sell us the lot and go find another place to call home."

Chuck stepped closer to the map. He'd never dreamed there'd be a problem here; he and Anne Marie just wanted fresh air and a place for the kids to roam, some new friends, new faces. He thought about the architectural drawings and blueprints they'd spent hours poring over.

"So what do you say?"

"I don't think so," Chuck replied brusquely. "We like

it out here. We've already made improvements on the lot and we've already got blueprints drawn up. We're ready to break ground.''

The other man cleared his throat and spoke up. ''Let me make it perfectly clear. Your name is Giancana and we don't want a Giancana here. Nor do any of the other fine upstanding citizens who reside in Inverness. Do you understand? Mr. Giancana, there will be no gangster in our subdivision. You, sir, are unwelcome here.''

''Unwelcome? You sure as hell knew my name when you took my money for the lot. You knew who my brother was.''

The two stared back with uniformly cold smiles.

''I repeat, you and your family are unwelcome here.''

''Why you—'' Chuck checked himself and began again, but there was an undeniable anger in his voice; he tried not to yell. ''Listen, I'm no gangster. I make an honest living running a motel—''

The gray-suited executive cut him off. ''We're well aware your motel, the Thunderbolt.'' He picked up a newspaper and added, ''As are our other homeowners.''

''It's a clean establishment. So clean, it squeaks. I'm not connected to my brother's business dealings,'' Chuck protested. ''I'm a different person entirely. And you can't shove me around because of my last name.''

''Mr. Giancana, we are being polite and civilized in this matter. We suggest you discuss this with your wife. Our offer to repurchase the lot at the same price paid originally will stand. Good day.''

''Same price . . . what kind of scam operation are you runnin' here? I've already put a lot of money in the lot. What the hell do you take me for?''

''Good day, Mr. Giancana.''

Driving home, Chuck went over the conversation again and again. It wasn't fair; he wasn't his brother. He'd had nothing to do with the Marcus and Moretti deal—hadn't even known about it until after it happened. Mooney never had said a word about it to him. And although he'd always wanted to be on the inside, he wasn't really. He wasn't a gangster. And he wasn't Mooney; he was his own man. It was the first time he'd ever said that.

Anne Marie was heartbroken at the news. "We aren't murderers or gangsters," she ranted. "How dare those people accuse us of something like that. I just want our babies to grow up right, to have a nice place to live, with nice little friends and a good school." She burst into tears. "I think we should move there, anyway."

The phone rang and Chuck talked for a moment and then went back into the living room. "That was the guy from Inverness. . . . He said there was something else we should think about."

"And what's that?" She patted her eyes with a mono-grammed handkerchief.

"He said we shouldn't be selfish, that we should think of our little boys. He said they'll be mistreated . . . abused. . . . Those were his very words, *abused* by the other kids. That they'll be outcasts and nobody will play with them."

"Nobody will play with them?" she repeated in disbelief.

"Yeah, because their last name is Giancana."

The following day, they sold the lot back to the grim-faced executives. Their American dream had ended.

Anyone else would have called Mooney, would have asked for his help. It seemed reasonable to think that if Chuck and his family had to suffer because of the things his brother did, they should at least benefit from the terrible power he could wield. But Chuck's pride wouldn't let him ask for help. He refused to bring his problems to his brother. "After all, it's Mooney who's the Outfit boss, who's under suspicion for murder, not us," Chuck told Anne Marie.

But because of their name, it seemed as if they'd been tried and convicted themselves. Chuck found himself calling for flowers for Anne Marie and using an alias. Mooney used an alias all the time—Sam Gold, Sam Flood—so, Chuck consoled himself, why shouldn't he? But he felt like a Judas, a traitor. Was he denying his heritage or was he protecting himself and his family?

The events of the previous weeks threw Chuck into a state of confusion. He'd never denied who or what he was. He wasn't ashamed. Indeed, it might not have been so bad to be called a gangster by the developers—if he'd actually been one. But recently, he had realized that although he might know all the Outfit guys, was privy to what was going on and probably talked to Mooney more than anybody else, he wasn't an actual member of the Outfit.

Mooney said New York's gun-and-saber shit was "the silliest thing I've ever heard of . . . grade-school stuff." But because Chicago didn't have a formal "initiation" and "secret society" like New York or adhere to some hocus-pocus Old Country rules for being "made," it was hard to tell who was a member of the Outfit and who wasn't. You just knew. You knew how high up the ladder a guy was by the men he hung around with, by how many soldiers he required to conduct business, or by the job he had.

Guys such as Needles, Nicoletti, and Alderisio—Mooney's chief executioners—were without question full-fledged members of the Outfit. But a guy didn't necessarily have to kill his way up—not if he had powerful friends to protect him from such dirty work. Jake Guzik had been a good example; Guzik hadn't had the stomach for murder, so Capone had killed his adversaries for him. Chuckie English was in a similar situation. But they were a rarity.

Being a member of the Outfit and being connected were two different things in Chicago. Being connected meant you did business with the Outfit. Leon Marcus was connected. Joe Kennedy was connected—as were Abe Pritzker and Moe Annenberg. According to Mooney, all the Presidents of the United States since Teddy Roosevelt had been connected. Celebrities ranging from Sammy Davis, Jr., to Jake LaMotta were connected. King Farouk was connected. There were hundreds, probably thousands, of people across the United States and throughout the world with non-Italian names and seemingly "clean" businesses who were connected.

Having connections meant having friends and associates who were in the Outfit. These relationships enabled a person to get things done in city hall, win government contracts, even get a loan. In at least one way, being connected was better than being a member, because a man could rationalize that he wasn't really involved in organized crime. But the bottom line was, if a man got a favor from an Outfit member, he was more involved than he imagined. He might get lucky and never have his marker called in or he might be called on to hit his best friend or take a fall on a murder rap for a total stranger. The possibilities were limitless.

Chuck's conclusion that he wasn't a full member of the Outfit was based on the job he currently had and the type of activity it involved. Running the motel, a job given to him by Mooney, meant he was connected, but the fact that the activity was all on the up-and-up meant he wasn't in the Outfit. Years ago, when he'd run punch boards, he was a member. But later, when he'd worked solely as a movie projectionist, he wasn't. Acting as a courier to Cuba was certainly an Outfit job.

Chicago's Outfit was a fluid, ever-changing animal with no spoken rules and no formalities. There were no conferences as there were in the movies. It was a look, a walk, the cut of a guy's clothes; whom he had dinner with and whom he didn't. By most of the guys' standards, Chuck was a member by virtue of being Mooney's brother. But in his heart, he knew that managing the motel put him on the fringe, not on the inside. And it was killing him.

He hadn't really given it much thought before, but now he'd started looking at the motel job as a pigeonhole. The place was clean and it was obvious that, without saying it, Mooney was determined to keep him that way, as well. "There's nothin' I hate more than bein' accused of somethin' I didn't do," he told his wife. "It's not fair."

The Giancana name had always opened doors, not closed them. But more doors closed as Mooney's name continued to find its way into the newspapers. With the publicity came a new set of obstacles for Chuck and his family. They finally found a new home in Lexington Fields, where there was fresh air and blue sky and a picturesque farm with a white fence and frisky ponies and horses grazing nearby. But almost as quickly as the moving vans pulled away, they began to feel the curiosity and rejection of their WASP neighbors.

That very day, two-year-old Mooney was playing outside when a boy came across the street, taunting him. "I'm not supposed to play with you. . . . You're a gangster. And so's your father . . . my dad says so." A hurt, confused expression crossed little Mooney's face; his parents quickly brought him inside.

Not long after that, their other son, Chuckie, began having trouble in school. The teachers seemed to single him out more frequently, and if there was a fight on the school grounds, everyone pointed to him. "He's a Giancana and they're all gangsters," the children would cry.

Since no one came right out and told Anne Marie and Chuck to their faces that they weren't welcome in the neighborhood, Anne Marie set out to make new friends, inviting the ladies over for bridge or tea, having couples over for barbecues and cocktail parties, baking cakes and cookies for all the families.

The intense effort wasn't for her own benefit; deep down, she was still the same shy, self-conscious girl Chuck had met a decade before, and playing the social circuit came hard. Instead, this was for her children. More than anything, she wanted them to be accepted. And that meant making a real effort to establish friendships with these Anglo strangers.

It was a discouraging campaign; sometimes she'd confess to Chuck that perhaps they'd made a mistake leaving their own people and moving to a place so foreign to Chicago's Little Italy.

She watched little Mooney develop into a quiet, thoughtful, and sensitive child—vulnerable to the older children's cruelty and name-calling. And she wondered aloud about his coming school years. "What will happen when the teacher calls out for Sam Giancana?" she asked Chuck again and again.

She saw an anger welling up in their other son, and though seven-year-old Chuckie never mentioned it, she was certain he was continually teased and mistreated by the other children at school; more than once he'd come home with a bloody nose.

Chuck tried to reassure her, but he was away from home more often now, throwing himself into work at the motel, trying to immerse himself in so much activity that he wouldn't have time to dwell on what was happening to them. He wanted to get on with his life even if he suddenly wasn't sure where it was going.

Perhaps Mooney also was uncertain about the direction his own life was taking. At least that possibility flitted through Chuck's mind late one night when his brother pulled up in their driveway.

Chuck had just gotten home from work at the lounge; it was after three in the morning. Instead of going to bed, he was sitting up in the living room, sipping a glass of wine. He'd just lit a cigar when he heard the car pull up to the house. When he saw it was Mooney, he opened the door.

His brother stood on the porch, holding a large package in both arms. Dressed in a suit and tie, just as if it was high noon on a workday, he seemed impatient, almost nervous.

"Hey, this is what I call service . . . right here waitin' for me, huh? Pretty good," Mooney said, smiling wearily. "Glad you're awake, Chuck. Let's talk." Chuck noticed the dark translucent circles furrowed beneath his brother's eyes as he walked into the lamplight.

Soon they were comfortably stationed on the sofa, package between them.

"I want you to take care of this for me," Mooney said, patting the package with one hand.

"Yeah . . . anything else?"

"Full of fuckin' questions, aren't you?" Mooney chided good-naturedly.

Chuck shrugged his shoulders.

"Just keep this. Okay? And don't ask questions."

"Hey, fine. No problem," Chuck said; he thought his voice sounded defensive.

"Hey, don't go gettin' burned up. . . . There's a half a million bucks in here. Okay? So now you know."

Chuck almost gasped. "So, what do you want me to do with it?"

"Hold it here at your place . . . hide it. Hide it good, too. Damned good. That's all. Just take good care of it. When I need it . . . I'll ask for it." Mooney paused and cleared his throat. "But . . . if anything should ever happen to me, Chuck . . . open this up right away. I want my sisters to each have fifty Gs and you and Pepe to split the rest. Got that? There's an envelope inside here, too." He tapped the top of the package for emphasis. "Do what it says." Chuck thought he suddenly detected a concern, a fleeting look of worry cross his brother's face.

"Hey, don't you worry about a thing. No problem. You know you can count on me."

"Yeah, I know I can count on you," Mooney said, and then he brightened. He started to laugh and stood up. "Shit, you tell me that all the time; I guess I should know it by now, huh? Jesus . . ." He looked down at his watch. "It's time for me to get the hell outta here."

The next morning, Chuck immediately wrapped Mooney's package in asbestos, making it fireproof, and placed it in the attic of their home, beneath the ceiling insulation.

For weeks, he was afraid to leave the house. "What if there's a fire?" he exclaimed to Anne Marie. "Imagine five hundred thousand dollars of Mooney's money gone . . . and after he trusted me, too."

He was therefore relieved when the phone rang late one

night with directions for delivery of what they had started to call "Mooney's package."

"The guy down in Mexico," the voice on the other end of the line said. "He said to tell you he needs the *package*. He said you're to have Anne wrap it like a birthday present with a big bow. A driver will pick it up tomorrow."

They did as instructed and it wasn't until years later, when Mooney was actually living in Mexico, that Chuck would recall "Mooney's package" and—putting two and two together—realize that the half a million he'd held for Mooney was just a drop in the bucket. Chuck would be told by Outfit guys that during Mooney's reign, his brother had shuttled millions across the border, using Father Cash as his courier.

But that June of 1957, Chuck wasn't focused on Mooney's international schemes. Instead, there was another onslaught of local publicity that captured his attention; Mooney's trial for the Wagon Wheel indictments came up and the case was thrown out of court for lack of evidence. "I called in some markers," Mooney boasted to Chuck. "I've got more important things to do than sit around listenin' to a bunch of asshole lawyers argue."

The papers all said Mooney sat through the trial bored and disinterested—which was accurate. But what they didn't know was that Chicago's Outfit boss had bigger fish to fry; his attention was once again focused on the Kennedys.

Initially, Mooney had given the proceedings in Washington little thought. He'd saved Joe Kennedy's life, after all, he reminded Chuck, and had little reason to think the man's sons wouldn't recognize the debt they owed.

But by early August of 1957, Mooney was following

the McClellan committee hearings more closely. The Teamsters had come under intense scrutiny, as had Dave Beck, its leader. And although the theft of union funds was linked to the Outfit, organized crime had not yet been scrutinized to any great degree. However, Mooney got the word from Washington that the Outfit would be investigated in greater depth. Obviously Bobby Kennedy was planning a full-scale attack on the underworld.

Ultimately spanning thirty months and three sessions of Congress, with three distinct phases of inquiry, the McClellan committee would first attack the theft of union funds by specific union officials. In its second phase, unions with a history of racketeering—like the Teamsters—would be investigated. But it was the committee's third and final inquiry into improper labor practices that would prove most sensational: a direct look at what were thought to be leaders of organized crime in America.

When his brother came into the motel on a typically windy fall afternoon in Chicago, Chuck could tell he was not a happy man.

"What the fuck is wrong with that Kennedy brat?" Mooney exclaimed. "Can you believe that little bastard Bobby is gonna go for the throat? It doesn't make sense. . . . Doesn't he know he's costin' his brother every union vote in America? And what the hell is wrong with his brother Jack, anyway? Shit, he's on the committee, too . . . and just about as bad as Bobby. Are they fuckin' nuts?"

Chuck looked into Mooney's eyes—black ribbons of rage, they reminded him of his childhood and the night long ago when Mooney had found his money stolen. Chuck hadn't thought about the terrible beating he and Pepe and his cousins had gotten in years. But now, searching his brother's face, he saw the same horrible, almost terrifying cruelty still residing there.

Mooney thought he was being played for a sucker. And he hated that probably more than anything. Chuck couldn't think of anybody who'd ever tried such a thing and lived to tell about it. He shook his head. "It doesn't make sense, these Kennedy boys. . . . What's Murray have to say?"

"The same fuckin' thing . . . Joe's got it handled . . . Joe's got it handled. Shit, old man Kennedy's out fiddlin' with whores in Tahoe at the Cal-Neva while Rome burns."

"Hey, Mooney, relax then. Kennedy must know things are under control. And Murray's got Washington wired, right?"

"Yeah, but you'd think I'd get a fuckin' answer. Sinatra's baby-sittin' the old man out west. Joe just keeps tellin' him and the guys that it's just a political move, just a game. Murray says the same thing."

"Hey, Mooney, like you've said before, Joe Kennedy owes you his life. You think he's gonna bullshit you about this?"

"He owes me more than that and he fuckin' well knows it," Mooney snapped. "We can't keep business movin' if we got these assholes up in Congress breathin' down our necks, now can we?"

"No, I guess not."

"Well"—Mooney managed a half smile—"we have more than a few aces. We've got a couple of senators who owe us big time."

"So what's the problem?" Chuck said, brightening. "You've always managed to keep your nose clean. You've got guys on every corner who owe you; you've got politicians in your pocket. Relax."

Mooney smiled hesitantly and nodded. "You're right. Let's have a fuckin' drink. It's been a long day."

The wheels of justice continued to turn in Washington as the weeks sped by. There was the usual bipartisan grumbling from Senate committee members. Republican Barry Goldwater was quoted as saying that the committee's young chief counsel, Robert Kennedy, was exerting too much influence over the proceedings. But the committee's chairman, Democratic Senator John McClellan, a down-to-earth Arkansas Baptist, defended Kennedy's judgment and aggressiveness. "He's tops," McClellan retorted to Kennedy's detractors.

There was an admirable vehemence in the young Kennedy's manner that was perhaps unsettlingly familiar to Mooney. At thirty-one, the task of acting as chief legal counsel to the committee must have been staggering, if not overwhelming. There were one hundred accountants, lawyers, and investigators reporting to the chief counsel, and on the horizon, over fifteen hundred witnesses to be called and twenty thousand–plus pages of testimony to be chronicled and analyzed.

Mooney saw in Bobby Kennedy—as he'd seen in Teddy Roe—a calculating juggler, a ruthlessly ambitious man. A man very much like Mooney himself.

CHAPTER 17

After the Depression, unions had flourished in the United States, and Chicago—due to the brilliance of Murray Humphreys, in particular—was no exception. Of all the unions, the Teamsters were the shining star in Humphreys's crown. Like the film industry's Screen Actors Guild, which Chicago effectively controlled, theirs was a commodity with deadlines. If meat and produce didn't arrive at the stores, it spoiled. If shipments of equipment or machine parts didn't arrive, factories ground to a halt.

The power this gave the Teamsters was particularly impressive insofar as it offered the capability to target a specific business or industry. A shipment's speedy or late arrival could often mean the difference between success and failure in the U.S. climate of increased competition. Enterprises could be targeted by the Outfit for takeover, ruin, and bribery. Or conversely, if certain executives played ball with the union and Outfit muscle, their competition might begin to experience devastating shipping problems.

The sheer genius of such schemes hailed back to 1944, when Humphreys had placed a tough little Sicilian, Joey Glimco, in charge of Chicago's Teamsters. The five foot four, beak-nosed Glimco didn't let the Outfit down; Chicago's Teamsters' membership skyrocketed under his leadership as he forced the union into everything from egg workers and florists to bathroom sanitation workers. Over the next twenty years, others such as Dave Yaras, Lenny Patrick, Red and Allen Dorfman, and Irwin Weiner spun off their own ''feeder'' enterprises. Mooney told Chuck that dozens of bogus companies—from resort and hotel development to health insurance and restaurants—were used by these men as fronts for schemes destined to bilk the Teamsters membership out of tens of millions of dollars. Most were created solely for the purpose of receiving immense loans from the Teamsters' pension fund. Once a loan had been made, the company quickly went bankrupt, bled dry by the Outfit.

With Dan Tobin's retirement as the International president, Chicago made sure a man they could do business with assumed office. Dave Beck, a tough organizer from Seattle, came in to head the International. As Beck's right-hand man, the Outfit selected a like-minded Detroit thug, Jimmy Hoffa. In these two, they had the ideal partners for Glimco's continuing schemes.

After the heat on Dave Beck became too intense, it was time for a change, and in September of 1957, Chicago pushed Jimmy Hoffa to a sweeping victory as president of the International Teamsters. By October of that year, with their boy Hoffa at labor's helm, Murray Humphreys stroking the national politicians, and Mooney Giancana calling the shots, Chicago was the nation's star ascendant. The circle of power was complete.

Rather than a circle, though, Bobby Kennedy seemed to view organized crime's involvement in unions as a noose—one that mobsters had placed around the nation's throat, holding innocent people in its stranglehold. Consequently, during the McClellan committee hearings, he and his brother Jack grandstanded—grilling and fawning and mocking one witness after another. Jack Kennedy had lost to crimebuster Estes Kefauver in his bid for the vice-presidential nomination in 1955 and he seized on this opportunity to make a name for himself.

While the McClellan committee was unveiling the second phase of its investigation during the summer and fall of 1957, most of the nation's underworld was riveted to the unfolding drama in New York.

Following Willie Moretti's slaying in 1951, and Albert Anastasia's rise to boss of the Mangano family, Vito Genovese had been steadily working behind the scenes to dethrone Frank Costello. In May of 1957, Genovese had sent henchman Vince "the Chin" Gigante to assassinate Costello. In a twist of fate, the single bullet merely grazed the boss's head.

Although Costello survived the attempt on his life, he would not survive the interrogation that followed. A piece of paper listing the Las Vegas Tropicana's gross receipts, found by authorities in his pocket after the shooting, elicited the scrutiny of the IRS. He was soon indicted for tax evasion. It was a victory of sorts for the double-dealing Genovese, but as long as Anastasia remained in power as Costello's protector and ally, Costello was technically invulnerable. Not to be thwarted, Genovese set out to remove Anastasia, eventually convincing Meyer Lansky and other Mob leaders that Anastasia's ''cowboy craziness'' and attempts to move in on Cuban casinos merited elimination. Shortly thereafter, Albert Anastasia was murdered as he sat in a barber's chair.

Unfortunately, the timing for such a power struggle in the underworld could not have been more inopportune; thanks to the McClellan committee, the nation would soon be watching their every move.

On November 13, 1957, Chuck and Anne Marie sat down to catch the evening news over some cake and coffee. Like other citizens, they were amazed to hear what Joseph Amato from the Bureau of Narcotics had said that day to the McClellan committee about the ''Mafia'': ''We believe there does exist . . . a society, loosely organized, for the specific purpose of smuggling narcotics and committing other crimes. . . . It has its core in Italy and it is nationwide. In fact, international.''

''Oh my God,'' Anne Marie said, shocked at such a possibility. ''Is that true, Chuck?''

''No . . . Mafia? What the hell is that? It's just a name some government guys made up, that's all,'' he replied, and asked for another cup of coffee, hoping to change the subject. In fact, he'd never really heard any talk of a Mafia, except perhaps that the guys in New Orleans liked the moniker. Mostly there was the Outfit, the Syndicate, the Mob, the Commission. And through the years, there'd been the Black Hand societies and the Camorra, but he suspected the word *Mafia* was largely a name used by crazy New Yorkers and Louisiana guys—and was now being seized by the media in an effort to identify the enigmatic animal called organized crime.

Amato's testimony was hailed as a landmark in the investigations and that evening the question was asked around the country in millions of living rooms: Was there really such a thing as the Mafia? Was there really an organization of Italian gangsters? Through a combination of sheer coincidence and Vito Genovese's ill-timed quest for power, on the following day, the nation and the McClellan committee would have an answer.

Only eleven months previously, Senator McClellan had rocked Middle America with his assertion that "There exists in America today what appears to be a close-knit, clandestine criminal syndicate." On November 14, 1957, the day after Amato's fateful "Mafia" testimony, that very Syndicate was staging a conference atop a wooded hill at the 150-acre estate of fellow gangster Joseph Barbara, in Apalachin, New York.

The word *Mafia* was again in the news. A raid conducted by the New York State Police and federal Treasury agents on the clandestine meeting of Italian criminals turned up a dozen union officials, a Buffalo civic leader, and fifty-eight known gangsters.

On further investigation, it was discovered that fifty had arrest records, thirty-five had convictions, eighteen were suspected murderers, fifteen had received arrests for narcotics, thirty for gambling. Of this group, twenty-two were involved in labor-union activities; twenty-two in import-export, olive oil, and cheese; nineteen in major groceries, vending machines, and construction; and seventeen in bars, restaurants, and hotels.

It was suspected that as many as fifty other gangsters had escaped through the woods and fields.

Two days later, Mooney stopped by the Thunderbolt Motel. He sidled up to the bar and, grinning impishly at Chuck, shook one silk-suited pant leg.

"What the hell's wrong with your leg?" Chuck asked.

"I'm shakin' those goddamned New York backwoods burrs off my pants." Mooney cackled.

Laughing all the way, they adjourned to Chuck's office for a private cup of coffee.

"Burrs?" Chuck continued, chuckling. "Damn it, I knew if anybody could outfox the coppers up at the conference, it was you."

"Yeah, you heard about Apalachin? It's all over the news, right? Well, I wasn't even gonna go originally . . . but I did it as a favor to Lansky and Costello. They didn't go because they had a good idea what pitch Genovese was going to make. But somebody had to be there. Shit, I had to run like a fuckin' rabbit through the goddamned woods. The place was full of briars. . . . I tore up a twelve-hundred-dollar suit on some barbed wire, ruined a new pair of shoes." He raised his hands to light a cigar, revealing a pair of magnificent oval-cut star sapphire cuff links.

"Jesus, it sounds crazy. . . ." Chuck tried to imagine his brother doing something so undignified as running in the woods.

"It *was* crazy," Mooney said, nodding. He sipped his coffee. "And man oh man, was it ever cold. Did you know leaves get real slippery when they're wet?"

Chuck shook his head.

"Well, they do . . . out in the backwoods this time of year." He laid his cigar in the ashtray and started to laugh. "You should've seen some of the guys slippin' and slidin' down on their asses, splittin' out their pants. Some of 'em went right down through the trees, right down the hill," he said, snickering.

"It sounds like it must have been a zoo. The news said the coppers were everywhere."

"Like ants," Mooney said.

"Well, I guess a lot of guys didn't get away, huh?" Chuck asked, repeating what he'd heard.

"Yeah, and they're ready to kill Genovese. . . . They all blame him for gettin' pinched," Mooney said.

He leaned back in his chair with an undeniable air of self-satisfaction. His eyes grew cold and hard. "Shit, Chuck, that Genovese, the cocksucker, thought he was gonna make himself 'boss of bosses' . . . and after he tried to kill Costello and had Anastasia hit, if you can believe that," he exclaimed, disbelief rising with the level of his voice. "See, Lansky, Luciano, Costello, Gambino, and I talked before the meeting. Gambino and I would go and they'd lay back. We'd play both sides . . . find out what the sneaky bastard was up to . . . that's all. No way was the son of a bitch gonna be my boss. The man's fuckin' crazy if he thinks I'd let him get away with that. Look what he's done to Frank Costello." He clenched his jaw as his lip curled defiantly around his cigar. "Genovese is a total fuckin' ass . . . but he's ruined now," Mooney said with a sneer. "Nobody'll ever listen to him again. Any boss worth his salt would have had the place protected. And I'm gonna make damned sure every guy in the country knows that." His eyes flashed with determination.

Clearly, Mooney was after Genovese. One thing Chuck knew about his brother was that he was unwaveringly loyal to a friend. Costello was the closest thing to that Chuck had ever known; Mooney would pull out all the stops to get rid of Costello's enemy.

Mooney had a special saying he'd picked up from his travels in the Middle East: "The enemy of my enemy is my friend." Anybody who was after Genovese was

Mooney's ally for now—anybody. Such a philosophy made for strange bedfellows, Chuck thought as he studied the expression on Mooney's face. But he said nothing about that, saying instead, "Definitely, you'd have had Chicago locked up like a fortress if they'd come here."

"That's right. And that's because I know what I'm doin'. I have my town under control." A cruel smile played across his lips. "But we're not done with the bastard yet. Just watch, pretty soon he'll be layin' in a prison cell. Too fuckin' bad, huh?"

It was almost as if the old Mooney was back. He was scheming and plotting and he beamed when he talked about his plans. When he was like that, he was invincible, untouchable.

The events of that November would have far-reaching implications. In Washington, while Bobby Kennedy and John McClellan were feeling vindicated, FBI director J. Edgar Hoover was seething with embarrassment.

For literally decades, Hoover had insisted there was no such thing as an organized crime syndicate. He'd scorned Estes Kefauver's assertion in the early fifties that an organized Italian underground existed in the United States. Recently, he'd pooh-poohed Kennedy and McClellan. Now, due to the events at Apalachin, he was faced with public ridicule for his lack of knowledge on the subject of organized crime. But perhaps, worst of all, his ego had suffered; he'd been beaten to the punch by a handful of New York cops along with the FBI's longtime rival, the Bureau of Narcotics.

Mooney said more than once that former FBI man Guy Banister was part of the Outfit's plans. "Remember me tellin' you about how we helped him nail Commies, run in punks free-lancin' car thefts, that kind of shit? Well, we got him set up with Marcello down in New Orleans when he took over the police department down there.''

Mooney also confided that J. Edgar Hoover himself had been on the pad for years. ''Costello worked the whole thing out. He knew Hoover was just like every other politician and copper, only meaner and smarter than most. Hoover didn't want an envelope each month—that offended his sensibilities,'' Mooney said, sneering. ''So we never gave him cash outright; we gave him something better. Tips on fixed horse races. It was up to him how much money he wanted to make on the information. He could bet ten thousand dollars on a horse that showed twenty-to-one odds, if he wanted . . . and he has.''

Getting the tips to Hoover was easy enough, Mooney explained. Frank Costello would hear from Frank Erikson, the country's biggest and most powerful bookie, about an upcoming fix on a race. Next, Costello would tell columnist Walter Winchell, and Winchell, in turn, would call Hoover. Hoover would hop in his car under the pretext he was working on a case and head for the track.

''He'd place a two-dollar bet at the window while one of his flunkies put the real money on the sure thing at the hundred-dollar window,'' Mooney said. He told Chuck that Costello never let the FBI director down; Hoover won every time.

''Nice and neat, for sure, and you can call it anything you want . . . but a payoff is a payoff is a payoff,'' Mooney insisted, chewing on his fat cigar.

With so much attention focused on Hoover, Mooney expected repercussions. ''After all, the guy's gotta make it look good. He's gonna have to stop chasin' Commies and car thieves and let the public know he's fightin' the Mafia.'' Mooney drew the word *Mafia* out with an overly dramatic sense of evil in his voice.

Mooney believed Hoover would be worried; if he came down too hard on his old "benefactors," he could be exposed or faced with the threat of blackmail from the underworld. However, if he didn't move—and move fast—he could lose funding for his bureau and his personal stature as a crimefighter.

"Hoover could be dangerous now. We've been on the same side before. We've helped him out with Commies and that shine, Martin Luther King, more than once," Mooney commented, shaking his head. "Now, the rules have changed. He's in a corner and he knows it. It won't matter that it was Bobby Kennedy who's to blame for the whole fuckin' mess. A guy like Hoover has only one choice when the heat's turned up . . . kill or be killed. The game now will be survival. I'll put money on him tryin' to get us before we get him." Mooney smiled. "This is gonna get interesting, Chuck, real interesting."

Immediately after Thanksgiving, on November 27, 1957, J. Edgar Hoover did exactly as Mooney had surmised, formally launching an FBI attack on organized crime with his Top Hoodlum Program, or THP. Agents were assigned to this new vendetta in towns across the nation, but Hoover made it known Chicago and New York would receive the lion's share of scrutiny.

Hoover even managed to turn his initial embarrassment at having nothing on the "Mafia" in his voluminous FBI files to a sort of public-relations coup; he gave the Bureau of Narcotics's "Mafia" a new name, La Cosa Nostra, Italian for "Our Thing." By coming up with this name—

one no one, including guys in the Chicago Outfit, had ever heard of—Hoover gave the impression of being better informed. Chuck decided Mooney was right; J. Edgar Hoover would be a wily opponent.

In Chicago, ten agents were assigned to the THP. Mooney had Murray Humphreys and Mayor Daley keep tabs on things and notified his men that the G were on the prowl. He'd gotten word from Washington that the whole thing was only temporary and that things would blow over just as they had in 1946 when Hoover had his fun with CAPGA—the code name given by the FBI for "reactivation of the Capone gang." But he was suspicious and on his toes, telling Chuck, "It's up for grabs now . . . and it's winner take all. In this deal, I intend to be the winner."

Not only did the events in Apalachin increase the surveillance of Outfit activities; they also resulted in a third investigation by the McClellan committee into organized crime and the "Mafia." Word circulated among the Outfit guys that suspected key members of the national organization could expect to be subpoenaed to testify, and sure enough, by April 1958, a subpoena would be issued for Mooney.

But for now, Mooney didn't seem overly worried; he confided to Chuck that he didn't expect to be served— even if a subpoena was issued. "They gotta make it look good," he stated matter-of-factly. "But, as long as I keep a low profile and don't go actin' too fuckin' obvious, Humphreys tells me he's got old man Kennedy's word they'll just keep sayin' they can't find me."

Chuck was largely unaffected by the turmoil created by the McClellan committee and Hoover's G-men. He reasoned he was on the outside and perhaps, at last, was seeing some benefit. As Anne Marie had said once,

"We're not gangsters and murderers." He knew he had nothing to hide; the motel was still clean, and if he'd committed any crime, the only one he could think of was being Mooney's brother. "The FBI doesn't investigate you for that," he told his wife while stringing multicolored lights around their Christmas tree that year. "It's no crime to have the same last name, now is it?"

More and more, it seemed to Chuck that having the same last name might be the only thing he and Mooney had in common. By this time, he'd expected to be at Mooney's side, a respected partner. But instead, there were now ranks of loyal soldiers and lieutenants standing between him and that dream. And, according to the other Outfit guys, the only men even remotely considered Mooney's equals were the New York bosses—Gambino and Costello. Certainly, Lansky was a top guy—but he was a Jew, which meant he was still on the outside. Ultimately, most of the guys Chuck talked to agreed that even these men didn't count; because there were really two Mobs—the one that ran New York and the one that was headquartered in Chicago and ran everything else.

Chuck believed this assessment of his brother's dominion was accurate; there were literally hundreds of examples to verify such an assertion. By playing matchmaker between the other bosses around the country, Mooney had elevated himself to the man in charge. He had New Orleans boss, Carlos Marcello, as a partner in Chicago's gambling ventures in Texas, Alabama, and Georgia. Santo Trafficante, Jr., was his "man" in Florida, reporting to Mooney, feeding Chicago casino dollars from Cuba and drugs from Central America, the Caribbean, and Asia. In New York, Mooney had aligned himself further—working since Albert Anastasia's death with Carlo Gambino to solidify contacts with the European rackets and drug trade. In exchange, when Mooney embarked on a European gambling venture—always his specialty and under his domain—he brought Gambino along for a piece of the action. Largely, Mooney's international deals involved Lansky and whomever else they needed to take care of at the time. But with each new inroad into a major racket or geographic territory, Mooney made sure he held the reins.

That spring of 1958, Chuck had been having a leisurely drink with Mooney at the Pink Clock Lounge, a bar located only a block from Chicago's Armory Lounge, when his brother suddenly stood up. "Let's go upstairs," he said.

Mooney maintained an apartment above the Pink Clock to accommodate his ever-changing bevy of girlfriends and one-night stands. Chuck had been there before and he always marveled at how well decorated and tasteful Mooney's places were. When it came to living it up, his brother spared no expense.

For the remainder of the afternoon, Chuck sat, glass of wine in hand, listening as his brother talked about everything from Apalachin and his daughters to Frank Costello and his gambling interests in Havana.

It had been decided, Mooney said, that the United States government, certain American investors, and the Outfit would "play both sides of the fence in Cuba"—sending arms and munitions to the rebels attempting to overthrow Batista while publicly backing the current ruler.

Joint Outfit/CIA involvement in international schemes wasn't without precedent, Mooney reminded Chuck. He'd helped former Chicago FBI agent–turned CIA man Bob Maheu with both a Saudi Arabian and Indonesian CIA operation before and—as if made-to-order—already had

Maheu's smuggling operation set up out of Texas. He'd worked with one agent or another over the years, he said, in the Middle East, Guatemala, and Asia, forming ties that came into action only when necessary. But when not needed for "patriotic" purposes, those ties served as potent protection for his illegal smuggling concerns.

In exchange for his underworld services, Mooney said the CIA looked the other way—allowing over $100 million a year in illicit drugs to flow through Havana into the United States. It was an arrangement similar to all the rest they'd made, he said. The CIA received 10 percent of the take on the sale of the narcotics, which they utilized "for their undercover slush fund." Such illegally earned monies were stashed away by the CIA in Swiss, Italian, Bahamian, and Panamanian accounts.

As the turbulence in Cuba had increased, it was only natural that the CIA would turn to its friends in the Outfit. Having invested millions in Havana, both parties stood to lose a great deal.

Mooney said he was putting everything in place. He'd sent Lewis McWillie to serve as pit boss of the Tropicana in Havana. McWillie was one of his soldiers from Texas, whom he said had previously worked with Jack Ruby and Frank Fiorini—aka Frank Sturgis—running guns south of the border as well as smuggling narcotics. When he wasn't working the casino, Mooney explained, McWillie would be assisting Johnny Roselli with their smuggling operations. Roselli still spent a large portion of his time in Hollywood and Vegas, but now he often floated from city to city, representing Chicago—and Mooney—much as a diplomat might represent his country's leader.

Pulling off this new plan would be simple, Mooney said, flicking his cigar with confidence. "The black-market weapons will be supplied to the rebels by the CIA.'' He laughed and added, ''But of course the CIA will buy them from the Outfit . . . with money they've made from their other deals with us. After all, they can't take money out of their budget to support both Batista and the rebels . . . how would that look to their fellow Americans? Anyway, we've got all the contacts for arms and we'll buy them with money we've skimmed from Hoffa and the Teamsters. We'll store them in a warehouse in Texas, then we'll ship or fly them to Cuba. The CIA'll get us the planes and boats . . . or I might try to set up a company to lease planes and boats to the government.'' He took a sip of wine and continued, expressing his confidence that Ruby would get the job done in Texas. ''He's worked with Trafficante and Marcello for me before on a few smuggling deals as a middleman with the cops and feds. Trafficante will oversee the operation for me. McWillie will team up with the CIA to deliver the guns to Roselli and one of Trafficante's boys and another CIA agent who will get them to the rebels.''

''Beautiful,'' Chuck said.

Mooney beamed. ''Yeah, beautiful.''

''Hey, maybe you'll get that government pension, after all,'' Chuck teased.

''Maybe,'' Mooney said, smiling. ''But I've got a bigger marker I'm waitin' to call in . . . shit, I may need to.''

''What's that?''

''I may have to get them to call off Hoover and his pack of wolves. Or do somethin' with Bobby Kennedy and that goddamned McClellan shit.''

Word had circulated that a McClellan committee subpoena had been issued for Mooney. To avoid being served, he'd spent a lot of time that year out of town, bumping into his associates wherever he went. In spite of the pressure he was under, Mooney seemed to thrive. He liked a good challenge, he said, and Outfit business was his entire world.

One day that spring, Willie Potatoes, platinum blond girlfriend at his side, strolled across the black and white terrazzo floor of the Thunderbolt lounge, and declared, "Guess what just happened in New York?"

Chuck was at a table with Rocky Potenza and Johnny Matessa, and in unison they kiddingly cried out, "What?"

Willie leaned down toward the trio and whispered, "Mooney and the guys got Genovese . . . got him on a narcotics rap."

"The bastard deserved it," Rocky piped up.

Willie turned to the blonde. "Go powder your nose, honey," he said, winking at the guys.

She nodded. "Okay, Willie."

"Take your time," Willie called out as she turned to go. Their eyes followed her tight-skirted wiggle through the lounge and out the door.

"You know how to pick 'em, Willie!" Matessa tipped his glass admiringly.

Willie just grinned as he sat down at the table. "Jesus, it's fuckin' hotter than hell out there," he said, wiping his forehead with a handkerchief.

"I'll bet it's hotter in New York." Rocky snickered.

"You bet it is," Willie agreed, chuckling. "Some bad weather blew in from Chicago."

"So, what's the deal out there?" Chuck asked, motioning to the bartender for another round of drinks.

A broad smile crossed Willie's face, exposing a toothy,

almost sinister grin. "Seems a guy of mine, he ratted on Genovese."

"A guy of yours?" Matessa gasped in disbelief.

Willie, pleased by the impression he'd made, laughed and nodded. "Yeah, a guy of mine . . . a Puerto Rican. Mooney used him to set Genovese up on a drug rap," Willie said with pride. "You know, that cocksucker Genovese's been trouble ever since he tried to hit Costello. Chicago supplied the Puerto Rican stool pigeon. The New York guys kicked in twenty-five grand apiece and promised the stoolie three grand a month for the rest of his life just to talk in court and give enough information on Genovese to send him to the slammer."

"Shit, I don't know if it's worth three grand to go up against a boss like that," Matessa said.

"Who the fuck cares?" Willie shrugged. "Like Mooney says, 'Use 'em when you can' . . . we'll make sure the spic doesn't get hit after it's all over."

It had been Mooney's idea from the start, Willie told them later. But even so, the other bosses all threw in support. Any deal they all agreed on, they all participated in. It was always like that; each guy contributed—whether it was money or a man. It wasn't that any one of them alone couldn't pull off the job; it was that by having each guy take a piece of a job, and assigning their respective soldiers and lieutenants to handle it, they were further removed, as individuals, from any possibility of repercussions.

For the setup of Genovese, Mooney called on Willie Potatoes, who, in turn, brought in one of his soldiers, a low-level dope peddler, Nelson Cantellops. Mooney didn't have any idea who the guy was—and didn't care. Cantellops was just a sap, he said, but a smart sap—tailor-made for their plot against Genovese.

Since Mooney supplied the plan and manpower, Lansky, Gambino, Costello, and Luciano supplied the dollars to finance the narcotics caper that would ultimately frame Genovese. For Mooney's part, he received another 5 percent of the take in Havana. The plan worked perfectly; Genovese was arrested, thanks to Cantellops's testimony and sentenced to fifteen years in prison, where he would eventually die in 1969.

Getting Genovese out of the way was a breakthrough. "He was the only guy with the balls to start a war," Mooney later explained. The other bosses, he said, he could work with or around. Only Joe Bonanno raised his ire, but he insisted, "He's afraid of his fuckin' shadow . . . and he's definitely afraid of me. I've got no respect for the guy at all. He's got no guts; whenever there's trouble, he runs out of town."

Bonanno had caused Mooney some irritation in Arizona. Like Vegas, Arizona was an area that was considered "open territory," meaning anybody with the muscle could operate there. Mooney had made swift inroads in recent years, sending Chuckie English out to Arizona to set up real estate deals, jukeboxes and vending-machine operations. Although Bonanno owned a home in Phoenix—a signal to Mooney that he was attempting to stake a claim and grab the entire state for himself—he was only a minor thorn in English's side, but a thorn nonetheless. More than once, Mooney had confided to Outfit guys that he'd like to see Bonanno taken out. "But the hell with it . . . he's not worth the bullet."

Chuck wondered, albeit silently, whether the reason

Mooney had chosen not to use violence to oust Genovese and the reason he was so tolerant of Bonanno had something to do with the McClellan committee. After all, he'd said that to escape testimony, he had to lie low. By June of 1958, many of his underworld associates, including Tony Accardo, had faced the committee—and Mooney had to be feeling the pressure. Chuck sensed that the day of reckoning was coming. How long could anyone with an ounce of common sense continue to buy the excuse that a man of Mooney's prominence couldn't be located?

And he certainly was prominent. Among the nation's bosses, Mooney was now known as the most demanding and merciless. He kept a tight rein on his soldiers and lieutenants; he knew they skimmed from the take and he always looked the other way—unless it was so large a theft that it was impossible to see it as anything but an insult and affront to his intelligence.

Fond of saying "Give me a man who steals a little and I can make money," Mooney had no problem with a thief. For a guy to steal a little was fine, but God help the man who pushed his luck too far. Mooney's reaction would be swift and brutal and he always made it a point to make an example of a transgressor. Such was the case that fall of 1958. He'd had just about enough of Gus Greenbaum's shenanigans in Las Vegas.

In the early forties, Meyer Lansky had possessed a vision for the dusty hole-in-the-wall town that was no more than a road stop with a diner and gas station. Las Vegas, Lansky believed, could become a glittering gambling mecca. After World War II, he convinced playboy mobster Bugsy Siegel to get things rolling. In short order, 6 million syndicate dollars were invested in the first Las Vegas casino-hotel, the Flamingo.

When it was discovered that the Flamingo's losses were due not to lack of business but to Siegel's rampant personal skimming, the collective order was given for his assassination. Chicago sent two soldiers to handle the job, and Siegel was murdered in Beverly Hills on June 20, 1947. Immediately, each city provided an emissary to take over the Flamingo, protect their interests, and pick up the pieces.

Chicago sent Gus Greenbaum, an old-time Capone man whose activities hailed back to the days of Prohibition. Greenbaum was a masterful gambling pro and virtuoso skimmer, as well as a trusted soldier who'd effectively handled the Trans-American wire service for Chicago in Arizona. Under Greenbaum, the Flamingo reported a $4 million profit his first year as manager; in reality, profits prior to Greenbaum's skimming on the Outfit's behalf had reached 15 million.

With proof positive that money, tax-free and lots of it, could be made in Las Vegas, Mob dollars poured in. New casinos and hotels were built in rapid succession, each more ostentatious and outlandish than its predecessors. Overnight, Las Vegas became a gambler's paradise, and the Syndicate called all the shots—a situation that would continue until the late 1970s, when organized crime was finally forced out by the FBI.

Initially, Cleveland's Moe Dalitz owned the Desert Inn, while Meyer Lansky controlled the Thunderbird. The profitable Dunes was held by a New England family. The Sands was run by Lansky and Costello, with actor George Raft and entertainer Frank Sinatra holding part interest. California and Cleveland families had a piece of the Stardust—but only after months of behind-the-scenes threats and legal wrangling and only until Mooney made his push and won the largest share. The Tropicana was held by Frank Costello and Phil Kastel of New York.

Chicago would ultimately rely on union funds—particularly those of the Teamsters—for its financial backing and controlled the Sahara, Riviera, and the garish neo-Roman Caesar's Palace.

After Marshall Caifano had been dispatched to Vegas by Mooney in 1953, others followed. Mooney sent Johnny Roselli early on to negotiate and muscle into other casinos; Johnny Formosa, his Indiana gambling lieutenant; Joe Pignatello, his first bodyguard-chauffeur; Gus Zappas and Jimmy James, both union henchmen; and Chicago bookie John Drew. They were all there with one purpose in mind: increase Chicago's piece of the action.

By 1958, Mooney's personal take from Vegas was over three hundred thousand a month. Just thinking about that much money made Chuck's heart skip. And it was only a small part of hundreds of deals that flooded into Mooney's hands; overall, he was bringing in $4 million a month, tax-free.

After Chicago had gained control of the Riviera in 1952, Mooney had moved Gus Greenbaum in as manager. A proven master at the art of skimming for the Outfit, Greenbaum displayed talents Mooney liked. But after Marshall Caifano had located the traitorous Willie Bioff—the man whose testimony in 1942 was responsible for the imprisonment of Chicago's reigning gangsters—working right under Greenbaum in 1955, Greenbaum's star suddenly tarnished. He became a flagrant gambler—losing up to twenty thousand a week—as well as an alcoholic and drug addict. And, most important, he began skimming voraciously for himself from the Riviera, beyond what

Mooney considered reasonable. Meyer Lansky, who also had a share of the Riviera, agreed with Mooney that Greenbaum had to go.

Mooney gave the job to one of his lieutenants, who, in turn, supplied the soldiers. In December of 1958, three Chicago enforcers knocked at the door of Gus Greenbaum's Phoenix home. The gruesomely tortured and mutilated Mr. and Mrs. Greenbaum would later be found dead, their throats neatly slit.

News of the brutal slayings of the Greenbaums spread fast, which was exactly what Mooney wanted. They were a graphic example to anyone who dared cross Sam Giancana.

It was a cold, windy January afternoon in Chicago. Chuck had had his fill of paperwork and was checking the stock behind the bar. He'd paused to admire the newly decorated New Orleans–style lounge, the white wrought-iron chairs and glass-top tables, when Chuckie Nicoletti, Needles Gianola, and his sidekick, Mugsy Tortorella, swaggered in the door. They sat down at a sumptuous corner sofa and ordered vodka on the rocks, telling the cocktail waitress to ask Chuck to join them. In the background, the jukebox blared a hit tune by the Everly Brothers.

After exchanging hellos, Chuck pulled up a chair. It had been quiet in the joint that day, thanks to the icy roads, and he welcomed a chance to shoot the breeze with the guys.

"So, how the hell you guys been?" Chuck asked, smiling. "Or better, where the hell you been?"

"I've been out in Vegas," Needles said, grinning, and held open his empty suit pockets. "Fuckin' cleaned me out."

Chuck nodded. "It's better to take a win and get the hell out—"

"Or cut your losses and run," Mugsy interrupted, smiling.

"You hear about Gus Greenbaum?" Needles asked, sipping his vodka. He shot a look over at Nicoletti.

"Yeah," Chuck said, shaking his head. "Coppers found him and his wife with their throats slit."

"Greenbaum was fuckin' skimmin' for himself, tryin' to steal your brother blind," Nicoletti said, his cold eyes glazed like frost on a windowpane.

"Yeah, he deserved what he got," Needles agreed, lighting a Lucky Strike with an elegant gold lighter.

"Pretty terrible about his wife, though," Chuck added offhandedly.

"Not really," Mugsy remarked, and shrugged his shoulders. "It'll make people know that Chicago isn't full of chickenshit assholes when it comes to a woman. That it don't matter to us one way or another."

"Yeah, it sure doesn't matter to Mooney," Needles added.

"He likes to set an example . . . a woman really gets everybody's attention. And so what, she doesn't mean nothin' to any of us."

"Yeah, fuck her," Mugsy chimed in.

"Hey, hitting a broad is the same as hitting a man . . . only she's got tits and a pussy. Who the fuck cares? The guy's not there to screw her, he's there to do a job," Nicoletti said with conviction.

Chuck lit a cigar. It was true, hit men didn't care whether they murdered a woman or not. They didn't care whom they killed. That was their job and they were good at it and they liked it.

He looked over at them on the sofa. For a fleeting moment, he asked himself what the hell he was doing with these guys. They did share a common bond; they were all after a piece of the American dream. It's just that some guys were willing to go further than others to get there.

CHAPTER 18

On the surface, there could have been no more perfect
alliance than that between John Fitzgerald Kennedy—described by Eleanor Roosevelt as a part of "the new managerial elite that has neither principles nor character"—and
Sam Giancana.

The two men had it all: brash arrogance and lust for
power, ruthless ambition and vast personal wealth. Joe
Kennedy told Mooney in early 1959 that together they
would be unstoppable.

Considered one of the nation's wealthiest and most influential families, the Kennedys owed their fortune and
political connections to a heritage that hailed back to the
sordid days of Prohibition. Likewise, Mooney Giancana
had risen from similarly humble beginnings. Now referred
to as Sam most frequently by his associates—although
Chuck still called him Mooney—he reigned supreme in
the nation's underworld, according to everyone from re-

porters to Outfit guys. Chuck heard from his brother that he had over a billion dollars a year pouring into his coffers.

"The flower may look different . . . but the roots are the same," Mooney often quipped when referring to the Kennedys, and then added, "Never be misled by appearances, Chuck. Once a crook always a crook. The Kennedys may put on airs and pretend to be blue bloods, but they know and I know the real truth . . . we're cut from the same cloth."

Among the many phone calls made to political bosses and old cronies by Joe Kennedy that winter, several were to Mooney. Wily as he was, Kennedy had foolhardily decided to dance with the devil, believing in all his characteristic arrogance that he could play with fire and not get burned as he'd done throughout his life.

For Joe, an eternal pragmatist, there were certain individuals, criminal or not, with whom he wished to be ingratiated in his tireless quest for a Kennedy dynasty. Without the support and muscle of the powerful underworld—a world Joe knew all too well—overcoming the obstacles to his son's nomination would likely be impossible. Kennedy coveted the influence wielded by his old "alma mater" and was cognizant of where that power now rested. A man who only a few years previously had refused to return a phone call to mobster and longtime friend Frank Costello would now reestablish his network with organized crime. And with that purpose in mind, he called once again on the one man who could bring the full force of the nation's underworld to bear on his son's bid for the presidency—Mooney Giancana.

When he heard from Joe Kennedy, Chuck's brother wasn't surprised; he'd been waiting for the old man's call, waiting to extract further promises of influence in the nation's capital. For the first time, Chuck caught a glimpse of Mooney's dream. Like everyone else—from common dago peddlers to policy-playing shines—he'd held his own secret aspirations, and at last they were coming to fruition. While other children had been told they might grow up to be President of the United States one day, somewhere along the line, Mooney had come to the conclusion that owning the President would be far better. Now, that opportunity had presented itself and his dream was almost within his grasp.

A curious courtship thus began in 1959 between the man who would be President and the man who would be king. The very idea of possessing so much power intoxicated Mooney, and silently, Chuck began to question whether the sly old man had found Mooney's Achilles' heel. His brother had said it himself many times: "If it makes a man's heart race, it's a weakness." Listening to Mooney describe his plans for the 1960 election, still more than a year away, while basking in the afterglow of a conversation with Joe, Chuck—for the first time in his life—felt an ominous sense of concern for his brother. He wondered whether Mooney had fallen for the seduction, fallen victim to a set of false promises from a man who probably would say or do anything to make his son President of the United States.

Joe Kennedy already owed Mooney his life, but obviously that was not enough—Mooney wanted his soul. And his sons' souls. He relieved Chuck by saying he didn't trust the old man; the McClellan committee, still in session, was causing quite an uproar among his cronies—and watching Joe's sons work the crowds taught Mooney everything he needed to know about trusting the Kennedys.

He knew he needed something more than his reputation for retribution to guarantee their compliance. To accomplish that, he called on Frank Sinatra.

Hollywood's relationship with the Outfit encompassed three decades. Chicago had muscled its way into show business and paid its dues with the imprisonment of some of its biggest bosses in the wake of the celebrated Browne-Bioff trial. Mooney had wisely continued the lucrative contacts with producers, studios, and entertainers; aside from supplying top talent for his Vegas casinos, it also allowed him to push the careers of fledgling stars who might later be exploited. But as much as anything, he enjoyed the high life and fast broads Hollywood afforded; since Ange's death, he'd rolled in the sack with literally dozens of curvaceous entertainers and wannabes.

Mooney's relationship with Frank Sinatra spanned close to thirty years, as well. In New York, Havana, Vegas, and Hollywood, he partied with Frank's Rat Pack, or "Clan," and its extended entourage of fast-living celebrities: Joey Bishop, Dean Martin, Jerry Lewis, Sammy Davis, Jr., Eddie Fisher, Elizabeth Taylor, Mike Romanoff, Jimmy Van Heusen, Peter Lawford, Natalie Wood, Robert Wagner, Shirley MacLaine, Warren Beatty, and Angie Dickinson. Mooney said that many of the women who clung to the tight-knit group were "party girls" looking for a good time and a new fur coat.

Out of respect for Sinatra, Mooney maintained a modicum of decency toward the entertainer's high-rolling friends, using them for openings and engagements when it suited his purpose—but, nonetheless, he held them in disdain. "Those guys around Frank are losers, prima donnas, assholes," he complained to Chuck. They made good money, he said, but they lived from check to check—

always in debt for jewelry or a loan or a too-long night at the tables. And all of them were always "lookin' for somethin' for nothin'."

In truth, he liked Sinatra; Mooney said Sinatra had class and knew how to party. He was also loyal in the extreme. Frank might throw his weight around the clubs and restaurants and possess a string of flunkies who pandered to his every need, but with Mooney, the tables quickly turned. He was nothing if not deferential. And he always managed to locate broads too dumb to ask questions but smart enough to know that Sam Giancana might help their careers. In the months preceding the Democratic presidential primaries, Mooney also liked the fact that Frank Sinatra was a friend of the Kennedys.

The FBI and his detractors would later claim that female escapades were the unmaking of Sam Giancana; but in that, they were sadly mistaken. Mooney never really loved a woman, nor ever jeopardized his power for one. He could give the appearance of romantic love when it suited his purpose—and had hundreds of times, quite masterfully—in pursuit of new, unconquered flesh. But to Mooney, women were expendable objects like shoes. "Wear them out, throw them away," he'd say with a chuckle. "It's nice if they're the best-lookin' shoes you can buy, but they're still shoes anyway you cut it . . . disposable."

Mooney knew that, conversely, the Kennedys had a knack for getting too involved with women. From his days and nights of revelry at the Cal-Neva in Lake Tahoe with Sinatra, Lawford, and the Kennedy brothers, he'd learned they were not only adulterous but emotional and jealous, as well.

According to Mooney, it was no secret that Joe's sons

had inherited their father's penchant for a good time. Since the old days, Mooney said Joe had frequented the Cal-Neva, placing bets and banging his share of broads every chance he got. And in the early fifties, Mooney confided, Jack had followed in his father's footsteps, secreting himself away in a discreet Cal-Neva chalet. Mooney himself had been at more than a few of the Kennedy Cal-Neva "parties." The men had sex with prostitutes—sometimes two or more at a time—in bathtubs, hallways, closets, on floors, almost everywhere but in a bed.

The Kennedys, Mooney gleefully reported, liked the thrill that came with the kinky and clandestine, "and the kinkier, the better." They liked to think they were above the morality of the "other classes." Mooney was convinced that if he could find the right woman, he might be able to put Jack in a corner. Mooney knew a chink in the armor when he saw one.

In mid-March, with the McClellan committee subpoena still floating around unserved and his daughter Annette's lavish wedding to an Outfit bartender looming on the horizon, he dropped by the Thunderbolt Motel on his way to the airport.

Chuck peered over a mound of paperwork and saw Mooney smiling back at him.

"Hey, I'm flyin' out to Vegas . . . wanna come along?" Mooney tempted. "Lots of broads and good food."

Chuck motioned at the paperwork and shook his head. "Sure, if you don't care if this joint goes under." He smiled wanly across the desk.

"Well, you sure look like you could use some more time in the sun to me," Mooney said, grinning. He was especially happy and relaxed; his tanned face seemed rested. "Aren't you gonna offer me some coffee or somethin'?"

Chuck called the motel's restaurant manager for a pot of coffee and then leaned back in his chair. "So it's Vegas now? Don't you ever stay in town anymore?"

"Shit, I gotta keep ahead of the posse," Mooney said.

"The G? That shouldn't be too hard for an old wheelman like you."

"Yeah," he said, smiling. "I don't think they could find their ass with both hands tied behind their back. Jesus, what fuckin' saps. You know, I found out how much those dumb bastards make and I couldn't believe it." He lit a cigar and leaned back in the chair, putting his feet up on Chuck's desk.

"How much?"

Mooney snickered. "Ten grand a year . . . and that's if they're lucky and Hoover likes 'em. Jesus, it's not worth gettin' outta bed in the morning for that. Workin' for the Outfit, some guys make that much in one week." He paused while a crisply uniformed waitress poured their coffee. When she left, closing the door, he continued. "Hey, I got it all figured out, Chuck . . . the Kennedys and all."

"Uh-huh," Chuck said, stirring his coffee while giving Mooney his undivided attention.

"See, just like the old man, Jack can't keep his hands off a broad. So"—his eyes turned cold and the smile dropped from his face—"we'll set him up . . . get enough dirt on Mr. All-American family man to ruin him for life. Promises or not, he won't step outta line then." He sighed and said with a tinge of remorse, "Humphreys tells me he wished he'd known about this sooner . . . he could have tied the illustrious Senator Kennedy up a long time ago."

He shrugged his shoulders and winked, smiling brightly. "But, it's never too late."

Mooney explained that he would get Frank Sinatra, already a fellow Kennedy carouser, to set it up out west. Sinatra was close to Peter Lawford, who was married to Pat Kennedy. Together with Murray Humphreys in Washington, Sinatra would be in charge of finding just the right girls to entice Jack.

"Murray will set up a place just outside the capital; he's already got it picked out. Real class. Top drawer and discreet for our publicity-conscious politicians. It'll be a 'hospitality suite,' " he said, chortling at his choice of words. "Murray'll get the girls in there. Frank can find a few, too, and then we'll entertain those politicians like they've never been entertained."

He stopped for a moment and gulped at his coffee with excitement. "Here's the best part, though. . . . I'm gonna buy the Kennedys' favorite hangout, the Cal-Neva. I'll have both joints wired from top to bottom and anyplace else the Kennedys go." He grinned. "Those tapes should be real interesting."

"Where the hell are you gonna get wires? From your friends at the THP?" Chuck said, laughing.

"No, fuck them. I've got it lined up with Hoffa to set it all up with Bob Maheu and the CIA. Hoffa's had the guys wire joints for me before. . . . They'll help me out this time. . . . Shit, they owe me a few favors."

"Well, what about Bobby Kennedy? You haven't mentioned him," Chuck pointed out.

"Yeah, I know . . . and he's the worst one of the bunch. He's a troublemaker, for sure. A cocky greenhorn little bastard who's too big for his fuckin' britches. Hey, don't worry about him. . . . I'll cut him down to size. Frank tells me he's pretty straitlaced, but he's played around. We just gotta get him in the right spot. Frank'll find a broad that'll do the trick.''

"You think Frank'll go along with all this shit?" Chuck asked.

"Are you fuckin' kiddin'? What choice does he have? Christ Almighty, he owes the Outfit. He'll go along because he'll do anything I ask. And he won't even know why I want him to do it. He won't ask questions, and if he did, I wouldn't tell him. He talks too much. He'll just do it." He paused. "See this?" Mooney held up his hand, displaying a beautiful star sapphire pinky ring. "He gave me this ring. I'm his fuckin' hero. Frank is one of the few people I know who will follow through.''

"You really like the guy, don't you?" Chuck said, slightly amused. Mooney wasn't one to show any sign of affection.

"Yeah, I'll be honest . . . the guy's got a big mouth sometimes, and for this deal he'll be just another fuckin' pimp. But he's a stand-up guy . . . he's a good guy. Too good for the lousy scum out in Hollywood." He stood up to leave. "Hold on, Chuck . . . this is gonna be my decade comin' up.''

He was probably right, Chuck thought as he watched his brother breeze out the doorway. The way Chuck understood it, the Kennedys didn't really need money—so they couldn't be bought. Unlike most politicians, if they did win the election, they wouldn't owe a bunch of favors. Likewise, Mooney sure as hell didn't need money, so he couldn't be compromised. But if he got the Kennedy brothers in a few unpleasant spots with broads, well, they'd be in a box.

Mooney continued to amaze him—the way he could

spot a guy's vulnerability. And then if he wanted to get him, he'd plot and scheme until the guy was so tied up, he'd never see the light of day. Obviously, Mooney knew what he was doing with the Kennedys.

Aside from talking with Frank, Mooney had other business to attend to in Las Vegas. He was skimming millions from the Teamsters' pension fund for the Stardust that year. And while the McClellan committee was, as he put it, "sittin' around on their asses, *talkin'* about the pilfering of union funds," Mooney was guaranteeing their illegal disposal. He had Murray Humphreys and Jimmy Hoffa put Red Dorfman's son Allen into power as manager of the fund, assuring the dollars he needed would be accessible.

Mooney's ventures into the hotels and casinos in Las Vegas were extremely low-profile. The Nevada Gaming Commission viewed having known mafiosi in their midst as highly undesirable, and therefore, when he checked in at the Desert Inn that March, he used the alias S. Flood.

On his travels, he often used the last name of women he was currently bedding or family members. Flood referred to Ange's sister Rose Flood. Paige, another name he frequently used, was derived from his fling with chorus girl Roma Paige. He often used the name Gold in Miami and New York because he said being a Jew got you instant respect in those towns. There were dozens of others, selected on a whim or as a joke.

Unbeknown to Mooney, the FBI had gotten word of his jaunt to Vegas and spotted him at the Desert Inn. The following day, March 25—almost one full year since it had first been issued—the McClellan committee's subpoena was served. Mooney was to testify before the committee in June.

Chuck was surprised that the prospect of going before

the grueling committee didn't faze Mooney; all he said was that he was too busy meeting with Joe Kennedy, working out the details of their agreement for Jack's presidential campaign, to let the McClellan committee become anything more than a temporary annoyance. It all seemed pretty convoluted to Chuck—one day the Kennedys were meeting with Mooney to get his backing and the next they were interrogating him like a common criminal before a Senate committee. But Mooney brushed all that aside, saying that once Jack Kennedy was elected, they'd go back to "business as usual" in the Outfit.

Mooney truly relished the notion of no longer dealing with Hoover's THP agents and the publicity their surveillance had brought. As of late, his picture seemed to hit the papers with increasing regularity in Chicago; he yearned for the old days and his incognito status. "It hurts business when you can't even take a piss without having the G look over your shoulder. I can hardly wait to see their faces when our new boy in the White House tells 'em to lay off."

The publicity surrounding Mooney was hurting more than Outfit business; Chuck's family was wrestling with constant rejection and condemnation. Chuck never brought up their hardship to his brother; he didn't think it was appropriate to whine about his petty troubles when Mooney was up to his eyeballs in Senate committee investigations, federal agents, and, most important perhaps, the upcoming presidential primaries.

Chuck had to admit, however, that little Mooney was strangely quiet and far too withdrawn for a normal four-year-old. Anne Marie told him their youngest son stayed to himself in the backyard or sat alone for hours by the fence, silently watching the horses canter in the fields. She said the neighborhood children teased him about having the same name as a gangster.

"Well, we can't change his name," Chuck retorted angrily. "Not now. But it'll get better. My brother's gonna turn everything around real soon. You'll see . . . things will settle down around here." Chuck hadn't really been angry at his wife, but he viewed the situation as unsolvable for now. Something he couldn't change, he didn't want to dwell on. The truth was, it killed him to think little Mooney was being ostracized because of a name—one Chuck had originally intended to be an honor.

Chuckie, their nine-year-old, suffered under the same stigma, but in his case, the stress took a different toll. Unlike his little brother, Chuckie was outgoing, rambunctious, and outspoken. When ridiculed, he fought back; they'd lost count of the notes from school and teachers' meetings, the bloody noses and torn clothes. The reaction from his classmates was so painful, Chuckie had even asked to go away to a military academy. Initially reluctant, Chuck and Anne Marie had begun to think that in light of the attention the Giancana name was now receiving, it might be best. At least he'd be protected there and away from the daily newspaper headlines that dogged his every step.

It seemed there would never be an end to the headlines. If it wasn't an exposé on Chicago's "Number One Gangster," it was something far more mundane. The press was obviously aware that sensational stories about mobsters sell newspapers. A flurry of such stories appeared on April 4, 1959, when Mooney's eldest daughter, Annette, married at Chicago's plush La Salle Hotel.

The papers all said it was a staggeringly expensive affair, attended by an honor roll of top mafiosi. And it was.

Mooney laid out $25,000 for the reception's seven hundred guests at a time when a typical middle-class American home cost $17,000.

Among the women, word spread that Annette wanted it to be the biggest bash the city had ever witnessed. Mooney complained to Chuck that she was "damned determined to make a scene. . . . She thinks she's some goddamned movie star, I guess she'll never grow up. But at least now some other man will have to worry about her."

The lavish affair, featuring Joey Bishop as headliner, was peopled by the most powerful members of Chicago's underworld. It reminded Chuck of his own marriage ten years previously—only bigger. "Annette'll probably do a couple hundred grand," Mooney whispered as he surveyed the crowd. He was obviously pleased, and he had a right to be; he'd earned every last dime paid in tribute to his daughter that day. He'd scratched and scraped and clawed his way to the top.

The publicity received in the wedding's wake only added insult to injury for Chuck's family. Mooney had held an uncharacteristically frank and open conversation with reporter Sandy Smith, and soon it appeared in papers across the country.

Again, Chuck's wife and children were bombarded with stares and whispers from the neighbors. "Maybe we should move back into town," Anne Marie said, sighing. "I can't take much more."

But Chuck wouldn't hear of it; he was certain Mooney was making inroads with the Kennedys and certain that, if Jack was elected, all their troubles would be over.

At a time when old man Kennedy was paying thousands of dollars to interest the press in his son Jack, the wealth of publicity Sam Giancana received was ironic. Scores of publications headlined two names that year: Kennedy and Giancana. The only difference Chuck could think of was that one's coverage was paid for in blood, the other's in dollars. "We've got a lot in common . . . me and the Kennedys," Mooney said in all seriousness. "The good thing is, nobody knows it."

J. Edgar Hoover, however, did recognize the similarity. He knew Kennedy's heritage and had compiled a dossier on Joe and his sons over the years. In fact, Mooney said he heard from former Chicago FBI agents Guy Banister in New Orleans and Bob Maheu out west that Hoover was watching the Kennedys with the same intensity given him. "Hoover blames Bobby for all the bad publicity he and the FBI got after Apalachin," Mooney explained. "He's got a hard-on for the Kennedys . . . no question about it. And that's good. That means Hoover and I are workin' on the same side. He just hasn't figured it out yet."

In June, while Murray Humphreys and Frank Sinatra were busily setting up a number of sexual lures for Jack Kennedy, Mooney was testifying before Bobby at the McClellan committee. It was all crazy to him, he said to Chuck later. "Bobby must know I saved his old man's life . . . that we're talkin' now. They're all nuts in that family," he ranted.

Mooney, who sported a toupee for the occasion to misdirect at least some of the press, took the Fifth Amendment thirty-four times and, to his credit, managed to maintain his composure during what he described as a "childish" attack from Bobby.

"I thought only little girls giggled, Mr. Giancana," Kennedy had taunted. Chuck's brother explained Mooney's laughter during the hearings: "Sittin' there, I couldn't help but laugh. . . . I was thinkin' about a night with his brother at the Cal-Neva. It was all so funny . . . I couldn't help it. What a bunch of fuckin' hypocrites.''

Although Mooney left Washington for business in Mexico determined to ''fix that smartass Bobby as soon as I get a chance,'' the actual outcome of the McClellan committee's investigation into organized crime would be inconsequential. Nobody in the ''Mafia'' went to jail as a result of testimony received by the committee. The worst thing to come of the thirty-month hearings would be the sensationalized testimony given by a low-level New York gang member named Joe Valachi, and the public embarrassment suffered by J. Edgar Hoover, which ultimately led to Hoover's personal war against ''La Cosa Nostra.''

Ironically, while the FBI was busy laying a trap for Mooney on his return to Chicago through customs, Mooney was conducting business in Mexico with another branch of the U.S. government—the CIA.

On his return from Mexico, Mooney ran into trouble at Chicago's Midway Airport. At customs, he agreeably submitted to a search, but when they found another man's driver's license in his wallet, his demeanor abruptly changed. After questioning, he was released, unscathed but ruffled. Again, he made headlines. And again Chuck's children were the butt of cruel jokes and pranks from their fellow classmates.

Following the irritating incident at the airport, Mooney dropped by the Thunderbolt. There, lounging by the pool with Chuck, he expressed puzzlement over the fact that the government—with its many branches—had so little collaboration and intercommunication.

His contacts in the intelligence agency had told him Hoover detested the CIA, was jealous of their power and budget, and bitterly resented the secrecy that shrouded their operations. "The right hand doesn't know what the left is doin'," he said, shaking his head in disbelief, squinting in the glare of the sunshine.

"What's that supposed to mean?" Chuck asked, pouring chilled Bloody Marys crowned with celery sticks into tall frosted mugs. He handed one to his brother.

"It means, like I said before, that I'm workin' for the government and half the government doesn't even know it." Mooney removed the celery stick and took a bite. "Bobby Kennedy is just too far down the ladder to know about it and J. Edgar Hoover can't find out because the CIA's afraid he'd blow the lid off the whole operation just out of spite. So, for now, I guess I'm fucked."

"Pretty thankless," Chuck commented. He was thinking about how differently people might react if they knew Mooney was actually helping the U.S. government.

"That's fine, though. I've made a lot of money with those guys. A lot of money."

"Yeah, well, you stand to lose a lot of money, too . . . look at Cuba. Since Castro took over in January, who knows?"

"So far, it's iffy," Mooney conceded. "But by backin' Castro, we may have saved our ass. You never really know, though, how a deal like this'll turn out . . . it's a crapshoot. We gave him millions to let us reopen the casinos. Maybe he'll see this as an opportunity."

"Maybe," Chuck said.

"Well, we do have a guy on the inside. With Castro makin' our guy Frank Fiorini his 'Minister of Games of Chance,' we should be covered." He sighed and thoughtfully sipped his drink.

"How about Trafficante? I heard he's in jail down there. A bad sign?"

Mooney's eyes narrowed and he nodded in agreement. "It *is* a bad sign. Marcello's worried about his drug rackets. . . . We could lose a lot down there besides gambling and Santo Trafficante. But I'll get him out. . . . Ruby's workin' on it. It's gonna cost me, though, because Castro knows Santo was real tight with all the old guard. I may have to go down to Havana myself. What the hell, I got investments to protect, right?"

Although he said nothing, Chuck believed he had investments of his own that were slipping away. In spite of Anne Marie's valiant attempts at friendship, their neighbors continued to behave decently but with suspicion. His two sons had almost grown accustomed to being left out of birthday parties and other neighborhood celebrations. With another Giancana wedding to attend less than a month after Mooney's tussle at the airport—this time, Bonnie was tying the knot with Tony Tisci, congressional aide to Mooney's political puppet U.S. Representative Roland Libonati—Chuck imagined he might be facing the last straw.

Both Chuck and Anne Marie were relieved to find that this time security was tight at the wedding and reception. Additionally, the festivities were held out of town, in Miami on July 4—a day reporter Sandy Smith traditionally staked out Tony Accardo's annual backyard barbecue in Chicago.

While Sandy Smith dutifully recorded the unusually subdued and oddly small Accardo party in Chicago, mafiosi were flying in from around the country to Miami. The two hundred tuxedoed guests at the Fontainebleau Hotel enjoyed a reception equal in extravagance to Annette's affair just three months previously—but this time, thankfully, Mooney gave no interviews to the press.

"I guess we can wait a while to sell our house," Chuck

said, smiling, as he and Anne Marie came back on the plane. Maybe it was all that sunshine, but somehow being in Florida always made things brighter. He patted his wife's small gloved hand. "We're gonna be just fine, Babe, just fine."

Even Mooney seemed to have been rejuvenated by the Sunshine State. He'd met with the Kennedys, he told Chuck, and "had it all worked out."

In late August, Chuck heard that Santo Trafficante had been released and allowed to leave Cuba. His brother said it was "a job well done by Jack Ruby," and as reward, he was giving him a small piece of a casino in Havana. "Things are smoothin' out," he remarked. "Maybe we'll stay in business down there, maybe not. . . . Santo got hurt pretty good, but he got out with as many dollars as he could and a lot of those dollars are mine. So far, so good."

By autumn of 1959, Mooney's attentions were turned once again to the political maneuvering of Joe Kennedy. He met with him at Chicago's Ambassador East on three separate occasions to finalize their agreement. Mooney said both Mayor Daley and Jack Kennedy were there, as well.

Although Chuck was curious as to the outcome of the discussions, he didn't pry; he'd learned long ago that asking too many questions when Mooney wasn't talkative was an unattractive trait. So he was forced to be satisfied with Mooney's sole comment on the meetings: "I'll have a lot to be thankful for by this time next year . . . everything is in place."

Shortly before Christmas, Chuck found Mooney in a more jovial, gregarious mood when he dropped by his home in Oak Park. Mooney offered him some eggnog and cookies and they retired, proper holiday nourishment in tow, tō his basement office.

This time, he wasn't bashful about discussing his progress. Chuck couldn't recall ever seeing his brother so pleased with himself.

"I got everything I wanted," Mooney abruptly announced, setting his glass down and lighting a cigar.

"Everything?" Chuck felt a growing excitement. If Mooney had in fact extracted some promise of protection from the Kennedys, his own family's troubles would be over. He silently said a prayer.

"Yep . . . everything. It's pretty simple, really. I help get Jack elected and, in return, he calls off the heat. It'll be business as usual. Of course, I said I'd keep it low-profile . . . after all, I'm not gonna be a fuckin' diplomat; I won't have total immunity." He laughed.

"What about Bobby?" Chuck hated to sound like a broken record, but Bobby was the one who really worried him.

"Bobby's taken care of. I asked them to get him off that damned McClellan committee . . . so they're gonna have him help run the campaign."

"Great," Chuck said.

"So you see, it's all ins and no outs for me when Jack's elected. I'll be on easy street . . . no more coppers, no more FBI, no more bullshit. No more Bobby. As far as my business will be concerned—Vegas, Teamsters, drugs, you name it—they'll all just turn their heads and they'll have executive orders to do it. Or else."

"No kiddin'?" Chuck said, startled by the magnitude of it all.

"Yeah, no kiddin'." Mooney lifted his glass and smiled.

A frown crossed Chuck's face. "Hey, did Joe say that . . . or did Jack? I mean, can you trust the old man?" Chuck had serious doubts about Joe Kennedy.

"Joe and I worked it out first, then Jack and I sat down. Jack knows the score. He knows how to play ball. Actually, he's not a bad guy to do business with." Mooney grinned, obviously pleased with himself. He began to laugh.

"What's so funny?"

"You should've seen Jack's face when I told him about me workin' with the CIA. I wish I had a picture."

"I bet. So you trust Jack's word, then, no double-dealin'?"

"Let me put it this way, I have myself covered in the event he suddenly gets amnesia."

"Yeah?"

Mooney grinned smugly. "I've already got enough dirt on Jack Kennedy and his lousy old man to ruin ten politicians' careers. I've got pictures, tape recordings, film, you name it, all safe and sound in a safe-deposit box. The American public would be real happy to see their President bein' serviced by three women and one of 'em a shine broad to boot. Yeah, if I ever need an ace, here's the key." He dangled a small gold key in Chuck's face and then slipped it back in his pocket.

Not content with the leverage he already had, Mooney was planning to arm himself with even more compromising information. "Frank's got it all handled with the broads for Kennedy. And there's more, all lined up, ready to go. Angie Dickinson's got a thing goin' with Jack . . . she's gonna go back and forth to Washington. We got some other girls, one Frank says is a dead ringer for Jack's wife . . . if you can imagine that." He shook his head and chuckled. "Frank's gonna introduce them. We're gonna get Jack in real deep with Monroe, too. . . . I hear he's been poppin' her. Hell, Frank tells me Bobby's even made a few remarks about wantin' to fuck her himself. Jesus, those Kennedy brothers are animals."

"Do the broads know what the deal is?"

"Hell no, they'll just think it's all coincidence or just a favor to Frank or me or that Frank's doin' them a favor introducin' them to the next President of the United States. You know, women eat that shit up." He grinned, popping a cookie in his mouth, chewing it thoughtfully. "To tell you the truth, Frank doesn't know for sure what I'm up to. . . . He thinks I just wanna make the Kennedys happy." Mooney laughed aloud.

"Right," Chuck said, his words laced with sarcasm.

"Right," Mooney echoed, grinning.

In January of 1960, secure in the knowledge that the dirt he was collecting would ensure compliance in his pact with the Kennedys, Mooney instructed Sinatra to start working to get Jack elected. He wanted him to "pull out all the stops," and that included getting all his friends on board, as well. "I told Frank to use every single trick in the book to get Hollywood behind Jack Kennedy. I don't just want the guy nominated for President, I want him to *be* President."

Soon after, Mooney burst into the Thunderbolt lounge practically bubbling over with joy. Certain Jack Kennedy would be President, Mooney was already flaunting the expected victory—still eleven months away—as if it was his own. He swaggered past the wrought-iron tables and up to the immense mirrored bar, proclaiming to Chuck, "We're all invited to the greatest show on earth. And it's gonna be worth the price of admission . . . every goddamned dollar.''

It was clear to Chuck that, for his brother, putting Kennedy in the White House would be a personal victory. Then not only would Mooney own governors and congressmen; he'd have what he called, ''a front-row seat at the biggest show of all.''

It took little insistence from Mooney for Frank Sinatra to plunge ahead on the campaign trail, inviting Jack to lavish parties, throwing campaign get-togethers at Pat and Peter Lawford's home. Sinatra convinced a bevy of stars— all who were tied to Mooney in one way or another—to support the campaign publicly.

Mooney said Frank was enamored at the prospect of wining and dining a President, of being able to call up his friend in the Oval Office someday. ''I think he's got it in his head he wants to be ambassador to Italy,'' Mooney said, laughing. In January, Frank invited Kennedy, already on the campaign trail, to a show at the Sands in Vegas, featuring his Clan buddies and the cast of *Ocean's Eleven*.

Kennedy went to Vegas and was treated like royalty— everything was on the house from the bedroom to boardroom. Slowly, Jack Kennedy was becoming more deeply involved with Mooney's world. Mooney might not always be present at the star-studded soirees, but his power seeped from every nook and cranny of the lounges, restaurants, stages, and boudoirs Kennedy now frequented with his brother-in-law Peter Lawford and celebrity friend Frank Sinatra. Each event was orchestrated by his unseen hand.

It was all working out even better than he'd anticipated: ''Kennedy loves to party, loves the celebrity shit. Frank's even gonna produce a campaign song for the guy using the song 'High Hopes.' You just watch, it's all gonna go to Kennedy's head and then he'll really fuck up. . . . You know what I always say, 'Play in shit long enough and somethin's bound to stick.' "

Mooney insisted Frank get some more girls in line right away and suggested he again invite Jack to the Sands in Vegas to introduce the "bait," as Mooney called it.

On February 7, 1960, at the Las Vegas Sands, Frank introduced his ex-girlfriend, the pretty brunette Judy Campbell—who later gained notoriety as Judith Campbell Exner—to Jack Kennedy. According to Mooney, Judy was little different from all the other women who flocked to Sinatra and his underworld friends in search of stardom, trinkets, or just a good time. But Frank reported to Mooney that Jack was immediately taken by this woman who reminded people of his wife, Jackie.

In March, when Mooney learned that Kennedy was bedding Judy Campbell on a regular basis, snatching time away from his political vote thumping every chance he got, he was close to ecstatic. He wanted Kennedy to have a "regular," someone he could eventually manipulate and use to his own advantage. With Judy Campbell, it appeared he'd struck gold.

Over the years, Mooney had utilized what to Chuck had become a familiar strategy: Whenever he wanted to know more about a man working for him, he became fast friends—lovers usually—with the guy's wife or girlfriend. Mooney moved slowly, circling his prey, imperceptible as a predator at first. He'd come around under the auspices of conducting some business deal with the woman's husband—making a new racket up as bait if he had to. Throughout his visits, he maintained the behavior of a perfect gentleman. After a while, he'd be "thoughtful" enough to take the woman a small trinket when he called on her husband—typically, a ring or bracelet. He always openly gave it to her in her husband's presence and therefore, ironically, his attentions convinced the guy that his own career was about to take off. "That's what ego will get you," Mooney would snort after bedding yet another man's wife.

Mooney would also take the time to call up and chat with the woman, "Just to see how you and my man are doin'," he'd say with all the charm he could muster. It was a charm that was considerable. Sometime along the line, he'd drop by with a fur coat. He waited, biding his time; he wasn't pushy. But it wasn't long before he had the woman in bed, revealing her husband's deepest secrets, his every weakness.

Mooney used a woman's infidelity to prove a point to her husband: He owned them and could take anything they possessed. Even if the guy never realized Mooney was banging his wife, it didn't matter. The important thing was for Mooney to know—to know he could destroy the guy anytime he wanted. With that knowledge, he always held the ace.

Recognizing his brother's pattern of seduction, it came as no shock to Chuck when he learned Mooney had told Frank Sinatra to introduce him to Kennedy's new plaything, Judy Campbell. After their "chance introduction" and dinner at Miami's Fontainebleau Hotel in late March, Mooney was ready to take it from there. True to form, he showered Judy with flowers and gifts and was soon seen with her on his arm from New York to Vegas. Jack knew of Mooney's friendship with Judy, he said, and saw nothing harmful in it whatsoever.

"Jesus, what an ego," Mooney said, chuckling. "The

guy thinks I'm just bein' a friend. He even suggested that maybe Judy could act as our go-between to set up meetings." He shook his head. "What an idiot."

Indeed, Mooney didn't seem to need a go-between; he met with Jack and Joe several times during the primaries, in Florida, New York, Chicago, and at the Cal-Neva in Tahoe. "Jack's worried about a few states," Mooney told Chuck. "Mostly West Virginia, because of the Bible Belt there and the coal miners' union . . . hell, the whole union vote back east is a problem." Referring to his Cal-Neva manager, Skinny D'Amato, Mooney said, "I told Skinny to tell Joe that I'll take care of West Virginia on one condition—that after Jack's President, Joe Adonis is allowed back in the country. The guys out east want Adonis back. Jack and his old man couldn't say yes fast enough . . . didn't have any problem at all bringin' a deported gangster back into the country. So we've got a deal for West Virginia."

Mooney paused a moment, then continued. "I did explain to them that once we get past the convention and start on the national campaign, the Teamsters can't come out publicly for Jack . . . that would look pretty fishy given what the McClellan committee did to Hoffa and his boys . . . let alone the stunts Bobby pulled. But behind the scenes, no problem . . . I've already got it worked out with Jimmy to skim a couple million out of the union for Jack's national campaign, based on Kennedy's agreement that Bobby will leave Hoffa and the Teamsters alone."

The East Coast states were a relatively simple job, but the hills of West Virginia proved a challenge. "We're gonna have to buy every fuckin' vote in the state," Mooney lamented as the May primary drew near.

The entire Kennedy family turned out in mass to help

ring out the vote for Jack in West Virginia, but Mooney
aid behind the scenes, away from the glare of the cameras,
vas where the vote would be won. He sent Skinny
)'Amato to West Virginia with a suitcase full of money.

In later years, the amount contributed by the Chicago
)utfit to the West Virginia primary would be put at fifty
housand dollars—however, that May, Mooney confided
hat because the state was deemed so critical, he'd put in
alf a million of his own money. "Jesus, we even had to
nuscle the taverns to convince 'em to play Frank's song
High Hopes,' on the jukeboxes. Those hillbillies hate the
dea of an East Coast Irish Catholic President."

Jack Kennedy had won every primary he'd entered.
With his victory in West Virginia, beating Hubert Hum-
hrey by a margin of 29 percent, it looked as if there would
e no stopping his quest for the nomination.

In anticipation of the July Democratic National Conven-
ion, the press hailed Kennedy as a new breed—a young,
harismatic idealist who offered America a breath of fresh
ir. Mooney found this portrayal especially humorous; like
veryone else, Jack Kennedy could be bought. He'd just
ad to use a different currency.

He kept close tabs on Kennedy's goings-on, thanks to
is wiretaps and Frank Sinatra. The Kennedy clan moved
nto the California home of Joe's old flame Marion Davies
 prepare for the convention in Los Angeles, and Frank
vas right there, doing a superb job as "social director"—
cting as bartender and matchmaker for his friends. Moo-
ey received daily progress reports; he was delighted.

At the convention, Jack wowed the delegates and press
nce more, winning on the first ballot. Mooney later told
Chuck that he'd discussed the selection of Jack's running
nate with Joe Kennedy and it had been agreed that a Texas

politician named Lyndon Johnson would be Jack's choice.
Early on in the primaries, Mooney said, Carlos Marcello
had made it clear that he wanted Johnson in the White
House, believing Johnson's political machine could swing
the South, an assertion verified by Jack Ruby, still Chicago's representative in Dallas. "Between Illinois and
Texas, we can swing the whole damned country," Mooney
said. "Joe liked the idea. . . . He owed Johnson more than
a few favors, anyway, even if it looked like they hated
each other. . . . Johnson put Jack on the Foreign Relations
Committee as a favor to Joe way back when and that
boosted Jack's career. So it was settled. Johnson's gonna
be Vice President."

Apparently, Joe was able to convince his son of the
wisdom of making Johnson his vice presidential running
mate despite the immediate fallout. Shocked Kennedy supporters—including Bobby—ranted and railed to no avail.
Lyndon Johnson's name was added to the Democratic
ticket.

Certainly, there had been elections before, but none in
which Mooney took so active an interest. Between his
transcontinental jaunts, he avidly watched the political
drama unfold. Chuck also found himself glued to the television, eagerly awaiting some tidbit of information. He'd
begun secretly to embrace his brother's dream of owning
the President—not for the power it would bring but for the
relief; his family was suffering more than ever due to the
notorious Giancana name.

Chuckie was now in military school, but it was his
youngest son who concerned him most; he didn't have the
same assertive temperament as Chuckie. Shy and easily
stung by the cruel comments from his classmates, little
Mooney was now in first grade and doing poorly in school.

"It's no wonder," Anne Marie said, wringing her hands. "The children act like they have machine guns and follow him around the playground going 'rat-a-tat-tat' all day long, saying he's a little gangster like his uncle." It seemed to Chuck that his brother had been reaping all the rewards of his position—piles of money, any broad he wanted, and, now, the ear of the next President. If Jack Kennedy actually won the election, Chuck thought it should be time for things to turn in his own favor.

He caught himself daydreaming about life after the election: There would be no more G-men shadowing his family, no more negative publicity. They could have neighborhood barbecues and cocktail parties; their kids could finally make friends and be able to concentrate on school so they'd go to college someday. Chuck hardly realized it when it happened, but by October, Mooney's dream had become his own.

Across the country, there were literally dozens of mafiosi who shared Mooney's dream, as well. With Jack Kennedy as President, there would be lucrative government contracts coming their way, friends appointed to high places, leniency in the event of a legal entanglement.

Even so, as Mooney explained to Chuck over dinner in late October at Meo's Norwood House, the Outfit was still "hedging its bets."

"We'll contribute to Nixon, too. They'll each get our support. Marcello and I together are givin' Nixon a million bucks. Just like we gave Lyndon Johnson a good piece of change. But of course, that's nothin' compared to what we've given Jack. Two million dollars on top of all the votes we've bought for the primaries. If it's close, we know we can steal the votes we need. But, if Johnson can't take the South and it goes to Nixon, well, we'll still come out on top. Not great . . . not as good as Jack . . . but in control.''

''You know, I can't understand why you don't just back Nixon, he's been the Outfit's boy for years. Why not now?''

''Because Kennedy is playin' ball with me . . . he's made some big promises. Nixon isn't in *my* pocket like Jack'll be. A lot of bosses own a piece of Nixon . . . we share the influence. Jack will be all mine.''

''Shit, I still worry about trustin' them. . . . The Kennedys are, well, look at Bobby.''

''Bobby doesn't even know what Jack and I have been talkin' about. He's out of the picture. He'll be just another goddamned lawyer soon. They've promised me they'll take care of him. Jack is gonna be President . . . not Bobby. Besides, if anything goes wrong, I've got a lot of shit on them.''

''Good.'' Chuck fell silent.

''You aren't convinced, are you? Jesus Christ, I've never seen you like this. Sure Nixon's ours, but Jack could be all mine. There's a big difference. Nixon's been good to us. . . . Hell, we like each other well enough, but you didn't see him do anything about Hoover, did you?''

''True,'' Chuck said, nodding. He'd heard that Mooney had met several times in Washington with Richard Nixon and that they'd actually gotten along quite well. ''We understand each other'' was how Mooney had put it.

''Granted, Nixon had his hands tied. . . . He couldn't . . . I mean, the heat was on too high just to try to bury Hoover. Nixon's done me some favors, all right . . . got us some highway contracts, worked with the unions and overseas. And we've helped him and his CIA buddies out, too. Shit, he even helped my guy in Texas, Ruby, get out of testifying in front of Congress back in forty-seven.''

''How's that?''

Mooney started to laugh. ''By sayin' Ruby worked for *him*.''

''You're kiddin'?''

''No, but the funny thing is between Murray Humphreys greasin' a few palms and Nixon sayin' that, the fed bought it.''

''That just proves my point,'' Chuck said. ''I still think your safe bet is Nixon.''

''Jesus, Chuck, you sound like a fuckin' broken record. Like I said, we'll hedge our bets. Just like we did out in California when Nixon was runnin' for senator. Shit . . . he owes us.''

''That's what I mean,'' Chuck insisted.

''Hey, would you rather have the milk or the whole cow? Me, I'd prefer the cow.''

''I hear you . . . but you don't know what the hell Jack'll do once he's elected. With Nixon, you got a track record.''

Mooney nodded. ''That's the safe way to play it all right. But the safe way isn't gonna get me where I wanna go and it never has. That's the problem with you, Chuck, you wanna always play it safe.''

A sudden look of hurt crossed Chuck's face and before he could hide his feelings, Mooney hastily added, ''Hey, that's okay, we're just different. You like runnin' a business. Me? I wanna run the country.''

CHAPTER 19

Not since 1916 had there been such a close election. On November 8, 1960, calls crisscrossed the country throughout the day and well into the night. To stay abreast of the returns personally, Frank Sinatra had posted himself at his L.A. office, where an open telephone line to Mooney's political fixer and Democratic National Committeeman, Jake Arvey, had been set up for election day. Sinatra received reports on the Illinois election each half hour. The news had been good; up until eleven o'clock, it appeared Kennedy had the election sewn up. But by midnight, the tide had turned and NBC news anchor John Chancellor predicted a Nixon win.

Chuck's heart sank, as he imagined Mooney's had as well, when he heard Ohio, Kentucky, Tennessee, and the western farming states had swung to Nixon. Worse, the critical state of Illinois was faltering. Without Texas and Illinois, Kennedy would never make it. Chuck would later learn that, in a similar rush of concern, Jack Kennedy had called Mayor Daley of Chicago from Hyannis Port. Daley, in turn, contacted Mooney, who reassured his associates.

Controlling Chicago's powerful black wards and his own Mob wards—nine in all—Mooney had turned the screws with all the muscle he could muster. He confessed later that swinging the election was like taking a "stroll down memory lane"—all the old tricks from his youth in the Patch came into play when his soldiers were mobilized in the name of Jack Kennedy.

To assure the election's outcome, guys either trucked people from precinct to precinct and poll to poll so they could vote numerous times or stood menacingly alongside the voting booths, where they made it clear to prospective voters that all ballots were to be cast for Kennedy. Occasionally, some misguided citizen declared his independence from such tyranny and in so doing drew the wrath of Mooney's zealots; more than a few arms and legs were broken before the polls were closed that day.

Chuck awakened the following morning almost afraid to turn on the television. When he did, he was ecstatic. The results were in: Jack Kennedy would be the next President of the United States.

In Mooney's wards, Kennedy had received 80 percent of the votes, while the rest of Chicago registered a respectable 60 percent margin. When it was all said and done, Kennedy carried Illinois by a mere 9,000 votes and in Texas had squeaked by to victory with a lead of only 28,000 votes over Nixon. Nationwide, he'd won by a margin of only one-tenth of a percent.

Outraged and correctly suspecting that the votes had been purposely falsified by certain Chicago precincts, the Republican party counted the Illinois vote and came up with a Nixon win of 4,500. At the call for an official recount, Daley balked as he'd been instructed and Nixon—who Mooney later said was pressured by his longtime underworld acquaintances and given a promise of help in the future—conceded defeat.

Overnight, Mooney's dream had become a reality: The man who would be king now shared the throne with the man who would be President.

Chuck had never seen Mooney so happy; he was a changed man. The mood swings and their accompanying scowls, silent rages, and omnipresent hostilities all vanished overnight. In their place was a relaxed, jovial man who played practical jokes, took the time to enjoy a good story, and laughed readily with newfound heartiness. Chuck felt a certain joy at seeing his brother drop the mask, if only momentarily.

Throughout Chuck's life, his own stability had been closely tied to Mooney's emotions, and now for the first time he thought he might be happy for more than a day or a week. "With Kennedy in office," he declared to Anne Marie, "Mooney will be on top of the world. . . . We've got four of the happiest years of our lives ahead of us."

Like his brother, Chuck eagerly anticipated the inauguration; life would return to normal. Mooney had been busy getting his plans in order and his men in line. Immediately after the election, he sent Murray Humphreys to Washington to massage the political machine. He also gave Frank Sinatra the nod to produce the biggest pre-inaugural gala for Jack Kennedy the country had ever witnessed.

In Mooney's eyes, everyone connected to the underworld—from two-bit soldiers to brothers-in-law—had to get what Outfit guys called "permission."

It wasn't that Mooney wouldn't approve of such an affair; certainly he was now one of Jack Kennedy's biggest supporters and therefore would naturally be in favor of Sinatra's idea. But for Sinatra, there was a formality to be served, a show of respect required. Proper Outfit etiquette demanded that he receive Mooney's blessing.

In the wake of the election, Mooney basked in glory throughout November—as did Daley, Sinatra, Marcello, and Lyndon Johnson. Each would claim the Kennedy victory as a personal triumph, if only privately. However, Mooney admitted to Chuck that the roles these men had played had been equally important and interdependent; it was their collective effort that had put Jack Kennedy in the White House.

Indisputably, Sinatra's celebrity status had served to mobilize hundreds of influential personalities, generating substantial campaign contributions. His star power had elevated the nation's presidential campaign and election to new political heights—that of media event, a phenomenon critical to gaining publicity and the popular vote.

Likewise, Daley and Johnson were crucial to the political machine. Historians might argue which state—Texas or Illinois—actually turned the tide. But the bottom line was that alone, neither would have made Jack Kennedy President of the United States.

As for Carlos Marcello—he rightfully believed his assistance was significant to the election's outcome. But Marcello's power and connections were largely limited to Louisiana and the relatively small electoral vote in the South.

According to everyone Chuck talked to, Mooney was currently at the hub of most illegal affairs nationally—with the exception of those originating in New York. Guys such as Daley, Johnson, Marcello, or Sinatra were simply spokes on a very big wheel.

Mooney wasted no time cashing in on his new connection to the White House, telling Chuck he'd already begun expanding his underworld network to include dictators, presidents, and smuggling czars—from nations as diverse as Haiti, the Dominican Republic, Iran, Lebanon, Italy, France, Nicaragua, Guatemala, the Philippines, and Laos.

Mooney also revealed he'd been in communication with his buddies from the CIA.

"It's beautiful," Mooney said one day at the Thunderbolt, playfully stirring his martini with a swizzle stick while the refrain of Bing Crosby's "White Christmas" played in the background. "The Outfit even has the same enemies as the government."

He glanced around the empty lounge, decorated for the holidays with stylish silver ornaments and red satin ribbons, and lowered his voice slightly. "I've been meeting with the CIA guys since last August; we're gonna hit Castro, Trujillo from the Dominican Republic, and some nigger in the Congo."

"*So*," Chuck said, lighting a cigar. "Don't leave me hangin'."

"Well, first things first," Mooney said, smiling. "You know, if we're successful, you might get that job in the Dominican Republic, after all."

"I won't hold my breath," Chuck commented. He'd practically given up hope of ever leaving the motel.

"Well, the big hit is on Castro, anyway. At least, for the Outfit it will be. After Kennedy takes office and Castro gets hit . . . everybody in the country will have to come through me." He smiled, lips curling around his cigar, obviously pleased at the prospect of being the undisputed "boss of bosses." "I don't care about fuckin' titles. . . .

I'm not a sap like Genovese. All I want is to know that I'm the boss. Titles don't mean shit.''

"Well, you really already have the bosses in line; I mean, they all practically kiss your ass now, as it is.''

"Yeah, Marcello, Trafficante, the guys out west, they know who's in control. Castro didn't wipe me out. I'm all right, if I don't look at what I'm losin' every day he's in power. But Trafficante, Marcello, Lansky, and all the rest of 'em—shit, they lost a fortune. The mistake some of 'em made was havin' all their eggs in one basket.''

"And you didn't do that,'' Chuck said tentatively.

"Hell, no. I got deals all over. But those guys were in a box when Castro realized they were close to Batista. So, he fixed them real good. Hell, you can bet he knows Marcello and Trafficante are tight with the Cuban exiles, too.''

He shook his head while puffing intently on his cigar. "We helped the CIA get guns to Castro, thinkin' the guy would repay us by goin' easy on our business down there. But Castro, the lousy bastard . . . I gotta hand it to him . . . he can't be bought. He says Americans are all crooks and pimps. He's a fuckin' double-crosser if there ever was one.''

"But he's pretty accurate in his view of Americans, don't you think?''

"Yeah, Castro's no dummy,'' Mooney conceded. He sighed. "So, the CIA finally woke up to the fact that Castro's closin' down American *business*. The government doesn't like that kind of shit. . . . After all, the CIA's lost their cut of the take from the casinos, too. So they offered me one hundred fifty thousand bucks for the hit . . . chicken feed. I told 'em I couldn't care less about the money. We'll take care of Castro. One way or another.'' He smiled triumphantly and raised his glass. ''I think it's my patriotic duty.''

Chuck had learned by now that most politicians were crooks, but these stories of Mooney's about the Outfit being paid by the government to hit other countries' leaders seemed hard to believe. ''If this stuff about the government killing guys is true,'' he said, ''why doesn't anybody ever hear about it?''

''Welcome to the real world, Chuck,'' Mooney said, leaning over to slap him on the back.

''The real world?'' Chuck's eyebrows shot up, half in anger, half in disbelief. Perhaps he was naïve, as Mooney always said, but he couldn't stand the idea that his country—one, he had to admit, he really did love—was so goddamned screwed up. The Outfit taking its piece of the action was one thing, but the government ordering hits on people—he found it all strangely depressing.

Mooney studied him for a moment. Their eyes met and his brother began speaking in a tone that to Chuck seemed patronizing. ''Yeah, Chuck, I've been tellin' you for years this is how it's played. You don't hear about all this because it's *secret, top* secret.'' He paused and searched Chuck's face. ''These guys are secret agents; they aren't supposed to get caught, and if they do, the government pretends they didn't know a damn thing about it. That's what *secret* means for Christ's sake.''

Mooney went on to say that CIA director Allen Dulles was the one who'd originally come up with the idea of taking out Castro. Two officials, Richard Bissell and Sheffield Edwards, were selected to put the scheme into action. For their liaison to the Outfit, Mooney said they called on Bob Maheu.

"The guy from the FBI?"

"The guy who used to be with the FBI. He has a cover, a detective agency. He's workin' for our Teamsters' attorney friend, Williams. That's how a lot of the guys work. Like Banister . . . shit, he's got an agency down in New Orleans now and is workin' on the Cuban exile thing with the CIA. Maheu and Banister work for the CIA all the time. They're good, damned good. And they've made me a lot of money."

After Mooney's initial meeting with Maheu, one arranged by his lieutenant Johnny Roselli, Mooney told Chuck he instructed Roselli to tell Santo Trafficante and Carlos Marcello he wanted them to provide the assistance necessary—their Cuban connections—to pull off the CIA assassination plan. Mooney made Roselli the go-between with Maheu and the CIA. Meanwhile, Mooney said he put Jack Ruby back in action supplying arms, aircraft, and munitions to exiles in Florida and Louisiana, while the former Castro Minister of Games, Frank Fiorini, joined Ruby in the smuggling venture along with a Banister CIA associate, David Ferrie.

The virtual blanket of men surrounding both the director of the CIA, the President of the United States, and Sam Giancana served to insulate them from even a hint of suspicion. And if not from suspicion, certainly from any direct tie to the events that followed.

As Chuck would conclude after their conversation that December, the Castro plot was only the tip of one iceberg, in a vast sea of icebergs, on a course charted by his brother and his undercover friends. It was a course that would result in the creation of a team of skilled men possessing the wherewithal to assassinate *any* world leader.

News of Bobby Kennedy's appointment as attorney general that December came to Mooney like a rabbit punch in the dark. The relaxed attitude he'd developed since the election vanished as suddenly as it had appeared. A seething anger simmered beneath his bitter disappointment.

The immediate question from Hoffa, Marcello, and Trafficante was, "What the fuck is Jack Kennedy up to?"

In an effort to get some answers, Mooney called Sinatra on the carpet. This was the guy he'd designated as one of his liaisons to the Kennedys, the man who'd assured him he had Jack under his thumb. "Eatin' out of the palm of his hand," Mooney yelled from behind his desk in his Oak Park basement one day. "That's what Frank told me . . . Jack's eatin' out of his hand. Bullshit, that's what that is." He slammed the phone down and threw it across the room.

Up until now, Mooney had relied largely on Sinatra and Murray Humphreys to keep him abreast of the goings-on with the Kennedys, but after Sinatra's most recent performance, he told Chuck he planned to have Roselli keep a closer eye on things out west concerning the Kennedys. He said he was also sending his old Havana Tropicana pit boss, Lewis McWillie, to the Cal-Neva in Tahoe in an effort to beef up surveillance of the Kennedys' frequent casino romps; he didn't intend to fall again for the overstated boasts of an egotistical entertainer.

The second person, after Harry Truman, to meet with Jack Kennedy in the Oval Office in 1961 was Chicago's Mayor Daley. It was no coincidence; Mooney expected to see a change in policy toward organized crime and see it fast. Having Bobby Kennedy as attorney general was not what he had in mind. He wanted answers. But mostly, he wanted reassurance. What he got was, "These things take time."

Finding that message unacceptable, Mooney took mat-

ers into his own hands—personally going to the White
House for a private meeting with the President. Their meeting, and the assurances he said he received, did little to
allay his concerns. He came back to Chicago dissatisfied
and, Chuck thought, more suspicious than ever of Jack
Kennedy's motives.

It had occurred to Mooney that Joe Kennedy, "the wily
old bastard," had had a brainstorm. By putting Bobby in
charge of the Justice Department, it could only be one of
two things: Either Bobby would put the clamps on Hoover
and tell him to lay off the Outfit as Jack and Joe had
promised or Bobby would be utilized as henchman, with
a virtual army of FBI agents at his disposal to destroy all
those to whom the Kennedys owed favors. The former
seemed hopeful but highly unlikely—it would be a behavior totally out of character for Robert Kennedy, the crimebuster of McClellan committee fame.

Slowly, Mooney came to the conclusion that the man
he'd envisioned slaving away behind a desk in some ob-
scure legal office after the election was to be his nemesis.
Bobby Kennedy, it appeared, had been placed in the position of attorney general to systematically erase all markers,
and Mooney knew he'd be on top of the list.

"It's a brilliant move on Joe's part," he said ruefully.
"He'll have Bobby wipe us out to cover their own dirty
tracks and it'll all be done in the name of the Kennedy
'war on organized crime.' Brilliant. Just fuckin' brilliant."

Just as he was coming to that conclusion, though, Mooney told Chuck that Jack Kennedy had done something
completely baffling: Kennedy had started sending him cop-
ies of confidential FBI memos through Judy Campbell.
Chuck would later learn from Mooney that the President
used Angie Dickinson and Marilyn Monroe as couriers

between them, as well. What documents these other two women carried, Chuck never knew—although, two decades later, when he heard sensationalized claims of women carrying correspondence regarding the Castro assassination between his brother and the President, he dismissed them as preposterous and laughable. Mooney wasn't one to correspond. Guys in the Outfit weren't stupid enough to get their picture taken in compromising positions, nor did they write incriminating memorandums or keep damning tapes that proved their wrongdoing. Bureaucrats, they were not.

Studying the documents Mooney received from the President proved to be an eye-opener. Mooney was startled to learn that the G-men's surveillance was highly detailed and incredibly extensive. He'd viewed the G-men as Boy Scouts, a nuisance, but basically nothing more. However, it appeared from the documents Jack was sending that the FBI was a bigger threat than he'd previously realized— there was at least one informant among his own ranks and extreme pressure to solicit more.

Mooney interpreted his receipt of the FBI memos, which were routinely conveyed from the White House, as evidence that his relationship with the President was solid, after all. He concluded—wrongly, as it turned out—that Hoover and his agents were merely present in Chicago now to "make it look good." He had Jack's word he would be kept informed of the FBI's operations and therefore would always be one step ahead of the game. Relieved, but still guarded and confused as to Bobby's role in the scenario, Mooney dropped the notion that Jack Kennedy had turned his back on his preelection promises.

Later, it would be discovered that Jack was sending Mooney only a carefully selected sample of the FBI memo-

andums issued daily to J. Edgar Hoover. Those Jack did
end said nothing, for example, of the wiretaps that had
y now been placed at Mooney's favorite hangouts, the
Armory Lounge and Celano's tailor shop.

Meanwhile, Bobby Kennedy, now ensconced as the at-
orney general, was orchestrating what would become the
argest attack on organized crime in the nation's history.
he young Kennedy compiled a target list of the country's
airty leading Mob bosses, and heading that list, just as
Mooney had predicted, was the name Sam Giancana.

The attorney general demanded that J. Edgar Hoover
intensify the bureau's efforts, going after the mobsters with
ae same zeal the FBI had used against the Communist
arty. To further his cause, Bobby brought the IRS on
oard to prosecute tax evasion by underworld figures.

As Bobby Kennedy prepared for battle, Mooney, despite
eing comforted by the FBI reports, didn't abandon his
wn surveillance of the Kennedys—nor did he ignore the
aitor he'd learned of through the memorandums, a man
e believed was William "Action" Jackson. He immedi-
tely put a contract out on Jackson and decided to increase
is surveillance of the Kennedy brothers.

Previously, in 1959, Mooney had given his man at the
eamsters, Jimmy Hoffa, the green light to bug locations
requented by the McClellan committee chief counsel,
obby Kennedy. Hoffa had gone to Hollywood private
etective Fred Otash for assistance in the project and had
elected sometime CIA operative and master wireman Ber-
ard Spindel for his technical expertise. Spindel frequently
ssisted the Outfit and CIA simultaneously.

Now, in 1961, Mooney said he called on Otash and
pindel again—to coordinate the wiring of every square
ch of the Kennedy haunts. Considered by both govern-

ment officials and the underworld as the "King of Wire men," Spindel was known for his sophisticated technology and cunning applications. At Mooney's behest, Spindel put a team of Outfit-CIA professionals to work, placing the Kennedys under a near-blanket of visual and electronic surveillance.

For the task of tailing the attorney general and the President, Mooney selected his CIA coconspirator Bob Maheu, telling him to put together a team of detectives that would eventually include Fred Otash and John Danoff. "I told Maheu I wanna know where the Kennedys are twenty-four hours a day, I wanna know when they go to the water fountain, I wanna know when they take a shit . . . and Bob's guys and the CIA can get it done," Mooney confided to Chuck. "I said a long time ago I'd never trust a Kennedy."

On April 4, 1961, when he learned of Carlos Marcello' deportation to Guatemala at the direction of the attorney general, Mooney's worst fears were confirmed: The Kennedys were pulling a double cross.

As Mooney had been since Castro's victory in January 1959, Marcello was a coconspirator with the CIA in gun-running operations and a fervent supporter of the anti-Castro exiles. It was an arrangement, Mooney said more than once, aimed at returning Cuba to its pre-Castro glory—meaning its lucrative casinos and vice rackets.

It was rumored in the Outfit that Bobby Kennedy was out to get Marcello because the New Orleans boss had refused to throw his support behind Kennedy on the floor of the Democratic National Convention; Marcello had always favored Lyndon Johnson. But whether or not this was the case, the fact remained that Marcello had been aiding other branches of the U.S. government. Unfortunately for

Marcello, neither his acts of patriotism nor his monumental donations to Jack Kennedy's campaign had impressed Bobby Kennedy sufficiently to grant him protection. It was a strong signal to Mooney, one he couldn't ignore.

He said his friends in the CIA were equally livid and were planning to secretly fly Marcello back into the United States, but nevertheless were currently too involved in overthrowing Castro's regime to divert much attention from the immediate task at hand.

That task was to assassinate the Cuban leader, now an avowed Marxist. Mooney himself had become deeply involved in the CIA's Cuban operations, so much so, in fact, that he offered one of his own "rising stars," Richard Cain, to the government agency.

An extremely handsome, dashing young man with a genius for mathematics, Cain—whose real name was Ricardo Scalzitti—was both fluent in five languages and a superior marksman who had been trained by the Chicago Police Department. He took to the CIA like "a duck to water," as Mooney put it, and the CIA likewise found him "tailor-made for a top-notch agent."

While in Miami training Cuban exiles in military operations, Cain did become a full-fledged CIA operative, according to Mooney. Like other intelligence personnel involved in the Cuban operation, he was "for the record" formally employed by a Miami detective agency that was, again according to Mooney, a CIA front.

Following the Bay of Pigs invasion, Cain would return to Chicago. Shortly thereafter, Mooney would receive the CIA's assistance in placing Cain in a highly sensitive position: chief investigator of the Cook County Sheriff's Office. It was a secret victory for Mooney. Cain would be second in command to Mooney's archenemy in Chicago,

Sheriff Richard Ogilvie, a man who'd made his reputation as a Mob-buster. Unknown to Ogilvie, Mooney would have a spy, a real one, in his midst.

Mooney confided to Chuck that spring that a CIA-instigated invasion of Cuba was in the offing, waiting only for the underworld's elimination of Castro.

To accomplish the latter task, Mooney said the CIA and Outfit shared the talents of a University of Illinois chemist and researcher, a man whose lethal chemical concoctions had been utilized many times over the years by both organizations.

The list of chemical weapons to be aimed at Castro was extensive and, according to Mooney, included poison-laced cigars; a lethal bacterial powder intended to be absorbed through the skin; toiletries spiked with a drug that, when splashed on the face or body, would induce a massive heart attack; a highly potent poison—"one drop and a guy's dead"—to be slipped into his food or drink; a cancer-producing injectable agent; and a slow-acting but lethal virus. There was even talk, Mooney confided, of utilizing radiation in the form of high-intensity X rays to induce cancer in their victim. But in the end, all attempts to assassinate Castro—Chuck heard of three—however sophisticated and devious they might have been, failed.

When they first undertook the plot to eliminate Castro, Mooney and his CIA friends didn't realize how difficult a target they'd selected; unbeknown to them, all food and drink were sampled in the prime minister's presence by political prisoners. Thus, their first attempt on Castro's life—slipping poison into a drink—had served only to alert him to a conspiracy and, in response to that threat, security was redoubled.

Chuck suspected that perhaps most central to the assassination plot's failure was the fact that most of the Cubans remaining on the island were—contrary to what the U.S. media would have had the public believe—happy with their new government. Additionally, Castro, a man surrounded by both loyalists and tight security, could not be easily murdered by a professional hit man; paid killers continued to be paid because they survived to kill again. Outfit guys weren't zealots who were eager to give their lives to silly political ideals. And even if a killer willing to sacrifice himself could be found, neither the CIA nor the Outfit could afford the exposure a tortured assassin's confession might bring.

This left only the Cuban locals as possible confederates. Mooney complained that there were few weak links to be located within Castro's regime; they'd tried pressuring several men close to the dictator and only one, a man named Cubela, had succumbed. After several meetings with the CIA, Cubela was arrested by Cuban counterintelligence and served thirteen years in prison.

Finally, the CIA decided to go forward with the invasion anyway. They planned to bombard the island's coastline with an army of Cuban-exile soldiers, mercenaries, and undercover agents, anticipating that the "disgruntled, oppressed population" would rise up and complete the overthrow. President Kennedy would approve military air support for the invasion and, within a matter of hours, Cuba would return to its previous state of glitter and greed.

What occurred instead was a horrifying fiasco. On April 14, six bombers left Nicaragua, less than half the number the CIA deemed necessary for the plan to succeed. Failing to demolish the Cuban air force, preparations began for a second strike, but the word came down that the President had ordered the strike canceled and the bombers never left the ground.

Meanwhile, a brigade of fourteen hundred courageous Cuban exiles on their mission to secure a beachhead at the Bay of Pigs was left pathetically vulnerable. Against Castro's two-hundred-thousand-man army, they didn't stand a chance. Kennedy received an urgent plea for air support on the morning of April 16 and was told that without his intervention, the invasion would fail. In an act that would dog his political career thereafter, the President denied the request. It was to be a suicide mission. Over one hundred men were killed and over one thousand captured by Castro's army.

On April 24, Kennedy released a statement taking full responsibility for the failed invasion. But behind the scenes, he blamed not only himself but also CIA director Allen Dulles, the director of covert operations, Richard Bissell, and the CIA deputy director, General Charles Cabell. Enraged, he vowed to "splinter the CIA into a thousand pieces," and shortly thereafter, the men he believed had caused him to suffer public humiliation and defeat were fired. Cabell angrily denounced Jack Kennedy as a "traitor."

Mooney was hugely disappointed by the defeat. Like the young President, he'd viewed the Cuban operation as a test of his greatness—a test he'd clearly failed.

Seeking vindication, Mooney and the CIA turned more urgently to their poison cigars, covert arms smuggling, and Cuban exile activities, while Jack tacitly approved military training camps, counterespionage, and exile raids.

Within the CIA, the dismay at having been betrayed by both the President and attorney general, as well as the

President's open promise to dismantle the intelligence agency's power, soon turned to hatred, creating a ripple effect that would blacken the moods of the men Mooney dealt with in his covert operations. These men expressed their outrage at the Bay of Pigs operation along with their fear that Kennedy now posed a very real threat to the CIA's continued autonomy, perhaps its very existence. Their highly vocal dissension served to confirm Mooney's own feelings about the Kennedys and made him even more doubtful of Jack's true intentions. It was in this turbulent climate that two of America's most powerful forces became allies. The Outfit and the CIA now shared a common enemy: the President of the United States.

There were other threats to Mooney's rule, as well. The Chicago FBI was attempting to exert pressure on the Outfit, and Mooney thought a lot of his problems could be laid at the feet of stool pigeon William "Action" Jackson. Mooney ordered his lieutenant Fifi Buccieri to make an example of the man—and the more gruesome, the better. Further, he wanted photographs taken so that everyone could see what would happen if they ever dared talk with FBI agents.

The murder of Jackson was the cruelest in the Outfit's bloody history. The three-hundred-pound loan shark was forcibly taken to a Chicago meat-rendering plant and hoisted onto a six-inch steel meat hook. There he remained, screaming in inconceivable agony, while Buccieri and his soldiers proceeded to ply their trade. They utilized an arsenal of tools that would have made the Marquis de Sade envious: ice picks, wrenches, bats, knives, razors, and a blowtorch. For added measure, they shot Jackson in the knee, rammed an electric cattle prod up his rectum, and on a whim, poured water on it.

Taking photographs of such horror only added to Buccieri's enthusiasm for the job; he and his cohorts tortured Jackson for two full days—around the clock—until at last the man mercifully died.

It was incongruous to Chuck that a man who could so easily call for another man's brutal execution could just as readily dote and fawn over a woman, all rough edges falling away while acting the "perfect gentleman." However, when it came to Phyllis McGuire, Mooney's latest girlfriend, his brother did just that.

Phyllis McGuire was a fresh-scrubbed all-American girl with a sweet voice that thrilled the public from coast to coast as a part of the singing trio of the McGuire Sisters. The trio had gotten its first break on television's "Arthur Godfrey Show" and had quickly graduated to star status with hit recordings like "Sugartime" and stints in night-clubs around the country.

Once Mooney saw Phyllis McGuire in 1958, he had to have her. And with that in mind, he implemented his tried-and-true methods of seduction—showering the pretty brunette with flowers, diamonds, and furs, picking up the tab for her gambling debts, and using his influence to maneuver the McGuire Sisters into lucrative nightclub engagements around the world. Soon the singing trio was at the top of the charts, cutting one hit song after another. And Mooney reveled in the attention that was created by having Phyllis at his side. A woman who was portrayed as a naïve country girl from Middletown, Ohio, Phyllis always seemed to enjoy partying with Mooney, living the high life with the likes of Sinatra and his Clan.

Mooney made Phyllis a permanent fixture between his romps with chorus girls, buxom starlets, and "business contacts" such as Judy Campbell. Their relationship never replaced his many other female escapades but, he said, merely added a "new dimension."

Anne Marie and Chuck met Phyllis in 1959 and thereafter entertained her and Mooney occasionally in their suburban home. They treated her like family, allowing her the opportunity to relax with her paramour. Away from the glare of press agents and photographers, Phyllis played pool in the basement with little Mooney, lounged on the patio, and walked in the nearby fields, feeding sugar cubes to the horses and their foals. Mooney thought the privacy Chuck's home afforded was refreshing, and therefore he visited often.

Chuck and Anne Marie found Phyllis to be a sweet girl, but childlike and frivolous. Her talent was quite obviously singing, not thinking. But for Phyllis to have been anything more than another pretty face would have come as a surprise to Chuck. Mooney never had surrounded himself with females who were intellectual giants. He liked to be in control, insisted on calling all the shots, and he didn't like women who were smart enough to ask intelligent questions. With Phyllis, he'd found a woman who would look up to him, admire his finesse, fall for his charm. Like all the rest, she didn't have to know the questions— because he'd always have all the answers.

As their relationship proceeded, Mooney began footing the bill for everything: a ranch in Vegas, Manhattan apartments, Beverly Hills condos. Phyllis McGuire might be a star bringing down well over a hundred thousand dollars a year, but, he complained to Chuck, she was always broke. "Celebrities throw their money away," he'd say disdainfully. "And Phyllis is about the worst . . . spends all her money on clothes . . . doesn't have two nickels to rub together."

As Mooney became convinced of her loyalty, he told Chuck he was purchasing more property out west, buying heavily in oil wells, and making extensive stock and bond investments—and putting some of them in her name.

In all his life, Mooney had never held so much as a car in his own name. He utilized countless soldiers, lieutenants, and family members as fronts for his own enterprises and holdings, but there was never any question as to who the real owner was.

Years later, Chuck would suspect that the lion's share of Phyllis McGuire's "wise investments" in antiques, fabulous jewels, oil—and on Wall Street—were actually made by Mooney and placed in her name. The jewelry, millions of dollars' worth, perhaps came largely from Mooney's old Costello "discount" connections; the millions of dollars in oil, from his friendships with right-wing Texas oilmen; the fortuitous Wall Street investments, thanks to information he received from insiders. If so, Mooney's legacy, not hit records, would ultimately make Phyllis McGuire a very wealthy woman.

While Phyllis enjoyed the material rewards of a relationship with Mooney, Chuck knew his brother was exploiting the affair, as well—using Phyllis's name, her credit cards, telephones, and apartments to further subvert the FBI. Aside from that, he simply found immense pleasure in being seen in the company of a beautiful star—and he took every opportunity to do just that.

Chuck was standing in the yard, admiring the budding trees in late spring of 1961, when the phone rang. His brother wanted to talk to him right away and they arranged to meet at the Thunderbolt Motel at noon. It was urgent. "It's about Phyllis," Mooney said, a note of concern in his voice.

At the hotel, Mooney explained that Phyllis needed a safe haven through what would be perhaps six months of a "difficult time." It would have to be a place where she could be assured total privacy: very hush-hush, no press, no nosy neighbors, and certainly no FBI. Could Phyllis live with Chuck and Anne Marie? Chuck gathered from the request that Phyllis might be pregnant and immediately agreed, relishing the opportunity to help his brother in any way possible.

It was decided Chuck would wait for his brother's call and then proceed to make all the necessary arrangements. But the call never came. And Chuck never asked what had happened—the word *omertà* ran through his mind whenever he considered inquiring. "Forget about it" was Mooney's only terse comment on the entire incident. It was never mentioned again.

During their affair, Mooney and Phyllis traveled constantly around the globe—to Acapulco, Puerto Rico, Europe, Latin America, and Hawaii. Under the guise of vacationing with the singing star or just following the McGuire Sisters' act, Mooney met with his international associates, exuberantly cutting one deal after another.

Sitting in Chuck's living room that spring, they laughed and talked of how they'd outfoxed the FBI agents time after time, Phyllis donning men's clothes and Mooney a disguise. It was a challenge to them to see whether they could walk right past an agent, "right under his nose," and never be noticed. They found it all immensely humorous, a game.

But on July 12, 1961, their game of cat and mouse with the FBI ceased to be entertaining. Mooney and Phyllis were returning from one of their many jaunts, this time from Phoenix, Arizona. En route to New York, their Pan

Am flight had a brief layover in Chicago. As they stepped off the plane, Phyllis well ahead of Mooney, the FBI waited to greet them. To Mooney's dismay, he watched as two agents hustled Phyllis down the concourse. Before he could follow, two more agents stopped him, identifying themselves as Bill Roemer and Ralph Hill. They proceeded to question him in a manner Mooney would later describe as snarling and aggressive. He informed them he had nothing to say and "suggested," as he continued to walk in the direction he'd last seen Phyllis, they leave him alone. Roemer and Hill had no intention of doing that and dogged his path, hurling an assortment of insults.

Mooney was more familiar with the duo than they realized. He'd put Bob Maheu to work digging up information on the agents in Chicago, and with one in particular, Ralph Hill, he said he'd hit pay dirt.

In recalling the incident at the airport, Mooney explained to Chuck that he decided "to drop a little bombshell on the illustrious Mr. Hill" and give him something to think about in the future. "So I said, 'You're the guy that's been fuckin' around with some of my girlfriends . . . well, I've got some affidavits . . . and I'm just waitin' for the right time to use 'em.' "

The look on Hill's face was nothing short of stunned, Mooney said, laughing with pleasure at the memory. "I had that motherfucker by the balls and he knew it. I shut him up real fast. I bet he can't sleep at night now that he knows that I've got concrete evidence of what kinda guy he really is."

Agent Roemer, however, was not to be deterred and a shouting match ensued. "He wanted me to throw a punch . . . that's what he wanted, the lousy cocksucker."

Roemer demanded to know whether Mooney was threat-

ening a federal agent, and with that, Mooney said he returned to the plane, emerging moments later with Phyllis's
hat and purse. When he did, Roemer seized upon the
opportunity to goad him once more. "That bastard started
whistlin' and sayin' I was queer. . . . I wanted to kill him.
People gathered around; we were screamin' back and forth.
Man oh man, it was fuckin' ridiculous.

"I got really pissed off and said, 'Fuck your boss and
your bosses' boss and his fuckin' boss, too.' Then Roemer
asked me who that was and I said, 'Jack Kennedy, that's
who.' He thought he'd be a smartass, so he got real cocky
and grinned and said he didn't think the President would
be interested in Sam Giancana. . . . What a dumb motherfucker. I told him, 'Hey, asshole, I have the lowdown
on all the fuckin' Kennedys and someday I'll tell everything. . . . Then the whole world will know what hypocrit-
ical bastards they are.' I wanted to tell that son of a bitch
a few more things . . . that I know everything about the
lousy FBI, every move they make . . . and that I get it all
thanks to the President himself. I'd like to have heard what
he would've said to that news."

In the aftermath of the airport confrontation, FBI surveillance increased. Chuck grimly shook his head as he noted
agents following him to work at the motel, shadowing his
errand running, sipping Cokes in his Thunderbolt lounge.
They'd gotten pushier, too—walking up to him at lunch,
asking to meet "for a cup of coffee." He refused to social-
ize, shaking his head politely and rejecting their efforts to
corner him.

Agents were following Anne Marie, as well. Whether it
was taking little Mooney to school, making trips to the
salon, or shopping at Marshall Field's and Bonwit Teller,
there was always a government sedan nearby, watching

her every move. Their neighbors had begun to act even more aloof, she said, and Chuck imagined the FBI had paid them visits, questioning them on "the Giancanas' habits, their comings and goings."

Under the microscope of government agents, the pressure started to take its toll. For his brother, it was still a game; if anything, he seemed to enjoy the challenge of dodging the tails and outwitting the "Boy Scouts."

"Can't you get Kennedy to lay off?" Chuck complained to Mooney, bitterness in his voice.

Always undaunted, Mooney reassured him. "Hey, they call this Camelot, remember? So relax . . . don't you know who's sittin' at the Round Table? We are."

Chuck could find no evidence that Mooney's assessment was grounded in fact. Mooney's having saved Joe Kennedy's life, his massive monetary contributions to Kennedy's election, the vote stealing that had clinched the presidency, the promises he'd extracted—none had any effect.

To the contrary, it appeared—despite Jack Kennedy's faithfully delivered FBI reports—that the Kennedys were out to erase any hint of obligation to their powerful benefactor. If this was Camelot, Chuck mused, it looked like Mooney was being made the court jester.

CHAPTER **20**

Mooney wasn't laughing. Sitting by the motel pool in the moonlight, Chuck studied his brother's tired, unshaven face. For six months, Mooney had struggled to hold on to the lingering belief that the presidency he'd bought and paid for would protect him. But by June, his personal dreams for Camelot were crumbling.

Since the first of the year, the last vestiges of Mooney's control over the Kennedys had all but fallen away. Quite ominously, Murray Humphreys was suddenly unwelcome in the Oval Office. Additionally, the Kennedys had formally snubbed Frank Sinatra, refusing the singer's invitation to vacation at his recently remodeled Palm Springs estate.

To bolster the logic of the insult to Sinatra, Bobby Kennedy pointed to a nineteen-page report prepared by the FBI highlighting Sinatra's connections to underworld characters. Faced with this damning document, Jack Kennedy called on Peter Lawford, a Kennedy brother-in-law and

Clan member, to break the news to Sinatra that he was persona non grata—henceforth the entertainer would not be welcome at the White House or at presidential social functions.

Sinatra, Mooney said, was dumbfounded and enraged. The singer's anger, however, couldn't compare to Mooney's, who confessed to Chuck that he'd considered having Frank hit but later changed his mind. "I guess I like the guy. Shit, it's not his fault that the Kennedys are assholes. But if I didn't like him, you can be goddamned sure he'd be a dead man."

To a guy in the Outfit, it made all the sense in the world to hit a man who let you down, whether it was his fault or not. To let him get away with a botched job could mean losing the respect of your other men—or worse, it might someday lead the cops right to your door.

The way Mooney saw it, Frank Sinatra was his middleman. And as such, he was expected to come through on a request or a promise he'd made. Sinatra had tried to be a big shot and it had backfired; Chuck imagined that, thanks to this screwup, Sinatra would grovel at Mooney's feet for the rest of his life. But, Chuck also had to admit, groveling was a hell of a lot better than dying.

Aside from the difficulties Murray Humphreys and Frank Sinatra were having with the Kennedys, there was other evidence of a double cross; word came down from Joe Kennedy to Cal-Neva's Skinny D'Amato that Bobby would not allow mobster Joe Adonis back in the country as had been promised prior to the West Virginia primary.

Then there was the plight of Mooney's associate Carlos Marcello of New Orleans. Only after a horrendous trek through the jungles of Guatemala, which Marcello enjoyed recounting as demonstrative of the Kennedys' brutality, had he managed to sneak back into the United States. Now, he was in hiding, as Mooney put it, "in his own damned country."

Further evidence of the deteriorating relationship came when Judy Campbell's calls to the White House were refused; the affair with Jack Kennedy had cooled considerably since March and, because of that, Mooney was no longer receiving Jack's FBI reports.

Overnight, Mooney's contact had been severed with Jack Kennedy, while Bobby Kennedy diligently worked to destroy him. It was all too clear to Mooney that the Kennedys had no intention of honoring their promises; more likely, they intended to annihilate him and thereby remove any trace of their previous relationship. The seduction had achieved its end; Mooney was a lover scorned. "If I was gonna get fucked, at least it shoulda felt good," he fumed.

The events of the past months were proof positive to Mooney of the ultimate double cross. Left unchallenged, his stature with the Commission and his men across the country would suffer irreparable damage. Quite simply, America's number-one Mob boss had never been made a fool of in his entire life—or if he had, the perpetrator of such an offense hadn't lived to tell of his accomplishment. Chuck didn't believe Mooney could ever, would ever, allow the Kennedys to be the first.

Leaning back in the lounge chair at the pool's edge, his brother sighed and lit a cigar. In the light of the flame, Chuck saw an older man, worn by determination. He silently recalled the time Mooney had been sentenced to prison at Joliet; it seemed like a century ago. Mooney had been so young then, just a cocky street punk. But he'd been Chuck's hero all the same. A sadness filled him, made him ache for Mooney's loneliness, mourn their loss of innocence. He'd never known anyone more totally alone than his brother. Once within his grasp, Mooney's dream had slipped through his fingers, and although he hadn't expressed his disappointment, Chuck knew the defeat was devastating.

Remembering the old days on Taylor Street, a wistful smile played across Chuck's lips. He longed for the simplicity of the street, its unspoken rules, its black and white reasoning. In the face of adversity, he was certain his brother would return there as well, to the ways he knew best.

Mooney broke the silence, clearing his throat as he gazed up at the night sky. "They think they've really got me, Chuck . . . that's what they think." He shook his head and sighed again.

"Well you've never been beaten before. Nobody's ever stopped you. *Nobody*."

"You're right about that." Mooney smiled wanly. "They've underestimated me . . . and to tell you the goddamned truth, that's good. Never let the enemy know your true strength."

Chuck nodded.

Mooney turned to look him square in the eye. "That mick cocksucker, Bobby, we got him on the wire calling me a guinea greaseball . . . can you believe that? My millions were good enough for 'em, weren't they? The votes I muscled for 'em were good enough to get Jack elected. So now I'm a fuckin' greaseball, am I?" He smiled, his eyes narrowing into small cobralike slits, and stood up. "Well, I'm gonna send them a message they'll never forget."

It was a formal declaration of war.

As he watched Mooney disappear into the shadows, Chuck wondered what his brother intended to do—and was afraid to guess. Whatever he was planning, it would be merciless, of that Chuck was certain.

Unlike the White House and Justice Department, the CIA had continued their head-over-heels affair with Sam Giancana. For months, activity had been fierce; Mooney had collaborated with the intelligence agency in covert operations ranging from the Castro assassination plot and Cuban-exile training to Latin American, Middle Eastern, and Asian operations. He'd also played a critical role in the CIA's international smuggling and money-laundering ventures. Along with his New York friend Carlo Gambino, Mooney had introduced the agents early on to the range of services that might be performed by Sicilian Mob financial wizard and Vatican consultant Michele Sindona.

Mooney confided that through their Vatican connections and shady banking deals, he and Gambino had assisted the CIA in pouring millions of illegally earned dollars into Sindona's illicit "slush funds." In exchange, the CIA contributed heavily to Catholic charities—some legitimate, others not.

For his service to the CIA, Mooney had been well rewarded in May of that year. As a favor—and, perhaps even more important, to conceal just how closely they'd been collaborating—Mooney's CIA associates had managed to get a Las Vegas wiretap case against Bob Maheu and Mooney dropped. "They risked their jobs for me to get it handled. . . . Now that's what I call loyalty," Mooney exclaimed.

Indeed, jeopardizing their own careers, Mooney said the CIA's top officials had confessed to Attorney General Robert Kennedy their agency's own involvement in the bugging of comedian Dan Rowan's apartment. Rowan was half of the popular Las Vegas comedy team of Rowan and Martin, which would later achieve fame hosting the hit television show "Laugh-In," and had been suspected by Mooney of romancing Phyllis McGuire in his absence. To allay Mooney's concerns, the agency had bugged Rowan's home.

Afraid of the possible political fallout, Bobby Kennedy was forced to back off and the case was closed. But the attorney general didn't retreat from battle, demanding the FBI rid the country of the man Outfit guys said he referred to as "that dago scum Sam Giancana."

For months since the primaries, using technical assistance that could be traced back at least partially to the CIA, Mooney had gathered damning evidence of the Kennedys' sexual exploits. And, in the weeks following his poolside proclamation of war to Chuck, he made it clear he fully intended to use this evidence, exposing the Kennedys' tawdry hypocrisies to the entire world. The time was right, he said. He now had the muscle and the necessary connections to the media to destroy the Kennedy dynasty once and for all.

But that would not be the case. There was one lingering problem with blackmail, a method Mooney longed to use. The fact was that, in exposing the sins of the Kennedys, the exact nature of the relationship between the CIA and Outfit might be exposed—just as had been feared in the case of the Dan Rowan wiretapping. Grudgingly, Mooney agreed early that summer with the opinion of his CIA cronies: Blackmail was out of the question; any information gleaned from their surveillance of the Kennedys would be used in more oblique ways.

For several weeks, Mooney lamented this decision.

Knowing he had enough smut to ruin the Kennedys forever and yet couldn't use it, embittered him even further. But eventually, and Chuck thought somewhat portentously, Mooney brightened, saying they would just have to come up with another, more lasting solution to the Kennedy problem: a solution embodied in Marilyn Monroe.

Marilyn Monroe had long been connected to the Outfit. Her first real break had come from a man Mooney and his lieutenant Johnny Roselli knew well—Joe Schenck, the Hollywood producer convicted and imprisoned back in the forties during the Browne-Bioff scandal. An aging seventy-year-old man by the time Mooney said he bedded Marilyn Monroe, Schenck nevertheless was still powerful in Hollywood.

Always on the lookout for potential stars through his relationships with producers such as Schenck, Roselli had been impressed by Monroe—and told Mooney so. From behind the scenes, Chicago quietly promoted her career and Schenck introduced the buxom beauty to another man Mooney said he often conducted business with, producer Harry Cohn. According to Mooney, both Schenck and Cohn enjoyed Marilyn's sexual favors in exchange for two-bit parts in films.

But by 1953, her two-bit days were over. After achieving household name recognition with her sensationalized nude calendar and the movie *All About Eve*, Marilyn catapulted to true stardom with the hit movie *Niagara*.

Although Mooney said she'd been a good investment, he also admitted she was a sadly driven woman. More comfortable with her clothes off than on, Marilyn readily traded her body and soul for what she imagined was success and fame.

Hers was a fantasy filled with conquered men and white

knights. And neither would be the case; for instead, she became the conquered, discovering to her endless sorrow that the men she envisioned as her saviors became, at last, her persecutors. Deceived countless times by countless men, Marilyn Monroe was the quintessential victim.

From what Chuck could learn from his brother, in the late fifties and early sixties, Marilyn's desire to achieve stardom, coupled with her childlike desire to please, was exploited by the Outfit, the CIA, and Bob Maheu, as well: Her sexual charms were employed by the CIA to frame world leaders—among them, President Sukarno of Indonesia. Mooney insisted that using Monroe as bait, the CIA had successfully compromised leaders from Asia to the Middle East. And Marilyn, perhaps more because she enjoyed the attentions of the world's most powerful men than for reasons of patriotism, had been a willing participant in the intrigue.

Throughout 1962, part-time Outfit-CIA operative Bernie Spindel's wiretaps had recorded the lovemaking of Jack Kennedy. According to Mooney, he had all of Kennedy's playthings—among them Judy Campbell and socialite Mary Meyer, as well as actresses Angie Dickinson and Marilyn Monroe—under surveillance. Sometime that spring, Mooney said he'd learned from Guy Banister that J. Edgar Hoover had confronted the President with FBI reports of the affair with Campbell and that, thanks to that, Judy's effectiveness had waned. However, he also knew that Marilyn and the President had been connected romantically since the Democratic National Convention—and that in March of 1962, Bobby Kennedy had become involved with her, as well. Marilyn, the orphan child of a dozen foster homes, now passed from one Kennedy to the other.

And, she told friends over her tapped phones, she believed she was falling in love with the attorney general.

The timing was perfect for Mooney. While Bobby and Jack were hurriedly severing their ties to their benefactors, they continued to believe that they themselves were untouchable. With Marilyn Monroe, Mooney would show them just how truly vulnerable they were.

By June of 1962, Marilyn's film career was losing momentum; she'd become unreliable and deeply troubled. Early that summer, Mooney told Chuck he'd had Bob Maheu and detective Fred Otash working on Marilyn's surveillance and in so doing had received a wealth of information about the starlet's habits, her emotional state, and stormy love life. From what he'd learned, Mooney believed Marilyn's use to Chicago and the CIA was dwindling.

Later, Chuck would surmise that Marilyn Monroe's knowledge of CIA-Outfit collaborative efforts coupled with her increasingly severe emotional instability had become a dangerous combination. And that by July, thanks to a failing relationship with Bobby Kennedy, she had become not only expendable but—when Mooney received reports of her threats to Bobby Kennedy to "blow the lid off the whole damn thing"—a frightening liability, as well.

According to guys in the Outfit, it was at this time that the CIA, fearful of exposure by the vengeful, drug-addicted Monroe, requested that Mooney have her eliminated. And Mooney, smelling blood, seized on the CIA contract as a way to achieve another objective, as well. By murdering Monroe, it might be possible to depose the rulers of Camelot.

One week before her death, a distraught Marilyn Monroe flew in to Lake Tahoe's Cal-Neva Lodge. Unbeknown to her, Mooney had orchestrated the invitation. Among the guests that weekend were Marilyn's friend Frank Sinatra and a man Mooney jokingly referred to as "Peter the Rabbit" Lawford.

At dinner that evening, Mooney, Sinatra, and Lawford watched as Marilyn drank herself into near oblivion, pouring out her heart to an uncharacteristically sympathetic Mooney Giancana. She sobbed to Mooney that Bobby Kennedy had refused her phone calls—she'd even tried to reach him at his home in Virginia, something that sent the attorney general, recently hailed nationally as "Family Man of the Year," into a rage. She was obviously crushed by the possibility that she was, as she put it, "nothing more than a piece of meat" to the two brothers.

That night at the Cal-Neva, seeing Marilyn draped nude across her bed, her blonde hair in a frothy wave cascading over one eye, had been a beautiful, if disheveled, sight, Mooney said. He stood at the foot of her bed, looking on as she spread her legs for him, running her hands enticingly along her thighs. He'd accepted the invitation. He'd had her before, he said—plenty of times—but more than ever, he'd wanted her now. Wanted to know that he could take whatever the Kennedys might have. Zipping up his silk trousers later, he'd laughed to himself. He'd had Marilyn Monroe's body. What he didn't tell Chuck was that he'd soon have her life.

One week later, Marilyn Monroe lay dead. It was all over the news that she'd committed suicide by taking an overdose of barbiturates—a tragic end to an already tragic life. But Chuck heard another, more sinister story circulate among the Outfit guys who frequented the Thunderbolt lounge.

The week following Mooney's tryst with Marilyn at the Cal-Neva, Chuckie Nicoletti told Chuck that Mooney had received word from the CIA that Bobby Kennedy would be in California on the weekend of August 4. That was what Nicoletti said Mooney had been waiting for. Mooney immediately flew to Palm Springs, California—ostensibly to attend a party at the home of Frank Sinatra. But in truth, Chuck imagined Mooney just wanted to be nearby when it happened, hoped to see Bobby Kennedy's face for himself when the nation's attorney general was implicated in the scandalous suicide of a rejected starlet.

Nicoletti said that three other planes also landed in California that week—in San Francisco—carrying four other men. Mooney had selected a trusted assassin, Needles Gianola, to coordinate the job. Needles, in turn, brought his sidekick, Mugsy Tortorella, on board and two other professional killers—one from Kansas City and one from Detroit. The four men had gone to California, under Mooney's orders, to murder Marilyn Monroe.

Eavesdropping nearby, where the electronic surveillance equipment had been set up by Bernie Spindel, the killers patiently waited for the attorney general to arrive.

Bobby Kennedy finally did appear at Marilyn's home, late on Saturday, accompanied by another man. Listening in on the conversation, Mooney's men ascertained that Marilyn was more than a little angry at Bobby. She became agitated—hysterical, in fact—and in response, they heard Kennedy instruct the man with him, evidently a doctor, to give her a shot to "calm her down." Shortly thereafter, the attorney general and the doctor left.

The killers waited for the cover of darkness and, sometime before midnight, entered Marilyn's home. She struggled at first, it was said, but already drugged by the injected sedative, thanks to Bobby's doctor friend, their rubber-gloved hands easily forced her nude body to the bed. Calmly, and with all the efficiency of a team of surgeons, they taped her mouth shut and proceeded to insert a specially "doctored" Nembutal suppository into her anus. Then they waited.

The suppository, which Nicoletti said had been prepared by the same Chicago chemist who concocted the numerous chemical potions for the Castro hit, had been a brilliant choice. A lethal dosage of sedatives administered orally, and by force, would have been too risky, causing suspicious bruising during a likely struggle, as well as vomiting—a side effect that typically resulted from ingesting the huge quantities necessary to guarantee death. Using a suppository would eliminate any hope of reviving Marilyn, should she be found, since the medication was quickly absorbed through the anal membrane directly into the bloodstream. There'd be nothing in the stomach to pump out. Additionally, a suppository was as fast-acting as an injection but left no needle mark for a pathologist to discover. In short, it was the perfect weapon with which to kill Marilyn Monroe.

Indeed, within moments of insertion, the suppository's massive combination of barbiturates and chloryl hydrate quickly entered her bloodstream, rendering her totally unconscious. The men carefully removed the tape, wiped her mouth clean, and placed her across the bed. Their job completed, they left as quietly as they had come.

It was at this point that Mooney had hoped "Act Two" of the drama would begin—that next, Bobby Kennedy's affair with the distraught, love-scorned starlet would be exposed.

But what Mooney hadn't counted on were the lengths Bobby Kennedy would go to to cover up the affair. Nor could Mooney assist in the attorney general's exposure by providing damning evidence of a compromising relationship with the starlet, due to the risk such an act posed to his own clandestine affairs with the CIA.

Nevertheless, Mooney had expected that hordes of police would be called in—Monroe's neighbors and housekeeper questioned, her home searched, and the scandalous discovery made that Bobby Kennedy had been there just hours earlier. In the wake of the investigation, it might also be suspected that the attorney general, along with a confederate, had administered a lethal dose of sedatives into Marilyn Monroe's bloodstream. That, to Mooney, would have been the ultimate victory. But that was not to be.

Instead, the killers listened over their wiretaps in the hours following the murder as a series of phone calls alerted Bobby Kennedy to Marilyn's death and ultimately mobilized a team of FBI agents to avert the impending disaster that Mooney had anticipated would follow.

Kennedy and Lawford, unaware there were other intruders in Marilyn's home that evening, seemed to believe Bobby and his doctor friend were to blame for her overdose and death. From the wiretaps, Needles and Mugsy learned that Kennedy had panicked at the prospect of being charged with the starlet's murder and implicated as Monroe's sexual playmate. He directed Peter Lawford and detective Fred Otash—ironically, one of the men involved in setting up surveillance of Monroe—to sweep the house before the authorities arrived.

Thus, there were to be no discoveries of Bobby's visit to Marilyn's home earlier in the day, no love notes or damning phone numbers connecting either Bobby or Jack to the dead sex symbol. Chuck would later hear that Marilyn's diary had disappeared that night and that J. Edgar Hoover's agents had confiscated the highly damaging telephone records, leaving little of substance that would implicate Bobby Kennedy.

Ultimately, Marilyn's death was termed a suicide and Bobby Kennedy was not mentioned publicly as either her lover or unwitting murderer until years later.

It had been easy for the public to swallow such a story. Suicide wasn't surprising, given Marilyn's known addiction to alcohol and pills. She was unstable—that was no secret—an emotionally disturbed woman who'd attempted to take her own life on numerous occasions. This time, she'd simply been successful.

Nicoletti told Chuck that J. Edgar Hoover's men from the Justice Department eagerly stepped in to protect the attorney general. Like the underworld, the FBI had the President and the attorney general under surveillance. But this was a coup for Hoover; Nicoletti said that Hoover thought he had the goods on the Kennedys and, from this point on, would call the shots.

For years, there'd be whispered speculation about Marilyn's death and, hearing countless theories, Chuck would always laugh cynically to himself. Some, like that offered by Peter Lawford, who insisted that Marilyn had merely committed suicide, were, to Chuck, simply obvious attempts to protect the Kennedys. Typically, the closer a theory about the CIA and Outfit collaboration came to the truth, the greater the effort to discredit its proponent.

By October, the story of the starlet's murder was old

news. That's the way it was in the Outfit: Life went on. You listened, didn't ask questions, tried not to think about the unpleasantries. And you got damned good at it, too.

Still, philosophical or not, Chuck found the FBI surveillance, now targeted at him and his family, especially demoralizing. Through the late summer and into the fall of 1962, he agonized about the constant stream of sedans parked outside his home or at the Thunderbolt Motel, and about the agents who sat at the bar sipping Coca-Colas.

His agony increased when Mooney suggested he sell the motel. "It's too hot to even have a drink in the fuckin' lounge," Mooney complained. "It's crawlin' with G-men in there. So sell the joint . . . I'll find somethin' else for you to do."

Although Chuck did as he was instructed, putting the Thunderbolt up for sale at half a million dollars in early October, the thought of being out of work sent him into a panic. He hadn't forgotten his months of waiting for a job before the motel had come along. When and if it sold, he wouldn't grovel for a handout; he'd press for the opportunity to go into something legitimate, preferably his lifelong dream of construction.

Chuck blamed the FBI for this turn of events in his life. As Bobby Kennedy's personal army of FBI agents slammed into Chuck's world with full force, he began to see his dreams for his children slipping away. With each new headline and television exposé, little Mooney and Chuckie sustained further injuries to their psyches. And in the midst of his depression, Chuck dared not think about the sale of the motel, secretly hoping that, despite the FBI's pressure, Mooney would tell him to take it off the market. It was better to go to work each day and face the G-men than not to go to work at all.

Anne Marie begged him to talk to his brother. "Please, Chuck, maybe there's something he can do. There must be. Why should we suffer because of him? It isn't fair," she said tearfully.

But in the end, Chuck said nothing to his brother about their misfortune. Nor did he ask that the motel not be sold. It just wasn't fair to burden Mooney further, he reasoned. Besides, his problems made theirs seem silly by comparison. He couldn't imagine complaining to the country's— the world's—biggest Outfit boss about something he felt certain would be viewed as insignificant. "Mooney's too big to be worried by us," he explained impatiently to Anne Marie. "He's got big things goin' on . . . bigger than some damned motel in Rosemont, Illinois. He's up to his eyeballs in international deals. And he's got his own problems with the FBI. He sure as hell doesn't need me goin' in and whinin' about our little worries."

Truly, for Mooney, the Thunderbolt was only one of hundreds of investments scattered across the globe; he gave its sale barely a second thought. Instead, he focused on a new venture, one that captured his imagination, if only momentarily.

In between business trips to Bern, Rome, Paris, and London, Mooney, the consummate deal juggler, made plans for what would be called the biggest star-studded occasion in Chicago's history: the grand opening of the Villa Venice.

Northwest of Chicago, in Wheeling, Illinois, the Villa Venice had been just another joint among the string of joints Mooney owned. But after Mooney invested $250,000 in its refurbishing, the dowdy stepchild was transformed into the swankest nightclub east of Las Vegas.

Chuck and Anne Marie always enjoyed the atmosphere

of a swank club, and this one rivaled the finest. A grand, canopied entrance awaited each patron's arrival. And beneath the canopy, a line of smartly uniformed valets graciously greeted the fur-draped women and their tuxedoed escorts as they climbed from gleaming Cadillacs, limousines, and Lincolns.

Behind the club, a small river snaked through a grove of trees. Floating in the moonlight were brightly painted gondolas with Venetian-outfitted gondoliers eager to take romantic couples on a watery, violin-accompanied journey.

Inside, the ambience was equally breathtaking. A grand foyer opened onto a sumptuous room dotted with linen-draped tables, each topped by lush maidenhair ferns, flowers, and flickering candlelight. Thick burgundy carpets muffled the footfalls of dozens of elegantly dressed waiters.

Throughout the opening week, drinks flowed and the sounds of elegant, subdued laughter mingled with the tinkling of crystal glasses and champagne flutes. An ornate wrought-iron railing separated the club's revelers from a gleaming hardwood dance floor, while onstage, stars such as Eddie Fisher, Frank Sinatra, Dean Martin, and Sammy Davis, Jr., crooned for hundreds of admiring fans.

That week, Chuck and Anne Marie were stationed front row and center. At their table sat Butch Blasi, Mooney's bodyguard, and his wife; Chuck English and his wife, Laura; Butch and Mary English; and the Potenzas.

Anne Marie, like the other women, was dressed to the nines. The scent of expensive perfume blanketed the smoke-filled air and there was a hushed excitement in the room, electrifying the night.

Other people were willing to pay hundreds, even thousands of dollars just to stand. And here Chuck was, sitting so close to the stage, he could smell Sinatra's cologne. This was what being Mooney Giancana's brother was all about, Chuck thought to himself as the uncertainty of his financial future and the problems with the G-men and Kennedys faded from consciousness. He leaned back to enjoy his front-row vantage point.

Glancing up toward the ceiling, Chuck caught sight of Mooney clowning around on the catwalk. Waving and making faces at the entertainers, he seemed on top of the world.

As Chuck watched Sammy Davis, Jr., onstage, he let his mind wander. He'd met Davis years earlier, when he'd accompanied Mooney's New York fence, George Unger, backstage at an Atlantic City nightclub. Unger wanted to collect on a twenty-thousand-dollar debt owed by Davis for jewelry. Unger and Chuck hadn't muscled Davis, but nevertheless the entertainer had been terrified at the sight of Mooney's brother. The name Giancana was as good as any bullet ever invented, striking fear into the heart of a man well acquainted with Mooney's Outfit tactics.

Davis was not the only celebrity who owed money to Mooney. Half of Hollywood was in his debt. Mooney said Jerry Lewis, Joey Bishop, Dean Martin, Peter Lawford, and countless other entertainers, sport figures and politicians owed him substantial amounts of money. How substantial, Chuck wasn't sure, but his brother complained about it every time their names came up.

Mooney might not have had his financial concerns squared away with his Hollywood associates, but during the opening of the Villa Venice, he managed to wrestle major dollars from Chicago's affluent gamblers. Guests of the Villa Venice desiring to indulge their interest in high-takes gambling were shuttled either to a nearby Quonset hut—a prefab corrugated-metal building set up specifically for the occasion with roulette wheels, card games, and slot machines—or to the classy Vernon Country Club. Mooney had at last built a monument to his power in his own hometown and, although it had cost the Outfit's boss a small fortune, it was apparent to Chuck and Anne Marie as they joined the club's famous entertainers for a late-night party that the Villa Venice was worth every dime.

When journalists would later report that the famous celebrities had performed for free—as they'd claimed to nosy FBI agents—Chuck would chuckle. Mooney said different and in no uncertain terms—he'd paid Sinatra and his Rat Pack buddies $75,000 each in cash for their appearances during the club's grand opening.

Mooney had an unwritten policy of always paying the people who worked for him, entertainers included, because he didn't want to feel obligated. He didn't ask for favors; he granted them. He hadn't asked whether Sinatra and his Clan would do him a favor and come in for the club's opening; he hadn't called in a marker that had forced them to leave their other engagements. He'd *told* them. And they'd been happy to comply.

It was true that Mooney had grown disgusted with Sinatra's lame promises of intervention with the Kennedys, but his dislike of the Rat Pack did nothing to cool his desire for profits. He made sure the biggest names were included in his extravaganza at the Villa Venice. He even went so far as to suggest to Los Angeles attorney and theatrical agent Sidney Korshak—a man once described in *The New York Times* as a major link between big business and the Outfit—that Dinah Shore be sent to Chicago. Not necessarily to sing, he told Chuck, but because she had a reputation as a great partier. Her absence at the opening was Mooney's only disappointment. And so far as Chuck could tell that was a mild disappointment indeed, because apart from a sexual tryst or two, using stars was all business. All business now, Mooney pocketed the rewards from the Villa Venice: $3 million in tax-free profit at month's end

Amid the glamour of the club's opening and Mooney's globe-trotting international intrigues, the FBI intensified its war against the Chicago boss and organized crime in general. In January of 1963, the cry went out from the underworld coast to coast to eliminate the Kennedys. And Mooney, who'd set himself up as the undeclared "boss of bosses," began receiving pressure from fellow mafiosi—particularly Hoffa and Marcello—to do just that. If he was the man with the wherewithal and government connections to put an end to the Kennedy regime, as he claimed, they wanted him to prove it.

To Chuck's private dismay, in early spring the Thunderbolt was sold, bringing fifty thousand dollars above the asking price from two well-known community figures, Rosemont's Mayor, Don Stevens, and the state highway construction mogul, Joe Greco. By May, Chuck was out of work. Dejected and with no word from Mooney or some new challenge, he went into the hospital for a hernia operation.

Lying beneath sterile white sheets, he gazed out the window into a world that now also seemed sterile. He didn't want time to think; he'd spent most of his life trying not to dwell on the anger, the pain, but confinement in the hospital gave him more than enough opportunity to evaluate his life—as well as Mooney's. A despair closed in around him. "How can things be so black in a room that's all white?" he joked feebly to Anne Marie.

Since he hadn't mentioned his personal concerns to his brother, Chuck was surprised when Mooney trotted into his hospital room, his face lit with an uncharacteristic broad smile. He sat down on the edge of the bed. "I just wanted you to know it's all taken care of," Mooney said, smiling mysteriously.

"What's taken care of?" Chuck asked, his eyes narrowing in suspicion.

"Things," he replied as he flicked his cigar in the ashtray and looked him in the eye.

Suddenly, Chuck was transported back in time; he saw his brother's face in the crowd, one eyebrow slightly lifted—could almost hear the whistling man's tune.

"You know I *always* win," Mooney said, standing up. And with that, he turned and walked out of the room.

In June of 1963, the local FBI agents instituted what they called lockstep surveillance of the Chicago boss—meaning, literally, that agents had been assigned to dog his every step. Mooney credited Agents Roemer and Rutland as having masterminded the surveillance technique; Agent Hill, the man Mooney had said he had "a lot of dirt on," declined to participate, transferring to another assignment. Mooney explained Hill's change of heart as "smart."

There was no attempt made at secrecy under this new program; the G-men openly dogged Mooney's every move. More than anything, Mooney took lockstep as a sign that the Kennedys were fighting back, that they were out to get him first. Certainly, it was with a new vengeance that the Justice Department now waged war on Sam Giancana.

Chuck imagined that the continuous FBI tail would quickly annoy his brother, but he never dreamed Mooney would react by taking legal action. On June 28 of that year though, at the advice of his attorney and son-in-law Tony Tisci, that's exactly what Mooney did. He filed suit against the Justice Department in the hope that he'd win a court injunction against the FBI for harassment, on the grounds that the agency was depriving him of his constitutional right to privacy.

For a reputed mobster to sue the government was unheard of—the headlines in the Chicago papers blared amazement. Chuck, like everyone else in the Outfit, had initially been surprised by the stunt. But Mooney was enormously confident, telling Chuck he'd win his case for what he called "two very good reasons." First, he said his civil rights were indeed being violated, and this he could prove in a court of law. And second, but more important, he'd win because by filing the suit he'd essentially called Bobby Kennedy's bluff: He was certain the attorney general would back down. As he saw it, Kennedy would have no choice: "I'll be sittin' on the stand holdin' a can of worms. And Bobby'll be scared to death I'll open it . . . because if I do, all their dirty little secrets will come out."

There was some risk involved in Mooney's strategy however. By taking the government to court, Mooney knew he'd have to go on the stand himself, swearing that he was a law-abiding citizen. He'd then be cross-examined by government attorneys—attorneys who possessed reams of documents detailing every aspect of his criminal history, enough ammunition to put him away for life. Under oath, Mooney would be forced to answer all questions posed by these attorneys or face binding contempt charges. Nevertheless, Mooney wasn't worried at all.

He said he'd heard that the local FBI agents were ec

static, thinking they'd somehow managed to trap Mooney Giancana and that the crime boss was in for a big surprise. Instead, it was they who were in for a surprise.

Attorney General Robert Kennedy claimed that the court had no legal right to rule on the FBI's conduct of surveillance. On that basis, the prosecution declined to cross-examine Mooney, and the court eventually ruled that the surveillance had to be reduced. Mooney had won.

But his victory was short-lived; that summer, the court of appeals overturned the earlier ruling and once again the FBI agents dogged his every step. Mooney was philosophical about this turn of events, as well as adaptable. To conduct business, he simply dodged the FBI agents and changed his routine, meeting associates in parking lots, cemeteries, and on street corners. Occasionally, he'd lament the FBI crusade, but largely he said little to Chuck, seething inside, perhaps, but seemingly satisfied to wait his turn at revenge.

Still out of work, Chuck toyed with the idea of striking out on his own. He had let Mooney know he wanted to go into a legitimate business, preferably in construction. But he'd heard nothing about such an opportunity from his brother and waited in silent frustration, afraid to act on his own without Mooney's permission or endorsement. He hated to think what his brother's reaction might be if he dared be so brazenly independent. "I have to be patient and lie low," he explained to his wife.

Indeed, any possibility of Chuck going outside the Outfit seemed increasingly remote. He resigned himself to waiting for word from his brother, spending his days miserably idle, frequenting the Outfit bars and dives throughout the summer and fall. But in so doing, Chuck heard the whispered comments. "Mooney's gonna have to do somethin' about the Kennedys,'' Needles insisted. ''Mooney's gonna fix them,'' said Milwaukee Phil.

The general consensus was that something had to give—and it wouldn't be Sam Giancana. Chuck refused to submit to curiosity; he didn't want to know what his brother's plans entailed. And he refused to worry about what lengths Mooney might go to, mostly because he was far more concerned with his own family's welfare than any national security issues that might damage the myth of a Kennedy Camelot.

On November 22, 1963, Chuck turned on the radio in his car and learned that President Kennedy had been shot in Dallas. Somehow, he wasn't surprised: He'd heard everyone from gas-station attendants to guys in the Outfit say, ''Somebody should get that goddamned Kennedy bastard.'' So finally, he thought, somebody had.

Several years would pass before Chuck would know the truth; and then, he would hear the entire incredible story from Mooney himself—but even now, deep down, he knew who had been behind the President's murder.

Still driving, Chuck saw the roadway and the surrounding countryside blur past him with the nauseating intoxication of a spinning carousel. Mooney's recent prophetic words now echoed in Chuck's ears—''. . . it's all taken care of . . . I always win.''

Later, when Dallas authorities announced the capture of a lone assassin, Lee Harvey Oswald—a man the media quickly portrayed as a schizophrenic nut—the 1933 assassination of Chicago's mayor, Anton Cermak, sprang to Chuck's mind. Initially, Oswald sounded strangely similar to Cermak's killer, Joseph Zangara. Chuck remembered hearing about Zangara from Mooney when he was a kid. Zangara had been a patsy, set up to appear to be a political fanatic, but was in reality nothing more than a rumrunner who'd owed the Mob too much money to refuse a job. Like Oswald, he'd also been described as an excellent marksman.

As more of the story trickled out over the following days, Chuck found himself dumbfounded that the nation could fall for such an obvious scheme. He'd always believed that the Outfit's one failing was its predictability. If you knew how they thought, you were never surprised, because their tactics were always the same.

But when the all-too-familiar name of Jack Ruby sprang across the airwaves, when Ruby killed Oswald right on TV, in front of the entire nation, there was no doubt left in Chuck's mind. His brother had ordered the hit. The CIA had known it all along. J. Edgar Hoover had turned his head. And the nation would never be the same.

CHAPTER 21

Just as the nation changed irrevocably after the fateful day of November 22, 1963, so, too, did the lives of Chuck and Mooney Giancana.

After almost a year of waiting for a job—a desperate time financially and one in which Chuck morosely spent his time sitting with his brother Pepe, shooting the breeze with old Outfit friends from the Patch—Chuck got word from Mooney to visit several Chicago builders, among them a man named Sam Pezzette.

Pezzette's firm gave Chuck the opportunity to demonstrate his special talent for construction. He soon discovered that he thrived on haggling with suppliers and tradesmen, and enjoyed meeting the continual challenge of scheduling and production.

That he could be really *good* at the business was, for Chuck, a revelation. He suddenly had an identity, an expertise, outside the Outfit. And that fall of 1964, armed with a new self-confidence and the blueprints for an ambitious large-scale building project, Chuck decided to pay his brother a visit.

He wanted nothing more than Mooney's blessing, having already secured financing for the $3 million project through both an area bank and the Chicago developer Jack Pritzker, owner of the Hyatt Hotel chain. But because Mooney was his brother and because it was "the right thing to do," Chuck offered him a third of all profits from the project as a courtesy or "tribute."

It was customary in the Outfit to pay tribute to one's sponsor or mentor. Paying tribute assured having a partner whose name could be far more valuable than any financial backing—lending protection and stature to the project.

But Mooney refused Chuck's offer with a simple "Thanks, but no thanks . . . keep it all for yourself." And so Chuck left having gained his brother's nod of approval *and* something more—his independence. For the first time in his life, at the age of forty-two, Chuck was striking out on his own.

Chuck brought in Sam Pezzette and made him his partner. First, they built homes in Rosemont, the west Chicago township where the Thunderbolt had been located. Then, they parlayed that success into other projects, constructing and selling thirty-eight apartment buildings. With his share of the profits from the sale of these apartment buildings, Chuck went it alone, financing the development of a shopping plaza. All this he accomplished without Mooney's financial backing—and he was proud of that. By 1966, for the first time in his life, Chuck felt independent, removed from the shadow of his brother's influence.

No longer technically "connected" to the Outfit, Chuck anticipated no further scrutiny from the G-men. However, to the FBI, he was still Mooney's brother, still a Giancana, and his change of employment had done little to cool their interest in his affairs. The agents were convinced Sam Giancana and Outfit money had bankrolled Chuck's new enterprise.

Mooney had his own troubles to contend with in the three years following the Kennedy assassination. There were rumblings among his younger, less powerful underlings, complaints that he was unfit for the job, that he was too "hot-tempered" and "high-profile" to run the day-to-day business of Chicago's Outfit. Mooney told Chuck he had that under control, but what continued to irritate him was the scrutiny of the FBI. The G-men continued to shadow him relentlessly, despite the fact that Bobby Kennedy—still attorney general until Katzenbach was appointed in 1965—no longer took a personal interest in gangster busting. In fact, after his brother's assassination Kennedy never again met with his special task force on organized crime.

But even with the loss of Bobby Kennedy, the man who'd given the FBI its Outfit-busting mandate, the bureau was still capable of dealing a powerful blow to Chicago's Outfit. Launching a highly publicized grand-jury investigation into interstate racketeering in May of 1965, the Justice Department targeted Chicago's Sam Giancana for destruction.

The following month, Mooney, who'd been granted immunity but refused to talk, was found in contempt of court and sentenced to the Cook County jail. The incarceration would drag on for a full year, until Mooney's release on Memorial Day of 1966, with the termination of the grand jury.

It was a long year for Chuck, as well. Mooney had sent word during his prison stay that his younger brother shouldn't visit. "No reason to bring on any more heat from the G than you already have," he said. Chuck found himself balancing the logic of Mooney's statement with his strong desire to see his brother. Ultimately, logic won out and he comforted himself with the thought that the imprisonment couldn't last forever.

Chuck hadn't realized how much he'd missed Mooney until he finally saw him, immediately following his release from jail.

His brother had gone to Chuck's suburban home, saying he wanted to outfox the G-men who'd been tailing him since his release. It had always been a place where Mooney felt comfortable, where he could relax, have some pasta, share a few laughs, and talk openly. Neither Chuck nor his brother considered the possibility that the FBI might be bugging their conversations. Such an idea had never been mentioned, perhaps because Mooney believed that only he and the CIA would resort to illegal wiretapping.

Alone in Chuck's rambling ranch home, the two brothers now reminisced about the old days. Mooney's gaunt face and thinning hair saddened Chuck; the past year hadn't been kind. But as much as Mooney looked different, little had really changed. In many respects, he was still the same cocky punk from the Patch—a charming, albeit sometimes sinister, rogue who, twinkle in his eye, liked nothing more than to display a new piece of stolen jewelry while extolling the virtues of a good game of golf. Chuck was relieved to find that Mooney's old 42-gang brand of confidence remained intact—that the arrogant swagger still lingered in his stride.

"I'm leaving," he suddenly announced in a tone filled half with pleasure, half with what Chuck thought was a tinge of regret. He sat back and lit a cigar.

"Leaving? Where are you going?" Chuck exclaimed, practically·rising out of his leather chair in surprise. Mooney's words sounded more final than those of a man simply going for a drive.

"I'm leaving for Mexico," Mooney replied.

"Mexico . . . what the hell for? For who? Why?" Chuck's string of questions poured out so rapidly, he startled even himself. He suddenly remembered Mooney leaving for Joliet—and realized that here he was some thirty-odd years later, and a grown man on top of it, and yet he felt the same panic, the same sadness he'd felt as a child at the prospect of losing his brother.

"Slow down," Mooney said, grinning. "Jesus, you'd think I was bein' run outta town on a rail." He chuckled, then said, "Sure, I'll miss Chicago, but it's gonna be terrific, Chuck." He paused. "Didn't you wonder why Hanrahan didn't go after me again? If he had . . . they coulda kept me in jail forever."

Chuck shook his head. He was aware there'd been quite an uproar when U.S. Attorney Hanrahan had backed down and refused to go forward with reimmunization procedures—on orders from Washington, the papers had said. There'd even been a rumor, which Chuck had laughingly dismissed, that Mooney was going to "turn," that he was going·to help the feds nail his fellow bosses.

"Well, they would've reimmunized me; that's what Hanrahan and the local G wanted to do . . . but the CIA pulled some strings with those cocksuckers at the Justice Department. All I gotta do now is take Dick Cain and work deals for the CIA and the Outfit . . . all over the world. We've got some big-name companies ready to act as fronts and supply the financial backing. There's lots of money . . . billions . . . to be made in Asia, Europe, the Middle

East, and south of the border. I'll still be runnin' things like I always have in Chicago. . . . I'm puttin' Teets Battaglia in charge here. He'll do what the hell I tell him to."

Chuck nodded in agreement. Mooney and Battaglia went back a long way.

"Overseas is where it's all headin', Chuck," Mooney continued. "I've got Trafficante on board for Asia. The Vietnam War is gonna make a lot of guys rich. I've got Marcello in line for the shit from Latin America. Gambino and I'll be workin' together on Europe and the Middle East. As far as Chicago's concerned, Teets and Accardo and Ricca can handle it just fine without me here." He put his feet up on the table in obvious self-satisfaction.

"Yeah, the government's sure been good to you," Chuck retorted sarcastically.

"*Hey*," Mooney said sharply. He leaned forward and knotted his hands into two tight fists. "Forget about the fuckin' G-men . . . I'm talkin' CIA. They're different. Like night and day. We've been partners on more deals than I have time to tell you about. You should know that by now, for Christ's sake."

"I guess I'll never understand, huh?" Chuck challenged, irritated by Mooney's cavalier know-it-all attitude.

Glowering, Mooney stood up from his chair, cigar in hand, and marched across the room. When he reached Chuck, he lowered his voice and hissed, "Maybe this will help." He fixed Chuck in a steely, impenetrable gaze. "We took care of Kennedy . . . together." He lifted his cigar to his lips and a cruel smile curled like an embrace around it.

There was a deadly silence in the room as Mooney walked back to the comfort of his chair. Chuck felt as if his mind had just gone blank, become an empty slate of shock, and, still, a million questions rushed in just as quickly. He finally knew for certain what he'd secretly feared all along; his brother had been right—the government and the Outfit really were two sides of the same coin. But hearing the truth—and hearing it directly from Mooney—left him speechless. He saw his hands tremble as he reached for the reassurance of a cigar.

"How's that?" Mooney said, smiling triumphantly from his chair.

Chuck could only nod. He cleared his throat and muttered, "I guess . . . I guess I see what you mean."

For the next hour, Mooney shared the darkest and most horrifying of his secrets. Deep down, Chuck wanted to tell his brother to stop, wanted to cover his ears. These were not, he thought, the secrets a man should know if he valued his life. But somehow he couldn't call a halt to the stream of words.

Chuck had already known Jack Ruby was not a stranger to Chicago. Ruby had been Chicago's, meaning Mooney's, "man in Dallas" for years, running strip joints, gambling rackets, and narcotics for the Outfit and running guns—and, he heard, narcotics, as well—for the CIA. All the activities were carried out under Mooney's direction largely through the insulatory channels of a small, trusted handful of lieutenants: Lenny Patrick, Dave Yaras, Paul Jones, and his old Cal-Neva pit boss, Lewis McWillie, as well as Mooney's Outfit Teamsters men Red and Allen Dorfman.

Ruby's murder of Oswald, an act that placed Chicago's Outfit and its leader squarely in the middle of the assassination cover-up for anyone who understood the Outfit hierarchy, was, as Chuck had already suspected, not inspired by a sudden outburst of patriotism on the part of a two-bit racketeer.

Mooney told Chuck that he'd kept Johnny Roselli as his liaison to Marcello, Trafficante, and the CIA, while concurrently directing his lieutenants to put Ruby in charge of overseeing the Outfit's role in the assassination, collaborating in Dallas with the government agents.

So it came to be that another Jack Ruby—a smart, clever man, one very different from the person erroneously portrayed by the media as an overzealous yet bumbling nightclub owner—played a major role in the events surrounding the murder of the President.

Ruby, Mooney told Chuck, had been a logical choice. The guy had previously demonstrated his extreme loyalty and ability to work with the CIA during the planning for the Bay of Pigs invasion. Mooney said he'd heard through Lenny Patrick that Ruby actually had come into his own while collaborating with his intelligence buddies; over time, the Dallas gangster had formed fast friendships with undercover agents—men like Lee Harvey Oswald. Indeed, at one point, Ruby went so far as to give CIA operative and Outfit pilot David Ferrie a job in his Carousel Club.

But there was another reason Mooney said he selected Jack Ruby for the job: His relationships with Dallas law-enforcement officers were unusually good. Since first coming to Texas, true to his Chicago Outfit training, he'd massaged the local cops and politicians, gradually getting to know most on a first-name basis. These friendships, Mooney said, had been extremely useful in overcoming problems "with the local cop in the street" in the aftermath of the assassination.

As the person representing the Outfit in Dallas, the task

had quite naturally fallen to Ruby to silence Oswald when he was unexpectedly captured alive. "Having Oswald alive . . . and in custody . . . put us on the spot, real good," Mooney said, chuckling. Chuck, for his part, didn't see the humor.

Utilizing his associations with the Dallas police force, Mooney explained that Ruby was able to gain entry to the police station—an astounding feat for a person the press later referred to as a "half-witted strip club operator"— both immediately after Oswald's incarceration and, more critically, during Oswald's transfer.

The look on Oswald's face at the sight of a man he knew, should have tipped the cops, Mooney admitted. "Shit, I heard they were queer for each other," Mooney said. "They sure as hell were friends. . . . Oswald knew what the story was when he saw Jack comin' at him. He knew he'd been made the patsy already and then he knew Jack was gonna take him out . . . but what the fuck was he gonna do about it then?" Mooney shrugged impassively. "It was too late."

Chuck knew from years of association with the Outfit that a guy in Ruby's position would have to go to any lengths to kill Oswald, who had the knowledge to blow the lid off the entire operation. There wasn't an Outfit guy alive who didn't think it was better to die in prison as a murderer—to be executed in the chair for that matter— than to die at the hand of one of Mooney's vengeful enforcers for a screwed-up job. The gruesome memory of Action Jackson's torture and murder still lingered. Ever the loyal Outfit guy, Jack Ruby did what he had to do.

Mooney said that the "alleged lone gunman," Lee Harvey Oswald, like Ruby, had ties to both the CIA and the Outfit. Oswald had been connected to the New Orleans

Mob from the time he was born; his uncle was a Marcello lieutenant who had exerted a powerful influence over the fatherless boy. Early in life, Oswald had formed a powerful alliance with the U.S. intelligence community. First, as an impressionable young man during a stint in the Civil Air Patrol with homosexual CIA operative and Outfit smuggling pilot David Ferrie—a bizarre, hairless eccentric whom Mooney said he and Marcello frequently used to fly drugs and guns out of Central America. And later, when serving in the marines during the late fifties, when Oswald attended a series of intensive intelligence training sessions run by the Office of Naval Intelligence in a top secret Japanese spy base. The short of it, Mooney said, was that Lee Harvey Oswald was a CIA agent.

Oswald had been a spy for the U.S. government in the Soviet Union, and had been trained to speak fluent Russian. He was not a Castro sympathizer nor Communist at all, as the misinformation that spewed forth from government agencies in the wake of the assassination had the public believing. In truth, Mooney said, "Lee Harvey Oswald was a right-wing supporter of the 'Kill Castro, Bay of Pigs Camp' . . . CIA all the way."

After serving the CIA and its military intelligence division in the Soviet Union, Oswald had returned to work at a company involved in top security projects for the U.S. government. Once back in New Orleans with his Russian wife, he was directed by the CIA to a man very well known to Mooney, former Chicago FBI agent and Commie-buster Guy Banister.

Banister's Camp Street detective offices were a front for CIA covert domestic operations as well as clandestine Outfit and Cuban exile operations—just as had been the case with the Miami-based detective agency in which Richard Cain had worked following his stint with the CIA where he trained Cuban exiles. Likewise, Mooney said Bob Maheu's Washington–Las Vegas detective agencies served a similar purpose. All were fronts, designed to cloak illegal CIA-Outfit activities and draw top-notch agents for the CIA.

When Oswald was sent to Dallas by his intelligence superiors, he met with Mooney's Dallas representative, Jack Ruby, at Ruby's Carousel Club and reestablished his relationship with David Ferrie. Oswald was also put in contact with another of Mooney's associates, a man Mooney dealt with through both his Haitian and Dallas dealings, the Russian exile and CIA operative, geologist George DeMohrenschildt. "That guy helped me make a lot of money in oil, man oh man, did he have the contacts with Texas oilmen back then. He introduced me to a lot of 'em, too."

Over the years, Chuck had heard the names of many oilmen mentioned by his brother as "business associates," among them Syd Richardson, H. L. Hunt, Clint Murchison, and Mike Davis—a man who was later rumored among Outfit guys to be connected romantically with Phyllis McGuire. Chuck had also heard the names of several Texas politicians, including Lyndon Johnson and John Connally, said by Mooney to have received substantial Outfit and oil-money backing.

Mooney now confided that the dollars raised for the hit on the President—each man involved in the assassination plot received fifty thousand dollars; Mooney said he personally received "millions in oil"—had come from wealthy right-wing Texas oilmen. Precisely who these financiers were, however, Mooney never disclosed. And following a code well-ingrained over many years in the Outfit, Chuck never asked.

Mooney told Chuck he sent Johnny Roselli to New Orleans to check out Oswald early on. "When I told Marcello what the deal was, he said he liked the way Oswald looked for the job and so did Banister. Roselli came back with the same impression. . . . 'He's perfect,' that's what Roselli said after he met him in Banister's office," Mooney recalled. Roselli returned to Banister's New Orleans office several times in preparation for Dallas, his last trip being in October of 1963.

Contrary to popular opinion, Oswald, Mooney added, had been a bright kid. His downfall had been his unyielding patriotism and malleability; he was easily manipulated.

In early spring of 1963, when the decision was reached by Mooney and his CIA associates to finalize plans for their elimination of the President, Oswald was the natural choice as fall guy. "They'd already laid the groundwork to make him look like a Commie nut, by goin' to Russia and with all that pro-Castro shit. He was perfect . . . he acted like a Commie . . . he smelled like a Commie . . . so they figured it would be no problem to convince people he was a Commie."

As he'd done with the Castro assassination attempt and other covert operations previously, Mooney told Chuck he relied on Roselli as his main conduit to the CIA—but only after he said he held an initial meeting with Guy Banister, Bob Maheu, and former CIA deputy director Charles Cabell, then employed in Maheu's detective firm. There was also a man Mooney described as a "covert operations specialist" and some top brass in U.S. military intelligence from Asia in attendance.

After this meeting, Mooney said that Roselli met "several times" with members of the original group as well as the CIA's Frank Fiorini. Roselli also continued to serve as Mooney's go-between to Marcello, Trafficante, and Hoffa men who were equally eager to see their nemesis, Jack Kennedy, eliminated.

Mooney said that the entire conspiracy went "right up to the top of the CIA." He claimed that some of its former and present leaders were involved, as well as a "half dozen fanatical right-wing Texans, Vice President Lyndon Johnson, and the Bay of Pigs Action Officer under Eisenhower, Richard Nixon."

The more Chuck understood about Mooney's plot and its multitude of players, the more apparent it became that there were few, if any, lines of demarcation between the Outfit and the CIA. There were no black hats and white hats; that was all a sham for, as Mooney put it, "saps to cling to." In many instances, the Outfit and the CIA were one and the same.

Such was the case, according to Mooney, with Frank Fiorini, Mooney's lieutenant who worked simultaneously with the government intelligence agency and would go on to become embroiled in Richard Nixon's Watergate fiasco under the alias Frank Sturgis.

The same held true of Richard Cain. Cain was an operative and Outfit man who secretly had worked as a spy for Mooney in Chicago Sheriff Richard Ogilvie's department Cain was now the man whom Mooney intended to make his confidante, international traveling companion, and CIA deal-maker.

From Mooney's point of view—one that Chuck couldn't help but embrace when faced with the facts his brother threw down before him—the CIA and Outfit had become so intertwined that to say there had been a conspiracy between the two overlooked the mere fact that they had become—for all practical purposes—one.

For all its apparent simplicity, Mooney said the Dallas assassination had taken months to mastermind; dozens of men were involved and the hit had been planned for several different cities—Miami, Chicago, Los Angeles, and Dallas. But ultimately, the President had been lured to Dallas, the city affording the best opportunity for a successful assassination. Mooney said both "Richard Nixon and Lyndon Johnson knew about the whole damned thing," having met with him several times in Dallas immediately prior to the assassination. What exactly was discussed between these men, Mooney didn't say.

"The politicians and the CIA made it real simple," Mooney explained. "We'd each provide men for the hit. . . . I'd oversee the Outfit side of things and throw in Jack Ruby and some extra backup and the CIA would put their own guys on to take care of the rest."

According to Mooney, the nuts-and-bolts planning had involved some of the top people on the Dallas police force; most conveniently, the mayor, Earle Cabell, was the brother of former CIA deputy director Charles Cabell. As the man responsible for citywide security, the mayor provided the police protection for the presidential motorcade. Mooney grinned. "They made sure it was so loose down there on the day of the hit, shit, a four-year-old could've nailed Jack Kennedy."

Chuck would later learn through the Outfit grapevine that Mooney solicited professional killers from several quarters. Killers, who the guys said, were required to be "top-notch marksmen": two of Marcello's men, Charles Harrelson and Jack Lawrence, as well as two of Trafficante's Cuban exile "friends." It was rumored that one of these exiles was a former Havana vice cop turned mobster and the other a radical-turned-corrupt U.S. Customs official.

From Chicago, Mooney brought in Richard Cain, Chuckie Nicoletti, and Milwaukee Phil, all having worked previously on "the Bay of Pigs deal." Mooney said that both Cain and Nicoletti were actual gunmen for the hit, being placed at opposite ends of the Dallas Book Depository. In fact, he asserted it was Cain, not Oswald, who'd actually fired from the infamous sixth-story window.

Mooney also alleged that the CIA had added several of their own "soldiers" to the team, using Roscoe White and J. D. Tippit as the actual gunmen—along with Frank Fiorini and Lee Harvey Oswald, the man Mooney said they intended to frame as the lone assassin.

During the operation, Mooney said the CIA upper echelon sequestered themselves in a hotel, surrounded by electronic equipment. With the aid of walkie-talkies, the men were able to secure their firing positions and learn of Oswald's whereabouts immediately following the hit. Mooney's backup, Milwaukee Phil, stood armed and ready to handle any last-minute interference with the shooters.

To eliminate Oswald, Mooney said the CIA had selected White and Tippit, who both—like Richard Cain, who'd served in Chicago's Sheriff's Department—held positions in law enforcement, on the Dallas police force. Under the guise of self-defense and in the line of duty, they were to murder the "lone gunman." However, Tippit had wavered, Mooney said, allowing Oswald to escape. Thus, White had been forced to kill his partner. "Probably the only real screwup in the whole goddamned deal."

"And the rest is history," Mooney said, grinning. "For once, we didn't even have to worry about J. Edgar Hoover. . . . He hated the Kennedys as much as anybody and he wasn't about to help Bobby find his brother's killers. He buried his head in the sand, covered up anything and everything his 'Boy Scouts' found. But there was a line into the CIA. If somebody knew too much, the CIA found out about it and took care of the problem." When Mooney used the phrase "took care of the problem," Chuck caught the tacit message being conveyed.

From what Mooney said that day, the CIA had indeed stepped in with immense efficiency and removed all traces of conspiracy. As for any evidence that Chicago's Mob boss was a participant in the events of November 22, 1963, Mooney said he was well insulated, thanks to his practice of delegating the details to his trusted lieutenants. Mooney—like the higher ups in the CIA—cared very little about the minute details of the plot's inner workings; the results were all that mattered. He'd met one last time in Dallas, right before the hit, with the top guys in the CIA group, some politicians, and the Texan assassination backers, and that was that.

Chuck had listened appalled while Mooney unveiled the story of the President's murder. Now, his brother suddenly looked away, falling quiet as he apparently searched for the right words. He turned back to Chuck and went on. "The hit in Dallas was just like any other operation we'd worked on in the past . . . we'd overthrown other governments in other countries plenty of times before. This time, we just did it in our own backyard."

He said the murder of President Kennedy was little different from the plot to kill Castro, the murders of Vietnam's leaders, that of Panama's president—or any of the other dozens of military/CIA–sponsored coups propagated throughout the world.

"On November 22, 1963," Mooney stated with chilling authority, "the United States had a coup; it's that simple. The government of this country was overthrown by a handful of guys who did their job so damned well . . . not one American even knew it happened. But I know. I know I've guaranteed the Outfit's future . . . once and for all. We're set here in the United States. So, it's time to move on to greener pastures. Spreadin' the Outfit's power and makin' a fortune in deals overseas are two of the best reasons I can think of to leave the country." He paused and smiled somewhat sheepishly. "And I guess we could add that it'll be damned nice not being tailed by the G."

Just days later, Mooney was in Mexico and Chuck was left alone with his terrible secret.

Thanks to his brother's revelations, Chuck felt he would now live forever in the shadow of fear. And that fear—the fear that came with knowing the truth—gripped him now. He even wondered how Mooney could have shared it, why he had laid it all out in such glowing detail, knowing it might jeopardize his life.

Chuck didn't know what the guys in the CIA were really like. He had a pretty good idea already; he didn't want to know the *full* truth. But he suspected he now had far more to fear from U.S. government agents knocking on his door than any Outfit henchmen. As the years passed, Chuck realized that sometimes he hated Mooney for that. Hated him more for confessing his sins than for committing them. Hated him for telling the truth. After all, the truth had never been a source of comfort to guys in the Outfit, himself included. "Ignorance is bliss"—that's what Mooney had always said, and Chuck decided now that his brother was probably right. Because if the wrong people found out how much he really knew, his life could fast become a hell.

Conversely, for a person who was perceived by the uninformed as a mere Chicago cop turned gangster, Richard Cain in 1966 was fast seeing his life become a heaven. Chuck heard from other guys in the Outfit that Cain was proving to have an astounding number of international contacts, and was putting some of them to work for Mooney in Mexico, where he introduced the Chicago mafioso to the president, Luis Echeverria, and his legal aide/consultant, Jorge Castillio. Cain and Mooney were also solidifying relationships with wealthy pro-United States power brokers in Peru, Venezuela, Bolivia, Panama, the Dominican Republic, Haiti, Argentina, Paraguay, Chile, Brazil, Colombia, British Honduras, Guatemala, Nicaragua, and Costa Rica.

It was to be an all-out, no-holds-barred Latin American push. Mooney settled into a lavish Mexico City apartment arranged by Castillio and went right to work, drawing on tactics he'd honed since the days of Diamond Joe Esposito, as well as on the expertise and mammoth resources of the recently formed CIA team of assassins and operatives specifically trained for Latin American clandestine operations. CIA insiders dubbed the team the "White Hand"—kiddingly, at first—an allusion to their joint venture with Mooney and the Outfit, or "Black Hand."

With his interpreter Richard Cain at his side, Mooney whisked from country to country in a whirlwind effort to develop the necessary political alliances. According to Outfit guys Chuck talked with, at the same time Mooney and Cain were setting up gambling junkets in Latin American coastal countries, they were pursuing highly lucrative narcotics and munitions smuggling and money-laundering schemes.

As a by-product of Mooney's "Black Hand" deals, the CIA "White Hand" gained a firmer economic foothold for its U.S. corporate sponsors. Oil empires, in particular, oozed into Latin America with ease, the wheels of commerce greased by the CIA.

The CIA profited as well, discovering through Mooney's bribe-friendly contacts new avenues for diverting their own "dirty money," funds garnered from illicit CIA activities.

To courier the millions of dollars that would soon pour across U.S.–Mexican borders, Mooney called on the Roman Catholic Church.

In 1958, Cardinal Stritch left Chicago to accept a position in the Vatican. Stritch's successor in Chicago, Cardinal Cody, proved in Mooney's estimation to be a stellar replacement. Mooney said Cody was a corrupt man who enjoyed the trappings of wealth and, therefore, welcomed a close relationship with him.

Father Cash, the Chicago priest Mooney utilized as a courier, had traveled under Mooney's orders across the nation and to Europe for close to two decades. With Mooney's move into the southern hemisphere, Cash was told to add Latin America to his itinerary.

During Mooney's tenure outside the United States, Chuck heard talk among Outfit men that millions of dollars flowed to Continental Illinois, a bank then heavily invested in Finibank, a Swiss bank owned in part by the Vatican and controlled by financier Michele Sindona, Mooney's Gambino connection. Some was couriered by Mooney's trusted lieutenants to Washington, D.C., where it was converted to bonds and then forwarded to Finibank or another Sindona-controlled European shell, generally in Rome, London, or Athens. But still more was carried out of Chicago to Mexico, under the safety of the priest's robes, to be placed in banks scattered throughout South and Central America, but most often in Panama. Often these funds were then diverted to Milan and on to the Vatican Bank in Rome, where they were easily transferred to Finibank in Switzerland—and straight into the hands of Michele Sindona and an up-and-coming Chicago priest residing in the Vatican, Paul Marcinkus. The CIA, eager to improve its own financial position, was said to have followed suit, dealing frequently and closely with Marcinkus and Sindona.

While Mooney struck gold on countless foreign coasts in 1967, Chuck met a different fate. That year saw one disaster follow on the heels of another.

At first, it had looked as if he was really going to make it on his own in the construction business—and make it big. Since 1964, he'd diligently established himself in Rosemont as an active community sponsor, becoming personal friends with area bankers and the mayor. Out of the Outfit's shadow, Chuck was finally prospering and living the life of a successful, upstanding citizen. He and his family began, once again, to live the American dream. But in February 1967, that dream suddenly shattered.

He learned later that the FBI had suggested to reporters at the *Chicago Tribune* and *Chicago Sun-Times* that perhaps Sam Giancana, although now absent, might still be investing in Chicago real estate and construction. For starters, the agents pointed to Chuck's thriving Rosemont shopping plaza.

A slight prodding in this direction was all it took to entice the headline-grabbing reporters, who'd found the

Chicago Mob scene dull since Mooney's departure. Within twenty-four hours, helicopters loaded with cameramen circled like vultures above the shopping plaza, and its legitimate shop owners were besieged. Chuck was soon bombarded with questions by aggressive reporters.

Faced with their damning accusations, Chuck rightfully insisted that his success was his own, that his brother had contributed not "one thin dime" to his real estate ventures. But the newspapers the following day told a different story and suggested in their headlines that Sam Giancana was indeed, up to his old tricks. After all, Chuck Giancana was Mooney's brother; it was obvious he served merely as a front for one of Mooney's many illegal money-laundering schemes.

Within hours of the newspapers' scandalous allegations, Chuck received a call from the bank that held the note on his shopping plaza. They'd learned that the insurance coverage on the property had been canceled, which was news to Chuck, and were calling his two-hundred-thousand-dollar note. Chuck had to come up with the cash or surrender the property.

Soon after the disturbing call, Chuck discovered that not just reporters but also FBI agents had been visiting his tenants and questioning his bank and insurance company. Evidently, the agents hoped this crisis would bring Chuck's brother out of the woodwork and back into the United States.

The month of February was a frantic one, filled with desperate calls to insurance companies and lending institutions; Chuck was determined not to go to Mooney for financial assistance. But at last, forced to admit that there wasn't a bank in the United States that would "touch him with a ten-foot pole" due to the FBI agents' relentless threats and warnings about dealing with an "undesirable character," Chuck resigned himself to the inevitable and sent a message to Mexico: He needed Mooney's help.

His brother's reply was simple and direct: "No way . . . unload the joint."

Chuck was stunned. Never in his life had he felt such rage. He'd never asked his brother for anything more than a decent job, and now, when he needed him most—when his family's welfare, his entire fortune, depended on it— Mooney had turned his back.

Two days prior to foreclosure, Chuck sold his shopping plaza. He was overwhelmed with bitterness. He'd felt the cool thrill of the brass ring in his hand, felt it wrested from his grasp—all because of who he was. Countless times he asked himself what he had done to deserve such misfortune; his only crime was being Mooney's brother, having the name Giancana.

Years later, he would pass the bustling shopping center and point to it with disgust. "It's worth three million today," he'd lament. "And I lost it all because of the FBI. I really was clean. Mooney hadn't done a damn thing for me for years. But that didn't matter to them. . . . They wanted Mooney and nothing would stand in their way. Ruining me financially was all in a day's work."

Following the loss of his real estate, Chuck's personal life took a nosedive, as well. The publicity exacted a terrible toll on his family. Anne Marie was no longer welcome at most of her friends' homes; Chuck's political and banking acquaintances shunned him like a leper.

His seventeen-year-old son, Chuckie, who'd long since left the strict confines of military school, was increasingly rebellious. First, he'd entered the Catholic high school, St. Viator's in Arlington Heights, but soon transferred to public high school. There, Chuckie continued to be haunted by the Giancana name, jeered and taunted by his classmates, made a scapegoat whenever a scuffle broke out. Unable to face the mounting pressure, he'd eventually dropped out, still a junior.

His personal and professional dreams collapsing, Chuck turned to little Mooney and saw a twelve-year-old boy hounded into solitude by the very name he'd once believed to be the ultimate honor.

A darkness enveloped Chuck's world, and with no future in construction, he went to work as a motion-picture operator. The blackness of the theater suited him well now. With just the endless reels of film as company, he sat alone, seething in anger at life's injustice. And he reviewed his life along with the movies. In so doing, Chuck saw more clearly than ever before how Mooney had left his lasting, destructive mark on every aspect of his own being.

When he thought about his brother's terrible political secrets, the word *omertà* rang in his ears, hammered in his brain. As always, he wondered why he loved Mooney— and hated him at the same time. He loved him, he guessed, because he'd been his childhood hero, more a father to him than Antonio. But he hated him for everything he'd done. Not just to him, but to everyone and everything he'd touched. It was because of his brother that his only dream, the only thing that had ever mattered, had been snatched from his life and discarded like some bad edit on the cutting room floor.

In its relentless effort to get at Mooney, the FBI had unfairly lashed out at Chuck. But the G-men hadn't beaten Mooney; they'd only succeeded in defeating one of his greatest victims.

CHAPTER 22

From Mexico, Mooney wielded his power like a sword.
Historians might later record his Latin American adventures as a "Mob-imposed exile," but, in fact, according to Chicago's Outfit guys, nothing could have been further from the truth.

Revenues generated from local rackets had declined in Mooney's absence. It was all too apparent that the Giancana approach—one in which all the angles were figured out—was sorely missed. Had Mooney hopped on a plane to O'Hare and settled back in as boss, he would have been welcomed with open arms. But that was not to be, because Mooney had set his sights on the international scene and was largely unconcerned with what he considered "small-town" issues.

If anything can be blamed for creating resentment among Chicago's Outfit men toward Mooney—a resentment alleged years later by investigators, biographers, and journalists alike—it was this lack of interest in the plight of his native Chicago, not his desire to seize control again.

Mooney never lost his hold over his stateside empire, and, according to the Outfit guys Chuck spoke with, he came back to town "on the q.t." on numerous occasions over the next eight years. Any Outfit guy who'd been run out of town, as was so often alleged Mooney had been— at least any Outfit guy with any sense—would never in a million years come back. That kind of thing got a guy killed—pronto.

Upon first leaving the country, Mooney had placed Teets Battaglia in charge as his boss in absentia, anticipating little need to travel back and forth between Mexico and Chicago. But Battaglia's conviction and imprisonment for extortion later that year had necessitated a visit from Mooney. Chuck heard that his brother had donned his usual disguise, a toupee, and secretly flown back into O'Hare to meet with Tony Accardo and Paul Ricca in an effort to select a satisfactory replacement for Battaglia in the late fall of that year.

Although Accardo and Ricca were not involved in the day-to-day affairs of the Outfit, nor possessed the power base to actually veto a decision made by Mooney, it was politically wise to include them in the decision-making process. And Mooney did that quite often over the years.

Mooney particularly respected Paul Ricca's opinion— although, that didn't mean he always followed it. In this instance, however, the three men wholeheartedly agreed on Joey Aiuppa as Battaglia's replacement. His empire secured once more, Mooney flew immediately back to Mexico. From there, he turned his attentions to overseas interests, leaving his Chicago soldiers and lieutenants with he job of guarding the spoils from old battles, won long ago.

Chuck stayed in touch with his brother's goings-on through several Outfit guys, among them Tommy Payne, an old Capone soldier, and Chuckie Nicoletti, Mooney's henchman. Sometimes he thought they gossiped more than most women. But in any case, the guys all kept him on the grapevine; they treated him as if he was on the inside, and he liked that. Besides, he didn't have anyone else with whom to talk. Since the FBI had divested him of his shopping plaza, none of the men from his days as a builder would have anything to do with him. Hearing about Mooney was about the only thing that gave him much pleasure—which was strange, given his bitterness at his brother's rejection. Strange but true.

By the summer of 1967, the FBI had learned of Mooney's whereabouts and encouraged former Chicago reporter Sandy Smith to do an exposé on his Mexican lifestyle. In response, Smith, now reporting for *Life* magazine, rushed to Cuernavaca, where he hired a helicopter to fly over Mooney's comfortable new residence, snapping pictures. In *Life*'s September issue, Smith chronicled the infamous history of the Chicago mobster, creating, to Mooney's extreme rage, speculation as to just what the aging mafioso could be doing in Mexico.

The FBI might have desired to maintain its surveillance of Sam Giancana as he made his way around the globe, the multilingual Dick Cain at his side, but Chicago agents were forced to content themselves with lesser members of the Outfit as their prey. Unfortunately for Cain, he was one of them. As part of a federal investigation, twenty-four Outfit members were indicted in 1967, among them Mooney's erstwhile interpreter.

Going back to Illinois to handle business for his boss, Cain was nabbed by federal agents on charges dating back to a 1963 robbery. He was held in Chicago to await trial and in 1968, Cain, along with Willie Potatoes Daddano, was convicted and sentenced to prison. Willie got fifteen years and Cain, rumored to have been aided by his agent friends, managed to scrape by with four.

Without his sidekick, Mooney continued his travels. He spent long hours in discussion with Meyer Lansky in Rio and Acapulco, traveled to Rome for a private audience with Pope Paul, and, occasionally, took time out from his busy schedule to vacation with Phyllis McGuire, entertain Mexican officials in his home, or play golf at a nearby country club. According to Chuck's family and friends, such was the life of a "retired mobster in exile."

In July of 1968, the FBI again attempted to shake Mooney from his Mexican headquarters. This time, however, their attempts took a sinister turn, involving Mooney's daughter Bonnie and her husband Tony Tisci. The couple now lived in Tucson, a city New York boss Joe Bonanno also called home.

To carry out the plan, Tucson FBI agent David Hale hired three area hoods. Their first target was the home of Mooney's daughter. Late one evening, shots crashed through its windows into the living room. Two weeks later, the homes of Bonanno and other gangsters were laid under a similar siege. More attacks and bombings followed. Thankfully, none resulted in injury or death. But to all the world, including Outfit members, this sudden outburst of violence signaled a gang war. Even the national Commission suspected as much and called an emergency meeting. A full year would pass before FBI agent David Hale would be named as the person behind the attacks. Upon this revelation, Hale resigned from the FBI, refusing to testify. A witness to the shooting at the Tisci home was found murdered, and with that, the case was closed. The FBI and its agent David Hale escaped prosecution.

Outfit members believed the attack on Mooney's daughter's home had been an attempt to lure the Chicago boss across the Mexican border. If so, they failed to wrest Mooney from his lair. Instead, he jaunted through South and Central America during 1968 and 1969, moving to a new residence in the posh Las Quintas section of Cuernavaca, a massive walled estate known as San Cristobal.

In April of 1969, Chuck crawled out of the darkness of his movie operator's booth long enough to learn some distressing news about his brother from Outfit enforcer Chuckie Nicoletti.

He'd stopped by the Lilac Lodge, a West Side Chicago haunt. Since it was well known as an Outfit watering hole, Chuck hoped to hear some word of Mooney's Mexican adventures. During the spring and summer months, Mooney's men—everybody who was anybody—often played a round of golf at the nearby Fresh Meadows Golf Club and sooner or later made their way over to the Lilac Lodge for a drink. When he walked in the door, Chuck spotted Chuckie Nicoletti, apparently alone, at a corner table. Nicoletti waved him over and ordered another drink.

Nicoletti was not what Chuck considered a brilliant conversationalist, but what he had to say on this afternoon while they sat sequestered in the quiet recesses of the Lilac Lodge captured Chuck's attention completely.

"Well," Nicoletti announced after they'd exchanged handshakes and had drinks in hand, "one more Kennedy out of the way, huh?" He smiled broadly.

"Yeah," Chuck murmured absentmindedly. He wasn't

in the mood to talk about the Kennedys and hoped Nicoletti would change the subject.

Instead, Nicoletti continued. "So Mooney did it again . . . goddamn . . . I'll tell you . . . your brother's a fuckin' genius."

"Did what again?" Chuck asked, sipping his martini.

"You know." Nicoletti lowered his voice an octave. "Hit Bobby."

Not wanting to appear ignorant, Chuck nodded and l a cigar. "Oh, yeah," he replied.

"Settin' up that guy Sirhan to take the rap, shit, didn it work like a charm? Of course," he added, winking, "th son of a bitch didn't have much choice."

"No, not much choice," Chuck agreed, wondering wh Nicoletti meant.

"Hey, when you work for the Outfit and owe 'em small fortune . . . and you can't cough it up . . . that what happens. Right? Shit, now that I think about it, was a lot like the Ruby and Oswald deal."

"Yeah," Chuck agreed.

"You know," Nicoletti whispered, "Oswald didn't re ally fire a shot. At least Sirhan did that much. But even he couldn't hit a barn, it didn't matter, 'cause Mooney ha another guy do the job on Bobby . . . some Mexican h probably dug up down south."

"Yeah, I saw it on TV . . . the murder," Chuck added not knowing what to say. Obviously, Nicoletti thought h was still very much on the inside with Mooney.

"Me, too," Nicoletti said, laughing out loud. "Ca you believe it? Mooney must like to nail those Kenned bastards in front of God and everybody. Sorta proves point, doesn't it?" His eyes narrowed.

"I guess so. Lets 'em know nothin' will stop him . .

not even a crowd of reporters." He felt his heart begin to race. Mooney, contrary to what the papers were saying about him being washed up, a has-been mobster, was still exerting his influence over the entire country, over the course of history. Chuck wondered whether the same people were responsible, whether the CIA was involved. Certainly the lack of any real investigation into Bobby's murder seemed suspiciously similar to what had occurred in the wake of Jack's death.

Nicoletti, warmed by his discussion of Mooney, began waxing nostalgic, talking about the old days in the Patch. "Your brother's just as tough today as he was thirty years ago, Chuck," he said, grinning. "Just as goddamned powerful. No, *more* powerful now. There's nobody . . . nobody who can fuckin' touch him now."

Tommy Payne would later tell Chuck that the Chicago Outfit had controlled everything at the Los Angeles hotel where the hit on Bobby Kennedy had occurred and that the other gunman—an Outfit hit man—was a "last-minute replacement" for a regular security guard. "It was all planned out . . . down to the last detail and covered up . . . just like the other brother," Payne confided.

Following his conversations with Nicoletti and Payne, Chuck felt the added weight of yet another of his brother's terrible secrets; and with this new knowledge, he'd never felt so alone in his life. Was it the proverbial "straw that broke the camel's back"? He really didn't know. But he did know one thing for certain: He knew too much. Too much about Mooney and too much about the CIA and the politicians who would sell their souls for power. He'd never be safe again; maybe his family wouldn't be, either.

The anger at realizing it was all because of Mooney was overwhelming. Something had died in him when he'd lost the plaza—his love, his trust in his brother had been all swept away. And there was little left to cling to now.

Whether it was out of self-preservation or moral outrage—he'd never honestly be able to say, but he suspected it was the former, less noble motivation—he vowed then with every fiber of his being to turn his back forever on Mooney and the world of the Outfit.

On May 23, 1969, Chuck Giancana's family legally changed their last name. Chuck had decided he wanted to extricate himself completely. He didn't care whether he ever saw Mooney again.

What he didn't know at the time was that he never would—at least not alive.

EPILOGUE

On June 19, 1975, staff members of the Senate Select Committee on Intelligence arrived in Chicago, Illinois. Their purpose was to arrange for the safe transport of Sam Giancana from his Oak Park residence—where he'd been sequestered since his deportation from Mexico the previous year—to Washington, D.C., for his testimony five days later, on June 24. Senator Frank Church and his committee colleagues were specifically interested in his connection to the CIA's Castro assassination plot.

Mooney Giancana, however, like so many other potentially explosive sources of information before and after him, would not live to sit before the committee. On the evening of the very day that Senate staffers went to Chicago, Mooney was murdered.

Since changing his name and severing all ties to Chicago's Outfit in 1969, Chuck had not spoken to Mooney; their relationship had been irreparably damaged. Over the years, however, Chuck had kept track of his brother's whereabouts through friends and family members. What Chuck knew of those years, coupled with what he'd gleaned from previous conversations with Mooney, only added to his suspicions regarding his brother's murder—as well as to his bitter disappointment in the government of the United States.

In the years immediately following 1969, Mooney continued to reside at his Mexican estate, San Cristobal. He traveled extensively, visiting not just European and Latin American cities but also the Middle Eastern cities of Tehran, Iran, and Beirut, Lebanon. In Beirut, Mooney had obtained membership in an exclusive country club, Chuck was told, and while based there had met with many of the world's most influential power brokers, including Mooney's "friend," the Shah of Iran.

Interestingly, U.S.–CIA relations with these countries were in their heyday during this same period. Mooney had once told Chuck that the Shah had been placed on the throne by the CIA. To accomplish that, Mooney said U.S. intelligence had utilized massive bribes and financed a coup to overthrow the Shah's predecessor, Mossadegh, in 1953.

For their efforts, the CIA remained fast friends with the corrupt Iranian government until the Shah's forced exile in 1979. Chuck thought it probable that Mooney's relationships in the Middle East also flourished during this period, given the inordinate amount of time he spent in the area. Some biographers would later claim that the Justice Department had succeeded in souring several of Mooney's Middle Eastern enterprises, but Outfit men told Chuck that J. Edgar Hoover's attempts to interfere with Mooney's affairs overseas never had any impact. Indeed, such an idea was laughable given foreign officials' willingness to accept handsome Outfit payoffs. Hoover and his FBI agents might strike fear into the heart of the erring American, but their authority was inconsequential elsewhere.

During the latter part of 1971, Richard Cain was freed from a Texarkana prison and quickly resumed duties as Mooney's international protégé and interpreter. The sheer number of Latin American countries the duo visited—countries of extreme interest to the CIA—bolstered Chuck's suspicion that Cain had resumed his clandestine CIA duties, as well.

If friends and family were to be believed, Mooney enjoyed a lavish lifestyle south of the border and was still very much in contact with his stateside Outfit supporters and CIA coconspirators: Carlo Gambino, Santo Trafficante, Carlos Marcello, and Johnny Roselli.

The Chicago Outfit's and the CIA's many Asiatic ties—by the 1960s, Mooney had several Oriental representatives working at his behest in Chicago and overseas—suggested that Trafficante had far exceeded all expectations in his Asian heroin-smuggling efforts. In fact, it would later be claimed by several historians that Trafficante had collaborated with U.S. intelligence in Hong Kong, the Philippines, Vietnam, and Laos.

It also seemed likely that Mooney, along with Marcello and Trafficante, continued to reap the benefits of an extensive CIA– Mafia–Texas cocaine-smuggling ring worth literally billions of dollars—a joint effort based in South America, Costa Rica, and Panama, which Mooney had described to Chuck during the Bay of Pigs era. Based on his brother's comments at that time, Chuck suspected the ring utilized offshore Texas oil wells to subvert the efforts of U.S. Customs.

As for the Gambino-European opium connection, there

was reason to think, based on Mooney's frequent trips to Rome, Bern, and Athens, that during the years following Chuck's estrangement with his brother, Mooney maintained his partnership in the Gambino enterprise.

Mooney's travels might also have served to further his relationships with the Vatican's Bishop Marcinkus and Michele Sindona.

In 1973, after several profitable and fast-paced years with Richard Cain at his side, Mooney and his friend were reported to have had a heated falling-out—one that led to Cain's departure to Chicago. It was not known by Chuck whether Cain also severed his ties with U.S. intelligence but he'd heard that, once back in Illinois, Cain made it known he was looking for investors in a Cyprus-Malta gambling junket—without the blessing of his mentor. Cain spoke openly of his displeasure with Mooney, telling virtually anyone who'd listen that he intended to proceed with the gambling venture against his boss's wishes.

According to FBI reports, Cain then met with bureau agents and asked to be hired by the Justice Department. The agreement called for him to continue his Outfit duties and act as a paid FBI informant. Whether or not the Justice Department was aware of Richard Cain's alleged CIA ties was never revealed, but according to FBI reports, he was indeed given the status of paid informant, earning a handsome "consulting fee" equal to that of the average annual salary of a Chicago agent.

In light of his FBI employment, it seemed strange that Cain—rather than mend his fast-souring relationship with the Outfit in an effort to gain information for the FBI—began an even more fervent denouncement of Mooney, seeking out dissatisfied mobsters as his cohorts.

For the informed, there were shades of the Tucson FBI

"dirty tricks" in this endeavor, although tame by comparison. Chuck believed, as did many of his fellow Outfit friends, that it was more likely Cain, rather than acting as an informant, was part of a covert FBI operation whose aim was to foster turmoil within Chicago's Outfit.

Told to back off by Outfit superiors, Cain continued his public ranting, claiming that one day he himself might become Chicago's boss. Such braggadocio was not only foolhardy, it was suicidal; Cain of all people should have known better.

Given his behavior, no one was surprised when Richard Cain was murdered on December 20, 1973. Obviously, he'd shot his mouth off one too many times; authorities ruled his death a gangland slaying and the case was closed.

But for Chuck, Cain's actions and the details of his murder raised some disturbing questions. Given his involvement with the CIA and FBI and—according to Mooney—in the presidential assassination and countless other covert activities, Cain's behavior and death deserved closer inspection.

According to police reports, the murder took place in broad daylight at Rose's Sandwich Shop. There, Cain lunched with several unidentified men. These men got up and left while Cain remained alone at his table. Soon after, two men, wearing ski masks and toting shotguns, entered the shop. They swiftly lined the diner's terrified inhabitants against the wall.

Witnesses reported that one of the gunmen sported a black glove on his left hand, a white one on his right, while his gloveless accomplice carried a walkie-talkie. Witnesses stated that the man with the walkie-talkie held it to his mouth and said, "Who's got the package?" He repeated this question several times until finally a reply came back: "Here comes a guy now; maybe he's got the package." Hearing those words, the strangely gloved man walked up to Cain and fired two shotgun blasts at point-blank range into his brain. After briefly searching Cain's pockets, the two walked rapidly out the door, disappearing forever.

There were several intriguing features to this incident. Certainly, it was unlike any Outfit hit in the history of Chicago.

Since the flamboyant days of Al Capone, the Chicago Outfit's professional assassins had shunned witnesses, preferring the cover of darkness to accomplish their ends. There was little question Cain could have been hit at night; his whereabouts were no secret to anyone in the Outfit desiring to harm him.

Another element that didn't make sense was the use of walkie-talkies; such a thing was considered "silly" by macho Italian killers.

But most interesting were the two mismatched gloves on the hands of Cain's killer.

It seemed probable to Chuck that the two gloves were a bold message from the collaborators in Cain's execution—a message only Cain himself would recognize. Very likely, they represented the two forces he knew all too well: the Latin American CIA "White Hand" and the "Black Hand" of Sam Giancana.

What Mooney's precise role might have been in the murder would never be known. Perhaps Cain was lured to the diner by Mooney's trusted lieutenants and then executed by his coconspirators from the "White Hand." It seemed certain to Chuck that Cain was not murdered by actual Outfit members, and based on Mooney's reported actions following the murder, it also seemed certain that

Mooney was involved in its planning. Had the "White Hand" executed Cain without Mooney's approval, Mooney would have rightly feared for his own life.

But in 1974, if he did harbor such fears, he gave no indication to family or friends. On the contrary, Chuck heard that security remained lax in and around his brother's massive, walled Mexican estate.

However, ill health did force a discontinuance of Mooney's travels that year. The majority of his international business was firmly in place, no longer requiring his constant personal attention, and therefore, according to family members, he focused his attention on his declining health while trusted emissaries handled the details of his global empire.

On the evening of July 18, 1974, Mooney may well have regretted San Cristobal's lack of security. He was attacked in his walled garden by four men, immigration agents, who dragged him, dressed only in robe and slippers, to the area jail. There he remained in custody until the following day, when he was driven to Mexico City.

From Mexico City, Mooney was flown to San Antonio, Texas, where he was met by the FBI. The agents gleefully served him with a subpoena to appear the following week before a Chicago grand jury.

Up until the day he was deported from Mexico, Mooney's position as a welcome alien there had seemed secure. Since his connections in the Mexican government went right up to the president, he was taken by complete surprise by his deportation. The FBI later claimed they were caught off guard as well, and had been forced to hurriedly prepare for his entry back into the United States. If neither the Justice Department nor the Mexican government was responsible for these events, it might be speculated the CIA orchestrated Mooney's deportation. But for what purpose remains a mystery.

One week later, back in Chicago and seated before the grand jury, Mooney was granted immunity—the prelude to a seeming reenactment of his 1966 grand-jury fiasco. But this time, older and wiser, he willingly talked—and said absolutely nothing of substance. The jury was forced to make do with his paltry testimony and, this time, Mooney went free. For the balance of that year and into 1975, his health continued to deteriorate. He experienced a serious gallbladder disorder and flew twice to Houston for surgery performed by the famous Dr. DeBakey.

On June 19, 1975, the day of Mooney's murder, the still-reigning "boss of bosses" visited with friends and family. Whether or not Mooney was concerned about his upcoming appearance before the Senate Select Committee on Intelligence was unclear; he apparently never mentioned it.

Chuck believed, though, that his brother would have met this new inquiry as he'd met dozens of hearings before by saying nothing of consequence. Mooney never would have revealed his vast knowledge of covert CIA operations, or any of the thousands of skeletons buried in the closet of Chicago's Outfit. Quite simply, the code of *omertà* ran too strongly through his Sicilian veins. Throughout his life, he'd clung to it like a badge; it was his code of honor. But to those unaware of this ethic, the specter of Sam Giancana testifying before the committee must have appeared as a threat of monstrous proportions.

Thus, by midnight, Mooney was dead, shot once in the back of the head, once in the mouth, and five times under the chin. And by dawn the next day, all the world would know was that another mobster was dead—murdered, of course, in true gangland style.

As reason for his murder, it would later be stated that Mooney became greedy, refusing to share with other Outfit members the wealth he'd accumulated during his sojourn in Latin America. If that was true, it was the first time in his life he'd been so inclined.

It would also be said that he was making a bid for power—a bid the Outfit had countered with his murder. Obviously recovering from difficult surgery, Mooney was in no condition or state of mind to make a comeback in Chicago—had one been necessary. In truth, he'd not lost for one minute the ruthless power for which he was known.

Indeed, Chuck learned that the week prior to his death, Mooney had placed a contract—rumored to have been requested by the CIA and a former U.S. President—on Jimmy Hoffa. The job was given to five soldiers: two from Chicago, one from Boston, one from Detroit, and one from Cincinnati. And one month later, Hoffa did, in fact, disappear and was presumed murdered by mobsters.

Evidence suggested that there might well be more to Mooney's murder than gangland retribution. There was the fact that, if what he told Chuck was true, he would have posed far more of a threat to his CIA associates than to Chicago's Outfit. His Outfit friends knew he never would have divulged damaging information; the CIA, rampant with spies and counterspies, crosses and double crosses, may not have been so certain of his loyalty.

In pinpointing Mooney's executioners, Chuck thought of applying one of Mooney's own adages: "Find out who's still alive and you'll find the killer."

That approach led quite clearly to a suspect. In 1976,

both Carlo Gambino and Johnny Roselli died—Gambino of a heart attack and Roselli by the hand of an unknown assailant in Miami. Carlos Marcello, Mooney's other co-hort, continued to be plagued by his alien status and—conveniently for those not wanting his part in the conspiracy known—began exhibiting signs of mental deterioration, thought to be Alzheimer's disease. Chuck heard rumors among the Outfit guys that such diseases were the product of modern CIA chemistry; it was said, but never proven, that Marcello's was, as well. Nevertheless, in June of 1983, Marcello's New Orleans kingdom formally collapsed with his imprisonment in Texarkana.

In fact, of all the major players Mooney said were involved in CIA covert activity, only Santo Trafficante remained alive and well. Trafficante was virtually untouched; his narcotics ventures in Latin America and Asia reportedly boomed. One had only to read the newspapers to see that the focus of underworld crimebusters was not on Tampa, Florida, but on its highly visible New York and Chicago cousins to the north. Accordingly, Trafficante conducted business without so much as a whisper of legal difficulty until just before his death due to kidney failure in 1987.

Under Trafficante's reign, Florida became known as the nation's major entry point for illicit drugs. Interestingly and inexplicably, Trafficante's involvement in the assassination of the President was never thoroughly investigated. Given his documented involvement with the CIA around the globe, this lack of scrutiny was compelling.

Applying Mooney's own method of deduction, Santo Trafficante appeared the most likely Outfit suspect in the orchestration of Mooney's murder.

That is not to say Trafficante was unaware of the code

f *omertà* to which Mooney adhered or that the Tampa mobster for a moment believed that his compatriot would actually talk to a Senate committee. Nor is it suggested that Chicago had somehow become part of Trafficante's territory or that Mooney was murdered without the support of the Chicago Outfit, but rather that Trafficante was simply given a job to do—just as Mooney himself had been so many times in the past—by the CIA. And to oversee that job, Chuck believed Trafficante solicited a Chicago representative of the Outfit and a fellow CIA coconspirator: Johnny Roselli.

Mooney's biographers, family, and friends would later insist that Mooney's killer was someone known and trusted. A hometown boy himself, Roselli could have assured that the proper individual was dispatched. Significantly, perhaps, the gun used in Mooney's murder—a .22 caliber weapon—was traced to Miami, Florida.

There also remained a persistent rumor that Mooney, sometime before his death, had begun questioning whether Roselli and Trafficante were "too close," and that Mooney had actually begun to mistrust his Floridian crony.

If Mooney's suspicions were well founded, and Roselli had indeed assisted Trafficante in a CIA contract on the Chicago boss, it could explain Johnny Roselli's own gruesome murder. Roselli's chopped-up remains were found floating in a sealed oil drum in Trafficante's home state of Florida in 1976, following Roselli's well-publicized interviews with reporters Drew Pearson and Jack Anderson and his top secret testimony before the Senate Select Committee on Intelligence.

Roselli's disclosures, involving the Mafia-CIA efforts in the Bay of Pigs and the Castro assassination attempt, demonstrated that he was a man who certainly knew too

much. Perhaps he was also the one man who could impli
cate Trafficante and the CIA in the murder of Mooney
Giancana, and, even more damning, in the assassination
of the President of the United States and his presidential
hopeful brother.

Roselli's testimony and murder soon after prompted the
formation of the U.S. House Select Committee on Assassi
nations and the reopening of investigations into the death
of the President.

Curiously, Trafficante did appear before both Senate
committees but, quite unlike Mooney and Roselli, experi
enced no ill aftereffects.

More deaths were to follow Mooney's and Roselli's—
some more suspicious than others.

Chuckie Nicoletti was murdered in 1977, immediately
after the U.S. House Select Committee on Assassination
determined he would be called for questioning. His demise
was chalked up as just one more Mob hit, although some
committee members evidently suspected differently.

George De Morhenchildt was also scheduled to testify
before the U.S. House Select Committee on Assassination
in 1977 and died on the very day he was to be questioned
regarding the President's murder. Despite the coincidental
nature of his death, it was ruled a suicide.

The list went on. Filled with names familiar—Jack
Ruby, David Ferrie, Guy Banister—and not so familiar.

For a serious student of history, there is good reason to
pause at Mooney's saga of corruption. There is also good
reason to question whether such immorality continues to
exist in this country, reaching into our nation's highest
office.

Sadly, it may very well be that this is, indeed, the case

To whit: the Pentagon Papers; Richard Nixon's Watergate; the Vatican bank scandal; the Iran-Contra affair; the graft and CIA involvement in the case of the Philippines's Ferdinand and Imelda Marcos; the Manuel Noriega–CIA connection in Panama; and BCCI. All bits and pieces perhaps of a much larger and more sinister puzzle. But all bearing the stamp of the CIA's entanglement with organized crime.

Most of those who were involved in the 1963 assassination of President John F. Kennedy have been murdered. Some have committed "suicide" or spent their final days in prison, while others still linger behind bars.

There are some men, however, if we are to believe Mooney's tales of Mafia-CIA counterintelligence activities, who've prospered and remained free. Amassing incredible power from careers deeply rooted in the CIA, these men have reached America's loftiest positions of authority, from which they continue to influence world events.

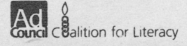